PRAISE FOR *THE LAST PARTY*

"Elegant . . . a vivid portrait of '70s nightlife."
—*Wall Street Journal*

"A fascinating account of Studio 54's hedonistic glory."
—*New York Observer*

"Who better to take us behind the velvet rope of that '70s mecca of
disco and substance abuse? . . . Haden-Guest's notorious excesses
might seem unseemly or pointless if he weren't able to collate them
into such perceptive pop chronicles. *The Last Party* is an assiduous
mix of memoir and reportage."
—*Newsweek*

"Engrossing . . . *The Last Party* is more than the story of Studio 54.
It is the Gibbonesque chronicle of the rise and fall of New York
nightlife from the postwar period to the present."
—Jim Holt, *Slate*

"One of the 40 Greatest Rock & Roll Books of All Time."
—*Blender*

"One of the fifty greatest music books ever. . . . Haden-Guest's forensic exposition of New York nightclub Studio 54 extends far beyond its reach, magically morphing into a unique calibration of disco itself. . . . Haden-Guest's major triumph is to steer the story away from the major figures who became emblematic of 54 at its late-seventies peak, instead providing fabulous insights into the minds of the coat-check girls, the drug dealers, and all manner of unsung alumni who allow the nightworld to swing."
—*The Observer* (UK)

"A deliciously sordid account of New York nightlife since the late seventies."
—*The Independent* (UK)

"Perhaps nobody was as well qualified to write *The Last Party*."
—*The Guardian* (UK)

ABOUT THE AUTHOR

Anthony Haden-Guest is a writer, reporter, and cartoonist. He was born in Paris and lives in New York and London. He long has published in leading magazines in Britain and America, including *Esquire, Vanity Fair, Paris Review, New Yorker*, and many others. Among his books are *True Colors: The Real Life of the Art World, The Last Party: Studio 54, Disco, and the Culture of the Night*, and a book of cartoons, *The Chronicles of Now.*

THE
LAST
PARTY

STUDIO 54, DISCO,
AND THE
CULTURE OF THE NIGHT

ANTHONY HADEN-GUEST

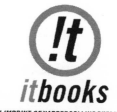

*it*books

AN *IMPRINT OF* HARPERCOLLINS*PUBLISHERS*

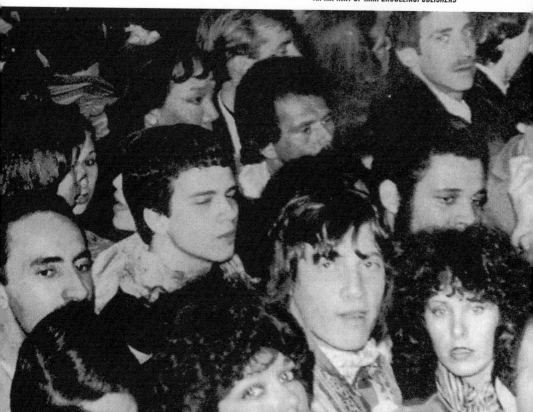

OTHER BOOKS BY ANTHONY HADEN-GUEST

True Colors: The Real Life of the Art World

Bad Dreams

The Paradise Program

ACKNOWLEDGMENTS

ALMOST ALL OF THE MATERIAL IN THIS BOOK has been derived from my own researches, whether by way of formal interviews, informal conversations, or simple observation. All but a handful of the people cited in the Cast List have, as readers will plainly see, been astonishingly generous, both with their time and in their willingness to share their experiences with me. So much has this been the case that I am almost reluctant to single out individuals, but I will say that this enterprise would have been both more difficult and very different without the help of William Hamilton, Arthur and Colleen Weinstein, Reinaldo Herrera, Scotty Taylor, Nile Rodgers, Maurice Brahms, Myra Scheer, Rudolf Pieper, Eric Goode, Mark Fleischman, Anita Sarko, Sally Randall, R. Couri Hay, Peter Sudler, Gwynne Rivers, Peter Gatien, Claire O'Connor, Fred Rothbell-Mista, Kelly Cutrone, Michael Alig, Stephanie Parker, and Elyn Wollensky. I will also say that Ian Schrager, who could have thrown formidable obstacles in my path, chose not to do so.

My path was also made the smoother by certain fellow writers. Helpful books have been few, but include *Disco* by Albert Goldman, *The Dancer from the Dance* by Andrew Holleran, *The Andy Warhol Diaries,* edited by Pat Hackett, and *Art After Midnight* by Steven Hager.

My journalistic sources, on the other hand, are so varied that I want to make a preemptive apology to anybody overlooked. The news reports and columns in *The New York Times,* the *Daily News,* and the *New York Post* have been crucial. So, too, Stephen Saban's columns in *Details* and Michael Musto's in the *Voice*. The impact of the magazine pieces by Dan Dorfman, Henry Post, and Amy Virshup has been noted in the book. Other magazine features that helped point me in several of the right directions include "Club Culture" by Brad Gooch and "Studio 54, Where Are You?" by Bob Colacello, both published in *Vanity Fair;* "Living and Dying the Great Adventure" by Albert Goldman, published in *High Times;* "Little Stevie Wonder" by Michael Gross, "The Comeback Kids" by Michael Daly, "The Ecstasy and the Agony" by Maer Roshan, Mark Jolly, and Norman Vanamee, all published in *New York;* "Lost in Music" by Vince Aletti, "My Life in Clubland" by Jim Fouratt, "The King of Clubland" by Frank Owen, and "Lullaby of Clubland" and "Busting the King of the Club Kids" by William Bastone and Jennifer Gonnerman, all published in the *Voice;* "Studio 54: The Mourning After" by Steven Gaines, published in *Fame;* and "Clubbed to Death?" by Mim Udovitch, published in *Details.*

I want to thank Jesse Kornbluth, who published "Royalton Flush" in *Vanity Fair,* for making his notes available; Brian Saltern for allowing me to use his journals; *Geraldo* for sending me tapes of its four (to date) Club Kids shows; and Screamin' Rachel for letting me quote from her song "Murder in Clubland."

Considerable gratitude is also due to several people at William Morrow, among them: Kathleen Antrim, copyeditor, for unsnarling my narrative; Jon Moskowitz, the editor who did the troubleshooting; and Paul Bresnick, my editor, who asked me a couple of years ago if I might be interested in writing a book about Studio 54.

CONTENTS

Now the night comes—
and it is wise to obey the night
Homer, *The Iliad,* VII

INTRODUCTION

to the It! Books Edition

TAMA JANOWITZ RECENTLY TOLD ME HOW PERPLEXED she would always feel whenever anybody asked whether she missed the eighties. The young novelist had, of course, been very much a part of the eighties Manhattan nocturne—Andy Warhol had filmed her first novel, *Slaves of New York*, and she had been one of his tirelessly Constant Companions—but, so far as she was concerned, this had just been ordinary life. "I was desperately sorry that I had missed the sixties," she said.

By the eighties, of course, the sixties had become a fully achieved narrative, a perfect arc, with its giddy moments of transcendence, its heroes, its tragedies, its marches, its music, its pictures, its costumery, its hair, its politics, its misdemeanors, its high hopes, its puffy egos and its hypocrisies, the whole being compounded of memory and imagination so that story becomes infused with fable. Hell, there were movies about the sixties.

And now, what do you know? Pretty much the same has happened to the hugely different period chronicled in this book.

Pretty much the same but not, of course, precisely the same. The shifts and changes that have occurred in the urban envelope allow us to see the world that *The Last Party* records from several radically different vantage points. For one thing, the tabloid celebrity culture was still in a fresh, even rosily gung-ho phase. It could get a bit feral at the time, of course— the photograph of Ron Galella wearing a football helmet to photograph Marlon Brando outside the Waldorf-Astoria some time after the actor had knocked his teeth out comes vividly to mind—but at least Brando, Elizabeth Taylor, and Liza Minnelli were Out There, usually without laser-eyed publicists and minders in tight black suits. The culture of tabs and paps was nothing compared to the engulfing negative zone it has become.

Emergent technologies have fed new and darkly ravenous appetites. Nowadays the secrets of the VIP rooms would be all over sites like Gawker, the meat of the cybergossips like Perez Hilton, and any perhaps indiscreet goings-on would be targets for pictures and video on mobile phones, shoved up on YouTube, Popbitch, and any number of other sites, and front-paged in the tabs.

So there's no hiding place. And if you doubt me on this, you could always check with Amy Winehouse, Kate Moss, or Christian Bale, as well as any number of belligerent models, out-of-control actors, rabbits-in-the-headlights fashionistas and room-to-let-upstairs socialites, who have been brought to attention in no doubt utterly misinterpreted images and/or soundbites, stolen in what they imagined were private moments. Meaning that these days only the willfully self-destructive will engage in the enthusiastic and sometimes limber naughtiness that sporadically took place in the VIP rooms (and VVIP rooms) during *The Last Party* days.

The thing was that the complicated society of the night was still fairly private, indeed covert, in the days before Facebook, Twitter, and whatever fresh gizmo is succeeding in blurring the lines between public and private. You might think that this notion of a private and sheltered Nightworld is contradicted by the addiction to extravagant self-display you will see pictured within. Wrong. Nightworld photographers were naturally focusing on taking pictures they could sell, meaning pictures of famous people, or of wholly or partially naked people and of extremely bizarrely accoutered people, preferably doing interesting things to each other. Most of the clubgoers were consequently left hiding in plain sight.

As for the naked, the silver-painted, and the creatively accoutered, well, back then they reveled in being the Special Attractions in a crowd of rubbernecking straights. Enter another eraser of the line between public and private: Reality TV. These days exhibitionism has gone mass-market. "I couldn't take the pictures I used to take now," says Anton Perich, who took some of the most delicately seductive photographs of Nightworld. "It's different. Now everybody is doing it."

The world of *The Last Party* was in many respects powered by being in recovery from the broody politics of Vietnam and Watergate, and it existed by its own fervent wish in a crystalline cocoon. But now dark scenarios are once again pressing themselves on our attention and they are darker than before. AIDS acquired definition and a name within the time span of the book, but most of the headline-gobblers that now menace us—bubbling glaciers, dying species, drying-up oil suppliers, and dwindling water, to say nothing of jihadists and runaway nukes—were furrowing brows mostly in academe. I'm not about to claim that everyone out 'round 'bout midnight these days has deep stuff on their minds, nor that it's back to the sixties, but the politics—the basic politics of survival this time around—are back on the menu. And high time, too.

I suppose one the most significant changes specific to Manhattan's Nightworld—and an unwelcome one to many city-dwellers, surely—is that it has become a shadow of the one you will find described in this book. Thanks to consecutive unsympathetic regimes in city hall and the power over the granting of liquor licenses robustly exercised by community boards, the nightlife of the city has grayed out.

It was at the memorial for Arthur Weinstein in late 2008 that I discerned a glimmer of hope that the color, the raciness, the edginess of Manhattan's Nightworld had not been nannied out of existence permanently. Well, you will learn more of Weinstein in the following pages, but he was one of the crucial figures in the world of *The Last Party,* and his memorial, at the High Bar on 48th Street, was attended by the artists René Ricard and Neke Carson; fashion folk including Steven Burrows, Michael Savoia, and Larissa; the DJs Anita Sarko and Johnny Dynell; Stanley Bard of the Chelsea Hotel; and such veteran clublords as Steven Lewis.

It was the beginning of the turbulent times that still continue. The headline of *The New York Times* business section that same Sunday had been stark: *Wall Street RIP*. But the reaction of the crew at Arthur's memorial was not without schadenfreude.

Steve Lewis was articulate. "The VIP will now be redefined back to what it was in the old days. Artists are used to starving so they will survive for sure. They'll be around," he said. "But the Lehman Brothers type, when they can't drop a lot of money, are completely irrelevant. He doesn't offer anything else.

"So the VIP in nightclubs will be an artist. Style will return. It's not how much you paid for it, but the style of the streets. This could be the kick in the arse that New York needs. We'll get the city back."

A nice thought. We'll see.

Anthony Haden-Guest

London 2009

PROLOGUE

NOT EVERYBODY'S MEMORIES OF THOSE YEARS ARE as clear as springwater but Antonia de Portago can summon up a specific evening at Studio 54 as clearly as though she were running it through a projector. De Portago, a French countess by marriage, a chanteuse with a punk band, the Operators, by calling, was sitting at a balcony table. "There were a few sofas and you could rest," she says. "We were a whole group. There was Elsa Martinelli . . . Helmut Berger. You know, who was in *The Damned*? . . . Mick Jagger . . . some of the Niarchoses . . . a girl from Manila . . ."

The balconies were halfway up the metamorphosed theater and quondam TV studio. On either side, people furtively sidled into the infamous unisexual bathrooms, not necessarily to pee. Beneath was the dance floor, pulsating with the beat of disco, which is very close to that of the human heartbeat, where dancers, washed in the surf of sound, dappled and splashed by light, shed the dull gravitational tug of quotidian life, and lost themselves in what was at once a voyeuristic jostle, like a fairground, and a domain of the self-absorbed, like a ballet for prima donnas only.

Over the dance floor, tubes studded with light bulbs, Flash Gordon style, were rising and descending and, higher yet, the spoon made its rhythmic journeys to the insatiable nose of the Man in the Moon, discharging a fizz of light. De Portago says the club was thronged with the Studio menagerie that night. She cannot remember the precise cast list, but it certainly must have included heavy squads of toffs in tuxedos and evening dresses; plenty of pretty preppy girls and boys; Studio employees, the waiters and busboys, bouncing around bare-chested in sneakers and gym shorts; and, of course, the camera bait.

The camera bait—those whose pictures showed up in the *Post,* the *News, People,* and magazines worldwide—would certainly, that evening, have included themselves. Also, other famous faces, and these wouldn't have been just predictables, like Truman Capote, Rudolf Nureyev, and the starlet of the moment, but beings who looked truly out of context as though they had winged in from a different movie, like a Republican senator in a heavy gray suit; or Andre the Giant; or an English duke; or the Reverend Sun Moon plus entourage; or Moshe Dayan; or Fred Astaire in a tux; or Vladimir Horowitz, who would have been capering around on the dance floor, protecting those valuable eardrums with wads of cotton.

Film would have been expended too on the fashion models and demi-señoritas who could be counted upon to pop a perky nipple as they threw themselves into choreographed frenzies on the dance floor; also those who had themselves painted silver, or gold, or costumed as pharaohs, cucumbers, or Angels of Death; to say nothing of such Studio-famous characters as Rollerena, supposedly a prim Wall Streeter by day, a dreamboat by night in a wedding dress and roller skates; and the man who danced with the lifelike marionette; and Miriam, the woman (by day a substitute teacher) in the see-through wedding-dress; and the septuagenarian party girl, Disco Sally. Finally, there would have been, as always, a handful of souls who felt that the sight of their naked genitalia should be a source of wonder and delight.

The dance floor was the former stage. Grouped around it were puffy banquettes. Beneath the balconies was the main bar, which was pickup central. Ignored by most was a discreet door in the wall that opened onto the stairs that led to the VIP Room in the basement. Above were the bleachers, the circle when the place had been a theater, now upholstered, according to gossip, in a material that could be hosed down daily. Just gossip, but it was not unusual to spot clubgoers enjoying a personal moment, possibly with somebody previously unknown to them. David Hamilton, the photographer, says: "You would look around and you'd see somebody's back. And then you'd see little toes twinkling behind their ears."

De Portago's group sat as though embedded in Lucite. "We were just sitting there for hours on end. For some reason we stayed at that little table for hours," she says. "And at one point I said, '*Oh, this will always last! This will never be over. This is too incredibly bizarre and pushed to the extreme!*'

"And they were all saying, 'Yes! It's probably going to be like this always.' We had a whole conversation about this. It was very odd. At that moment we could see it as if we were observing the scene from another planet. We could see a mini-cosmos of what was going on.

"And I said, 'Oh, this will never end! This is too wonderful.' It was so intense. Oh, so intense. 'It can never go down from this plateau.' "

De Portago laughed a silvery opera-inflected laugh, then said, "Boy! Was I wrong!"

Not completely wrong, as it happened. A new Nightworld, as I shall call the culture of the night, had indeed been born. Steve Rubell, the most visible progenitor of Studio 54, once observed that five thousand people in New York went out several nights a week. Within ten years this battalion had become a division, an estimated sixty thousand. What it was they were looking for—in some cases, are still looking for—was earthly, like a warm body or a toot of cocaine, and also unearthly: a moment of transcendence as much as a night on the tiles. That is something with which these chronicles will be concerned.

These tens of thousands were the army moving through Nightworld. The celebrities are the trophies, proof of sucess, like human equivalents of the stars in a Michelin guide. But the real shock troops of Nightworld are the club owners, the impressarios, the performers, the publicists, the columnists, the purveyors of carnal delight—whether the meat or the vegetables of pleasure—and these form a bizarre, self-absorbed social ecosystem. Uptown, downtown, black, white, or shades between, straight or gay, these are the ones who make up Nightworld and inhabit it; and with their convoluted goings-on too these chronicles will be concerned.

Nightlife, especially in big cities, certainly in New York, is seductive, and sexy, often raucous, and occasionally dangerous. With little clubs popping into being and being squooshed, and huge ones becoming huger and atrophying, the Nightworld that bloomed at Studio 54 went through every sort of odd transformation. Nightworld, for all of de Portago's incredulity, did indeed become more bizarre and more extreme. And the intensity of the attention that it began attracting in Studio times has exacted a price.

★　　★　　★

"Are you going to tell the truth? About everything?" Fred Rothbell-Mista asked me fiercely. Rothbell-Mista has worked from A to Z in New York clubland and his question made me quail. There are such different truths. Consider Studio 54 itself. Most are still starry-eyed about the place. "To me, it was about freeing the body. The girls would take off their tops, and dance," says Myra Scheer, who worked there, talking about a certain "purity." A few are bittersweet. Chen Sam, Elizabeth Taylor's late publicist, is said to have observed, "It's not that I don't remember Studio 54. Studio 54 was not a place for memories." Barbara Allen de Kwiatkowski says, with equal opacity, "Studio 54 was not a harmless place." Lilian Carter, the former president's mother, was taken on her first visit there by the party promoter George-Paul Rosell. Quizzed about it in the Russian Tea Room the following day, she said, "I don't know if I was in heaven or hell. But it was *wonderful*!"

Timothy Leary, of all people, was skeptical. "Oh, Anthony," he said not long before his death, "you're romanticizing it. It was just a very good nightclub." Leary was wrong, I think. Somehow that chunk of property happened to become psychic real estate, like the Haight-Ashbury in San Francisco during the 1967 "Summer of Love." The Haight-Ashbury was often squalid and poor, despite Flower Power and its trappings, and many of those who congregated there came to dim or sticky ends. But it was seen, both at the time and later, as a real location where fluid, random, and abstract energies focused for a historical moment. Steve Rubell was the first to admit that Studio 54 had its dreary nights, even in its glory time, but Studio 54, a real location too, nonetheless occupies a niche in history. And like most niches, it is full of shadows.

The shadows can be glimpsed in the archives of the paparazzi who fed off Nightworld. These are weak on lovely images but strong on telling documents. The tabloid photographers, like Ron Galella, Sonya Moskowitz, and Robin Platzer, worked fast and focused on celebs. Marcia Resnick was an "art" photographer, trawling the Mudd Club. Wolfgang Wesener was ubiquitous in the artscapes of Area, and Anton Perich specialized on finding ravishing unknowns, muses of the nowhere zone.

Working through the boxfuls of images taken by Richard Manning, or RPM, as he calls himself, one of the hardest-nosed paparazzi, a man with a white beard and a ponytail, was a particularly intense experience. Here are Elizabeth Taylor and Betty Ford, each wearing something diaphanous, each with a bodyguard, wearing Truly Bad Hair; here is Michael Jackson with an Afro and Michael Jackson in pale shantung and an ascot; here is Steve Rubell dancing with Margaret Trudeau, her eyes wide and heavy-lidded, like those of a succubus; here are Barry Diller and Rod Stewart in the DJ booth; and here is Christie Brinkley, with permanently sideswept hair, as though being escorted by her own personal wind tunnel.

Here is a sequence of Christina Onassis, her weight whooshing in and out like a squeezed concertina. "She's dead," RPM said matter-of-factly. Rudolf Nureyev dancing with Rollerena. "They're dead," he adds. Here is Cher— "Before she got her implants"—and here is the man who looks like a futurismo Harpo Marx, with HERPES VIRUS inscribed on his costume; the maître d' of Mortimer's restaurant in a pin-striped suit; the Jewish couple in Nazi regalia, she sporting a swastika on her panties. And on, and on, and on.

The phenomenon of Studio 54 seemed to be born of nothing, as though lightning had bloomed in a clear black sky. Of course, this was not the case, and it wasn't just the energy of sex, drugs, and rock-and-roll. The complex energies that would surge into Nightworld had been pumping from unrelated sources for years.

Discos already had a history. They sprang in the first place from a postwar European enthusiasm for technology and American pop music. Arguably, the first discos were in France, and credit for coining the word "discothèque"—a play on cinémathèque—has been claimed by Brigitte Bardot's director husband, Roger Vadim. In the late fifties and early sixties the modish Paris discos were Castel's and Regine's. Le Sept, which was largely gay and a favorite of Elizabeth Taylor, was a hit in the early seventies. There were lively discos in the Rome of La Dolce Vita, which likewise invented the paparazzi, and discos quickly burgeoned in Europe's big cities and other playgrounds of le bon ton such as the Côte d'Azur, Marbella, and Acapulco.

As a fledgling reporter in the sixties, I wrote up the (then) little more than a decade's worth of history of discothèques for a slippery-paper magazine while covering the opening of a new London contestant, Sibylla's. The London discothèques included Annabel's, a subterranean haunt on Berkeley Square, Wips, and the Ad Lib, which I described as "the chosen haven for the gilded mafia of the pop scene, with its nightly Beatle or Stone, and the supporting fashion-photographers, satyrs in this urban Arcady." It was in the discos of mid-sixties London that you could actually see society morphing into new shapes. They were the arenas where artists and photographers from the middle or working class, like David Hockney, David Bailey, and Terry Donovan, designers like Mary Quant and Ossie Clark, and a hairdresser like Vidal Sassoon met with the young of the smart set on equal terms. There was plenty of narcissism and general silliness, but there was also an explosive release of energies, a huge sense of possibility, a sudden openness. Ray Davies of the Kinks sang, "Everyone's a star." This was the dress rehearsal for Studio 54.

Manhattan was also pulsing with discos through the sixties and very early seventies. They included Ondine, Shepheard's, and Cheetah, the brainchild of Olivier Coquelin, who had started Le Club, and Steve Paul's basement club, The Scene, where Tiny Tim had been the opening act until his discovery by haute hippiedom. Also lively were the Electric Circus and Salvation, which was owned by Bradley Pierce and photographer Jerry Schatzberg. "Salvation was great. But Schatzberg sold out to a fellow who owned a car fleet dealership in the Bronx. He was in the drug business but no one knew that. Weird type of people began to come in," says Jonathan Farkas, a habitué. "There was a beautiful woman called Patsy, who was always around there, who was murdered. Then the owner was found in the trunk of a car. And it was closed." Schatzberg points out that his former partner is now a Roman Catholic priest. "The club finally lived up to its name," he says.

But, as heavy political weather settled in, both in Europe and the United States, nightlife lost its zest, and clubs settled into quietude. In New York, the upper classes roosted contentedly in El Morocco and Le Club, joints where a little wildness went a very long way. Evangeline Bruce, a doyenne of the time, complained to *Women's Wear Daily* that Society was suffering a "premature hardening of the arteries." Among the young, the action wasn't in the clubs but on the streets, in the communes, the squats. "Liberation" was much praised, but a liberation sixties style. Stokely Carmichael, the Black Panther, when asked what should be the position of women in the struggle spoke for many radicals, in spite of the token respect paid to the likes of Germaine Greer, replied "prone." Homosexuals, seldom then called "gays," had a voice but by and large, liberation was pursued by, and for, the benefit of straight men.

The awesome speed with which the political temperature dropped was discussed in an interview with the mercurial French savant, Jean Baudrillard. The interviewer, Sylvère Lotringer, fretfully observed that "May 1968 swept down on France like an avalanche, and no sooner had it appeared than it disappeared, mysteriously, practically without a trace."

Baudrillard mused, "Then where has all that energy gone? Nowhere—certainly not into socialism, in any case. It must have been reabsorbed somewhere—without necessarily remaining underground, so as to emerge later. . . ."

Bingo! It did reemerge. In America, Utopian dreamers, soured by Vietnam and Watergate, became apolitical. "Liberation" went mainstream as "Fun." This was first noticeable in the straight world. In July 1976, Plato's Retreat was opened in a Manhattan brownstone, with Larry Levenson as the "Mr. Outside," then moved from place to place. As a new New Yorker, I was frequently required to take visiting Euros on guided tours, and I was struck by the uninhibited women there. Plato's was amazing, not least in its timing. Nothing really started happening there till way after dinnertime. The main arenas were a huge oblong of conjoined mattresses, a Jacuzzi, and a pool, which was in frequent splashy use, so had, as per regulations, a lifeguard. "Ma'am," a lifeguard told a young woman broodily, "nothing in the world is going to get me into that pool."

Gays too were grabbing their market share of the sexual revolution, and clubs sprang up to respond to this demand. Blue Flettrich, an organizer of the Islanders, a group of gay club zealots from Fire Island, believes that it was out there that the gay discos first flourished, and that the jukebox was replaced by a live DJ to keep out the Mafia. "I remember how amazed people were to see somebody standing in a plastic bubble," Flettrich says.

David Mancuso opened his first Manhattan place in 1970. It was in his loft on the Lower East Side, so it was called the Loft. Indeed, all of Mancuso's subsequent places, and he is still in business at the time of writing, have been called the Loft, too. Mark Jacobson, a writer, discovered the Loft when he was working as a cabbie. "I got to take all these gay guys to a warehouse. And this guy invited me in. And I thought, fuck it! I'll just go. The Loft was the first time I was in a room where the majority of people were gay, and everybody was having a real good time. It was a breakthrough. Even for a beatnik hipster like myself."

Andrew Holleran describes the more avid customers of a later gay club, the Tenth Floor, in his novel *Dancer from the Dance*, much of which is set in the disco world of the time.

THEY SELDOM LOOKED HAPPY. THEY PASSED ONE ANOTHER WITHOUT A WORD IN THE ELEVATOR, LIKE SILENT SHADES IN HELL, HELL-BENT ON THEIR NEXT LOOK FROM A HANDSOME STRANGER. THEIR NEXT RUSH FROM A POPPER. THE NEXT SONG THAT TURNED THEIR BONES TO JELLY AND LEFT THEM ALL ON THE DANCE FLOOR WITH HEADS BACK, EYES NEARLY CLOSED, IN THE ECSTASY OF SAINTS RECEIVING THE STIGMATA. THEY PURSUED THESE THINGS WITH SUCH DEVOTION THAT THEY AC-QUIRED, AFTER A FEW SEASONS, A HAGGARD LOOK, A LOOK OF DEADLY SERIOUS-NESS. SOME WIPED EVERYTHING THEY COULD OFF THEIR FACES AND REDUCED THEMSELVES TO BLANKS.

Not all took their pleasures so sternly. "We were coming off the sixties," says Joyce Bogart, who was a young TV producer and soon married Neil Bogart of Casablanca Records. "It was party time. I used to stick my little short hair into a cap and go in as a guy. And I would dance. It was the whole love of music." That was crucial. "What I call early disco was well before it became a mainstream crossover thing," says Nile Rodgers, who became a disco star with Chic, and later produced albums for Madonna and David Bowie. "It was really more of a black thing. I remember records like 'Dreamworld' and the Joness 'Sugar Pie Guy.' Even though I first heard these in predominantly white clubs, like Le Jardin and Tamburlaine. Tamburlaine was where they filmed *Klute*. That was really the start of disco and disco music in New York. That set up the vibe."

It's easy to see what disco was reacting against—the preening and angst of the singer-songwriters and formulaic rock bands like REO Speedwagon and Journey—but it's more complicated to unravel the strands that went into the seamless disco weave. Barry White, yeah. Isaac Hayes, sure. James Brown, absolutely. But, also, examples of what was not yet called "world" music would sometimes lodge themselves in the food chain, like the odd African or Islamic record. It was to do with the whim of whoever was spinning the records. David Mancuso, for instance, was big on "Wild Safari" and "Woman," by a Spanish rock group, Barabbas.

The core of disco, though, was black. "It was definitely R&B dance music. That was where it originated," Nile Rodgers says. "Then it took on more blatant sexual overtones because of the gay movement, and there was residual free sex stuff left over from the sixties. It seems to me that disco—from when I first recognized it as a musical form—was the most hedonistic music I had ever heard in my life. It was really all about Me! Me! Me! Me!

"It was the exact antithesis of hippie music that had preceded it. It wasn't about save the world! It was about get yourself a mate, and have fun, and forget the rest of the world. In a strange way that was very therapeutic. When I was political, and a hippie, we talked about freedom and individuality, and it was all bullshit. You could tell a hippie a mile away. We conformed to our non-conformity. Whereas disco really *was* about individuality. And the freakier, the better."

Baccio, a white DJ, who began in 1970 and has worked a slew of venues, used to go to Philadelphia every Monday and buy a stack of 45s from the Gamble & Huff warehouses. Bacho worked venues as distinct as Plato's Retreat and the Ice Palace, a successful gay disco of the mid-seventies. How did he program for Plato's, where the point wasn't dancing but fucking? "It's the way you put it together. It's mostly from the heart. It's more an emotional type of thing. There were times I had people cry.

"Even when I worked at the Ice Palace," Baccio said. "At four-thirty in the morning, when I played 'Last Dance,' the people were in tears. In tears!

"That was the rush. Can I tell you something? You felt like *God*. Like a total rush! You knew that they were out there to dance. And to sweat. If I was doing my job, the walls would be . . . *wet*."

"Last Dance" was an iconic number by Donna Summer, who was herself the iconic Disco Diva. Summer, who was from Boston, had gone to Munich in 1968 to play Sheila in a road company show of *Hair*. She was one of seven children of a Catholic family and she was a religious-minded young woman. Her appearance in *Hair* was a spiritual experience, sixties style.

It was during *Hair* that Summer met the songwriter, Paul Jabara. Summer stayed on in Europe to appear in *Godspell, Porgy & Bess, Showboat,* and *The Me Nobody Knows,* and she began to make a career singing what the Germans call *schlager,* meaning "cream," the word for their own soft pop music. She had a couple of hits, one of which, "The Hostage," went to number one in Germany, France, and Belgium. Her producer was Giorgio Moroder.

Moroder comes from Bolzano in northwest Italy. He had begun as a performer himself. "I worked a month in a hotel here, a month there," he says. "I did about ten songs in English. I did some Beatles songs. I made a little money. A hundred and fifty, two hundred dollars." Moroder soon became a producer, specializing in what would be called Euro-disco. "I started actually with Kraftwerk. They had their first hit in 1975, I think, with 'Autobahn.' And there were several other groups, like Tangerine Dream from Berlin.

"The disco songs we had before 1975 had drums. Just normal drums, like a rock group," he says. "Then in 1975 we started to put in the bass drum. We called it 'four on the floor.' One, two, three, four! We kind of exaggerated." Moroder didn't personally much care for the sound. "But you watched people dancing and as soon as the song came out with that kind of heavy bass, people liked it."

It was Donna Summer who drew Moroder's attention to "Je t'aime," the duet, apparently recorded in bed, between Serge Gainsbourg and Jane Birkin. "I can do a record like that," she said.

"You?" Moroder said, looking at his *religiose* singer. "Come on! You're not sexy!"

But Summer already had a song working. "It kept on going over and over in my mind," she says. "Love to Love You, Baby" It *was* quite a sexy song for a churchy girl, of course, but Summer explains that it wasn't her singing it, not exactly. "Marilyn Monroe," she told me firmly. "That was Marilyn Monroe singing that song, not me. I'm an actress. That's why my songs are so diverse. With Whitney Houston songs, you know, it's always Whitney. I'm almost the complete opposite of that."

Summer never did get the song finished to her satisfaction. "I would allow myself to feel the music, and be part of the music, until I felt the words," she says. "And I came up with whatever the song was about. And I never got that far with this song! I just got to the part where I kind of imagined myself as the character doing that . . . and not knowing that it was finished, not *thinking* that it was . . . thinking that I was going to go back and write the lyrics . . ."

It was finished enough for Giorgio Moroder. He produced a three-minute single and put it out. Nothing happened. This suited Donna Summer fine. "In all honesty, I never intended this song to be a hit," she says.

Neil Bogart of Casablanca heard "Love to Love You, Baby" at MIDEM, the annual music biz trade fair in Cannes. He liked it a lot.

Neil Bogart had never done disco, but he was a brilliant hustler. He had originally kept Casablanca afloat by sending out quantities of an album of moments on Johnny Carson's *Tonight* show. "He shipped more than he should have because he needed to refinance the company," says Joyce Bogart. As long as the Carson albums were actually out in marketplace, they represented value, and by the time they flooded back, Casablanca was aloft and Bogart was swiftly doing well from the infantile pop generically called Bubblegum and from the novelty group, Kiss.

Bogart played his Donna Summer record at a party when he got back to Los Angeles. "People were saying, 'Hey! Play that again!'" Joyce Bogart remembers. "He played it again, and again, and again, and again. And finally he said to me, 'I'm calling Giorgio!'"

"It's the middle of the night. And you're calling Giorgio?"

"I'm calling Giorgio . . ."

"He woke him up. 'Giorgio, you have to make this long. You have to make it twenty minutes or something. Just do it! And I'll get it played.'"

Moroder produced a seventeen-minute cut. There had been long rock cuts, like Iron Butterfly's "In-A-Gadda-Da-Vida" and Isaac Hayes's "By The Time I Get to Phoenix," but nothing in dance music, and certainly nothing so racy. Casablanca's publicist telephoned Summer to discuss a promo tour. "Are you sexy?" she asked her. "Would you pose nude?"

"No. I would not," Summer said flatly.

Neil and Joyce Bogart caught up with Summer in Amsterdam. "That was when we found out she could really sing," Joyce Bogart says. This wasn't just about a hit. It was about a career. Bogart hired Billy Smith, a legendary record plugger and got into the act himself. "Neil Bogart called and asked if I would play 'Love to Love You, Baby' at midnight," says Frankie Crocker, who was at WBLS, and perhaps New York's leading radio DJ. "He was getting some resistance to it because of the suggestive lyrics or whatever. I had heard it in Paris in a club. I said what are you talking about? Will I play it at midnight? I'm going to play it in the middle of the day."

On December 29, 1975, a featurette in *Time* headlined SEX ROCK described it as a "marathon of 22 orgasms." The reporter, who did not divulge how this precise count had been made, also noted that "a poll of North Florida high schools revealed 984 of 1,000 unmarried girls sampled had become pregnant listening to pop songs."

The single became a mighty hit. Donna Summer instantly moved back to the United States, her German painter–husband in tow. She would be followed, in due course, by her producer, Giorgio Moroder.

Other Euros were flooding into Manhattan too, with dramatic impact on Nightworld. Regine Zylberberg, for instance, arrived with sister, Evelyne, to stake her claim in the mid-seventies. The Zylberbergs, who are of Belgian Jewish origins, had transplanted to Paris so effectively that Evelyne was crowned Miss France at a beauty pageant and Regine became a famous nightlife *animatrice*, meaning a cheerleader of chic. Regine, who introduced Paris to the Twist, and ran her own club, Regine's, had launched further clubs in Rio, Bahia, and Monte Carlo. Manhattan was an obvious target, so Regine hired Peppo Vanini, who ran the King Club in the Palace Hotel in St. Moritz, with a modish manner of chronic fatigue. Regine's opened in the glimmery innards of Delmonico's on Park Avenue in May 1976.

The transition from Paris to New York was not painless. The first announcement, which was printed on paper the color of canned salmon, said *"What to wear? Ladies: Evening elegance. Gentlemen: Ties."* Ties! "We found we were getting all the wrong people," Peppo Vanini says.

But the right people, necktied or not, who promptly began filling Regine's were a bit too right for some. "We were tired of Regine's," says Bill Oakes, who ran RSO Records for the Australian, Robert Stigwood. Oakes was going out on nocturnal sorties with Nik Cohn, a Dublin-born writer who had a contract with *New York* magazine. "People went to Regine's in jeans. The revelation we had in Brooklyn was finding that you had to wear proper clothes," Oakes says.

The disco they discovered in Brooklyn was called 2001 Odyssey. Its clientele was mostly working-class, straight, and Italian. Vito Bruno, a figure in Manhattan's Nightworld, who began as a bouncer there, nostalgically describes the rascally business practices of Odyssey's owner, Charles Rusinak. "Charlie would turn the music off and tell everybody they had to leave," he says. "Everybody would go out of the back door, and get on line, and pay to come back in again. Back in the old days, when there wasn't much competition, you could get away with murder."

Cohn's visit to the disco, which led to him crafting a long piece for *New York* about a young man called Tony Manero, was also practically his last visit, as some of his fellow new journalists suspected. "Nik came over to me when he was closing the piece," says Mark Jacobson, who worked at *New York* at the time, as I did also. "He said, 'Do you know anything about Brooklyn?'

"I said, 'Well yeah. A fair amount. I mean, like I *live* there.'

"He wanted me to drive him around so he could see. He wanted to get a couple of street names."

Cohn is a vivid writer. He is also a writer who knows when a piece has movie plastered over it. He gave a prepublication copy of "Tribal Rites of the New Saturday Night," which came out on June 7, 1976, to Kevin McCormick, with whom he had been working on another movie project. McCormick read it and speedily gave it to Robert Stigwood.

Stigwood called his lawyer, and partner, Fred Gershon, in some excitement.

"I see a hundred-million-dollar movie," he said.

"There *are* no hundred-million-dollar movies," Gershon said. "You are crazy."

"This is a hundred-million-dollar movie," Stigwood said. "Get the rights."

Gershon, still in awe at Stigwood's prescience, says, "Disco was happening. But it was not yet the worldwide craze it became. It was the very smart set and the gay set. Which was sometimes the same set. It hadn't spilled over. But Robert saw this was happening in Brazil. The year we went on the maiden voyage of the Concorde from Paris to Rio, Rio was rough, and very exotic, and the music never stopped. He saw it happening in England, France, Germany. It was going down the social strata. Five years earlier it would have been deemed effete for men to even be on a dance floor. Now men were becoming peacocks. It was Robert's instinct that a Tony Manero existed in every community in the world."

Gershon got an option on Cohn's article for $10,000. McCormick, who was twenty-five, was assigned to produce. The veteran producer Ray Stark pounced before Cohn's deal had been finalized, so Stigwood nailed it down offering the writer a first shot at the screenplay for a guaranteed $150,000, as well as percentage points in the soundtrack album. ("Points" are a percentage slice of the net.) This was at Nik Cohn's insistence. The soundtrack, which was to include such Stigwood artists as the Bee Gees, would obviously be important to the movie. It seems to have been the first time a writer got points in an album, certainly when the property was a magazine feature. It didn't seem much of a first, though. Soundtrack albums seldom did much business.

Stigwood hired a director, John Avildsen, after seeing a rough cut of *Rocky*. Avildsen soon made his presence felt, insisting that a writer he felt comfortable with, Norman Wexler, who had worked on *Joe* and *Serpico*, do the script. Wexler was hired, a fact Nik Cohn, laboring away on his own script, was not made aware of. Now the movie had to be cast. "We were in the Beverly Hills Hotel. I was sitting in the living room of, I think, Bungalow five," Gershon says. "I hear a screaming in the bedroom! Quick! Quick!"

He hurtled in. Stigwood was watching *Welcome Back, Kotter*. "That's Tony Manero!" Stigwood said, pointing at John Travolta on the screen. Travolta got a three-picture deal. "It was very unusual, but very typical of Robert's belief in himself," Gershon says. "It guaranteed that John Travolta would be paid for three pictures, even if the first one bombed. But Stigwood owned him, the way the old studios used to own an artist. Like a chattel."

Stigwood and McCormick loved the Wexler script. In the late fall of 1976 they began assembling a production team. The production was being run out of a former gynecologist's office on the ground floor of 135 Central Park West, where Stigwood had a triplex penthouse.

It was then that the problems began. "John Avildsen had been struggling. As he began getting more successful he began getting . . . lost in the process," McCormick says. He insisted on bringing in yet another writer. He also decided that Travolta was A. a rotten dancer and B. too fat. Jacques d'Amboise was brought in to remedy the first problem, Sylvester Stallone's trainer to take care of the second. Travolta shed twenty pounds.

So far as locations went, there was some discussion of using a new disco where construction was nearing completion: Studio 54. "Stigwood said, 'It's just down the road from my office. Wouldn't it be better than going to Brooklyn?'" Oakes remembers. They decided against it. Other discos they looked at didn't work out either, like Les Mouches. "The ceiling was too low," McCormick says. Brooklyn it would have to be.

"We were planning to shoot principal photography in January 1977," Fred Gershon says. The studio was Paramount. Stigwood was dealing directly with Barry Diller. "Barry was as sharp as a tack and tough as nails," Gershon says. "But he also had the ability to step back and say, 'I don't agree with you but I will defer to you.' Had he not done that, there would have been a debacle, because he was under a lot of pressure to make this a PG movie.

"Ratings had just come in. Robert made this an R movie. Unheard of! The words 'fuck' and 'suck' and all kinds of stuff. How are the kids going to get in? There were many fights. I think Robert allowed a few 'fucks' and 'sucks' to be taken out. As a concession.

"The other incredible thing was the music. There was no music! The Bee Gees were working in January 1977 in a Paris recording studio called the Château. Robert and I were at the Plaza Athenée, negotiating with the Rolling Stones to leave Atlantic Records and come to RSO. The Stones were at the Georges V. I think Mick was registered under the name of Mr. Mercedes Benz."

Stigwood learned that Prince Rupert Lowenstein, the Stones's longtime business manager, was meantime holed up in the Beverly Hills Hotel, and keeping Ahmet Ertegun, the customarily unflappable founder of Atlantic, apprised of goings-on. "Every one of our memos were being used to bludgeon Ahmet," Gershon says. "Robert finally said they were getting very, very greedy. Very, very, *very* greedy!

"And Robert and Ahmet were very old friends. Robert had had it. He said I've gone the limit on this deal. He sent Ahmet a bottle of Louis Roederer on his account." A memoir of a deal undone.

Stigwood refocused on *Saturday Night Fever*, and flew to New York. It was shortly before shooting was to begin, and the colossal success of *Rocky* was not making Avildsen easier to handle. McCormick brought Stigwood up to date. "He doesn't want to use the Bee Gees," he said.

He could see the Australian's pale, slightly protuberant eyes goggle.

"And that was it," McCormick says. The three had a meeting in Stigwood's apartment. The telephone rang as they were getting going. Stigwood picked it up, listened, and turned brightly to Avildsen. "There's good news and bad news," he said. "The good news is that you've been nominated for an Academy Award. The bad news is that you're fired."

It was poor timing for the director to indulge in auterism. *Saturday Night Fever* was to be a producer-driven movie as surely as disco is producer-made music. A substitute director was hastily hired. His name was John Badham, and his previous feature had been a baseball movie, *The Bingo Long Traveling All-Stars and Motor Kings*. "Can you shoot this script?" Stigwood asked him. Shooting finished in time for the opening of the movie's almost location: Studio 54.

ACT 1 : NIGHTS ON FIRE

TAKE YOUR PARTNERS

MAURICE BRAHMS GOT INVOLVED WITH MANHATTAN'S
Nightworld entirely on account of John Addison,
who arrived from South Africa in the early seventies.
"He was a second cousin of mine. He stayed with me
in Brooklyn," Maurice Brahms says. The cousins
were unalike. Brahms was of middling height, garrulous, straight, and dressed like a businessman,
whereas Addison was tall, gay, secretive, and elegant.
Brahms had a front-stage demeanor, like an actor doing monologue. Addison liked to lurk in the wings.
But the cousins got on fine. Both were ambitious,
tough, and sharp, and both could grip a dollar hard
enough to make it squeal with pain.

Maurice Brahms had been in the restaurant business since he was seventeen. "My father bought a restaurant for my uncle, but he died after a couple of
years. I took it over," Brahms says. The place was the
Colonel at 101 Park Avenue. John Addison had an
uncle who owned a parakeet business in Ventura
County in Southern California, and he himself had
studied horticulture in South Africa, but horticulture

not being huge in Manhattan, he signed up with Ford as a model. "He did well from day one" says Jerry Ford. He worked with Francesco Scavullo and became a long-term lover of the photographer. Addison also took a backup job as a waiter in Yellowfingers, a restaurant in midtown on Third Avenue. Unlike most MAWs (Model Actor Waiters) Addison quickly decided he liked the restaurant business. Preferred it, in fact, to the glam drudgery of modeling.

Juice bars were big in those days. Addison opened one up not far from the Ford Model agency, under the 59th Street Bridge. He called it Together. "He was a night person and I was a day person. I never had a nightlife," says Brahms. "He opened up my eyes. When I saw how many people were going out at twelve o'clock at night. And paying five dollars for a Coca-Cola and five dollars for admission! And I had a restaurant and I would get thirty-five cents for a Coke and they would scream and yell it was too much money. I said what the hell am I *doing*? I should be doing what he's doing." That's part of the magic of the night, the way that the moon and stars, though invisible, smothered in the contaminated skies of big cities, nonetheless manage to charm silver and gold out of pockets that are zippered shut in the daylight.

Fancy clubs at the time, like El Morocco and Le Club, were straitlaced, if not completely straight, so Le Jardin, which was on two separate floors in the Diplomat Hotel on West Forty-third Street, the penthouse and the basement, was a breakthrough. Though fashionable straights were made welcome, "Le Jardin was essentially gay. And there were some very pretty women there," notes Bill Oakes of RSO. "Which was obviously one reason gay discos broke out. Women could go and dance there without guys hitting on them." Also welcome were every sort of exotica. Patti Smith sang at Le Jardin, for instance, soon after making it at CBGB as chanteuse. Le Jardin was stylish, with bowls of fruit and cheese on tables. It was a bellwether of what was to come.

Brahms and Addison started to make the rounds of Nightworld. The place that Brahms found riviting was a gay club, Flamingo. Flamingo had been started in 1975 by Michael Fesco, a former Broadway dancer, a gypsy in the chorus of *Irma La Douce*. It mostly had gay male members, who each paid six hundred dollars a year. Flamingo was in an upstairs loft space, and there were two stunning women on the door, with gardenias behind their ears and Tuinal smiles. Since there was some fear of drug busts the club had an unlisted

telephone number, but initiates knew they would find it under Gallery for the
Promotion of People, Places, and Events at 599 Broadway.

Michael Fesco, a club owner and promoter, says that running a gay club
at the time was a breeze. "For the seven years that I was at Broadway and
Houston, we never had any problem with the neighbors," he says. "Everybody
was gay, queer. Who cared? Now it seems like everyone cares. AIDS came
along and the whole gay issue became a kind of a phenomenon. And we got
into a lot of trouble with the religious right and rednecks around the country."

The only women regulars at Flamingo, the Tuinal smiles aside, were a
couple of disco music nuts. "I would haul along the latest records in a milk
crate or a canvas tote bag," says one of them, Robin Sciortino. The club was
famous for the intensity of its ambience and for its theatrically inventive parties.
"There were Black parties and White parties," says a habitué, writer Stuart Lee.
He remembers a live pig scarfing down copies of *Vogue* and *Harper's Bazaar*
that people would toss into its pen, and set pieces such as a Crucifixion with
the models dressed as Roman legionaries, and a Jesus Christ who would, from
time to time, turn his eyes heavenward and ascend a cross.

Maurice Brahms, a straight middle-aged businessman, wasn't offended by
the Flamingo's inventive cabaret at all. "I saw a tremendous potential for the
gay market that wasn't being utilized. All the clubs that they had were raunchy
and secondary," he told me. Even Flamingo itself didn't scratch the surface. "If
people will pay this much for soda with a jukebox, my God, what if somebody
built a real club for the gay population? It could *explode*."

Brahms began to nose around looking for a venue. He finally lighted upon
a former envelope factory at 653 Broadway. "You had those Hare Krishna
people there. And the landlord was getting only two hundred dollars a month,"
Brahms says. "The landlord asked me for a thousand dollars a month. I told
him, 'I'll give you twelve or thirteen hundred, but I want a lease of fifteen
years. Where I can do whatever I want.' He gave me everything I wanted. He
thought I was crazy.

"I spent like a hundred and fifty thousand dollars opening that club.
That was unheard of, to put that kind of money in. It was painted black inside, with neon balls. And it had no name outside. I felt the whole mystique
of the place was to make a person struggle to find it. There were mirrors on

the sides. If you looked in the mirror, the neon balls just went on forever."
Which gave the club its name: Infinity. Brahms says, "We advertised in
Michael's Thing, a gay magazine, and we did a membership, and I said,
'COMING SOON! COMING SOON! with a penis sign . . . and then IT'S
FINALLY COME! . . . ' "

And as part of the decor there was a six-foot penis of pink neon at Infinity's
opening in the fall of 1975. "I made two openings, one for eight o'clock and
one for ten o'clock," Brahms says. He had invited his straight, or at least uptown
list, for eight, assuming they would clear the place to make room for the downtown gay crowd. "But at ten-thirty the room was still so crowded," he says.
"Nobody left. There were probably two thousand people in the street. That
was the market I had really targeted, and they couldn't get in."

"We didn't have anyone at the door with a guest list," Brahms says. "It
didn't exist. It's wonderful when there's no other place to go. I was the only
place to go. Nobody knew how to *spell* discothèque." Brahms's fingers fluttered
through clippings. "Donna Summer and the Pointer Sisters. They were just
there, partying. Nobody paid them. They paid admission when they came in.

"My policy was: Everybody pays! I wasn't there to become famous. I was
there to make as much money as I possibly could." His fingers flew through
his press clips and he found a 1975 headline in *Women's Wear Daily*: DISCOS
HAVEN'T PEAKED YET. "If they only knew! If they only knew!" he crowed.
"Here's some of the crowds we would get . . . everyone was magnificent . . .
Giorgio Sant'Angelo . . . Franco Rossellini . . . Calvin Klein . . . *I mean, everyone paid!*

"In this club you would see gays, straights, transvestites, bisexuals, movie-
stars, paupers, everything. Givenchy used to bring in Bunny Mellon. I didn't
charge her. She'd come in for fifteen minutes just to make him happy. He was
one of the few people I didn't charge. I didn't have the heart."

"I didn't realize how smart you were," Brahms's landlord grumbled later.
"You stole this from me."

It was at Infinity that Brahms met Steve Rubell and Ian Schrager.

Don Rubell, Steve Rubell's brother, the elder by two years, is a gynecologist and, along with his wife, Mera, a substantial collector of contemporary

art. For my information, he punched out an abbreviated version of the brothers' backgrounds as though he were filling out a form. "Started lower-middle class," Rubell said. "Became middle class. Grew up in Brooklyn. My father, who had wanted to be a dentist but because of the Depression had taken a job in the post office initially, was also a tennis player, and was the champion of New York City. When it became viable to earn money teaching, he became a tennis pro."

What were his father's strengths? "He *won*. He was a great athlete. My brother and my father were built very similarly. On the small side. Wiry."

He and his brother grew up living a "typical neighborhood existence," Don Rubell says. His brother's need to connect showed itself early. "We would live a large part of our life at the tennis courts," Don says. "Steve had a zillion friends and would drive us all slightly crazy. Even when he played, he would constantly be talking to people through the fence. He would be talking to people all the time."

Don Rubell is six foot two. Steve Rubell, who was very short as a boy and finally reached five five, later described his horror of Friday afternoons, which were when the father measured his sons. Nor were things better in school. "I'd go into class. People would say, '*You're* Don Rubell's brother?' " he said to writer Jesse Kornbluth. "You wonder why I want people to like me?"

Don, moreover, had gone to Cornell; Steve was rejected by Cornell and went to a more run-of-the-mill college, Syracuse, in upstate New York. Ken Auletta, the writer, was twenty-two, in his first year as a graduate student there and was a resident hall adviser. "That means you got free tuition, room, and board," Auletta says. "Your responsibility was to live on a freshman floor in a dormitory with thirty to sixty freshmen. You counseled them if they needed it.

"Steven was on my floor. He was a great tennis player," Auletta says. "But he was having trouble academically. He would come and talk about it. He was a very sweet guy. He had a sweet smile and these big, goofy eyes. And I knew they thought he would be a star. A tennis star. Just the opposite in the world.

"His academic weaknesses were across the board. He wasn't stupid. He just wasn't applying. He basically didn't give a shit about school. It wasn't like he was a wise guy or had a surly attitude or was depressive. He was worried about it. And his tennis coach was worried about it. He was not bounced out. But he was marginal."

Steve played tennis for Syracuse in the Eastern Intercollegiates in his first year, but this experience put him off looking for a future in the game. "I'd see great old tennis players in the stands, drunk and talking about the past. I didn't want to peak so young," he told Kornbluth. Since Rubell's father had wanted to be a dentist, Steve duly signed up to study dentistry. He flunked and transferred to history and economics. He stayed on a couple of years after graduating and picked up a couple more degrees, one a master's in finance.

It happened that Ian Schrager grew up a few blocks from Rubell, but he was a couple of years younger, and the vagaries of districting took them to different schools. But Schrager, too, went to Syracuse. One day he got into horseplay in a dorm. His opponent was something like six foot four, one of the college basketball stars, but Schrager wouldn't knuckle under. It was this that caught Rubell's eye. There were marked differences between Rubell, who was exuberant, with elastic features and—still guardedly—gay, and Schrager, who was shy, introverted, bonily good-looking, and straight, but the two swiftly formed one of those youthful friendships that are usually the most enduring in life.

Rubell was draft material on leaving Syracuse and joined the National Guard along with a Syracuse friend Bob Tannhauser. When they sensed their unit might be headed to Vietnam, "Steve managed to get us into a military intelligence unit in the Army reserves," Tannhauser told writer Michael Gross. "He had this knack, this desire to be where decisions are made. He wanted to direct what was happening, and he was so charming and disarming, people immediately embraced him. I hadn't even gotten my uniform and Steve was already the assistant to the company commander."

Steve Rubell joined a brokerage firm in Wall Street after leaving the military. "He gradually grew to run the back office," Don Rubell says. "There was a company at that time called Steaks 'N Ale that was being franchised. And Steve found a great location, I think on Queens Boulevard. And it was so good the parent company decided to use it for their own.

"I remember the night it happened. He was furious. And he stayed up all night, chewing up pencils and breaking pencils. By the next morning, there were just thousands of fragments of pencils in his room. He thought this would be the end of his life. Then he decided that he would never do that again. He would only go on his own."

But Steve Rubell had decided that the restaurant business was for him. His first places were a functional eatery in Bayside, Queens, and a fancier place in New Haven, Connecticut, called the Tivoli. "It was wonderful. A classic restaurant," Don Rubell says. Steve moved to New Haven and lived there for a year. What attracted him to the restaurant business was what attracts many amateurs to running restaurants, bars, and clubs—the idea that you spend your time not with numbers or with things, but with people. Neil Schlesinger, who had been at Syracuse with Rubell, and became his partner in these ventures, says gastronomic adventure was far from the point. Steve Rubell was a steak-and-potatoes guy. "He would say the best surprise is no surprise," Schlesinger says. Cookery was not his forte. "He knew nothing about restaurants. He couldn't turn a hamburger. He couldn't pour a glass of milk," Schlesinger says. "I could clean a coffeepot. I could fill up the salt and peppers."

Ian Schrager had begun to practice real estate law in 1974. Steve Rubell approached him and signed him up, with a retainer of one thousand dollars. It was his job to organize a rapidly swelling chain of Steak Lofts, some of which were doing poorly. "It was robbing Peter to pay Paul," Schlesinger says. He told Rubell they would be far better off with just a couple of successful places. "Steve called me soon after. He said, 'I've done a deal,' " Schlesinger says.

Another restaurant.

One of the final pieces in Rubell's restaurant empire was the Inn of the Clock, a place he took over in the twin towers alongside the UN Building, only to find that the building wouldn't let him run a smokestack to the roof. "That was a problem for a steak restaurant," as Don Rubell puts it, rather understating the case. The place was another bust, and the Steak Loft chain was teetering on the brink.

With typical brio, Rubell decided to open his most ambitious eatery yet. His newest Steak Loft was to be in a venerable stone building, which had until recently been the clubhouse for a golf course on land owned by the City Parks Department in Douglaston, Queens. Ian Schrager came in on the deal, too. Now as a full partner.

★   ★   ★

Ian Schrager, whose office was on Park Avenue midtown, would venture out into Manhattan's nightlife, as any young man would, in particular to such then lively clubs as Nepenthe and Hippopotamus. Living in New Haven, Steve Rubell was somewhat the homebody. He didn't drink, he would sometimes smoke a little pot, but his working habits didn't include late hours. Then he moved into Manhattan and shared an apartment with Neil Schlesinger. This arrangement continued for eight years, first on Eighty-fifth Street, then in the Bristol on Fifty-sixth and Third, and Schlesinger remembers nightlife slowly coming to his roommate's attention.

The Hippopotamus, which was run by an old Nightworld hand Olivier Coquelin, was the first club Rubell went to with any regularity, but soon he and his cronies, most especially Ian Schrager, were also going to Infinity, where they met Maurice Brahms, and to Le Jardin. Schrager was both astonished and impressed by what he saw. Not just the size and vigor of the gay culture he saw about him, but the general mixing and melding of different groups of people, the breaking down of social barriers of race and class, and the sight of people willing to stand in line, often in rotten weather, for the privilege of spending their money awed him. For Steve Rubell, though, it was just party time and the homebody was soon addicted to going out. It was during this time that the former jock made some new nocturnal aquaintances: Quaaludes, cocaine.

Schlesinger remembers that it was in Le Jardin that Steve and Ian first saw Bianca Jagger. It was puppy love. "If she sat down, they would sit down. If she left, they would leave. If she went to the bathroom, they would go to the bathroom," Schlesinger says. "Of course, she didn't know they were alive."

Rubell gave a party in one of his own joints. It was for Ian Schrager's then girlfriend, Ellen, and it was in the Inn of the Clock. "That was one of the best parties there ever was in this city," Neil Schlesinger says. That was also when the light went on for Ian Schrager. He, the lawyer, and Steve, the restauranteur, would be a perfect combination to enter Nightworld. Rubell took little persuading. The partnership was, on the surface, curious. The gregarious and extraoverted gay and the introverted straight would always be social opposites. "In general, Steve stays too long. And I leave too soon," Ian Schrager said later. But, as at college, that very lack of overlap made the fit the better. Rubell and Schrager set out together to study the terrain.

The reigning Nightlords were John Addison and Maurice Brahms. "We started talking about doing things together," Brahms says. "Steve could charm your pants off. You could hate him one day and love him the next day. He just had a charm about him. But," he adds, "even when he was stoned, when he used to come into Infinity with his mouth open, dribbling from the Quaaludes, he was always watching . . . always looking . . . always trying to gather information. There are a few people in the world who are able to function well, even when they are stoned out of their minds. And he was one of them. Anybody who thought they could take advantage of him because they were drugged, they were *wrong*."

That was the wisdom of the morning after, though. This was still bright evening.

Brahms introduced Steve and Ian to the elusive John Addison. The foursome, or the couple of twosomes, Brahms and Addison, Rubell and Schrager, got down to talking night business and agreed to an ambitious five-club deal. The profits were to be split up evenly among the four. Three venues were agreed upon right away: one was to be in Washington, D.C., one in Boston, and one in the house beside the golf course in Queens, New York.

Work began on the building of the clubs in Queens and Boston at roughly the same time. The look of things was going to be crucial. John Addison had a crystal ball built in New York for the Boston club and hired a driver to take it there, a fledgling fashion photographer named Arthur Weinstein.

Weinstein had been brought into the picture by a lighting designer, Ralph Bisdale. Weinstein had been walking down Twenty-first Street and had looked up and seen an illuminated window. "It was on the first floor. It was lit up so gorgeous. I was a kid. In my early twenties," Weinstein says. He walked up the stairs, knocked on the door, and walked in. "I said, 'Wow! This is a beautiful place.' " It was an after-hours club that Bisdale ran. "He was the one that opened my eyes to everything. He knew Addison, Brahms, everybody." Nightworld makes converts, like art and religion. It is *serious*.

It was thanks to Bisdale that Weinstein was hired to make a delivery for Addison. He took a friend. "We drove a truck up to Boston with the largest disco ball ever made. In history. It was humongous. It had to be at least fifteen feet wide," Weinstein says. "New York to Boston is not one-two-three. It's like up to a six-hour drive easy. So, *of course*, Addison wanted the delivery, and us to turn around and drive the truck back."

They finally made their grimy arrival. Richard Bernstein, maestro of the *Interview* magazine covers, was decorating the place with huge pictures of poppers (amyl nitrites) in irridescent colors. The building, at 15 Landsdowne Street, was an art nouveau pile with a history. For years it had been the Boston Tea Party, a famous venue for live rock concerts. The Grateful Dead had played there one New Year's Eve. The first time the Who ever played on American soil, it was in the Boston Tea Party. Led Zeppelin likewise. After the Tea Party had folded its napkins, the building became Cabaret After Dark. A nightperson of the time describes it as "a kind of run-down beat-up gay club." This was now going to be the four partners' first joint club.

The disco ball dropped off, Weinstein and his partner turned around and drove straight back. Weinstein was living then, as now again, at the time of writing, in the Chelsea Hotel on West Twenty-third Street. "I get back. I'm dying. I'm dead. I never heard of cocaine in those days. He leaves an envelope here for me. Guess what's in it? *Fifty dollars!*

"I call Addison up. He was at the Enchanted Garden. 'If you don't come over here with two hundred dollars right now I'm going to drive the U-Haul right into the fucking river. Do you think I'm kidding? *Try me!*'

"And that's how I met Steve. He came over to the Chelsea. He called and said, 'I'm parked in the front.' "

Rubell was sitting in an old Cadillac. He gave Weinstein a couple of hundred bucks. "He liked me from that moment on," Weinstein says. It was mutual. He went out to Queens and met the four partners together.

The humongous disco ball was emblematic, as were the Bernstein popper pieces. The disco look was being born. Ungarnished lofts and ramshackle basements were yesternight's news, and the sheer look of things was going to be important in the new disco palaces. Some elements would be nostalgic, like the disco balls themselves, and some, like Infinity's neon penis, would be borrowed from the gaudy over-the-topness of burlesque shows, the Vegas aesthetic. Others would be taken from Nightworld's arsenal of special effects, like the strobe, borrowed from fashion photography, which caught dancers in a snowblind dazzle, freezing them, moment by moment, like a Muybridge photo strip, and like the luminescent spermatazoa that used to slip over the walls, ceiling, and revelers during the classic light shows of the sixties.

One characteristic bit of sixties modernismo was devised by Ron Ferri, an artist from Narragansett, Rhode Island. It was called the "Translator," and coded music into electrical pulses that activated a flashing light system. You could say that Ferri was fulfilling a project of the Decadents of the nineteenth century, who had dreamed of sense swapping. In one of Rimbaud's poems each vowel was a color, and the Marquis d' Esseintes, the hero of a novel by Joris-Karl Huysmans, would inhale scents as though they were a symphony. The "Translator" made ear-to-eye transactions, turning thumping sound into fractious light for the new decadence; and in the mid-sixties Michael Butler, the producer of *Hair*, commissioned Ferri to design a nightclub in a Chicago town house, Le Bison.

Ferri wired his Translator into a thirty-foot wall of incandescent light bulbs, which could act mellow or crazy, depending on the sonic feed. He was also making neon sculptures. "I would use all these different gases and they burn different colors." John Addison, who had been introduced to Ferri by Scavullo, saw disco opportunity in the neon pieces. "He contacted me and said, 'I'm doing a project,' " Ferri says. " 'And I want your work. We're going to do five clubs.' "

"We?" Ferri asked.

"John said he has two partners. But he didn't want to introduce me to them. Because they were from Brooklyn and they were *really vulgar*."

We were talking in Ferri's apartment. He gave a sudden hiss of a laugh, like escaping steam, at the memory. "I said, 'Well. That's nothing to do with me, John.' "

Ferri was introduced to Addison's really vulgar partners, Ian Schrager and Steve Rubell. "Steve and I, we hit it off, like *that*," he says.

The new club was to be primarily gay, like Le Jardin. Addison, Rubell, and Schrager, who were working on a tight budget (Brahms being a somewhat absentee partner), spruced the place up, painted it, and installed Ferri's floor-to-ceiling neon pieces. Nobody could think of a name. "Why don't you just give the address of the place?" Ferri suggested. "Just call it 15 Landsdowne Near Fenway Park." They did so and opened the doors, not knowing what to expect.

"People were standing in the rain, waiting to get in. *Five thousand people, standing in the rain!*"

Just what happened next depends on whom you are listening to. Rubell later said, "I was really there only one day. And from the beginning I knew I was going to sell it."

If John Addison had thought he could use the energy of Rubell and Schrager, he hadn't counted on the way the two could absorb, internalize, *learn*. These processes are part of any kind of creative growth, and they can seem brutal, because whoever is doing the learning makes the newly absorbed knowledge part of their own chemistry. "What John didn't know was that they would just pick his brain and throw him out. Which is exactly what happened," Maurice Brahms says.

"They got the knowledge of how to build a club. They knew which sound person to go to, who the designer was and who the light person was. They got the information they needed."

Actually, Ian Schrager and Steve Rubell never denied that John Addison was a progenitor. Schrager, in particular, has insisted on the importance of Addison's role in creating a club that both harnessed the gay energy coursing through New York and was hospitable to other energy sources too.

Arthur Weinstein has a dry, droll take. He had it figured that first meeing. John Addison had taken Rubell's and Schrager's measure right away. They all liked each other. "Why not? They were all cowboys," he says. "But even then, I was green behind the ears, you look at these guys and . . . Yeah! *They're really going to share in the profits from the two clubs? Divvy it all up?* They're going to report what they make to each other and sit down like gentlemen?"

He gave his distinctive, sardonic laugh. If irony were an Olympic event, Arthur Weinstein would be a contender for the gold. "Yeah. Oh yeah!" he says.

Rubell and Schrager went to Queens, leaving Addison the club in Boston. It was all secretively handled, Nightworld style. They must have felt the subject was buried. Indeed, three years later, when a journalist, Henry Post, looked at Studio 54 for *Esquire*, he wrote: *They don't remember to whom they sold (the Boston club), Rubell and Schrager now say.*

John Addison, who was unmentioned in the piece, kept the Boston club awhile. It is now owned by John Lyons and his brother Patrick, who arrived in Boston soon after Rubell and Schrager skedaddled, and who currently constitute the four-hundred-pound gorilla of Boston nightlife. John Lyons says, "The problem was John Addison had—I don't know whether you would call it a lawless attitude or a can-do attitude—he had his way of doing business and believed in things being fabulous and flamboyant. Many times that flew in the face of Boston licensing authorities and Boston police and Boston fire department. He had a certain way he wanted to do something and he would just do it."

I asked whether Addison simply had a New York attitude?

"I've lived in New York. I'm perfectly familiar with the New York attitude," Lyons said. "John Addison had a New York attitude *times ten*."

It was in New York that John Addison proposed to take the battle to Ian Schrager and Steve Rubell.

The third club was supposed to have been in Washington, D.C., but the five-club deal was doornail-dead.

The New York disco was the one in the house beside the golf course in Douglaston, Queens. Rubell and Schrager had rented it earlier from Restaurant Associates, a chain of eateries that had the lease from the city. They decided on a name for their disco, Enchanted Garden, and began designing and hiring straightaway. Scotty Taylor, a nineteen-year-old five-foot-seven college kid, gave his girlfriend, who was looking for work, a lift there in his tiny Alfa, then went in with her to check the new joint out.

The next thing he knew, Taylor had accepted a job as a waiter. He had his first sight of Steve Rubell the next day. Taylor says, "Steve had got parachute pants and tight black shirts for everyone to wear. He turned to me and said"—Taylor went into an approximation of the nasal timbre Rubell would never shed—" 'Go ahead and try it on!' So Steve kind of took notice of me that night."

Opening night was a noisy bash. Taylor began the evening as a waiter but quickly decided he didn't care for it. "Going around, asking people if they wanted a drink! I was embarrassed." He demoted himself to busboy. "I collected the glasses . . . I washed them . . . I was a one-man army." Scotty Taylor was cheerful and as hardworking as a pit pony, qualities that commended him to Rubell; Rubell and Schrager both admired hard work.

Scotty Taylor knew that Steve Rubell was gay, although Rubell was not one to make public display of his private life. "In the beginning, he used to have beards. You know, he would have a girl hanging around," he says. Rubell was seeing a blond young man who he would introduce as his "cousin." "Steve asked me one day in the Enchanted Garden," Taylor says. "He said, 'Are you straight?'

"To me straight meant do you do drugs? *'Fuck no!'* I said. *'Me? Straight?'*

"He said, 'You want to go to a party tonight?'

"I said, 'Yeah!' We got in a car. They closed at four o'clock. It was about five-thirty in the morning. We drove down lower Broadway. There were two black doors at 653. We went in the door. It was Infinity. There were two thousand guys. And it hit me! Steve saw the expression on my face and he went, *'I thought you said you weren't straight?'*

"I said, 'I thought you meant did I do drugs!' I felt embarrassed. But Steve was cool."

It didn't affect their relationship one whit. If Rubell took to somebody, he took to that person. Richie Notar, a seventeen-year-old from Queens, was washing dishes. "A gentleman comes in," Notar says. "I smile, as I pretty much do. He says, 'What do you do here?' I said, 'I'm washing dishes.' He said, 'No!'

"Oh great! I'm fired. What did I do?" Notar says. "He said, 'I like your smile, buddy. You should be around people.' It was Steve Rubell."

Next thing, Notar was busboy-cum-driver. "He had a broken-down powder blue Lincoln Continental. It was something out of *Superfly*. It was the ugliest thing you've ever seen," Richie Notar says. He was baffled because the club was so sleek. Its ornamentation was changed weekly. There was a Playboy pad–type "game room" equipped with backgammon boards, pool tables, and electronic pong. There was a special room for the amorous, furnished with sofas the size of beds.

"The Enchanted Garden was a great precursor to Studio 54," says Robert

Caravaggi. Though he was a college junior, his father, Bruno, was an owner of Quo Vadis, a restaurant in Manhattan popular with le bon ton, so he knows what he was talking about. "It cost fifteen dollars to get in and it was mobbed," Caravaggi says. "It was all kids from Brooklyn, Queens, Long Island. It was wild. They didn't bother to go downstairs to do drugs. They did them on the table. There were rooms with themes—all this was before Area—and there was this one room overlooking the golf course. You could see Manhattan in the distance, maybe fifteen miles away. And you could see that that was where Steve Rubell wanted to go."

Because everybody who did go to Enchanted Garden agreed that it was a terrific-looking place. But just who was it that did go? Enchanted Garden was in *Queens*. When the rest of the world thinks about New York, they mean about Manhattan. The odds that partygoing Manhattanites are more likely to have dined, drunk, and danced in boîtes in London, Paris, St. Moritz, Miami, and Los Angeles than in Queens, Brooklyn, the Bronx, and Staten Island bounce off the scale.

Manhattanites have a whole xenophobic repertoire to deal with humans who happen to dwell in the outer boroughs. They mock their accents, deplore their dress codes, and have names for them—BBQs (for Brooklyn, Bronx, and Queens), Bridge and Tunnels (for the ways in and out of the city), and 718s (for the Brooklyn and Queens area codes). In *Saturday Night Fever* John Travolta's arrival in Manhattan is depicted as though a Neanderthal were suddenly to find himself stumbling among Homo sapiens, and Melanie Griffith, a commuter from Staten Island in *Working Girl*, is shown sporting her Big Hair, leather coat, and lots of jewelry, like the totems of some peculiar tribe. This prejudice made Steve Rubell, who might have become a Brooklyn dentist, crazy. Not least, because he shared it. Big time.

Steve Rubell needed allies for his assault on the foothills of fame. Like Billy Smith, the record promoter. "Billy kept on saying you've got to come to Enchanted Garden! You've got to come to Enchanted Garden! These guys are going to treat you real nice," Steven Gaines, then a young journalist with a lot of heft, says. Originally from Brooklyn, he had moved to Manhattan when he was in his very early twenties. He had been editor of the rock and roll biweekly,

Circus, but now wrote the "Top of the Pop," column for the New York *Daily News,* which went beyond music into the popular culture at large.

"So I finally agreed," Gaines says. "And they sent a limousine to pick me up in Manhattan and drive me to Queens. There was this very, very pretty but very Queens-type club. The problem was the landing pattern at Kennedy airport. The jet planes would go right the hell over this place and there would be this tremendous noise every fifteen seconds. So they just pumped up the music.

"And that was where I met Steve Rubell. I was introduced to him as another gay man. As far as I knew, he was always out. He was a gay man who owned this club with a straight partner. And then Rubell kept on trying to get me back out there. He wanted me to write about it in 'Top of the Pop,' " says Gaines. He did return to the club. "I became friendly with Steve but I didn't get to know Ian. He was always very distant. He really was one handsome stud. We all used to tease Steve about how handsome Ian was and he used to roll his eyes like *I know*! I think Steve had a bit of a crush on Ian."

Rubell would often buy dinner for Gaines in Manhattan. Gaines never did write up the Queens club in his column, and if Rubell was irritated he was too smart to let it show. Actually he and Ian Schrager were spending more and more time in Manhattan. They went to Infinity. They went to Hurrah. They went wherever there was stuff to be *learned.* They also went to private dinner parties in Ron Ferri's apartment on East Sixty-seventh Street. Ferri knew a whole set in New York. He had been married to a model and they had shared an East Side town house with the designer Angelo Donghia and the couturier Halston. "Halston was one of my closest friends. We were together all the time. But *Halston never went out,*" Ferri says.

So Halston did not meet Rubell and Schrager at Ron Ferri's little dinners. But many others did. "The people I had invited were snobs, of course," Ferri says. "They would say, *'What are you doing with those awful people?'*

"All those people who were dying to get into 54 later—trying to catch Steve's eye to get in. They didn't want to see him in my place because he wasn't anybody important." Steve Rubell was uncowed by this. His attitude was why should these people pay attention to me? He would have to *make* them. It was Ron Ferri who suggested to Rubell and Schrager that they should talk to one of Manhattan's most bravura nightpeople. She was doing special nights at Infinity. Her name was Carmen D'Alessio.

MANHATTAN À LA MODE

2

CARMEN D'ALESSIO, FIRST OF THE PARTY PROMOTERS, A true pioneer in a brand-new profession, celebrity-driven fun, has no recollection of her first sighting of Steve Rubell and Ian Schrager. But Steve Rubell had a vivid memory of *his* first sighting of Carmen D'Alessio. "Steve told me later. They showed up in Infinity to check me out," says D'Alessio. She has eyes like black enamel, a smile at once knowing and ingenuous, and she is given to whoops of laughter, so throaty as to be practically visible, like her native Peruvian butterflies caught in an updraft of tropic breeze.

"I was giving a party. They spotted me the first time, from what Steve told me later, on the shoulders of Sterling Saint-Jacques," a young black man, who had made a reputation as a hot dancer in clubs. Hubert de Givenchy had seen him on the floor and had cast him directly as a catwalk model. D'Alessio says, "I was dressed in one of my Giorgio Sant'Angelo outfits. I had taken off the skirt and was wearing the bathing suit. It was white. So they immediately decided that this person had to be their PR! You know, in

Queens." She gave her hoarse laugh. "In their Enchanted Gardens. So they started pursuing me from that moment on and they wanted me to come and see the place.

"Of course I told them it was out of the question. I said I have *nothing to do* in Queens. I don't know anybody in that part of the world. I don't think I can even bring press there. Why don't you try hiring somebody locally? I don't know how to help you . . ." D'Alessio thought she had seen the last of this on-the-make duo from some wasteland of unchic.

Carmen D'Alessio comes from a land-owning family in Lima. She arrived in Manhattan in the sixties, speaking five languages, and landed a job with the United Nations. It wasn't exactly bliss for a fun-loving girl—the UN's internal climate is a clammy gray fog. The delegates and the secretariat do not kick out the jams when they give their parties. So D'Alessio did not have to mull it over when Lili Townsend, an American friend, who was opening up the Yves Saint Laurent boutique in New York offered her a job doing public relations. That was 1969 and Yves Saint Laurent was God.

"That same year Valentino opened his first boutique on Madison Avenue," D'Alessio says, and she was duly poached. It so happened she was going out with Enrico Tucci, a Swiss movie producer at the time. The following year, they married. Tucci wanted to return home and Valentino transferred Carmen to work on the PR for his haute couture house in the Via Gregoriana.

She stayed until 1975. "I learned a lot about glamour and fashion. And I was exposed to a lot of international people of the first level," she says. "But I was tired of my second husband. Tucci was involved in the movie business. I was tired of that whole scene. I was ready for the excitement of New York."

That was inevitable. Carmen came back and moved into the Meurice, a building on Fifty-eighth Street. That was inevitable too.

The Meurice was the New York GHQ of what *Vogue's* Diana Vreeland had called the "Beautiful People" and *Women's Wear Daily's* John Fairchild had abbreviated to the BPs. Those in and out of the Meurice in those days included Nastassja Kinski, Helmut Berger, and Dialta Cardini, a blond Florentine of fey beauty, and the niece of the Briton, Sir Harold Acton.

"There was Marina Cicogna and Florinda Bolkan . . . Franco Rossellini, who sometimes was going out with Doris Duke," Dialta says. "Susan Sarandon was there with Louis Malle. But first I put him there. Silvia Martins, who went to the Sherry Netherland with the excuse of photographing Richard Gere, and they were together for years . . . Clio Goldsmith . . ." The Meurice would know its ODs, but was better known for its highly charged emotional life. Sometimes the whole building seemed to be panting. "It was as much fun, the Meurice, as Studio 54," Dialta says.

Fun was not the whole issue for Carmen. There was also money. She had a Brazilian friend in New York, Peter Martins, who owned Tropicalia, a club on Second Avenue. He asked her to organize parties there on Tuesdays and Thursdays, which had been the slowest nights of his week. "I thought this sounded great—to throw parties, have a good time, and get paid on top!" D'Alessio knew as many fashionables as she needed from her Valentino days. (It has always been said she disappeared with the Rolodex. Wrong. Her life was her Rolodex.) D'Alessio burbles, "Before I knew it *Women's Wear Daily* labeled Tropicalia the chic place to be on Tuesdays and Thursdays."

Maurice Brahms first cast eyes on D'Alessio in Infinity. "My wife, Viviane, saw her dancing and pointed her out to me. She always used to come with these great-looking guys. My wife said I should talk to her. She seemed to know a lot of people." They talked. "So obviously I was stolen by Maurice Brahms," Carmen D'Alessio says breezily.

Brahms says, "Even though the club was extremely successful at the time, I was always looking for new things. So we developed an additional night. A Wednesday night. Carmen didn't have any money. She was starving! I wish I remembered the deal. I think she got a dollar a person she brought in. She would make six or seven hundred dollars a week, I think. That was okay in 1975, 1976." He sighed. "Now the deals are totally different . . ."

D'Alessio says, "I made Infinity famous by doing two enormous parties. One of them was Carmen's Carnival and the other was the Bicentennial. So there we are! And Infinity was in *The Wall Street Journal* as a phenomenon, for making tons and tons of money!" *Women's Wear Daily* did a half page on Carmen's "Brazilian carnival." The copy sniped that *" 'celebrities' were in a minority,"* but ran little pictures of Franco Rossellini, Uva Harden, and Calvin

Klein. The *Journal's* article ran on the front page on May 4, 1976. It was head-lined A DISCOTHÈQUE DJ HAS TO BE A MASTER OF CONTROLLED FRENZY, and it focused on Infinity's disc jockey, Bobby DJ.

Maurice Brahms was not named. His partner, Joe Levy, was referred to only as "one of Infinity's owners, an insurance man who prefers to remain anonymous." This was Nightworld discretion, Old World style. It was not to last for long.

Arthur Weinstein was as surprised as anybody to find himself running the hottest new disco in town.

Weinstein, one of three sons of a New Jersey realtor, had slipped by the draft and at eighteen was already living in the East Village. He was a radical. "I was living with some Black Panthers on East Seventh Street. Actually they were in jail. I was living with the women. That was better. This was the Stone Age." He became a fashion photographer, did well enough to work for *GQ*, and fell in love with a model, Jessica Lange. He followed her to Los Angeles when she left to make *King Kong*. "Then I needed a loan. She couldn't believe I came out without my return fare," Arthur says. "I said this is *me*. Remember?"

Back in Manhattan, he had grown disenchanted with photography. "I could hardly sustain myself," he says. "You realize no matter how great you become, there's millions just like you. And after a while you have looked at so many portfolios and seen so many girls and played so many absurd games that the fashion business is all about."

In this, he saw eye to eye with one friend, the former model, John Addison. Addison gave him a job in Le Jardin as a waiter. "It was outrageous," Arthur says. "All you had to do was get some drink tickets. Then when the customer pays, you keep the money. I was coming home with a thousand bucks in my pocket." This wasn't, he explained, robbing Addison—"he was a great guy"—it was just that a successful club is a cash machine and it was accepted that functionaries tap in at different levels of the ziggurat. It is very orderly, held to a sensible scale, like systems of bribery in foreign lands.

Arthur was then going out with Colleen Mudery, an auburn-haired woman from Pennsylvania, half Polish and half Irish. He says, "Maurice had Infinity. I wanted to do a place. But I never in a million years thought I'd meet anyone who would put the money up. Colleen told me she knew somebody the first time we met. I thought it was bullshit."

The somebody was named Robert Boykin. Arthur persuaded him that since Infinity was open only on Fridays and Saturdays, there was room for a competitor. The two set off on a real estate prowl and looked over a former TV studio on West Fifty-fourth Street, which Arthur admired, but which Boykin thought too big. They picked a smaller place on Broadway and Sixty-second Street. Boykin put up $150,000 and gave Arthur half of the club. The disco opened as Harrah's but there came a stinging letter from the Reno casino whose name they had purloined and they quickly called it Hurrah.

Hurrah was a hit. Arthur fell gladly into that sensual continuum available to Nightworld's inner core. He and Colleen were living on the West Side, but he was playing around, and when he started spending most of his time in the Fifth Avenue apartment of a rich girl who was also a model, Colleen decided on a show of will. She took a beau, an abrasive-tongued fellow named Paul Garcia, an actor, who worked mostly as a model. "Arthur tried to ban Paul from the club," Colleen says. "I said it's as much my club as yours."

Things came to a head when Arthur kidnapped their mutually owned dog, a saluki called Mushy. "We walked across Central Park and talked," Colleen says. "I was wearing Charles Jourdan sandals in two feet of snow. Arthur suddenly said it was like baseball . . ."

"Baseball?" she asked, puzzled.

"You don't break up a winning combination . . ."

John Addison had folded Le Jardin. Infinity and Hurrah ruled the night.

One day Carmen D'Alessio was having lunch with Ron Ferri in Gino's, a fine old-fangled joint on Lexington, where zebras pranced on the pink walls, which was just as well, because some of the patrons would have likely seen them there anyway. When, what Carmen later learned was a prearrangement, Rubell and Schrager happened to walk by in time for coffee. "So they appeared," she says. "Really charming, both of them. And they ended up inviting me for dinner."

Carmen, who was with her future third husband, Rick, liked Thai food, so Steve and Ian took them to Uncle Thai's. "This was the good old days of drugs and alcohol and whatnot," Carmen says. "So first of all they ordered the entire menu—they did this to impress me—then we went through I don't know how many bottles of wine, and we got stoned. They had *everything.*

"At the end of the night when they said, 'Would you like to come with us to the Enchanted Garden?' I said, 'Let's go anywhere!' " Another husky chuckle. "I was amazed of the fact that the place was not a dive like I had thought. It was beautiful. So then I decided that I was going to help them. Not as a promoter, because I still insisted I could not bring them people or press. But I was going to give them themes. So that they could invite their own following of, you know, Queens, or wherever."

D'Alessio's first theme party was the Thousand and One Nights. "I brought Pat Cleveland"—a supermodel avant la lettre—"and I told them to have camels, real camels, and elephants, and to do the whole trip, and the bartenders were sultans, you know, bare-chested, with harem pants and what not. So it was amazing."

Rubell and Schrager grew ever more ambitious. Richie Notar remembers being assigned to ferry "a bald-headed man . . . a little chunky" in from Manhattan. Duly made-up, this turned out to be the drag diva, Divine. There was an appearance by Marilyn Chambers, the former model who had graced the cover of a box of soap flakes before graduating to porno stardom in *Behind the Green Door.* "They went so far as to have a Gay Night," Richie Notar says. "It was just a label they put on to scare away all the Guidos from Brooklyn. It was the best night of the week."

It was at Carmen D'Alessio's instigation that Paul Caranicas and his partner-lover, Antonio Lopez, the fashion artist, filled two school buses with celebs and ferried them out to the nightery, and that Grace Jones performed free. "I took Egon there and Calvin Klein," Carmen shrieks. "All this in Queens! The moon!"

It cost Carmen her Infinity deal. "I fired her," Maurice Brahms says succinctly.

Queens might be Queens, but Brahms had an instinct about Steve Rubell.

Then Carmen D'Alessio was approached by one of her set, the German male model Uva Harden.

THE GERMAN MODEL, THE ISRAELI PLAYBOY,
THE PERUVIAN PARTY GIRL
& THE NEW YORK BUSINESSMAN

3

THE ACTUAL BUILDING AT 254 WEST FIFTY-FOURTH STREET
was put up by an idiosyncratic fellow called Fortune
Gallo, who stuck his monogrammed crest up here and
there on the walls. It was designed to house a project
of Gallo's, the San Carlo Opera Company, and it
opened its doors in 1927. Soon enough the opera
company was forced to eke out its budget by renting
the premises out for theatrical productions. By 1930
the opera company was gone and the place became a
theater, the New Yorker, opening with the first, and
last, New York production of one of Henrik Ibsen's
less effervescent plays, *The Vikings*. Between 1933 and
1936 the premises survived as a theater restaurant, the
Casino de Paris. In 1937 the Federal Theatre Project
leased the building and gave it yet another name, the
Federal Music Theatre.

The Columbia Broadcasting Company took it
over six years later, and for three decades the space
functioned as a soundstage for radio and television,
pumping the *Jack Paar*, *Perry Como*, *Jack Benny*, and
Johnny Carson shows into the ether, along with *Beat*

the Clock, What's My Line, The $64,000 Question, and *Captain Kangaroo.* Ed Gifford, who was with CBS says it was called Studio 53. "All the studios had numbers," Gifford says. "We had 52, 56, 57. Studio 43 was up on Vanderbilt Avenue. Studio 53 was this one. I know, because I was an associate director of Studio 53 back in the fifties."

When CBS finally went to Hollywood, the final curtain seemed ready to fall, but the New York slump—memorable for the *Daily News* headline FORD TO CITY: DROP DEAD—arguably saved the building from the wrecker's ball. Its existence was no secret; many Nightworlders looked it over, as the disco boom frothed and foamed, not just Boykin and Weinstein, but Maurice Brahms and John Addison. They were preparing to open another disco, though "I saw the space and I loved it. But I was already fully committed to New York, New York," Addison said.

Everybody seems to have decided the old theater would prove a mouthful too big to chew. Everybody except Uva Harden.

Uva Harden, the man who found Studio 54, was from the German port town Hamburg. "He was blond with blue eyes. The ideal Teutonic male," says the Finnish model Ulla-Maija Maki, adding with the affectionate exasperation that Uva inspired in so many, "he was a brainless pretty boy." Harden married in Germany, and his wife, who was half German and half Japanese, bore him a son. The marriage then went sour—his wife had had him thrown into jail on one occasion—so he came to Manhattan in the early seventies and began to do well as a fashion model.

Uva Harden was a charmer. He was part of a brash set. "It was a fast crowd. We were all very young and traveling all over the world. Uva protected me," says Barbara Carrera, the model he married in 1973. "But he was very into hallucinogens and coke."

Uva and Barbara were married for three years and stayed on warm terms after their divorce. He was always working on plans to do something more substantial than modeling, something that might bring him up to the economic level of his buddies. Opening a nightclub that would outdo anything he had seen in Europe or New York was a notion he had played with from the middle of the decade. "He would go around looking for *the* location for the idea he had," Carrera says.

A number of Uva's well-heeled friends agreed that he would make an excellent front man for a disco. One was Erroll Wetson, who owned a chain of hamburger joints and was married to the Amazonian model Margaux Hemingway. Wetson, who had let it be known he was looking for space for a disco, heard of something that sounded just dandy: a studio that had been constructed for the photographer Bert Stern. Stern had been a hugely successful photographer both of fashion and the famous—he had taken perhaps the best-known photographs of Marilyn Monroe—but amphetamine addiction had undermined his empire, and the studio was up for grabs.

"I brought Uva and Gordon Butler over," Errol Wetson says. Butler, a sleek entrepreneur of Lebanese origins with a pitted face, was very much part of the crowd. "I said what do you think of it? Gordon, you put up the money. Uva, you'll bring the fashion industry—the straights and the gays and the Europeans. I'll be the mastermind behind the damned thing and conceptualize the club." Erroll Wetson says he even had a name for the place. It was, after all, a photographic studio. "I said we'll call it Studio," he recalls.

Wetson was in the middle of negotiating the deal when Uva Harden, who like many charming unbrilliant people could be headstrong, as though obstinacy could be a sort of substitute intelligence, told him to call a halt. First, he said, they should check out another venue that had been brought to his attention, a disused theater on West Fifty-fourth Street.

"So I went over there with him," Wetson says. "We went in the back door on Fifty-third Street. It was black, and we got some light, and I actually started to lay out the concept. I said the bar should be here . . . movable sets . . . the flyers and the drop . . . it would be a little sleazy, a little sexy . . ."

Uva had notions of his own, too. "He had ideas for lasers and lighting. He got the idea from the studio equipment that was there," Carrera says. "Uva would always come up with these wonderful ideas. And he would even go through with them *diligently*. But right before it would take off, the self-destruct button went off . . ."

Several members of the set, Gordon Butler included, seemed keen to get involved. They would sit around and talk it up. "I named it the Studio,"

Wetson says. "And because the address was 254 West Fifty-fourth Street, in a round table conversation somebody threw out the name Studio 54. It was the address. The concept of the studio—movable sets, the actors being the audience, the audience being the actors—was mine. A hundred percent. No one else's. Unquestionably." But, as so often happens, especially when some of the enthusiasm of the interested parties may be stimulants-based, things went into slow-mo when the prospect of actually parting with dough drew closer. "A lot of times people are very slow on the draw," Wetson says.

The impatient Harden began showing the premises to friends like Howard Stein, then one of New York's principal promoters of rock concerts. He was also sounding out other financial prospects. One was Sidney Beer, an older man, who was a schmatta manufacturer from Brooklyn. He calls himself Uva's best friend and still talks of the young Teuton with angry affection.

"He calls me one day and says I have found a *groovy place* for a discothèque," Beer says. "So he takes me down. I look over this gigantic place and I was very interested. I said, first, get an engineer's report. What would it cost to put this place together? He comes back a few days later. He had spoken to the landlord. We could cut a very good deal—a fifteen-year lease, a twenty-year lease. He said it'll cost you sixty thousand dollars.

"I said, 'Idiot! It'll cost you three or four hundred thousand.' At the time I had lost a fair amount of money in the stock market. So I tried to get some friends to invest."

Sidney Beer also notes that his work on the project extended to naming the unborn club. "Uva found it. I made the name," he says. "It was on Fifty-fourth Street. I said, 'Let's call it Studio 54.'

"Uva, do like I tell you! It's a good name. It's easy for people to remember—where the street is and what the club is. So it's God's truth! I made the name." His friends couldn't come up with the money, though. "So I backed off," Sidney Beer says.

Another friend whom Harden approached was called Yoram Polany. Polany, who had British and Israeli passports, was living in the Bahamas. "I was doing some real estate development. We had bought property in Paradise Island," says Polany. "Uva came down one day," Polany remembers, saying that the German model was with a cute blonde from someplace in the Midwest. "Uva was always very drunk, very, and he was always looking for money,"

Polany says. That time, though, Uva was very specific. There was a place he had discovered that would be a tremendous venue for a club. Polany had never done business in New York but he was always looking for an interesting deal, and what could be more interesting or sexier than a discothèque?

Yoram Polany visited New York two or three weeks later. Uva Harden took him to the theater. Expecting little, Polany was astonished. "CBS had moved their television operation to the West Coast," he says. "But they were maintaining the place. They had a crew there, just a skeleton crew. But everything was running. The place was amazing. It was ninety percent ready. The sound system was in. It had the balconies with seating. It was literally *there*." He also noted that the place was next to a parking lot and that the Fifty-fourth Street police precinct was just down the road. "So there wouldn't be any problems with drugs," Polany explains.

Polany had a partner in his Bahamian dealings. This was Frank Lloyd, who owned the swell Marlborough Gallery, a Lichtenstein-based corporation with imposing spaces in London and New York. Polany told Frank Lloyd about the proposed club and offered him a partnership. "He said, 'Yeah! Go ahead and do it,' " Polany says. "So I began negotiating . . ."

Curiously, Polany also came up with the name. "Studio 54," he says. "That was my name. I chose that name because it was Fifty-fourth Street and it was a CBS studio. And why not? It's a great name."

Neither the German nor the Israeli seems to have bothered his head overly much about a case unwinding in the New York State Court of Appeals. In this, Frank Lloyd—whose jocular art world nickname was "Frank Lloyd Wrong"—stood accused, along with other executors, of defrauding the estate of one of his artists, Mark Rothko, of several million dollars. Since the case had been crawling along through six years of litigation, the club would doubtless be open long before it was settled.

Polany and Harden returned to the Bahamas and took a couple of young women out on one of Frank Lloyd's speedboats. "The motor conked out. So they called a coast guard who towed them in," Beer says. The women got off. "It got fixed. But they didn't blow out the noxious gases in the hold. It blew up. Uva was turned the other way. It went up his back." Both men had fourth-degree burns all over their bodies. Polany spent three months in the hospital in New York and was unable to return to the islands. "I couldn't stay in the

Bahamas in the sun," he says. Uva Harden was in hospital a few weeks longer. His friends say he never fully recovered.

So it was that Polany had stronger reasons to make a go of it in Manhattan when he returned to negotiations. But his negotiations became increasingly tough, both with the two landlords, and indeed with Uva Harden.

"Basically he wanted to be an equal partner," Polany says. "But I said to him, 'Uva, this is a deal that's going to cost a quarter of a million dollars, if not more. You can have a finder's fee.' So we started falling out a little bit . . .''

Nonetheless, they continued with the nuts and bolts. Polany talked with the police precinct. "Everything was done according to Hoyle. Right? At least, I felt so," he says. Disc jockeys were approached and detailed plans were drawn up for the embryonic club, which was called Studio 54. Also, Uva Harden asked Carmen D'Alessio to do the publicity. "I loved the place from the moment I set eyes on it," she says. "And I could see the future or something like that. Because up until then there had been nothing like it in New York. This was the first time I was being shown a theater for a club. And I could already envison that this would be the ideal place for fashion shows and for movie and TV shoots. This could work twenty-four hours out of twenty-four. This was a winner!"

But the lease was still unsigned. "We didn't want to sign anything without a liquor license commitment," Polany says. "I filled in all the documentation. And for some reason the liquor license wasn't coming through. I didn't understand why. I just felt we were getting the runaround."

A first application for a liquor license had been filed with the New York State Liquor Authority in August 1976. It stated that Yoram Polany was to be the chief stockholder, with Harden as a partner, and that the backing was to come from the Chase Manhattan Bank of the Bahamas. The SLA turned it down on the grounds that it was unhappy with their lack of information about the sources of the funding. A new application was swiftly filed revealing that the Marlborough Gallery Inc. owned 93 percent of the stock. This was turned down too.

It was then that the New York State Court of Appeals handed down what was described as a "landmark decision" in the Rothko case. The conduct of the executors, primarily Frank Lloyd, was described as "manifestly wrongful and indeed shocking." Fines and damages amounting to $9.25 million were imposed. On Tuesday March 8, 1977, the Manhattan D.A. Robert Morgenthau announced that a grand jury had indicted Frank Lloyd on February 24 on two counts of tampering with evidence, charges that could land him in the pen for eight years. An arrest warrant had been issued and Interpol had been put on the alert. Actually Lloyd was sitting it out at his family retreat on Paradise Island in the Bahamas.

Polany applied again, this time on his own account, but the situation was fraught. Erroll Wetson, who was monitoring the process, says, "If you miss three times, you lose the deal. You don't get paid any money back for the lease or your start-up expenses." Polany was summoned to the District Attorney's office and learned the D.A. had not been overjoyed to find that he was himself the owner of four Rothkos. "I was told that they didn't believe it was my money and would I appear in front of a grand jury," he says.

Polany said yes, rather to their surprise, he feels. He testified, and produced ten years of receipts on his Swiss bank accounts and fairly voluminous records. "You know, having worked in Hong Kong and various places, and always paid taxes, I had receipts," he says. "They realized that this was genuine money, not funny money. I showed them I could justify an investment of a quarter of a million dollars." He says he got his application for a liquor license approved. All was set fair.

That is Yoram Polany's version. A spinning disco ball, mounted with mirror fragments, is a fine metaphor for Nightworld generally, though Carmen D'Alessio saw it differently because for her, Frank Lloyd's taking it on the lam had changed everything. "Suddenly with his going, there was no more investor. And I decided to approach Steve and Ian," she says.

Uva Harden, who had grown frustrated with the snail's pace of the project, agreed to let Carmen initiate a meeting with the twosome from Queens. Polany, after all, still hadn't come up with a liquor license. His own rich pals seemed to be sleepwalking. Errol Wetson, who saw himself as effectively Uva's silent partner, says that some money had already gone into the project but there was "a question of credibility." Uva Harden's credibility. He was sociable, well liked in the fashion world, a good party guy, but would he be a reliable director? "He made irrational moves," Wetson says. "He was sometimes known for shooting himself in the leg." Wetson has a vivid memory of a dinner in Uva's midtown apartment. "A bunch of us were there. Gordon Butler. Barbara was there. This one, that one," he says. "Midnight, listening to some music. We had just finished dinner. *And the money was in the room!* Each guy would have thrown in fifty, twenty-five, whatever it was. The money was in the room. More than the money. More than necessary. But Uva had a buzz on him. He said he was going to go out to Queens that night. And would I go with him? He wanted to meet with these kids who had a club out on the island in Douglaston, and Carmen was taking him. I said, 'She's bringing you out there and you're going to do business at midnight? What kind of deal are you going to make at midnight? You're not going to speak for my position. Stay here. We'll make a private meeting. But we will discuss the deal with our own inside group only. Let's do this rationally. You've got a buzz on.' "

But Uva Harden felt he had been sitting on his hands long enough. Off he went to meet Ian Schrager and Steve Rubell. Larry Gang, an attorney and something of a party animal himself, gave him some sensible advice before the meeting. "I told him, 'Uva, before you let these guys see the property, make sure your end is covered,' " Gang says. " 'Otherwise, you'll wind up getting screwed.' He said, 'Don't worry about it!' "

They met. Carmen later took Rubell and Schrager to the old theater. Like so many others, they were daunted by its sheer size. "They asked me, 'Do you think you can fill it?' " Carmen says. "And I said, 'I will!' "

Uva proposed a new partnership to Rubell and Schrager. He asked for 22 percent. "Uva knew a lot of people around town. He was going to be the front man and promoter of the place," Larry Gang says. His option on the property had lapsed, though.

"That was on a Sunday night. By Tuesday or Wednesday of that week, Steve and Ian told the landlord to draw up the papers for the lease," Gang says. "I was at a dinner party on Beekman Place on Friday. Yoram came in, very happy. He said, 'Guess what, guys! Our liquor license has been approved.' And Uva's face turned white. Because he had not told Yoram what he had done."

Shortly after Carmen D'Alessio and Larry Gang, who was acting as Carmen's attorney, met Steve and Ian to discuss her own relationship with the club. The meeting was in Ian's legal office on Park Avenue. "They offered Carmen five percent of the club," Larry Gang, who was trained as a chartered accountant, says. "I asked, 'What do you mean five percent? Is that a five percent ownership interest? Five percent of the gross? What does all this mean?'

"Ian said, 'No, no. That's five percent of the *net*.' "

The net is the gross, minus expenses, so it is nebulous, where the gross should be easy to figure. Count the people paying to get in. Look at the cash register tapes at the bar. Gang hammered away at the duo, urging them to give D'Alessio a percentage—say 2 percent—of the gross. "They were good guy, bad guy," he says. "Steve was the good guy, Ian was the bad guy. Ian was the one who kept saying, 'No. We can't do that.' "

The light bulb clicked on. "It was then I knew they planned on skimming. They planned on skimming from the *beginning*," Gang says. He took Carmen aside. "I told her, 'Five percent of the net with the cash being counted by Steve and Ian, you could very well end up with nothing. Maybe what you ought to do is just take a flat salary. I said this also knowing that Carmen wasn't a U.S. citizen." Carmen D'Alessio settled for a salary, plus a slice off the door for her own special parties.

Yoram Polany has some darkly baroque detail to add to the scenario, dating from just before Rubell and Schrager came on the scene. "Uva was getting a bit funny," he says. "And I could see I would have a lot of problems with Uva because one couldn't give him the percentages he felt he had coming without him putting up money, which he didn't have. And then a strange thing happened.

"Uva rang and said, 'Please, could I have lunch with some people.' We were three weeks away from opening. I was busy with disc jockeys and public relations and the logos and everything else. He forced me to have lunch. He said, 'You must. You owe it to me, and it's very important.' We met in the Algonquin Hotel. Uva introduced me to this young Jewish-looking fellow. I forgot his name. Brian, I think. No second name.

"The other one was an Italian-looking fellow named Frank. He must have been about sixty-five. We had lunch together. You know how crowded the Algonquin Hotel is? We had a separate table in the corner. It was the only table with flowers on it. It was totally secluded. Like there was a . . . cordon sanitaire. And waiters buzzing around, but very discreetly.

"Uva left immediately. Didn't stay for lunch at all. Left me with these two people. Brian made polite conversation. I didn't know who these people were.

But I was there. Then somehow I think Brian got the nod. He got up and left, and there I was sitting with Frank. Frank was a nice, polite, little Italian fellow. And he said he wanted 10 percent of the gross. Just like that!

"I said, 'I'm really very sorry, Frank. But I wish I knew what this was all about. Because I've already got a partner and we're not interested. The thing is fully financed. Et cetera, et cetera.' And he said to me, 'I don't think you understand. *We would like to have ten percent of the gross.*'

"You know, ten percent of the gross is like twenty-five, thirty percent of the net. And then the penny dropped. I said to him, 'Frank, am I having lunch with who I think I am having lunch with?'

"He said, 'I don't know who you think you are having lunch with. But I think the answer is yes.'

"And I started laughing. This was like in a book. And my next question to him was 'How do I know that somebody else isn't going to come and ask me for ten percent of the gross?' He said, 'After lunch I'll show you . . . ' "

They finished their lunch. Frank's driver then drove them to the Brooklyn docks and Frank took Polany into an office. "Wherever he went, these big tough seamen were coming up, and it was like he was the pope," Polany says.

Polany was convinced. Actually, he was *more* than convinced. "I said, 'Frank, I'm a nice boy from London. I just scraped away from death on a speedboat. I'm still recuperating. I don't know my way around New York and I wouldn't like to be involved.' "

The family that controlled the Brooklyn docks at this time was controlled by Antony Scotto's uncle.

He telephoned his own Frank—Frank Lloyd. "I said, 'Frank, we're selling,' " Polany says. "He was very annoyed. He said, 'We've spent all this time and effort. Now at the Fifty-ninth minute, you want to get out?' I didn't want to tell him why at the time. But Frank was going to sit in the Bahamas or Switzerland and I was going to be *there*."

Yoram Polany got out of the club business posthaste.

Uva Harden's relationship with the Rubell/Schrager Studio 54 was short-lived. "They gave him shit," Sidney Beer says with dolorous indignation. "They let him come in a few times. They gave him a couple of thousand dollars. It was heartbreaking. Uva was bitter. He was a wonderful guy. He just wasn't too bright."

It was Errol Wetson's doing that Uva got any money at all, by his telling. "When I found that he negotiated himself out I had to go there and collect the money," Wetson says. "Because those guys didn't respect the deal they had made. But they were still at that moment little *pishers*. They had to respect me, walking in and saying, 'Come on! I want the money, and *deliver*. Go get the cash, and bring it here.' "

As Studio prospered, Uva persevered. Unfortunately what he persevered in was one of those bumbling rake's progresses, which were so much part of those times, and ours. His burns had put him out of modeling but John Casablancas had put him in charge of the man's division at Elite. He was there when the journalist Henry Post was writing about Studio for *Esquire*. "That year was a tragedy for me," Uva told Post about his brief period at the helm of Studio. Of Ian and Steve, he just said, "I don't wish them any harm."

After six months Uva was fired from Elite for conspicuous drug use. He opened a restaurant on Sixty-fourth Street between Lexington and Third. "It was called Uva's," says Larry Gang. "It attracted a good crowd at the beginning, because of Uva. But the food was terrible and the service was worse. He, I, and Gordon Butler got stoned one night, took a knife, and cut his name out of the awning. And that was the end of the restaurant. It closed down after that."

Uva then decided to start a model agency of his own. His first partner was a Mexican, Roberto Troyat, whose father had built up Acapulco. "Troyat blew forty, fifty, sixty thousand dollars. Uva was a gofer, bringing girls and bullshit like that," Beer says. "Nothing ever happened."

Uva then came up with financing from new partners—a couple of young Saudis, Sidney Beer, and a former oilman of Lebanese origin, Saleh Izzedine— and he actually did start an agency. It was called Ten and boasted three famous names on its opening, Barbara Carrera, Ulla-Maija, and Lynda Carter, who was Wonder Woman on the TV series. This was impressive and meaningless, because Carrera was segueing into acting, Ulla-Maija was designing, and Lynda Carter wasn't really a model at all. But it opened with a bang. "Ten is my number one concern. It is a business and a pleasure," Uva told *Night* magazine.

"I was impressed that he had an office and bookers," Ulla-Maija says. The shadows were drawing in, though, shadows of a silvery whiteness.

"We didn't know how badly he was involved with drugs," Sidney Beer says. "He used to steal checks from the back of the checkbook. I found out about it. I called up the boys in Saudi Arabia. I said there's forty thousand dollars missing. I'll put it up. But I'm resigning right now."

The Saudis got on the next plane. The agency was a goner. Another victim of cocaine's white death.

Uva drank more and began to bloat. "He had put on about fifty pounds the last time I saw him. I hardly recognized him," Larry Gang says. With Studio 54 at its roaring height, Uva Harden hired a Toyota, drove it from New York to Los Angeles, sold it, and vamoosed to Europe, a warrant fluttering in his wake.

STUDIO 54, WHERE ARE YOU?

4

THE ENCHANTED GARDEN HAD BEEN RECOMMENDED TO
Jack Dushey by a lighting designer who was working
on his house. "We were looking around to do an
outrageous party for my kid's bar mitzvah," says
Dushey, who was in real estate, specializing in buying
up stores. He was lukewarm to the suggestion at first.
"I said no. I'm not going to drag people out there,"
he says. He visited, and was won over. The party,
which featured disco music, was a wow.

That had been in the winter of 1976. Dushey had
got into conversation with Rubell and Schrager.
"They had mentioned to me about doing a club in
the city. And I had said I would be very interested in
doing something like that," Dushey says. Later that
winter they met again in Acapulco and resumed the
discussion. "When I got back to the city, they called
me and showed me the space," Dushey says. "I
thought it was fabulous." He went with them to Hurrah a couple of times, and was introduced to Carmen
D'Alessio. Jack Dushey agreed to back the club.

This was all just as well, because the magic had

dimmed at the Enchanted Garden long before Steve and Ian cast their eyes on Fortune Gallo's former opera house. Douglaston is one of the sedater parts of Queens and the neighbors of the former golf course were not amused that a bunch of would-be Tony Maneros were gunning their penile motorcars, peeing on their lawns, and tossing beer cans into their walkways in the early hours. Under unremitting local pressure, the City Parks Department buckled and agreed that Rubell and Schrager should be chucked out. Which wasn't a breeze. First, the lease was not held by the city, but the previous occupants, Restaurant Associates. And second, they had a Manhattan lawyer, none other than the belligerent and well-connected Roy Cohn, who had been introduced to Steve by John Addison, his longtime lover. "John had plenty of time to regret *that,*" Maurice Brahms says gloomily.

It is traditional for New Yorkers in the club and bar business to be cavalier about picayune details, like regulations and bills, and this was a tradition to which Steve Rubell and Ian Schrager were true. The list of warnings and summonses they were pestered with included a summons for selling liquor without a license. In October 1976 they stopped paying Restaurant Associates rent and they were finally ousted the following year. "They took everything that wasn't nailed down," Janet Cotton, the lawyer who handled the case for the parks department, told Henry Post. "When I met Rubell, I thought he was a very naïve young man, which was the wrong impression." On October 25, 1977, a judgment came down that they owed Restaurant Associates $73,724 for equipment rental. Steve Rubell failed to pay, took no notice of a subpoena, and was fined $1,784 on March 13, 1978, for contempt of court. Given what was roaring away on West Fifty-fourth Street, contempt of court was presumably as fair a description as any.

Scotty Taylor had moved from the Enchanted Garden to a brand-new Steak Loft, Rubell's fourth, which was up in Westchester. "He let his cousins, Jeff and Steve, manage it," Taylor says. "These guys, they were from the garment center. They knew nothing. Steve only hired people in restaurants that never worked there before. He didn't want anybody with habits. He liked to train them." The Westchester joint was "making money, but kind of running amok," as Taylor puts it, and he was fed up with waiting tables in a genteel suburb anyway.

Steve Rubell was generous with Taylor. "He gave me silverware when I

got my first apartment," he says. "He let me take stuff from the Steak Loft."
Rubell sometimes needed coaxing, though. Construction had started at Studio.
Taylor told him, "Steve! I want to work there!"

" 'Nah! I only want muscle-bound gay bartenders. . . .'

"To him, I was like a little straight boy from Queens. . . .

"But during the day, they would need help. So I was like Johnny-on-the-
spot. I would take garbage and stuff out of there. I would drive into the city
and do whatever they wanted."

The drudgery of demolition and construction work took a year. "What I
actually put up was a few hundred thousand dollars, actual cash," Jack Dushey
says. "The balance was guarantees to the contractor. It was my contractor, so
he was expecting me to pay. If I remember correctly, the cost was somewhere
in the region of six or seven hundred thousand by the time we got the doors
open." Steve Rubell did not allow himself to be overwhelmed by the camaraderie of labor. "All the construction workers were like, 'Yeah! We can't wait
until this place is opened,' " Scotty Taylor says. "He said to the head guy, 'I
don't want to see one of them in here. This isn't a place for them. It's not
about that.' "

By the beginning of 1977, putting together a team to create the club had
become the priority. Steve Rubell was determined that the media attention
that had mostly eluded him in Queens would be his in Manhattan. Carmen
D'Alessio could be relied on to bring in the Eurotrash, which would take care
of, say, *Women's Wear Daily,* but meat-and-potatoes media was also crucial, so
Ed Gifford and his wife, Michael, were essential hires. The Giffords had been
in business since 1968, and they had had a kind of rich hippie client list, including a couple of Broadway shows, *Hair* and *Godspell,* and a church, the
Cathedral Church of St. John the Divine. "My kids thought that for us to be
involved in the decadent Studio 54 was just a terrible thing to do," Ed Gifford
says.

The Giffords found the setting up of Studio rather astonishing. "Schrager
was the son of a garment center guy and Rubell was the son of a postman.
These guys really didn't seem to have their finger on the pulse of *anything,*"
Ed Gifford says. "But they managed to do something quite brilliant. Nobody
ever could understand how because Rubell and Schrager never let the left hand
know what the right hand was doing. They never held a meeting where every-

one who was involved with the creative process sat down and exchanged ideas. They kept everybody away from everybody else. But they assembled the most gifted people in New York."

Rubell and Schrager walked in on florist Renny Reynolds unannounced. Reynolds was a partner in a new design firm, and was quite the thing because of a slew of parties he had done, including the shipboard launch of Yves Saint Laurent's scent, Opium. "Steve and Ian came in on a Saturday or Sunday afternoon when I was sitting there, painting this wooden floor," Reynolds says. "They sat on the floor as I painted, and we talked about design." In Reynolds's unsurprising opinion, the best designers were his new partners, the designer Ron Doud, the architect Scott Bromley, and the environmental lighting whiz, Brian Thompson. All were hired, the approach to Scott Bromley and Ron Doud being made by Carmen D'Alessio early in 1977. Two names famous on Broadway, Jules Fisher and Paul Marantz, were hired to do theatrical lighting. Renny Reynolds's assignment was "interior landscaping." The final design began to be put together.

"Ian was very nervous about the whole thing and very indecisive," Scott Bromley says. "I think we went through four hundred million permutations and combinations. But I remember walking in to see the space with Ron before meeting Ian or Steve. I said, 'Ron, this is how it is going to work. Wherever the floor comes into juxtaposition with the stage, there will either be a step up or a step down. The stage will be the dance floor. *Because everyone has always wanted to be on the stage!*' "

It was also now that the name was finally agreed upon. "They were sitting around, thinking up a whole bunch of dumb names," Ed Gifford says. "Michael said, 'This place used to be called Studio 53. My husband worked there. We're on Fifty-fourth Street. So why don't you just simply call it Studio 54?' She came home and told me about it."

Steve Rubell was thoroughly aware that something else was crucial: word of mouth. Nightly, either alone or with Ian Schrager, he would patrol his soon-to-be competition, culling the cream of the membership in his own inimitable style. Brian Saltern, a nightbird, recorded the following exchange in Hurrah. "One night I was introduced to a guy always there, stumbling around and slurring his words," according to Saltern.

"How ya doin'?" I asked.

"Hey . . . howaryaa? I allwhays see ya here."

"Yeah. I dig it here."

"Yeah, me toooo."

"You look like you're having a good time."

"Yeaah, I teenk I takin tooo many Quaaaylooodes. I wan' your name en address . . ."

Saltern scribbled the necessary info on a matchbook.

"Tanks . . . my naaame's Steeeve . . . uhhh . . . Roooobellll . . . ess gonna be caa . . . caaalled Stoooooooodio ffffifdy fffoooo . . . ess gggonnna be a beeeg ccclubb."

Right, Brian Saltern thought.

Marc Benecke, a nineteen-year-old student at Hunter College, with fair hair, a face that is all profile, and a voice sounding like nutshells cracking, happened to be having lunch one day with a friend who had been offered a security job with the embryonic club. After lunch, they walked across to the West Side to have a look at it. Benecke was introduced to Steve Rubell, then they went around the corner for coffee.

Benecke, who was raised in Brooklyn and Paris, says, "My mom was very active in Democratic politics. I was working for Eugene McCarthy when I was twelve. I was heading for a career in law or politics. I didn't have any idea about nightclubs. I didn't really want to go to them." It was the beginning of April and Steve, who had taken an instant liking to this poised and formal young man, asked what he was doing for the summer. "I said, 'Nothing.' He just clear out of the blue asked, 'How would you like to work here?' I said, 'Fine.' "

Joe Eula, the fashion artist who worked with Halston, had heard of Steve Rubell. "He was a friend of a friend of a friend," he says. Eula lived a couple of blocks away and strolled over to the theater about a month before the opening. "It was just complete chaos," he says. "I met this nervous widget of a guy who I just immediately fell in love with because he was so far off the wall. *Is it going to be a success? Is it going to make it?*" Eula told Rubell another discothèque was just what New York needed.

Not everybody thought that. Stuart Lee, a writer, was with a group of gay friends in Julius, a bar on Saint Marks Place, when somebody mentioned that there was a party that night in a new disco in some old theater. "It was a construction party. Before the opening," says Lee. "Construction parties," as the name implies, are given before a place is fully ready. They are like fittings for a custom-tailored suit. "We drove up there. We saw Marc Benecke," says Lee. "We didn't know who he was, of course. We asked if we could go in. There was no crowd, no velvet rope. I think we paid fifteen dollars. There were only about ten people in this huge place. I remember thinking we've got the Flamingo, we've got Twelve West. *Who needs this?*"

Joanne Horowitz, a young woman from Roslyn, Long Island, was introduced to Steve Rubell by Neil Schlesinger, whom she had been dating since they had met at Enchanted Garden. Horowitz was a secretary at Universal Pictures at 445 Park Avenue. "I used to get the *Celebrity Bulletin* every day across my desk," she says. "I said to Steve, 'Listen! I know where the celebrities are. Give me the invitations and I'll invite them to the opening.'

"I was hustling. The girl on my right had been there for nine years. The girl on my left had been there for twelve years. I knew I wasn't going anywhere. I was like *this is my ticket out.* Steve said great! No money was discussed at that point. I was formally there from two months before the place opened up. I had no title. I was a young kid. Steve said, 'Okay, let's see what you can do. You do a good job and we'll sit down and make an arrangement.' "

Steve duly sent a bundle of invitations to Horowitz at Universal. *The Wiz* was in production at the time, so Michael Jackson and Diana Ross were in town, as were Henry Winkler, Warren Beatty, and Kate Jackson. "I sent them all invitations, with letters saying this is going to be the new hot club and blahblahblah," she says.

The actual day before opening, a young man, Michael Overington, walked past the door of the club. "I got this feeling. *Something's going to happen here,*" he says. He asked for a job. Any job. He was hired as a janitor. That same hectic day, the bartenders and busboys were called up to the balcony and issued uniforms, which were an unabashed steal from those at Le Jardin. "Steve said I want everyone to be very cool . . . very relaxed," says Richie Notar, whom Rubell had brought from Queens along with Scotty Taylor. They were issued gym shorts and vests. "The shorts were gray. The vests were gray with black trim. I'll never forget them," Notar says.

Things were ready to roll. The morning of the opening, the *Daily News* ran a tiny item, with a jokey headline: STUDIO 54, WHERE ARE YOU? It was, after all, just another disco. Manhattan seemed ready to welcome it with a yawn.

Nikki Haskell was a clubgoer. She had grown up in Beverly Hills and had been taken to see Jimmy Durante and Carmen Miranda perform when she was five. "The Daisy was like the beginning of the disco story," she says. "There was the Whiskey a Go Go but the real chic place was the Daisy. It was on Rodeo. I was just out of high school. I went every night." When Haskell moved to New York, she took a job with a brokerage house. And went to more nightspots. "Le Club was the place to go. I hated anybody that would take me out that wouldn't take me to Le Club. 'You're not taking me to Le Club? That's it!' I liked Le Jardin, but it was such a pain in the neck getting in. They didn't want you to come in if you were straight. They didn't want girls. You had to wear boots, you couldn't wear open-toed shoes. It was a complicated story, very peculiar."

She still has no clue how she got on the opening list for Studio. She and a date were having an early dinner at Elaine's with Ivana and Donald Trump, who had recently married. "I said, 'C'mon! There's this new club opening tonight. Why don't we go?'" Haskell says. "So we got to Studio 54 and there was nobody there. We were like the first. We knocked on the door." A few other revelers arrived. Haskell was acquainted with several of them but neither of the Trumps was. "Donald hadn't built Trump Tower. Nobody knew him in those days," Haskell says.

Weird history was in the making that night, which was April 26. They banged on the door. Nothing. They waited, and waited. People were willing to suffer a bit for their fun back then. "About fifteen minutes later we were just getting ready to leave, and they opened one of the doors. They didn't even know we were waiting out there. It wasn't cold." Nikki Haskell, her date, and the Trumps walked in, followed by some others, maybe half a dozen in all. Haskell showed the invitations. "We walked around. They were still adjusting the lights and fixing the music." Myra Scheer, the publicist who worked Studio's parties, says that the very first song played was "Devil's Gun."

"About half an hour later there were fifty or sixty people there. We kept on saying, *'Gee! I wonder where everybody is?'* " Haskell says. A reporter from *The New York Times* came, looked around, and left early, because he had to make the late city edition, much to Ed Gifford's irritation. "Then it filled up a little more," Haskell says. "By dribs and drabs. I remember Margaux Hemingway came in. By eleven o'clock the place was semi-crowded." Too crowded for comfort. Some tried to leave. Haskell says, "People were going to the front doors, people were going to the side doors. *They couldn't open them.* All the doors opened out. A thousand people all of a sudden had converged on Studio 54, and there were so many people, pushing the doors, and pushing on top of each other. It was a physical impossibility."

Randy Wren, a wannabe publicist, had been given a couple of press passes by John Carmen, the publicist, for whom he had briefly worked as an assistant. He went with his roommate, Paul. "I was in an alcoholic stupor. Hazy, crazy," Wren says. "So we took the subway and there was like a million people there. We were all Brooks Brother'd up, we looked great, but we were tripping our brains out, so we pushed and the Red Sea parted. I felt like Cleopatra, making my entrance into Rome. I felt I should have my own show on Broadway. Halleluia! What fun!

"Cher and Margaux Hemingway were each on the dance floor. They were dancing by themselves, and there were all these photographers. It was right after Anita Bryant and Dade County and all of that. So Fred and I jumped onto that almost empty dance floor. And suddenly we were swamped by photographers too. It was *who do they think we are?*"

Wren thinks this was at about half past ten, which was also when Robin Leach arrived. "I took Brooke Shields there. I was covering it for CNN," says Leach. A journalist from greater London, England, Leach had come to New York in 1963 with the British rock and roll invasion, and had been working for the tabloids ever since. This was his first television assignment in the field. He and his preadolescent celebrity date were introduced to Steve Rubell, who took them up to the DJ booth. They looked down on the leaping phosphorescene of the dance floor, astounded. "We thought we were just covering the opening of an ordinary nightclub," Leach told me in his orotund *Lifestyles of the Rich and Famous* tones, a sort of papier-mâché baroque. "All of us knew that night that we weren't at the opening of a discothèque but the opening of something historical, that was going to change the shape of the way people lived, or played. Everything had come together in one place. There were no rules. Sodom and Gomorrah met the High Street that night."

Meanwhile Studio staffers were trying to calm the roiling crowd. Ed Gifford got on the telephone to the *Times* news desk. "Frank Sinatra's sitting in his car outside. He can't get *near*. It's a madhouse," he barked. They could hear sirens wailing down the street. Nikki Haskell still remembers the panicked look on people's faces. Among them would have been that of Geoffrey Holder. The tall designer, who went with his wife, and Michael and Ariane Batterbury, both gastronomic journalists, was assailed by disquiet. "There were pillows on the stairs. And women with high heels. It was dark with flashing lights," he says. He tried a fire door but found it locked. "Panic time!" Holder says. The Holders and the Batterburys managed to get out of there and departed.

Hollywood di Russo was Renny Reynolds's date, and they arrived at about midnight. Di Russo is a makeup artist, who was freshly arrived from Texas, and she had brought a contingent of fellow Texans along with them. They arrived in a pickup truck, which promptly lost a door to an assertive limo. "It was complete pandemonium and *The Day of the Locust*," she says. "Steve was standing on that . . . thang, and he saw us and hollered Renny's name, and we were inside with a fistful of drink tickets. It was the silver spoon and the Man in the Moon and it was like . . . ohmigosh!"

Richard Turley had dinner with a group at the modish Lexington Avenue restaurant Holbrooke's. It was well after midnight when they decided to go on to Studio, and without great expectations. "There was this thing that had been in the *Daily News* that morning," he says. "There had been a whole series of nothing discos opening that were trying to get publicity. The *News* was just belittling the idea of another huge, boring, unsuccessful disco.

"I got there a little late. There were over a thousand people outside. The place was locked up like a fortress." Turley's group included a doctor with a jeroboam-sized bottle of Quaaludes. They were outside well over an hour. "We were three or four layers back," he says. "And there were thirty or forty layers behind us. We all took a Quaalude. They took about fifteen or twenty minutes to kick in.

"The doctor started handing them out. About thirty people standing around us took them, and then everybody started having this mad sexual orgy. All the men had their dicks out . . . the women were showing their tits . . . everybody was feeling everybody else . . . the crowd was moving in waves . . . all of a sudden you would find yourself next to someone you didn't know . . ."

It was about one by the time Richard Turley was swept in through the great gaping doors. He looked around and realized something with blinding certainty. "This was a completely unique zeitgeist," he says. "Some little voice said, 'In your lifetime there's never going to be anything like this. Don't miss a moment!' "

Arthur Weinstein arrived from Hurrah at about midnight and slipped in with no trouble. He had been curious about his new rival, but not too apprehensive. As he looked around the tossing dance floor, a spotlit spawning sea, his complacency was sucked out of him. Everywhere, there were tranced grins, lighted gizmos rising and falling, the comic book spoon journeying to the lunar nose, cheering, black ties, silver face paint, and famous faces coming into focus for a wink before dissolving into the throng. It was pure theater magic. "Suddenly Steve was on the floor with Bianca Jagger," he says. "It was snowing confetti on them. It was a scene from a movie. I said, 'Holy shit! This is it. *I just got destroyed!*' "

Didn't he feel a bit odd to be looking at his own commercial death?

"No. I didn't. I felt great too. They totally destroyed us but they took two months. I've always been proud of that."

Jim Fouratt, another Nightworlder, insists 54's success was guaranteed when Arthur either sold or gave Rubell Hurrah's membership list. "That's total bullshit. Steve and Ian came all the time. They *knew* our list," Weinstein says. "It really hurt me to see Hurrah go down the tubes. I took it personally. I didn't understand, like I do today, that it's just business. I was stupid enough to think that people would be loyal." A bark of laughter. "They built a better mousetrap and people came," he adds. "And at least I was destroyed by the greatest club that ever came down the pike."

That not only did just about every one of Joanne Horowitz's movie star invitees actually show up for the opening of Studio, and also that they had to endure ignominy like everybody else, suggests that those were still unjaded times. *"Warren Beatty never got in! Kate Jackson never got in! Henry Winkler never got in!"* she wails. "I was really upset the next day." But one of her list did get in, and the unputouttable Cher aced Margaux Hemingway out of the picture pages. "She was on the front page of the *New York Post* and the *Daily News*. The front covers. Huge pictures!" Horowitz says. "That sort of set New York on fire because really up until then they didn't put celebrities on the covers of newspapers." Steve Rubell and Ian Schrager got the message. "Ian sat down with me and this was the deal," Horowitz says. "I was paid $250 for bringing in a major celebrity. I was paid $125 for bringing in a medium-sized celebrity. I gave up my job at Universal right after the opening."

There was a "dinner for the disgruntled" the following night, says Lester Persky, a lawyer-turned–movie producer, who had been with Warren Beatty when they failed to get in. "There were several people there who had been pushed aside. We went over with Steve Rubell to ensure that we would get in next time," Persky says.

That weekend Renny Reynolds was in Steve and Ian's backstage office. On Monday the place was to be closed, and they were reviewing plans for the coming week. "It was ten-thirty in the morning and the phone rang. It was Halston," Reynolds says. "Well, this was big-time. Steve at that point wasn't known by anybody, and this was Halston . . . *Oh my God! What was happening?* . . . Halston wanted to have a birthday party that Monday night for Bianca Jagger. Steve thought for about half a second. He didn't say, 'Oh, we're closed.' He said, '*Of course.*' "

That is one version. All histories are subjective and a history of the Studio years can be particularly a bouquet of blurs. Steve Rubell would later say that he had been introduced to Halston by Bianca Jagger one night in Hurrah. Also Joe Eula, who worked for Halston as an illustrator, had gone to the opening of 54 and the next night and the next. "From the minute the door opened, you could smell success," he says. "There was nowhere else to go. You had that thing on Fourteenth Street where people put fists up asses. Crazy places. So I was coming in in the mornings and I would have to sleep for five minutes because I had come straight from 54. This literally the first week."

Halston had always been reclusive. The Iowa-born designer had been dressing the rich and fashionable since being taken up by Babe Paley, but he was little known at large. "Halston wouldn't dare go out," says Joe Eula. "Halston never went out a day in his life, unless it was under cover or under a great shroud."

Now, though, Halston was eaten alive by curiosity. Soon the designer, with the sleek hair and perfect smile of an old-fangled matinee idol, and green eyes as shiny or unreadable as the glass eyes of a doll, or of the camera lenses in whose glare they seemed forever caught, would be a part of that coterie that would sweep Studio 54 up to the next level.

HELL ON THE DOOR, STAIRWAYS TO PARADISE

5

NOTHING HAD BEEN ACCORDING TO PLAN. LATER STEVE Rubell admitted that he had been reconciled to the notion that Studio would be slow during its first summer. He had imagined that everyone would be out in the Hamptons or on Fire Island, that things wouldn't really get going until September. The Jagger party was a fluke. "When Steve got off the phone we flipped into action to make it happen," Renny Reynolds says. "I called everybody I knew in New York to come and blow up masses of white balloons. Ian went over to the theater where *Oh! Calcutta!* was and I went to the Claremont Stables to arrange for the horse. We kept going for three days. We did a drop. A theatrical drop is a baglike thing that's a folded piece of canvas between bars. You just drop one side and all these balloons flutter down. Which was the start of a lot of that. We did Ping Pong balls . . . confetti . . . feathers . . ."

A bevy of famous folks descended on the club that night. "We had been told to keep all the media out," Ed Gifford says. But Steve Rubell wasn't hard to persuade to let in just one photographer, and Gifford had called Dick Cork-ery, who was then with the *Daily News*. Inevitably, a crew of other photog-raphers got in too, and they were ready for action when a lithe black couple, naked but for a slathering of gold paint, led in a white horse, and Bianca Jagger hopped into the saddle, rode her photo opportunity, dismounted, and was presented with a cake.

It was about half past ten. Ian Schrager, who was there with a girlfriend, disappeared into the night, but Rubell was at the center of the party that raged on. "Jeez! I couldn't believe what was going on," Corkery says. "I was pho-tographing people who were conked out of their minds. Some of the pictures, they're really like they're in another world. Mick Jagger was sleeping on one of the banquettes. Yeah!"

The photographs of Bianca Jagger on the white horse broke all over the world. "Bianca's party was the catalyst," Benecke agrees. "It just snowballed from there. Studio opened on a Tuesday. The next couple of nights weren't as busy. But that picture started the ball rolling. It was that soon."

Steve Rubell was thoroughly aware of his partner's reclusive temperament. He was astonished by the fact that he would leave a scene thronged by just the sort of people they had dreamed of attracting, all the same. "I can't believe you left," he told Ian the following day. But Ian's early leavetaking set a pattern that would persist. He would increasingly lose himself in the process, the pro-duction, while Steve would be buoyed up by the people, as the Studio phe-nomenon gathered strength.

It was a preliminary tremor of a social upheaval that would prove much more enduring than the populist revolution of the sixties: the coming of the Celebrity Culture. In the early seventies Time Inc. had hired Richard Stolley, formerly editor of *Life*, to launch *People*, a magazine based on its "People" column. It was not welcomed by all in-house. "I think there was more op-position to it in the company than outside," Stolley says feelingly. The first issue came out in 1974. Columns also began to sprout afresh in the dailies. Liz Smith had been first asked to do a gossip column by the New York *Daily News* in 1974. A skeptic, she dallied two years before signing up. "I said, 'Well, I don't think people want to read gossip anymore,' " she says. "I guess I just thought the Winchell thing had ended."

In fact—and here the success of Andy Warhol's *Interview* might have been pondered, to say nothing of "Random Notes" in *Rolling Stone*—a new phase was beginning. *New York* ran "Why Everybody's Talking About Gossip" by Alexander Cockburn on the cover of its May 3, 1976, issue. Cockburn dated the phenomenon to "the last few months. Gossip" he wrote cheerfully, "has crawled out from under its stone and is now capering about in the full light of day." *Newsweek* ran a "Gossip!" cover story on May 24, illustrated by a caricature of forty-five top gossipees, from Betty Ford to Liz Taylor, and soon *The New York Times* launched another celebrity-based mag, *Us*.

With two or three exceptions, tops, every one of the *Newsweek* forty-five made a documented appearance in Studio 54, and because of the coverage the club began receiving, it could easily seem that it was the famous faces that provided the frisson there—the sightings of Elizabeth Taylor playing with the lights, Mikhail Baryshnikov on the dance floor, Betty Ford on a banquette, Sylvester Stallone at the bar—but this was far from being the case. It was a particular moment in the growth of the Celebrity Culture, too. It would be equally fair to say that the famous came to Studio 54 because it was a slice of the "real" world where they were highly unlikely to be hassled, and that they felt secure there, admired but at ease among the costume people, cosy among the glitter.

Soon that window would slam shut. Liz Smith adheres to a theory advanced by *The Washington Post*'s Sally Quinn, which was that people had become hooked on the heroin of Watergate and needed to come down on the methadone of gossip. "Watergate and Chappaquiddick changed the climate of everything," Smith says. "Ever since then the press has acted in an increasingly open, ravenous, and sometimes irresponsible way. They've stopped protecting *anybody*." The complicit rituals of the celebs and the media would become increasingly bitter, and Studio 54, which began as a sanctuary, would become just another part of the show.

It is a Manhattan myth, a chunk of urban folklore, that Studio 54 never had a dull moment after Bianca rode the horse. James Hammond, a Briton and a habitué of Hurrah and Le Jardin, went to the club with his American wife, Sharon, and Andy Warhol about three weeks after the opening. "We sat in some bleacher seats with Steve Rubell," Hammond says. "He had a paper bag with a bottle of Dom Pérignon in it and some paper cups. He said, 'I haven't got my license yet.' And he started dispensing the champagne in these coffee cups.

"There was hardly anybody there. It was virtually empty. Two or three people, and loud music. Urggghhhh! I thought *hopeless*. What a place. I felt sorry for poor old Steve Rubell."

By his next visit, though, the astonishing phenomenon was out of control. It began with that notorious door, and the velvet cord strung along brass stanchions outside the door. At the beginning, opera house pomp wasn't the point. "Studio 54 was in a terrible neighborhood. The West Side was nothing. It was to keep out prostitutes and pimps," Ian Schrager said. Of course, what it ended up keeping out was the everyday world. The frumpishly dressed folks from solid neighborhoods, those normal people, once supposedly proud to lead private lives like characters in Norman Rockwell illustrations or Frank Capra movies, now changed utterly into a media-saturated lumpen proletariat, aching for glimpses of the fabulous.

Marc Benecke played second fiddle to Lynn Barclay, a veteran of the door at Arthur and Regine's, on the actual opening night. "It was just a total, overwhelming experience," Benecke says. "Just throngs of people. All these people dressed up, and the drag queens in their incredible costumes." Soon, though, he had the job's measure. Steve Rubell always preferred people he had created himself, and three months later Barclay was gone and Marc Benecke had become second only to Rubell himself as a Studio icon. He was quickly far, far more widely known than Ian Schrager.

Steve Rubell impressed on Benecke the paramount importance of the mix. "We called it casting a play," Marc says. "Or tossing a salad." That was an image the pioneer of the Steak Lofts would return to again and again. "We don't want all tomatoes. When you have a lot of lettuce, you have to mix in other ingredients. Sure, some big tomatoes get in all the time," he said. Rubell impressed on another doorman, Chris Sullivan, the importance of the *look*. "Steve had a whole philosophy. Basically, the whole thing revolved around what kind of shoes people wore."

What it came down to, according to Al Corley, who occasionally took over for Benecke in 1978, was a sentiment that was at once droll and a bit disturbing. "You know Steve's basic line?" Corley says. " 'Just make sure you don't let in anyone like me!' Basically what he was saying was, I would not let myself in. It was a joke, but there was some truth to that. Or Ian. I mean, you would never let Ian in. If Ian wasn't in, he would never get in. And he knows that."

The aching want from the crowds at the door was the aperitif. The place had been a theater, and it remained a vehicle for sensations—anticipation included. You were swept within, perhaps gliding in with the golden slipstream that got in free, and you would feel pulsing waves, as if from a core of energy. "It made you come alive," says Pierre Prudhomme. "You would begin to hear the music . . . you knew you were in for another adventure."

The hallway was physically a prologue, and it was fully exploited for the parties thrown on Halloween, Valentine's Day, New Year's Eve, and on special occasions. One of the main planners was Karin Bacon, who had got her start as a hippie, helping organize the first be-in in Central Park. One Valentine's Day, she stationed harpists in the hallway. "We didn't just get one harpist," she says. "We had like *twelve* harpists. And they were all in costumes and they were all in makeup. But getting these harpists to play together was hard. Harpists are so individualistic."

The parties, the spectacle were Ian Schrager's particular delight. "He is very intense. Which made it very exciting to work with him," Bacon says. "Because it was always so important. He worked hard on all of the detail. It wasn't just the theme. He cared what the *makeup* was like. Every single detail.

"Once Ian wanted to have dwarfs in chains, sort of groveling around on the floor. That was one of the times I could not agree with him. I found these midgets on Long Island, who were completely well-proportioned people. They were performers. I dressed them up and got a dinner for them. Everything was mini-size. They were having this little feast when you walked in. They were drinking this champagne and they got a *little high*. . . .

"A lot of my research was just finding the right people. It was really being a detective." It was decided to make Studio look like a street in Shanghai for the birthday party for Tina Chow, the wife of the restaurateur Michael Chow. "I had to find Chinese people who looked gorgeous," Bacon says. "Ian would always say how much it should cost, and I would figure out something, and we would negotiate.

"But he could never really get his juices going, and make a decision until the *zero hour*. It was just horrendous. I would beg and plead for him to decide. Make up your mind! Because I would have all these people on hold. Dancers, costumers, choreographers, makeup people. Are we going to go with it? Is it going to happen? He would just drive me crazy."

Hollywood di Russo was also there before the Chow soiree, for which Renny Reynolds had done the flowers. "It was nine P.M. And nobody had paid us. We didn't know why they wouldn't pay. They went through phases like that. Maybe it's the way men communicate with men? It had taken us twelve hours to put everything up. It took us thirty minutes to take it down. As soon as Renny pulled the decorations down, they instantly flew in his face with the dough. It was thousands. It took us two hours to put everything back," di Russo says.

"Ian is an incredibly bright man with an incredible amount of energy," Reynolds says. "Whenever he's working on a project he talks to absolutely everybody, and finds out what they think." It was Reynolds who suggested doing a party for Dolly Parton. "Ian was totally not into it," he says. "The thing that swung it was Norma Kamali. He was seeing Norma at the time, and Norma loved country and western." Reynolds did up the party with stuff from a farm he was renting in Bucks County. "We had big wine barrels we filled with corn," he says. "I had a farm wagon that we brought in and piled with hay. We had chickens in a pen."

It was enjoyed by most, but not the party girl herself. "Dolly came and was *completely freaked out* at the number of people there. She had not had a Studio 54 experience," Reynolds says. "She was real nervous about this whole deal and went up to the balcony. She sat up there for a while. She was *not* a comfortable lady there."

He likewise has vivid memories of the party Allan Carr threw for *Grease*. Reynolds decided to put some fifties cars around the club. "I called various places and it was impossible," he says. "Nobody wanted to rent a car to Studio 54. So I found this little auto museum down somewhere in New Jersey. They agreed to bring these cars up." Six cars duly arrived at midday on the day of the party. Michael Overington was in charge, having swiftly risen from being janitor to manager. "That's what Ian calls my Horatio Alger story," Ovrington says. It was at his suggestion that the gasoline was emptied into the gutters of the street before the cars were brought into the club. "They always claimed it was John Addison who called the police," Renny Reynolds says. "Everything bad was always blamed on John."

The police were soon on the spot, and the fire department. Reynolds remembers that Jack Dushey arrived, and that all of them, Steve and Ian included, had to push the cars down to a gas station several avenues away, while Ian tried to calm an anguished museum curator. His anguish was not unjustified. "There was a 1950 Chevy convertible that got a bit trashed because people climbed in and burned the seats. So we ended up having to pay for new seats," Reynolds says. "But the party was wild. Fabulous."

If Ian was the producer, Steve was the director. In Studio 54's earliest weeks, Carmen D'Alessio had been the *animatrix,* the locomotive. Not for long. Ian Schrager was so much in the background that he acquired the nickname Greta, but nobody whooped it up at the parties more than Steve Rubell, and refueling himself with killer quantities of Quaaludes and cocaine, he was every bit the madcap host. "Sometimes he would use this little truck, like a kid's playground truck," says Baird Jones, gossip writer and promoter. "There would be this mix of naked pagan Rome and black tie, and he would roll around, so high, in this kid's truck."

Steve Rubell, the guy who couldn't stop talking on the tennis courts in Brooklyn, the live wire of the army reserves, had found himself. It was remarkable. Of course, Steve was ingenuous, enthusiastic, and eager to please, but so are any number of hustlers who merely manage to annoy. Rubell had something that went beyond this. "Someone once described him very well," says Don Rubell, his older brother. "He said that Steve had this ability to perceive fantasies—people's fantasies that they didn't know about themselves. He took people out of their context and put them in the context where they really wanted to be. Whether they realized it or not. He was able to take people from one form of life, whether they were senators or presidents of airlines or executives with major corporations, and put them into an environment where they were able to act out things they had privately always wanted to do."

Not only were hard-shelled socialites captivated, but so were the most twitchy and gun-shy stars. Of course, Rubell *needed* the stars, the celebs, but there was nothing calculating in his manner around them. He was as over the top, as shamelessly star-struck as any autograph hunter or reader of the tabs, and would remain so, despite his own rise to boldface mention in the columns. Just as he adored his family, just as, in a way, he adored Ian Schrager, Steve Rubell adored celebrities.

The point has often been made, both by those close to Rubell and employees who watched him closely, that Steve Rubell disliked being alone, that he both generated energy, and was needy when it wasn't around. "He could be sad. Very lonely, and he needed a lot of enouragement," says Chris Sullivan, a Studio employee. This is a pretty normal urban plight, and Rubell surrounded himself with a group of friends with an equal appetite for media attention.

None of the core group—who quickly achieved a first-name status in the tabs as Liza, Andy, Truman, Bianca, and so on—was created by Studio 54, but what they got from Studio was an astonishing drenching in gossip column and tabloid fame. Truman Capote found in Studio a replacement for that "real" society that had dumped him after *Esquire* had published his nonfiction fiction "Le Cote Basque." Andy Warhol's fashionable silkscreen portraits of the seventies had been widely pooh-poohed by the high art world and he was wistfully aware that he wasn't seen as being in the same league as his fellow popsters like Roy Lichtenstein. In Studio, Andy was the famous artist. Halston, once a household name at a grandee level, now became a household name in trailer camps and retirement homes. "The vehicle for Halston's re-ascent was Studio 54," says Joanne Creveling, the fashion publicist who had worked for him. This created a closeness among the group that was not illusory. "They were a sort of version of Frank Sinatra's Rat Pack," says Don Rubell. "Steve was involved with that tremendously. They loved each other's company. They loved their energy. And they did everything for each other."

Arguably, also, Studio 54 was one of the single most effective showcases for newly visible gay clout, a demonstration that it was possible to be gay without being non stop camp, tolerated by straights for entertainment value. The writer Jeffrey Hogrefe has observed that *The Best Little Boy in the World,* a 1973 novel by John Reid, introduced the gay overachiever in fiction. In the same vein, it was Studio 54 that delivered the goods in real life. It did so most famously in the shape of a small tight group that soon acquired the nickname the "Velvet Mafia," a term used mostly by less successful gays. David Geffen, the movie and music magnate, interviewed by Jonathan Van Meter for *Out* magazine, said that the term was "silly." He added, "If they mean a group of people who are bonded to each other by virtue of friendship, *yes,* call it anything you want."

It was not just the rich and famous of whatever sexual predisposition who were favored by Steve Rubell and Marc Benecke at the door. "He would let the limo drivers in," says Baird Jones. "He used to say that the perfect party was like a tossed salad," wherein the choicest vegetables were not necessarily the "most important." Some just seemed to . . . fit in. Stella, a young dancer, whom Antonio Lopez had drawn for *Vogue* a couple of times, was addicted to Studio because she loved the freestyle dancing that had replaced the Hustle which was still the rage in her own borough, Queens. "I used to have a crush on Steve. A mad crush!" she says. "Because there was something about him that was not intimidating. A little-boy essence. Years later I ended up working for him and being his friend and I told him I had had a crush on him! He was, 'No . . . no . . . no' . . . He didn't believe me!"

Suddenly there was a new elite in Manhattan, a Praetorian Guard, a social commando unit. It could be startling to run into a fellow regular in the light of common day. Nikki Haskell, who kept her job as a stockbroker for some months after Studio opened, says she would be in an elevator and somebody in a conservative suit would be standing alongside her. "And you would see a little piece of glitter in her hair," she says. "And you knew she had been at Studio 54 the night before. There were always these little telltale signs."

Haskell was a member of what might be called the peerage of the velvet cord, people who not only enjoyed access to Studio, but who could get *other* people into the place. "It got to the point where I became really popular," Haskell says. "Everybody would come from all over the world and call me." Haskell had usually dated fellow brokers, "but they didn't like Studio. They didn't really want to go there. So *that's* what stockbrokering was like." Haskell gave up her $300,000-a-year job and looked around for something more amusing to do.

Susan Blond, a former Warholette, who was now on the PR side of Epic Records, was also known to be a favorite of Rubell's. Any time a band or a music executive hit town they were likely to call Susan Blond. Like Haskell, Blond was a Studio addict. "People would say to me, 'Where do you live?' I would say, 'I live at Studio 54' " she says. (Charles Suppon, the designer, actually *did* move to be closer to Studio 54.) Blond said she had three priorities in life. "My first priority was getting ahead in business, and becoming a vice president, which I did. My second priority was Andy Warhol and anything to do with him. And my third priority was Studio 54. So my husband of the time, who had no interest in Studio 54, was like priority number seventeen or something. So that was why *that* marriage didn't work."

Some of those with no apparent problem on the door could be pretty exotic, like Irwin Schiff, the "Fat Man," a blimp of a con man, with ready access to free drink tickets. Or Dominick Montiglio, a Gambino enforcer until he went into the witness protection program. "You know, when I was in the life, it was great. I mean, we got respect," the former hood reminisced wistfully to writer Jeffrey Goldberg. "I got in once at Studio 54 ahead of Burt Reynolds . . ." Wiseguys were part of the salad too.

Journalists, by and large, were also welcome, but naturally were treated as provisional VIPs, important as long as their jobs were important, and so much the worse for them if they didn't get *that*. Steven Gaines, for instance, was persona grata as long as he was at the *Daily News*. "One night I went to Studio 54 and word had spread like wildfire that I had been fired, as it does when one loses a job at a magazine or a newspaper," Gaines says. "Steve came up to me and said, 'What are you going to do?' He seemed more upset by it than I was. Like I had no future or something.

"So something flashed into my mind. I said, 'You're still going to let me in here. Aren't you?'

"And then this look crossed his face. I realized that he was going to have to, but my privileges were really going to be gone. That was a very important moment to me. Because when you write a column, you think that everyone loves you. And when you lose the column, you realize that they didn't really care about you *at all*."

This had a measurable effect. When I myself came to live in Manhattan in 1976, the social order seemed to be ruled by the same network of families that had always ruled. That changed with astonishing speed, and Studio 54 was an agent of change. "All these Racquet Club guys, the people who used to go to El Morocco, the guys who ran things socially," says the writer Michael Stone. "Suddenly they found themselves standing outside Studio with their dicks in their hands."

★ ★ ★

The lords of the door were aware of their might. "Sweet it is, when on the high seas the winds are lashing the waters, to gaze from the land on another's struggles," wrote Lucretius. The Roman poet was writing in the first century B.C. but might as well have been describing the emotion of those wafting into Studio 54 as they disengaged themselves from those being denied entrance. "At times you certainly were on a power trip," Marc Benecke says. "People would always tell me I was playing God or whatever, but I was under a lot of pressure, *intense* pressure, most of the time, especially when there was a sea of people out front, which was more often than not. I knew that to keep the energy high I had to adhere to a certain standard.

"Steve was much more friendly and outgoing with people. Steve was able to go up to somebody and be buddy-buddy with them while turning them away. I couldn't do that. My thing was not to talk to them. I would just zero in on somebody I knew was going to get in and frankly pretty much ignore people who I knew weren't going to get in. And the funny thing was when I did change tactics and say to people, 'I'm really sorry. You really don't have a chance. Maybe you should come back another night.' They would just stand there for two or three hours anyway."

Many were happy just to stand there. Michael Musto would go with a friend Bill Ellis. Both toiled on the deranged outer fringes of the Celebrity Culture. Musto, who is now a columnist at the *Voice,* was then working for a fanzine. "It was filled with stories like 'Farrah "Leaves" to Be with Sonny Bono' and it turns out she's left the house to be on TV with Sonny but you wouldn't learn that till page one hundred fifty," Musto says. Ellis, who is now with *Billboard,* was working for a publicist. "Studio had just opened and I thought I would never get in," Musto says. "I was just a kid from Brooklyn. We would just stand outside for hours and hours, and that would be a full night's entertainment, just watching the celebrities' limousines pull up, and see who would come out of them. We didn't even try to get in."

One night they were standing there when actress Sylvia Miles arrived. "I had interviewed Sylvia Miles for this fan magazine, and sort of knew her. I said, 'Let's scream out her name,'" Musto says. "It didn't work. She didn't even turn around. We just came across like idiots, screaming 'Sylvia! Sylvia!' But that was fine. To me, that was a fun night."

Sentimentality was not encouraged at the door. Scotty Taylor once took his mother in. "Steve saw me walk her in. He came running after us," Scotty says, and emulates the nasal spurt. " 'Where are you going? You've got to tell her to leave?'

"I said, 'Steve, I'm not kicking my mother out!' And I walked away from him. And he was fuming. But he didn't throw her out."

Celebrities, of course, got the nod. Lesser-known celebrities were identified to the security muscle who would sometimes have to create a flying wedge and pluck them out of the throng. Other desirables were picked out too. "We coded everything for security," says Roger Parenti, who worked with Benecke for a while. "Marc and I never really touched the ropes. We used to stand on that little standpipe out there so you could see out over the crowd. The tag '302' meant the police department was coming up, to let them in. 'Regency' was for the gay crowd. 'Regency Gold' was Alexis de Rede approaching the ropes, maybe. 'Regency Bronze' was not so wealthy, the trendy Christopher Street crowd, more Versace-dressed, perhaps. A black would be 'Mustapha.' If you saw two black guys you wanted in, it would be 'Two Mustaphas Center Ice.' Marc was a big hockey fan."

There were also, of course, the Flamboyances. Some were famous. "Grace Jones came in naked. Quite a few times," says Chris Sullivan. "Probably more than she should have. Because after a while it became boring." Some were just "Disco-Famous," like Rollerena. Others were loyal to the point of addiction, like Mariam, Disco Sally, and the man whose escort was a man-sized marionette. Others wore getups geared to special events, like celebrating the opening of the Treasures of Tutankhamen at the Met. "I remember twenty-five guys, all dressed as King Tut and chained together," Larry Gang says. "I remember a guy in a doctor's outfit, wheeling his patient in on a stretcher, with a tank of laughing gas attached, with twelve tubes coming out of it. This guy was giving free hits to everybody."

Ingenious plans were hatched. Larry Gang recalls being telephoned by a young woman who asked for the loan of five hundred dollars. He asked why. She said she wanted to rent a horse. She and a girlfriend planned to get into Studio for the Halloween party as dual Lady Godivas. Gang came across with the dough. The women stripped, saddled up, and arrived. "Steve was out in front," Gang says. "He looked them over. 'Okay. The horse can come in. But you girls have to stay outside!' he said."

Gang heard that the horse did get in, behaved itself, and was returned to its riders, who took it to a club with a less-demanding door policy.

Getting in did not necessarily guarantee staying in. There was also the phenomenon, if individuals got too wild, of the Second Bounce. "There was this fellow who was Latin American, who would always come in a suit," artist John Scribner says. "He would go into a side room, take everything off, put on a bath towel, and parade around the dance floor, doing this *hooting and screaming*. And he would do a whooping kind of thing, like an Indian war dance. The floor would immediately clear. And he would have his own little kind of territory. I remember one night that he was quite drunk, and Rubell was up in the disco booth. And this guy bent over, and mooned him. Steve immediately alerted the bouncers. It was one of the snowstorms of the late seventies and they threw him bodily into the snow. He lost his towel and he was like lounging in two feet of snow. I think somebody took pity and gave him an overcoat."

The doormen would be offered the usual inducements to allow entrance. "I've been offered thousands," Roger Parenti says. "Usually when the Saudis would come up. They would have New York City police with them. They were the ones that would give out the tips—the Saudis themselves would not do that—the end of the night or the next day or however they did it. Unfortunately—I hate to say—they got wise. They started giving out twenty-dollar tips when they were expected to give hundred-dollar tips."

One night a group showed up in formal Arab jellabas. Parenti didn't let them in but sent them on to the Studio wannabe, Magique, where a friend of his was working the door. "They gave him a check on the way out. That's like having no tip at all. Twenty dollars is better than a check," he says. Not that night. "From what Jeff told me, he got a two-thousand-dollar tip. I honestly believe it's true because Jeff bought himself a car shortly after that."

Other favors were not stuff you could put in the bank. These were often made available in what Studio employees called the Candy Room, a little room with mirrored walls next to the coat check, so-called because this was where they kept the big bowl of candy that was brought out for departing revelers at the end of the night. "The Candy Room was put to other uses by some of the doorpeople," Roger Parenti says. "What would happen very often is that there would be four or five gals standing outside at the end of the night. That room back there was where we dropped our pants," he explained. "We were young," he added. And the gals *did* get into Studio 54.

Power not only corrupts; it becomes whimsical. Komar and Melamid, artists recently arrived from Moscow, understood Studio at once. "Every good establishment has a limited access. There are always the *nomenklatura,* the special people," Melamid says. A rich folklore soon spread about the Studio door policy. Benecke and Rubell were each a stern *arbiter elegantiae* with regard to what people were wearing, which was perhaps more tolerable from Marc Benecke, who would look crisply preppy, than from Steve Rubell, who would usually be dressed for a hot dog stand or a bowling alley.

"There was a time I was wearing a particular sports jacket. A guy comes up and says how can I get in?" Benecke says.

"Well, you should go buy this jacket. They have it at Bloomingdale's," Benecke told him.

The man returned the following night wearing the jacket.

"He still didn't get in!" Benecke says with an involuntary snicker at the memory. "It was amazing to me that anyone would do that. But there was such a fervor. Such a need to be inside. And to be part of that."

Sometimes the lords of the door would be so overweening that they propelled themselves into a comedy universe. A plenipotentiary from a country in West Africa was refused admission and stalked off, announcing that he was going to sever diplomatic ties with the United States. Benecke refused admission to the president of Cyprus under the impression that he was actually the president of the Cypress Hills Cemetery in Brooklyn. The need would sometimes go to such astounding lengths that it would elicit from Rubell and Benecke a need to push, to see just how far people would actually go, like schoolkids on a dare. "There was this girl that wanted to come into the club. She was a ravishingly beautiful woman. Okay?" Baird Jones says.

"Steve told me to tell her if she took all her clothes off, she could get into the club for free. She took all her clothes off." He paused, and suddenly yelped with a sort of weird glee. *"And she had to go to the hospital with frostbitten nipples. I am not making this up!"*

Marc Benecke admits there were follies on the door. "It was part theater outside. That had a big part to do with it," Benecke says. "I was as guilty as anybody else."

Marc remembers being outside with Steve one evening. "A couple came to the door. A very good-looking guy and his not as attractive wife. They were from Ohio. It was really late at night. The guy explained the whole thing, how they had just got married, how happy they were.

"Steve listened to the whole thing. He said, 'You can come in! Your wife—she can't!' "

When I asked if the newlywed had come in alone, Benecke said yes, and laughed explosively.

Steve Rubell's friends would sometimes take him to task for the velvet rope. Joyce Bogart, for instance, who with her husband, Neil, was close to both Steve and Ian. "Steve!" she scolded one night. "You're cruel to these people. They stand outside all night long. It's cold! This is ridiculous."

He dragged her outside. "The door is yours for the next hour. Who are you going to let in and who are you not going to let in?" he said. He took her to the fire hydrant and said, "Get up there!"

She got up. "It was one of the hardest things I have ever done," she said. "You want to let everyone in. But what he said before he left was if you let in too many people who look as if they come from the outer boroughs, no one will be interested in coming next week. The truth was I didn't change his door policy. It was very similar to what he would do."

People would go to great lengths to get into Studio 54. Chris Sullivan made a small business out of it before he actually got a job there. "My brother, Mark, and I couldn't really afford to go there," he says. "But at the back, facing Roseland, there was a fire escape that went all the way to the top of the theater. And there was a door." Chris would lurk out in front, locate a group of Euros with no shot of getting in, and direct them to meet his brother in the rear. He would then pay his fifteen dollars, walk up the back stairway, and unlock the door. Mark, meantime, would be shepherding something like fifteen or twenty Euros up the fire escape, charging them twenty-dollars a head. "I think we did this for about six months," Chris says. "We used to make two, three, four hundred dollars a night. Then one night I opened the door and the alarm went off, and I felt this arm grab my neck. I am about six foot one, but I was all bones and skin, and Studio 54 had really big bouncers." He was tossed out undamaged, and the Sullivan Studio tours went out of business.

Others continued. "We would have this situation where people would climb down from the building next door in full mountain-climbing gear. With ropes around their shoulders. They were trying to get into the courtyard," Baird Jones says. Barbed wire was put there as a deterrent. It was ineffective. "They would tangle in the barbed wire and fall to the cement pavement which was ten feet below. I remember where this guy had really screwed himself up and they got a stretcher. He was being brought through the lobby to the ambulance and he was really hurt." The man had shimmied down a cable for three stories, then fallen thirty feet, landing in an alley outside the window of the room occupied by Lisa Wright, who operated the coat check. He had broken his neck and left wrist. "And you could see him, trying to scope out the inside of the club. Trying to *see it*. Desperately!" Baird Jones says.

There was one death at least, according to Jones. "This guy got stuck in a vent trying to get in. It smelled like a cat had died. He was in black tie," says Jones, bubbling and hissing at the bizarrerie of the misadventure.

The people on the wrong side of the velvet cord would mostly be docile. A few might get sour, mean, angry. "At times, it got really hairy outside," Benecke says. "I'm very sensitive to people. I can usually tell when real tension is building. One time I decided to again change my tactics. A regular customer had too many people, or some problem. I walked him back to his limo. And all of a sudden the guy starts choking me. Of course, it made me even more standoffish." Unsurprisingly, Marc Benecke, who lived on Fifty-seventh Street, would sometimes ask a security guard to walk him home. The door and security were so nervous about being pelted with bottles that they would sometimes clear potential projectiles from nearby garbage cans for several blocks.

And sometimes worse happened than misbegotten throttling attempts. Roger Parenti remembers standing by the rope with a security fellow named Monty. "It was pretty late. Probably close to four o'clock," Parenti says. "He made the mistake of sticking his head over the rope a little too far. This guy walked up and gave him a shot. I've never seen anybody take a punch like that. Monty was out like a light, propped up against the door. Our security needless to say ran out to get hold of the guy. Steve Rubell was right behind the door and he stepped out, saying, 'What happened, Roger? What happened?' "

Parenti pointed up the street to where security had the sucker-puncher on the ground. Parenti says Rubell shouted, "Don't let them hurt him! Don't let them hurt him!" and hared up the street. Parenti assumed this was "for obvious legal reasons. We were afraid they were going to kill the guy." Not so.

"He got there . . . he looked around . . . he had these cowboys boots on, with tips. And he started kicking the guy in the head, saying, 'How dare you hurt my friends?' . . . That was the way Steve was. He certainly wasn't violent. That was the only time I saw him lose his temper."

Baird Jones claims a young woman pulled a gun on him when he wouldn't let her in. "It was just simply a terrifying experience," he says.

Chuck Garelick, the head of Studio 54 security, agrees things could get difficult. There was the time a disgruntled fellow who had been refused admission tried to crash the VIP entrance on Fifty-third Street. Literally crash. He was driving an Oldsmobile at the time. Or the time Chuck was standing at the front door. "A car whizzed by," he says. "Somebody yelled out 'Hey! Asshole!' I looked, and there was a rifle pointed at me. And I kind of let that slide by because he didn't shoot.

"After you finished a busy Saturday night, you were dead tired. It was about seven in the morning. You sat down and had a beer before you walked out because you were so wound up. You finished the beer. You opened up the back doors and went out onto Fifty-third Street. One morning there must have been about six of us. We weren't using the employees' entrance. We walked out through the entrance where the garbage goes out. It was closer and we were dead. The next we knew, these guys were out of a car across the street. They'd been waiting. And they just started shooting. Above our heads. Chips of brick flew down. We dived onto the ground. I personally tried to get very friendly with the underside of a car."

The shooters took off and the cops from the police precinct down the block set off in pursuit, movie-of-the-week style. They chased them down to the Village, then, as seldom happens in movies-of-the-week, lost them.

"More than likely it was people who couldn't get in," Garelick says.

★   ★   ★

High-society melodrama being a favorite style of Eurotrash, it was only natural that there should be a ripe example soon after the glittery caravan swept in strength into New York. It was perhaps almost as natural that the player should be the doyenne of Studio 54, Carmen D'Alessio. D'Alessio was then divorced from her husband Enrico Tucci, but they remained friendly and both continued to live in the Meurice, she in 9J and he in 11J. A mutual friend arrived from Europe, an art dealer, Franco Rappetti. He was quite a dashing figure, Rappetti, at once private dealer to the extremely rich Baron Thyssen and the paramour of the baron's fourth wife, Denise.

Heini Thyssen had begun spending millions on American art, and Rappetti got no cut on those deals. The baron's New York dealer was Andrew Crispo. Reppetti flew to New York. "I admired his honesty," Crispo told me. "He came and said, 'Andrew, you want to sell pictures to the baron? You pay me a commission.'

"I said, 'Franco, forget it! I'm not interested.' "

Crispo had done no business with Thyssen for a year. Denise Thyssen had tossed Rappetti, and his hold was slackening. This time he returned to New York racked on both his professional and emotional fronts. "Denise had been with him for ten years. But she was getting ready to exchange him for a younger ski trainer that she found in Gstaad," Carmen says.

Rappetti checked into the Waldorf. He was suicidal. "Enrico thought he might need the company of friends to soothe him," Carmen says, so Tucci asked him to stay in the Meurice.

Carmen D'Alessio, arriving home from a meeting at Studio, was agog to find that somebody had just taken a fatal dive from her former apartment. Rappetti had landed on the roof of a Volkswagen truck in his underpants. The small window through which he had exited the building had been opened with such force that it had stuck. Eurogossip refused to believe that Rappetti had taken a flier. Conspiratorial ideas were advanced. "Franco would never be seen in public in his underwear like that. He was so fastidious," Dialta Cardini asserted roundly.

Carmen D'Alessio disagrees vigorously. Tucci's new wife had actually been writing letters in another room at the time. "He continued to be depressed," she says. "He left ten grand and a gold chain on top of the night table. It happened at three in the afternoon. There were no drugs, or orgies, or ridiculous items that have been mentioned right and left. There was nothing else. That's exactly what happened."

The body was identified by Diane von Furstenberg. Baron Thyssen came to New York and arranged for the corpse to be returned to Italy. Andrew Crispo took care of the details. Thyssen had ordered a casket of such portentous size that Crispo learned a special plane would be necessary. It would cost $150,000. "Isn't that a bit expensive?" Crispo asked the baron. Doubtless contemplating all those commissions, Thyssen said, "Believe me, it's a bargain."

No wonder, Dialta, who is now the Principessa Dialta Alliata di Montereale, has written a Meurice-based movie script.

In the spring of 1977 a tall man with skin the color of vanilla yogurt and a rocker bouffant of black hair walked into the downstairs bar and asked for a drink. "A Stoly and tonic," he said. The barman was Scotty Taylor. He dished out the vodka. "That's two-fifty," he said.

The man looked at him. His eyes were beetle-black, shining, unblinking. "I don't pay," he said.

Taylor had been increasingly baffled by the esoterica of the free list. He looked the man over. He wasn't a celebrity. He didn't look like a journalist. He didn't even look like a publicist. "Tell me who are you?" he asked. "I want to know."

"I'm Arthur Weinstein. I own Hurrah . . ."

Taylor's mood switched. In Enchanted Garden Steve Rubell used to chatter about Hurrah. Also he knew it was the place that Studio 54 was wiping out. "You don't have to pay for anything at this bar. Ever," he told Weinstein. One of those spontaneous alliances that mesh together to form part of Nightworld had just sprung into being.

He met her in Studio. She was a woman in her mid-twenties with straight blond hair and she was living with somebody in L.A. who put her into rock videos and she was taking the inevitable acting classes. She had come east for a couple of weeks because everybody, but everybody in L.A. was doing too many drugs. She was with a guy with a closed textbook of a face, apparently a big wheel of a lawyer in the music biz.

This suit clearly viewed him with sour suspicion, but had to leave them together in Studio because he had an early-morning plane. Ontario.

They chatted. She had a high voice and a deliciously flaky laugh, particularly when she was discussing her arrest record, which was juvenilia mostly, like being picked up with a couple of other drug-deranged girls for unspecified misbehavior during a Pink Floyd concert. She went home with him. The lawyer had left her two hundred dollars' spending money. And she had her return ticket to L.A. "He's got the smallest thing you ever saw" was her main comment about the lawyer.

They murdered Charles awhile, and got out of their clothes.

Next morning he spotted something curious about a framed photograph on his wall. She had stuck a passport picture–sized color snapshot of herself over somebody else's face. She stayed in bed, sniffling. She blamed the cocaine.

He took a bath. She perched herself on the lavatory seat, and chattered about her plans for the day. She planned to go to the Museum of Modern Art, of which she had heard good reports, and she was meeting a girlfriend for lunch downtown. It took him a second to realize that she was pissing. She was artless as a child, he decided. Except most children wouldn't do that. Would they?

He went out to have a set of keys made for her and spent the day in a magazine office. She was in the apartment? How had she liked MOMA? She had decided to buy a hat instead, she said, and she brandished pale nails, newly done by the manicurist in the Pierre. They looked like pale beetle wings. The friend with whom she had been planning to have lunch had vamoosed on a Cindy Lauper tour.

That night they went to Studio. Of course.

They had coffee in the morning. She went out shopping. He read her agenda book while she was out and inventoried the things in her bag. The agenda book was big, but only contained pages of random squigglings. Her things included gold high-heeled shoes, a pink leopardette wrap, white plastic open-toed sandals, and a short skirt of silver-painted leather.

That night they went to Studio.

Next day he suggested that they try the Mudd Club, but, it turned out that rockers bored her witless. She spoke of the time she got into a chat with somebody with long hair, broke off, and said, "Oh, I'm sorry. I thought you were a girl."

"No. I'm a rock and roll star," he said sulkingly.

She had said, or says she had said, "Oh really? Same thing."

So that night they would go to Studio or, perhaps Xenon. But first they met up with a couple, friends of his. The woman was named Fiona. They dined at the Lone Star Cafe. She and Fiona were physically very alike and quickly grew to loathe each other. Indeed, she querulously complained that Fiona had poured beer on her white sweater. "I didn't. But I will," Fiona had snapped.

He decided to take her home. In the cab she decided that Fiona had been jealous, and raged with a wild and jagged streak of poetry. "It's always shiny on my planet. There's no dark and I am luminous," she said. She gestured downtown in the direction of the Lone Star Cafe, Fiona, and all other life-shriveling forces. "So fuck you up the ass," she added, making the appropriate gesture.

He scribbled all this down in the bathroom later, keeping a tap running for camouflage. There was no disco that night, but some Charles. They made love gently and, in part because of the liquor he had taken on board, forever.

She complained of bad dreams the next morning, giving harsh little coughs, like a cat. She got up at noon, and wandered around in a pink top, with no bottom, drinking from a bottle of Molson's ale, then patted her tiny tum. "I'm getting fat. I hope I'm not pregnant," she said, and giggled. "Yay! Mama! Another one down the tubes . . ."

She had decided to stay on till Halloween, perhaps doing some waitressing. There was, you see, no Studio 54 in Los Angeles, and many too many brain-dead rockers. She was unexpectedly resigned when he said it was time she find somewhere else to stay. Heartbreakingly so, really, but he hardened himself. A woman friend of hers called with an address. He scribbled it down on his pad, then wrote her out a copy. Wanting her out of the place he volunteered to take her there by taxi. When they were in the neighborhood, she didn't know the address.

He said, "I gave you the address."

"You wrote it down. I thought you had it."

"It's your address. Why would I take it?"

He was late for an appointment, and furious, but went back to the apartment, feeling very noble to consult his pad, then drove her to some grotty building in the East Thirties. There, he thought, that wipes the slate clean. He didn't ask for her telephone number.

The next morning he found her copy of the list. It had been in his pocket all the time.

Three nights. Pretty good going for a Disco Romance.

CLUB WARS

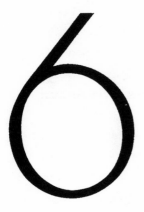

THERE WAS A NEW COMPETITOR: NEW YORK, NEW YORK. I was at a preopening party there after the premiere of *The Children of Theater Street,* a documentary produced by Earle Mack. The party had been filled with pirouetting balletomanes, so the club seemed cool and silvery.

New York, New York was at 33 West Fifty-second Street, a building that had housed a legendary hangout of the Walter Winchell epoch, Toots Shor's.

Its owners were Maurice Brahms and the very much behind-the-scenes John Addison and it had been done up by the fancy designer—and former housemate of Halston and Ron Ferri—Angelo Donghia. New York, New York occupied three floors and the prepublicity made much of the fact that one of those floors was a restaurant, so the place wasn't just a trashy discothèque. It was gray, glittery with mirrors, it had a red lacquer dance floor.

I asked John Addison, a smooth, pleasant fellow, what his capitalization had been. "I don't want to give you phony figures, like everybody else will," he said. His solution was to give me no figures at all. Anyway, as so often happens when money is no object, it ran perilously short before the completion of the disco. Addison took the necessary steps, flying to Switzerland to take money out of one of his accounts. On March 6, 1977, he was nabbed by customs officials for claiming to be an American citizen while crossing from Canada. The feds interest in Addison intensified when he was found to be carrying an undisclosed $199,350. This was seized.

Addison hollered for his lover-cum-lawyer Roy Cohn, who assigned the problem to his partner, Tom Andrews. "Andrews got somebody in Switzerland to sign an affidavit that it was their money. Which it was not," Brahms says. "The government returned John's money and Andrews got a fifty-thousand-dollar fee for that." Tom Andrews—and Roy Cohn—had also, of course, gotten an intimate look at the not always wholly legal way that John Addison and Maurice Brahms conducted their affairs.

The official opening was on May 18. Blue and red beams of light roved, as if looking for targets, with unnerving effect, and the crowd was a glorious mix: jowly types from Doubles, blow-dries from Regine's, and discoids in varying degrees of funkness (the Peasant Intellectual look was pretty big for some reason). West Fifty-second Street had been "Swing Street" before the war, as Liz Smith reminded her readers in the *News*. She rhapsodized:

SOCIALITES FROM LADY KEITH TO JEROME ZIPKIN TO THE GILFORD DUDLEYS OF PALM BEACH TO THE UBIQUITOUS NAN KEMPNER WERE IN THERE OGLING THE MADNESS ON THE RED LACQUER DANCE FLOOR.

NEW YORK, NEW YORK ISN'T YOUR ORDINARY SLEAZE DISCO JOINT; IT'S GOT GLAMOUR TO SPARE. AND JUST IN CASE THERE ISN'T ENOUGH NORMAL SMOKE IN A NIGHTSPOT, THIS PLACE HAS FAKE SMOKE PUFFING UP OVER THE DANCE FLOOR. DON'T WORRY, IT'S CREATED BY DRY ICE FOR DRY TONGUE-IN-CHEEK-TO-CHEEK DANCING.

HUSTLE ON OVER TO SWING STREET. YOU'LL GET YOUR MONEY'S WORTH AT NEW YORK, NEW YORK.

Neither Maurice Brahms nor John Addison was mentioned in the piece, though. Both preferred to be mantled in the traditional obscurity of Night-world. Big mistake. It was quickly made plain that it was no match for Studio in the celeb flash department when it couldn't even secure the après-première party for New York, New York, the movie which starred Robert de Niro and Liza Minnelli. "We should have had it," Brahms says, peeved to this day. Liza Minnelli showed up at Studio after the movie, and Joanne Horowitz made sure that the world's press were made aware of this.

Within months New York, New York was catering to just the sort of working-class night-on-the-town clientele who would never get past Benecke's beady eye a few blocks north. "That's where the money is. And they think you're doing them a favor when you let them in," crowed Brahms to a reporter. "I'm in it for the money. For the joy, the satisfaction, the accumulation of money. It is a bad part of my personality."

He observed that his operating principle was Don't Trust Anyone, but he admitted that he didn't necessarily listen to anyone either. "That's another bad part of my character," he said. "Burying my head in the sand, even when the rest of my body is exposed."

Two astoundingly tall young women were sitting at the main bar in Studio, preening, dipping gracefully into their tall drinks, then looking around Studio, necks distended. One wore black tights and Maid Marian boots; the two of them looked at once graceful and sweetly ridiculous, like wading birds. The light was floury, a whoosh of particles swirling around dancers, who were turbulent as spawning salmon on a dark light-flecked pool of a dance floor. Decibel by decibel, a track of disco was pounding its way up a sonic Richter scale. "There's Margaux," one of the women noted.

"Where's Warren?"

"Warren's coming . . ."

Their eyes bounced around, searching out Milos, Mischa, Mick, or just about anybody whose name got printed in boldface. The AstroTurf was as black as factory smoke, and springy, and you could discern a private party coming into focus within the formless population of the club.

A cake came magically into being on the bar. It was the evening of May 21, and I had been invited to a birthday bash being thrown for Guy Burgos, the ex-husband of a neice of Winston Churchill. Some of the more volatile guests began to form a conga line. "I have three hundred friends that I see every night at discothèques," Burgos crowed. "D. D. Ryan found this place in the Hamptons and there were two thousand people there." He marveled. *"Two thousand!"* The more volatile guests got ready to sing songs.

At that moment some men showed up dressed as cops. Scotty Taylor, who was tending bar, later said that he at first assumed they were a bunch of Village People wannabes. "A guy asked me for a drink," Taylor remembers. Something made Taylor nervous and he busied himself with clearing away glassware. "I said, 'Uhhh! Talk to Eddie.' And when Eddie served him the drink, they handcuffed him." They were not dress-up guys, but actual cops from the midtown precinct, and they were headed by the State Liquor Commissioner, Michael Roth.

Two cops approached the bar at which I was standing. The two tall women looked them over with pupils as sharp as pins. "This iz'n my idea," mumbled the smallish cop. He was standing at shoulder height to them, staring into their bosoms as though they might be wired for sound.

The second, more forceful cop said, "Everybody's gotta leave."

They began to shove bottles together.

A third cop came over. "Only the full ones," he instructed.

The small, glum cop began tumbling bottles of amaretto into a sack.

Things wilted. It was as if a cold draft had blown into an overheated conservatory. Steve Rubell suddenly popped up at the bar. He was wearing his usual sloppy jacket, and he was angry but given the circumstances he was enormously composed. "Michael Roth is running for attorney general," he told me fiercely. "He knows this is the way to make the papers. We are what's happening."

Actually, it hadn't been quite that programmed. Earlier that evening Michael Roth had been at the theater, a Republican party benefit, held beneath the aegis of the party boss, Vince Albano. Afterward there had been a dinner at Gallagher's on West Fifty-second Street. Earl Wilson, the elderly gossip columnist for the *New York Post,* approached Roth and asked whether Studio 54 had got its liquor license yet.

"I said no, they had not," Roth remembers. "Earl Wilson left the party and came back half an hour, forty-five minutes later. He held his notepad up, pencil in hand, and said, 'I was just over at Studio 54. They've got a big crowd over there and they're selling alcohol. What are you going to do about it?' "

What the angry Roth did was drop by the midtown north police station en route to Studio, where he bought two drinks. He then had Rubell, Schrager, and two bartenders arrested.

For a number of interested parties it had, of course, been payback time. Various federal agencies had been getting calls from tipsters about Studio 54 as soon as it opened. Their charges were highly detailed, and accurate. "It's beyond me that they would invest all that money and do that," Albert Yocono of the Department of Consumer Affairs said of Rubell and Schrager's attempt to keep the place going on those one-night-at-a-time catering licenses. "It makes no sense. They don't have a certificate of occupancy, they don't have a cabaret license, and they don't have a public assembly license. The old pieces of paper they have aren't worth anything." Captain Patrick Casey of the Division of Fire Prevention said, "I guess they figure they are above the law."

"These places are springing up like mushrooms after a rainstorm. It's difficult to deal with legislatively," said Michael Roth resignedly.

A summons had been served on April 27. A first court date for May 6 had been adjourned. Now Roy Cohn was to take care of Studio's problem, arguing its case in Manhattan Criminal Court on June 6.

Guy Burgos's guests sang "Happy Birthday" post-bust anyway. "We'll be open tomorrow night," Rubell promised departing guests. The two tall young women stood outside, wondering whether to go to Hurrah or to New York, New York. They wound up going to both. As, indeed, did I. The word later was that many, many thousands of dollars' worth of Baggies and vials of cocaine had been found stuffed down the back of those comfy Studio banquettes.

Studio *was* open the following night, and Guy Burgos had his birthday all over again, and a new cake. "I stamped in it," he said. "It was creamy." Studio was now dry, though—a vulnerable condition for a brand-new club.

Much of the sniping at Studio had, of course, come from other clubs, and it was peculiarly intense. From the very beginning Studio's competitors sensed a certain delirium about the way the place was operated and grumbled at what they had to be getting away with. "Most of the commissioners are upstate. They're undermanned. They won't do anything till they have to," said Geoff Jones, the manager of El Morocco. "These fellows! You steal something till you get caught." He grew nostalgic for the days when he would cheerfully have barred anybody from his club just for wearing brown shoes.

Patrick Shields, the tall, urbane manager of Le Club said, "They just don't have class. Le Club has been around seventeen years. There's an awful lot of money coming into New York. European money. And mob money. Here they are handing over the money at the door. How are the tax people checking up on this? How are the feds and the city getting their money? That's what I want to know."

This did, indeed, seem worth looking into. "We have methods," John Waldman Somebody from the U.S. Attorney's Office told me in an appropriately mysterious fashion, and spoke of ongoing "investigations."

"We will be watching," said a spokesman for the intelligence division of the IRS. "We have teams covering areas broken down by zip codes." The teams ran from one to five people. The IRS added that "they don't have a responsibility to file until the end of the year."

Studio 54's five-month period as a juice bar presented Rubell and Schrager's opposition with a window of opportunity. The landscape of Nightworld had become various. There was the uptown contingent, which was for a John Held, Jr., Pete Arno–styled crowd, old money and new floozies, and included El Morocco, Le Club, and the latest addition, Doubles. Doubles was in the basement of the Sherry Netherland and had infuriated El Morocco by poaching its staff. It was neither the first nor last Manhattan nightspot to model itself more or less directly on Annabel's, Mark Birley's club on Berkeley Square, but perhaps Manhattan is the wrong neck of the woods for an Annabel's clone because Doubles looked like—and was about as much fun as—a sore throat.

There was Regine's, of course, and a newer place, Olivier Coquelin's Cachaca. "Which is not a disco. I *invented* disco. Now I do something new," Coquelin said. There were low-life discos with names like Club 54 and Starship Discovery, and there was Les Mouches, which had a nice loucheness and was frequented by Imelda Marcos. An aptly named dive on Madison, La Folie, which had opened in February, was all marble and glimmer. It had extremely bad École de Paris paintings on the wall—a late Van Dongen, a poor Kisling— and a date one evening told me that painted eyes were disquietingly set in the bowls in the ladies' room. "Look what a good time everybody is having. they've never heard about cool," she said charitably. The owner might just as well have signed a noncompete clause with Rubell and Schrager. Patrick Shields said, "These are not the kind of places that are built to last. It's like Nathan's floating crap game from *Guys and Dolls.*"

Infinity was waning, too. "What's hurt us is the hassle of going downtown," Maurice Brahms told me. The rumor offensive against the beleagured Studio 54 was unabated. "I don't want to blurt out anything. But I saw one of their security men open his jacket and take out a nickel-plated pistol," another club owner told me.

Ian Schrager cheerfully admitted that they knew they were ignoring the liquor laws. "It was expedient," he told a reporter. "We are aware of the law. I *am* a lawyer." Roy Cohn appealed the SLA decision. Among those who publicly supported the club were Calvin Klein, Andy Warhol, the *Daily News* columnist Liz Smith, James Brady, who was then editor of *New York,* and the patrician politician Carter Burden.

The decision against Studio 54 was reversed by Judge Hyman Korn. Michael Roth raged, "This gives the green light to people who want to operate without a license." But Studio got its license in October. It had survived its five dry months in fine fettle.

Studio 54's next exposure to media fire came in the liveliest periodical of the time, Clay Felker's *New York* magazine. Dan Dorfman's widely read money column there, "The Bottom Line," focused on the club in October. This, it went without saying, meant focusing on Steve Rubell (in his column, Schrager and Dushey occupied a bracketed sentence shorter than this one). "We had dinner. We went to Patsy's," Dorfman says. Patsy's, a favorite Manhattan joint of persons like writers, and characters who have sometimes had the full attention of the feds, was Rubell's choice. "There was a guy there, a well-known mobster. As we walked by, Steve said, 'How ya doin'?' He said, 'Hi, squirt!'" Dorfman says, still impressed.

Dorfman, a bantamweight like Rubell, with a high voice, bushy black hair, and a fondness for sheeny bronze clothing and ties that shriek like sirens, watched goggle-eyed as the hungry club owner ordered a mighty plateful of chicken, sausages, and mushrooms and attacked it with his fingers. "He was eating with his hands. He was getting this stuff all over himself. It was disgusting to look at!" Dorfman recalls. A waiter hurried over with a clean napkin. Unnecessarily, Rubell felt. "I'm not chic," he said blithely.

By Dorfman's account, names were dropping from Rubell's mouth like coins from a jackpotting slot machine, his eyes were darting around the room, and the meal was constantly interrupted by greetings for passing acquaintances and three telephone calls. Afterward, they took off for Studio. It was 11:30, still early. There were thirty-five people at the door.

Dan Dorfman floated around awhile, then went home and duly turned in his column.

Dorfman's article was headlined THE ECCENTRIC WHIZ BEHIND STUDIO 54 and it was published in the issue of November 7. "I really liked Steve. I really liked him," Dorfman told me later. "He was a personable guy." His column reflected that and it also reflected that Dorfman, like most journalists, could be horny-hided and naïve by turns. He describes, for instance, a couple embracing on a sofa, and quotes Rubell: "I don't care if they want to make out here. I want people to be themselves, like in a Fellini movie."

Dorfman wrote:

WHAT'S YOUR SEX LIFE LIKE? I ASKED THE UNMARRIED RUBELL. I FIGURED IT HAD TO BE MARVELOUS, CONSIDERING THE BEVY OF BEAUTIFUL GALS ABOUT. I WAS WRONG. "IF THERE'S SOMETHING LEFT WHEN THE PLACE CLOSES, I TAKE HER HOME," HE SAID. "BUT MY BUSINESS IS THE MOST IMPORTANT THING IN THE WORLD TO ME. I ONCE HAD A WONDERFUL GIRL AND SHE SAID, 'IT'S ME OR THE BUSINESS.' I SAID, 'THE BUSINESS,' AND NOW SHE'S GONE."

The magazine ran the column with a single picture, a snapshot of Steve in the club with Diana Ross. As a caption they ran a fine bit of Rubell bragging: "Profits are astronomical. Only the Mafia does better."

In the body of the text Rubell is described as being "skittish about talking figures," but his caution wasn't much of an improvement on his bravado. Dorfman quoted Rubell thus: "It's a cash business and you have to worry about the IRS," he pleaded. "I don't want them to know everything."

Some understood the impact straightaway. Ed Gifford read the Dorfman column and showed it to his wife, Michael. "These guys have sealed their doom!" he said.

Ian Schrager, too. Dan Dorfman returned in the aftermath of the piece.

"Steve was okay. He loved publicity," Dorfman says. "But Schrager went wild. Schrager went crazy. Schrager *glowered* at me when I came in next time. And Steve said, 'Heyyy! He's a reporter. He's a reporter.'

Ian finally addressed him. "He said, 'I didn't like what you did. I didn't like what you did!'"

Dorfman told him, "Look. This is what he *said*." He adds, "Steve was lovable . . . friendly . . . he spoke very openly. How many people would say we make more money than the Mafia? You've got to be out of your mind to make that comment. And it was repeated in a number of papers."

It was also characteristic that Dorfman wasn't cold-shouldered when he made many, many return visits to Studio 54. "There's never been a place like that for any reporter who was half alive," he says. "How could you not walk out with three stories? There were so many interesting things going on. Forget about the dancing, and the excessive drinks, and the grass they were selling all over the place. Forget about the upper balcony where the guys were making love. What really counted was there were so many people there, they were drinking, they were relaxed, they talked about other people. It was Storyland! That was what it was. It was *Storyland*."

DISCOMANIA

7

"*SATURDAY NIGHT FEVER* WAS EDITED IN BROOKLYN. IT was brought out like a little secret," says Bill Oakes. "Paramount people used to ask me, 'How's your little disco movie, Bill?' as I walked across the commisary. We were doing *Grease,* which they had much higher hopes for."

Oakes had been assigned to do the soundtrack album. He did the mastering, as the process is called at Capitol. "We started at midnight and went on till dawn, and by this time I was absolutely fried," he says. "This was October or November of 1977. I had been listening to disco for so long, I never wanted to hear the stuff again. I just wanted to get it over with.

"The word was that people had had enough . . . the Deadheads were coming back . . . Heavy Metal was making a run at it . . . That's it! Let's move on. We've got *Grease* in the can. Let's move on! Tom Petty was auditioning for a label deal with Capitol that night. I thought that sounded interesting. But they kept calling me down the corridor with the master.

'C'mon! We've got to listen to another track! Tavares, pumping away.' Great! I won't have to listen to it again."

Oakes got the master tape. "I was going to hand it to the record company, and then they would do what they would. It was in the back of my car. I was between La Brea and Hollywood as dawn broke. I found I was sitting behind a truck with this bumper sticker that said 'Death to Disco.'

"I was sitting there, thinking perhaps it is. It's too late! It's too boring to think of. I drove home, and left the master in the car. . . ."

The premiere for *Saturday Night Fever* was on December 16. There was a dinner at Tavern on the Green, then everybody went on to Studio for a party for Bianca Jagger. The inevitable horse was brought on and a great many doves were released. "The doves all got fried by the lights. There was a guy sweeping up these dead pigeons with a broom," Kevin McCormick says.

Saturday Night Fever did make Stigwood's hundred million. Plus. The record made even more, selling twenty million plus double albums. "You couldn't keep them in stock," Gershon says. "You had a cardboard sign saying YES, WE'LL HAVE MORE *FEVER* BY THIS AFTERNOON . . . YES, WE'LL HAVE MORE *FEVER* BY TOMORROW . . . that kind of stuff."

Jill Fuller, the daughter of a Texas oilman, who was then married and living in Brazil, says, "I saw *Saturday Night Fever* and decided to get a divorce. I came to New York and went to Studio 54. There was a party for Tennessee Williams. Yay!"

During that winter's most brutal snowstorm, Studio was full. "People went on skis," Peppo Vanini says.

Discomania had begun in earnest.

Nile Rodgers had been bowled over by disco. Rodgers, who is both a performer and a producer, says, "I think of Carol Douglas . . . Gloria Gaynor . . . Eddie Kendricks from the Temptations when he did 'Girl, You Need a Change of Mind.' I can remember these records being played in clubs for hours at a time. Certain songs became anthemic. The longer the record, the better."

By the time Studio had opened, though, Nile Rodgers had become unhappy with the notion of being considered a disco musician. "At that point the bohemian aspect was all lost. Now you had Frank Sinatra doing disco records. You had Dolly Parton doing disco records. You had anybody doing a disco record, to get a hit."

Nonetheless, Nile Rodgers and his partner Bernard Edwards were the creators of one of disco's monster hit groups, Chic. It was typical of disco groups, however, in that although they were hugely successful, they were also faceless. "I would go to Studio but I wasn't part of the hip crowd yet," Rodgers says. "My girlfriend went to the Fashion Institute of Technology and she knew Marc Benecke. She was the one who would get me in.

"But now we were known as the new whiz kids in music. Grace Jones was having a performance and a party there. It was a big show, and we were almost like her guests of honor, because we were really popular. But we were faceless, which was by design, by the way.

"It was snowing. That night both Bernard and I were in black ties. I still remember to this day. I had a Cerutti dinner jacket and Bernard had an Armani. We were killin'. I probably had a wing-collar shirt, with a decorative front, but not lacy. Pleated, with studs. The whole bit. Spectator shoes. You know, two-tone. Because that was our Chic outfit in those days. We had big afros. Really, really big afros. That was the thing. A big afro, and dance.

"We really were done up to the nines. You know, Grace Jones! And we were Chic. We wanted to look Chic." He gave a dry, rolling laugh. "We wanted to *smell* Chic!"

They presented themselves at the back door. It was snowing. The doorman eyeballed them. "I don't see your names on the list," he told them.

"No. We're on Grace's personal list," Nile told him. "We're probably going to produce her next album."

He didn't find their names on that list either.

They said, "Well, look under Chic . . ."

"What? Shit? I don't see Shit here."

Frustrated, they went around to the front. "I thought that by now Marc Benecke knew me because I had been there many, many times with my girlfriend and with a guy who used to manage Fiorucci," Rodgers says. "Everybody who would work at the boutiques would get into Studio 54. *But Marc totally disregarded us.* He didn't give us a second look.

"I'm waving and jumping. Meanwhile I'm going to see Grace. This is important to us. We're about to make what we felt would be the most important record of our lives. Because up until that moment we hadn't worked with any stars. No good! He wouldn't let us in. Meanwhile, we had three or four records burning up the discos at that point.

"Our lives before we had our hit were fun and interesting, but it was tough to make it. Now we had made it and we had the ultimate rejection. We felt, one, we couldn't get into this big event. Two, Grace Jones would think we were fuck-ups." They hoped they would be missed. That somebody might come out. They stuck it out till about one. "We stood there as long as we could take it. Until our feet were just finally way too cold. We were really totally dejected. We felt horrible."

They trudged to Nile's apartment, which wasn't far, on Fifty-second Street between Eighth and Ninth avenues, through the snow. "We were so furious," Nile says. "We bought a bunch of coke and marijuana and champagne. Because we were dressed great. So we had our own little private party, Bernard and I.

"We resorted to using music therapeutically, which was what we had always done up until that point. Bernard and I started jamming, just guitar and bass. We were just yelling obscenites . . . *Fuck Studio 54 . . . Fuck 'em . . . Fuck off! . . . Fuck those scumbags . . . Fuck them! . . .* " And we were laughing. We were entertaining the hell out of ourselves. We had a blast. And finally it hit Bernard. He said, 'Hey, Nile! What you're playing sounds really good.'

"I said, 'What do you mean?' Because we weren't trying to write a song. We were just having a good time, venting our anger and frustration.

"He said, 'I'm telling you, man! That shit sounds great.' "

They fooled around with the stuff Nile had been doing, and came up with a chorus.

"We said, 'Damn! That sounds like a song. This is cool.' And we wrote a whole obscene song about fucking Studio 54, and those assholes. But it had melody, and texture, and form. And we said, 'This is hysterical.' So we recorded it. We made a little demo. And after we laughed, we said, 'You know, this is really catchy!'

"We changed 'Fuck Off' to 'Freak Off.' But that sounded lame. Then we realized that the biggest dance in America at that time was called the Freak." It would be about the dance. They focused on Chubby Checker's famous "The Twist." "That was what Lionel Ritchie calls the Code Vibe. It's like a template you set up. It was like magic. We changed one word, 'Off' to 'Out,' and the floodgates opened up." (The song was called "Le Freak.")

"Within twenty-five to thirty minutes, we had the biggest hit record of our lives. It's still the biggest hit single in Warner Brothers' history. And as far as copyrights are concerned it's the third largest in the history of music. After 'White Christmas' by Irving Berlin and 'Rudolph, the Red-Nosed Reindeer' by Johnny Marks. We sold six million copies of the single and we stopped it because we felt it might cut into the album sales. To this day we feel ridiculous, because who knows what we might have achieved."

No wonder Nile Rodgers now counts Marc Benecke a friend.

There's no hatred or anger left in the song. "Not at all! Not at all!" Nile Rodgers says. "Music is our friend. Our lover." That was how he dealt with the anger. "It worked. It worked countlessly."

Rick Dees was a writer of novelty songs who hadn't done too well with his first offering. "A Sears catalogue came out and a man's penis was showing through the bottom of his underwear. They forgot to airbrush it out. It was on page 602," Dees says. "Page 602" was the title of his first novelty song. "I think it sold eleven copies," he says. "That was 1974, 1975. I was twenty-three."

His next novelty song was "Disco Duck." He put it out on a tiny label, Fretone Records. "Then we sold the master tape to Robert Stigwood through his representative, Al Coury, for three thousand five hundred dollars. *Thirty-five hundred dollars!*

" 'Disco Duck' sold four million. It was number one for almost a month. To ride that wave was an amazing experience. It was beating Paul McCartney and Chicago. Can you imagine the angst of having one of your masterpieces at number four, and you look and something called 'Disco Duck' was at number one?"

Dees saw a bit more than $3,500; since he was paid a penny royalty per record, he picked up another $40,000. "Then I was asked if I would mind if they put 'Disco Duck' on the soundtrack to *Saturday Night Fever*. I said, 'Fantastic!' My agent went and negotiated the deal. You can hear it as John Travolta is teaching dance in a dance class.

"Well, negotiating a deal that you're in the soundtrack is not the same as that you're going to be on the soundtrack album. It would have been easy to say, 'Just make sure you put it on the album.' The Stigwood organization would have said, 'No problem!' Lo and behold, the *Saturday Night Fever* album comes out. I run out to get the album. It's got the Bee Gees . . . KC and the Sunshine Band . . . The Tramps . . . nowhere, Rick Dees.

"That's about ten cents an album. *It sold 25 million copies.* Now we're talking about a loss of $2.5 million." Dees gave a manic chuckle, rather a Disco Duck chuckle as a matter of fact. "So the duck became an albatross, hanging around my neck," he said. His next disco novelty, "Dis-Gorilla," did okay, but lightning did not strike twice.

CLUB WARS HEAT UP

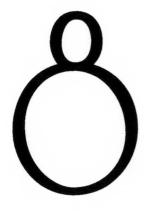

THE BINARY PRINCIPLE SEEMS TO BE PRACTICALLY A LAW of American business. If there is a *Time,* let there be *Newsweek.* Should enough mouths guzzle Coca-Cola, up will pop a Pepsi. Thus the nova flare of Studio dictated that there must be a competitor—that should be the same but just different enough—particularly when it was plain that New York, New York wasn't cutting the mustard. The competition, when it came, was also launched by a duo, so unalike as to make Rubell and Schrager seem like peas in the pod: Peppo Vanini and Howard Stein.

Vanini, then in his late thirties, was from Lugano, Switzerland. A former manager of the King's Club in the Palace Hotel, St. Moritz, he was a man who knew the social topographies of Europe, both the cobwebby interrelationships of the heirs to defunct monarchies and principates and the mark, franc, and lira-weights of the Europlutocrats. He had been brought to New York by Regine, but it was rumored that relations between he and his diva boss were poor.

Howard Stein is a New Yorker. A springy, dapper man, his black hair slick as polish on a balding pate, he has a bright grin but can switch from charm to chill in a nanosecond. Some attribute this to like father like son—Howard's father, Jack "Ruby" Stein, had been a loan shark, who ended up floating down the Hudson, sans head. About this, Stein is overly sensitive, although most of the grand young Euros in New York had family histories at least as baroque. Stein was one of New York's main producers of rock concerts in the late sixties. "Bill Graham was my major competitor. He was very successful with the Fillmore East on Second Avenue," Stein says. "I was doing shows at a theater in Westchester County. I was like Castro. In the hills. Taking little shots, making forays, while he controlled the market in New York City. I did a Sonny and Cher concert when they were still wearing *alpaca vests*."

Bill Graham quit New York in June 1971. One last concert had featured Frank Zappa, and John Lennon and Yoko Ono, who spent part of the gig with her head in a brown paper bag. His last-night lineup included The Allman Brothers, The J. Geils Band, and the Beach Boys. "I immediately went to New York and opened up the Academy of Music," Howard says. It was on Fourteenth Street in what had been New York's Metropolitan Opera House during the teens of the century. Howard Stein opened with the band Traffic. "It was a secret that a small number of people knew. About this new industry. The British Invasion," he says. "Where you could pay a band between $500 and $5,000 and it could make you $10,000 . . . $25,000 . . . $50,000 . . . I remember paying $2,500 to Pink Floyd. On their last American tour I think they grossed $65 million."

The dream was over. What could you say?

"Suddenly all these obscure rock and roll bands had very powerful attorneys, very powerful business managers, and agents, and the deals they were offering were terrible," Stein says. "They were delegating promoters like myself to being caterers, limousine orderers, drug dealers, and pimps. To wait two years to get a big band like the Rolling Stones, they would make you lose fortunes on smaller bands in the same stable. When you finally got the Rolling Stones, there was a limited upside. You got paid $25,000 while they grossed millions of dollars. And when you booked a marginal band there was an unlimited downside."

People started giving him a hard time. "It all changed. It just all changed simultaneously. I remember Cat Stevens telling me that he wasn't coming on-stage because the crabs on his backstage menu were not Alaskan King crabs. Or Alice Cooper complaining because the beer had to be in cans, not in bottles. Some promoter saying we had to take the green M&M's out of the batches. Nobody appreciated *This Is Spinal Tap* more than I did.

"I knew that it was time to leave. I had a little omen. The Academy of Music had a marquee—a traditional theater marquee. I was doing a Grateful Dead concert. The marquee sign said HOWARD STEIN PRESENTS THE GRATEFUL DEAD. And it dropped its P. When I went to work that morning I saw HOWARD STEIN RESENTS THE GRATEFUL DEAD. And I knew the whole world had now discovered my secret. That I hated this industry!"

What Stein hated was "having no input into the musical productions . . . into the sounds . . . into the lights . . . into the advertising campaigns . . ." but he also hated being taken for a sucker, and thought he might effect a change by whaling into the agents. "I'm not going to buy all these automatic losers in order to get the Rolling Stones. I'm just not going to do it anymore!" Stein told them.

The agents said, "Fine!" They didn't call him anymore. Other suckers were beating their doors down.

"Then when I decided I needed them, I called," Stein says. "They didn't take my calls." He realized he had been "quasi-blackballed from the industry."

Actually Stein didn't really care. "I was stupid enough—I'm *glad* I was stupid enough—to think that rock and roll was dying. And that it was being replaced by disco," he says.

"So I was bumming around, wondering what to do." That was when he had a crucial chat with Peppo Vanini. "I met Peppo at Regine's. He used to have all his Euro friends to his home in Bedford for Sunday soccer games. I was always the goalie because I couldn't kick. He was completely disenchanted with Regine. I was disenchanted with the rock and roll industry." They decided there was room for a competitor to Studio 54.

The chosen building, 124 West Forty-third Street, had been designed to look like the theaters in London's West End and built in 1918. As the Henry Miller theater, so named for a producer, it had premiered Thornton Wilder's *Our Town*. Then, as the Park-Miller, a porno house, it went from straight to gay to straight to broke. Stein and Vanini raised $2 million for a makeover and set to work. The opening, which I was assigned to cover for *New York* magazine, was scheduled for early June, just thirteen months after the opening of Studio.

Joanne Horowitz was hired away from Studio to do the PR. Two disc jockeys were hired away from other clubs, one from 12 West and one from Flamingo. Lynn Barclay, who had worked with Marc Benecke at Studio until being canned some months before, was hired to work the door. Doug Trumbull, the special effects whiz, who had worked on both *2001* and *Close Encounters of the Third Kind*, had been commissioned to create a "Mothership." This was a $100,000 spaceship that was to cover the club's entire ceiling, and that. . . . well, it was going to wipe the smile off the face of the Studio Moon, loving spoonful or no. That was for sure.

The day before the opening, things were as hectic as might be expected. There was no liquor license yet, Vanini admitted. He was terse about Regine. "She wanted me to work from two in the afternoon till six in the morning. I couldn't do it," he said. He added that after the breakup "she sent a letter to the immigration." Around us, longhairs in white hard hats were still fiddling in the innards of Trumbull's Mothership. "It has thirty thousand different possibilities," Vanini said. When I asked would it be working, "I hope so," he said, eyeing me aslant. A coat of dark green paint was being slathered onto a wall. Why the spinach green? "That is the sexiest color in the world," Vanini said. "Do you know how we chose it?" He took a bill from his pocket and pressed it against the wall, crowing, "Dollar green."

That night I went to Studio. Steve Rubell and I stood overlooking the balony. A whole crowd of people had come along in evening clothes from the Belmont Ball, so there was a fitful black and white threshing below. Rubell professed to be unfazed by the grab at his market share. "There are other successful places. People go to Flamingo on a Saturday night," he said. "When New York, New York opened, there was less talk, but I was more worried. No question. A discothèque is a personality business. I'll take care of my house. I'll take care of my homework." Candide in Nightworld.

I asked him if he was going to the opening. "No. I wouldn't go. It's their party. It's their night. But there are no disco wars. Disco wars—it's *silly*."

Steve Rubell could lie just the way he did everything. Engagingly.

In fact, many people had been looking forward to payback time. Not a few souls, after all, had found getting into Studio a bruising business. "We were going to do a party at Studio 54," said an executive from the Elite model agency, "but then we heard about Xenon, and I said to Johnny Casablancas, listen, there's this new club. Why don't we do it there? Listen! I hate Studio 54. I hate them *terribly*. Sometimes they don't let me in. Sometimes they don't even let John in. Anything not to give them business."

Steve Rubell acted unperturbed. "We had the Martha Graham party. We have the *Grease* party next Thursday." They turned down parties all the time, he said. They had turned down the Rugby Ball. They had just turned down a party for *Billboard* magazine. "I don't know why he turned it down. Maybe he didn't want the aggravation," a *Billboard* editor said. "We didn't feel the people were the most desirable," crowed Steve Rubell.

It was the day of the opening. A photographer was shooting a model on the dance floor. "Drop the dress," he instructed. "More leg. Right to the . . . end." Howard Stein, relaxed before, was pale and nervous. The problem was as obvious as it was insoluble: the opening party. Seventeen hundred and fifty people had become charter cardholders. "It has to be snotty or it won't work in New York," Stein said. At least twenty-five hundred had been invited to the party, and this didn't even include the discomanes, who would come any-way. "The people in costume expect to get in free," Stein said. "And they get quite angry if they don't." Permissible occupancy was sixteen hundred. It was hoped that some would leave early, and others arrive late. Hope is a lovely thing.

Meanwhile, the uninvited were hollering. Upstairs, aides had their ears soldered to telephones. "Xenon?" said a Italian princess with hair like a lightning-struck fruit bush, listened to a caller, and begged, "Please don't shout at me." Howard Stein ducked his head into the room. The Italian said the shouter was a man whose wife had tossed the invitation. He wanted another. Stein made a frantic X with his arms and dodged out of the room.

Some hours before the opening I trotted along to a private party in the Fiorucci, the fashion store that was mainlining disco, and later punk, into the culture at large (Kenny Scharf and Keith Haring both did stuff for Fiorucci and it was Fiorucci that introduced break dancing to the Upper East Side). "Macho

Man" was pumping out of a speaker system. People were dancing. A man in Turkish leopardette trousers was pogoing by himself. Another young man in a grubby mac with pink-rimmed eyes was either a real punker or an everyday loser who got into the party by pure luck. There were colorful attractions. I was cajoled into throwing dice by a punkette. The dice formed phrases. The first two I got were "We're hot" and "We're wet." The third combo was so enticingly crude that I quit while I was ahead.

A cluster of us, Xenon-bound, made for the exit. This was an illuminating spectacle. Discothèques at least have opaque walls. When you were in, you were in. Fiorucci had big plate-glass windows which afforded a wonderful view of the high times within to the crowd outside who had failed to impress the ambulatory muscle beside the door. A violet dusk was falling. The dancers danced in the radiant interior. The watchers watched from the pullulating murk. The zestfully cruel teaching of an early father of the Christian Church came to mind: One of the chiefest of the Pleasures of the Blest is watching the Tortures of the Damned. Yes. But it was also dandy to have the Damned watching *you*.

We arrived at Xenon at nine. "Come back at ten," they said. "Things weren't quite . . . ready." Okay. We went to a neighborhood restaurant. By the time we got back, a crowd was growling and swirling outside, uselessly waving tiny oblong cards denoting their extreme importance. Charter card-holders, no less! We made a characteristic disco entrance, which is to say we were muscled in, averting our faces from the imploring eyes of one's dear old friends, lest they try to piggyback, dragging us back into a foul swamp of failure, impotence, anomie; our comfort being the certain knowledge that one's dear old friends would have been every bit as craven as ourselves.

It was worse inside. A moment to catch the breath. "It's like the fall of Saigon," observed a writer with firsthand knowledge of the subject. What there were, in abundance, were the discomanes. A man in black, wearing white gloves, a bowler hat, and a mirror where his face should be. Rollerena. A mysterious rhinestone jogger. Various Studio regulars. Each in turn provoked tumescence from the paparazzi. Above us were silver streamers and balloons. The Mothership, however, was still a no-show.

Further icons trundled on. A person swaddled in jungle green mosquito netting, topped with a head-sized globe of multicolored wool. A man wearing a dinner jacket above the waistline, underwear below, and shiny spike-heeled shoes. More splatter sounds of camera action, but all previous contenders were overruled when the silver people arrived. A man and a woman, naked apart from the genital regions, and looking like a couple of chromed hood ornaments, were in our midst, and energetically dry-humping on the dance floor. The paparazzi went insane and the other attractions drifted off sulkily into the margins.

Inner-core celebs were hard to spot, though. Tony Curtis was rumored to be someplace and a Pet of the Year was preambulating around, performing her duties. A local TV star told Mariel Hemingway how she could make sure she made it onto TV coverage of the opening. The way she could do it was by dancing with him.

It was getting hotter. The Mothership was rising and falling as promised. Did it wipe out Studio? No, but it was okay. Movie producer Robert Evans arrived with Liv Ullmann; another crystal forest of flash sprang up. Peter Frampton was said to have dipped in and departed. But it was getting hotter and hotter. Kissing a cheek was like plunging your face into warm soup. It seemed time to move on. Or back.

Back in Studio 54 Steve Rubell had been more jittery than he had let on. Long before midnight his doubts had subsided as there was a washback from Xenon. The most disgruntled had been those who had failed to make the cut, despite being armed not just with invitations, but special laissez-passers. Bob Colacello of *Interview* and Claudia Cohen of "Page Six" among them. "Ethel Scull and I couldn't get in," said a bland young man, "and Andy told me he couldn't even get close to the door."

"John-John Kennedy couldn't get in. Now he's here, dancing barefoot, celebrating his flunking Andover."

"They didn't recognize Edgar Winters and how many albino rock stars are there?"

Susan Blond was emotional. "Coming back here was like coming home," she declared.

Monti Rock III approached. Monti Rock III, a former hairdresser, had not only been a momentary disco star—Disco Tex and the Sexolettes—but had played the DJ in *Saturday Night Fever*. What's more he looked the part, with a full complement of rings, artful makeup, and a white aviator scarf, but his expression was that of a hanging judge on a bad day, because he hadn't got in either. "You know what I think?" he demanded.

"Who the fuck needs it? I was invited. I got dressed up all for nothing. They can kiss my Puerto Rican ass."

Soon even the people that had gotten in were back. Bob Evans, Liv Ullmann. The local TV star was asleep alone in the balcony. At two in the morning, a bubbly Steve Rubell grabbed the public address system and, refraining from mentioning Xenon by name, thanked "everybody for being here." He declared an open bar.

"I feel I just had a baby," he told me later. He clenched himself into the shape of a cashew nut, a pale little bundle of pure joy.

The day after its maladroit opening Howard Stein and Peppo Vanini closed to regroup. Howard Stein spoke to me somberly of the two thousand gate-crashers, the collapsed security stanchions, the horrors. "All we saw of the celebrities was a face peering through the window of a limousine," he said. "Peering, and driving on. And I'm glad they did." Stein also said they planned to reopen in a few weeks.

It fell to me to tell Rubell that his rival was shutting its doors. "They're closing? That's too bad," he said. His concern seemed real. But he found it hard to believe they would soon be reopening. "They're having another grand opening?" he said disbelievingly. He repeated the question three times.

Xenon reopened on June 7. The Mothership never did do its stuff properly. "What they didn't realize is that when you do a movie, the prop only has to work once," Larry Gang says. "When you do something in a disco, it has to work about five times a night. I think maybe it worked one time."

That apart, they quickly established themselves. The Elite agency's Moët & Chandon party, for instance, took place on July 17. Studio diehards nick-named Xenon "Xerox" or "Studio 27," but it was more than number two. "I went to Studio 54 a great deal. But I basically went more to Xenon," says Ahmet Ertegun of Atlantic Records.

"Steve was very gracious," Howard Stein says. "What he did do was he competed. And he hurt both of us. After we opened was when he really opened up the complimentary admissions to the world. Instead of just VIPs getting in, anybody who didn't have two heads got in free. To compete with Xenon."

So far as the more outré Nightworlders went, Xenon never held a candle to Studio. Michael Musto, who is no stranger to striking costumery, says that he and a friend dressed up in expensive quilted kimonos one night. "Marc didn't notice. He wouldn't even look at us," Musto says. "We had to go to Xenon. It wasn't even second best. It was death. Xenon was okay if you were going back and forth, but if you were just resigned to it, it was seriously depressing."

The Eurotrash felt very differently. "Studio clearly had the advantage in fantastic and flamboyant gays. They clearly had a majority of celebrities," Stein says. "We, on the other hand, had an amazing number of American and European socialites. And we had our own celebrities, people who were at my club every night for years, like Sylvester Stallone and Robin Williams and Christopher Reeves, who I'm not sure would know what the club looked like. I mean, they never left the office.

"The last thing. In the sixties and early seventies, if you wanted to know the young politics, the fashion, the drug habits, the sexual mores, it was right in the middle of my industry. Right in the middle of Woodstock, the Fillmore, the Academy of Music. If you wanted those same questions answered in the late seventies and early eighties, it was right on the dance floor. Or the basement of Studio 54 and the offices of Xenon. So. Voilà!"

Enough of Studio. High time to go, move it along there, but the so-called women's room was pandemonium. Cissy heard an indignant female voice rising from the group milling around one of the stalls. "I didn't come here because I wanted a snort," the voice squeaked. "I came because I wanted to use the john."

Lots of mirror action too. Whoever it was who was padding on makeup to Cissy's left was a man, almost certainly. Along to her right a girl of perhaps nineteen with the fine bone structure of a bird's skull and a suety amphetamine complexion was applying Max Factor's Erase to a humdinger of a black eye, expertly, like she knew what she was doing.

Cissy found her date, an inexpert roué, lurking outside, as though she might disappear with somebody else. Which had, of course, been known.

They went on to Xenon. It looked like a hot night. Cissy spotted a couple of tennis stars cruising the downstairs bar. Rollerena was skating magisterially around in his flappy white wedding dress. The pudgy young blonde—who was not, repeat not, despite what would be said later, the as-yet-undiscovered Madonna—was dancing naked and self-absorbed atop a plinth while the throng of incoming preppies were trying not to goggle too overtly and the middle-aged celebrities had settled down at the important tables— the ones on the far left with RESERVED signs—and loomed as permanent as windows in a church. The men wore dark gray suits, the women had shiny helmets of hair and all wore the pro forma look of profound boredom, a boredom that coated them visibly, like candy-coated fruit.

Cissy and the roué didn't dawdle, though, not tonight. They went to the upstairs room right away.

The upstairs room was up the circular stairway through a first office, down a corridor, past a couple more, and into . . . a small dull office. By day it was Howard Stein's office and it was small and dull, even for an office. Peppo Vanini's office was alongside. You couldn't hear the music there, though you could maybe sense its pulse like the heartbeat of a pachyderm. There were no predatory paparazzi, no colored lights, no dancing, no fresh pretty things from out of town or other places entirely, no naked women standing on plinths, no vulgar fun. There was just them, the inner group, and that was what made the dingy office special, a still center in a churning world.

Tonight's core group—most of whom at least knew who each other was—was appropriate. It included a rock producer, one of the few in his loutish world who was considered sortable, meaning go-outable with (and she—as the would-be decadent suspected—had done so). Also there was a good-looking Colombian who positively stank of money; an aperitif heiress who had left Milan for São Paolo because of the Red Brigades and São Paolo for Manhattan because of the sheer taedium vitae; an upper-class journalist who talked noisily about pussy; and the German heir to an industrial fortune. Covertly Cissy compared herself to the Colombian's girlfriend, a lanky disco-blonde with shiny satin pants and boobs that came to a point like miniature dunce caps.

They sat there. Did some blow. Drank scotch.

Sat. Yammered more. Blahblahblah. Did some more blow, which tasted like the blade of a steel knife. Really. More people drifted in. Everybody had come on from somewhere else. They had been to the Mudd Club and Doubles and Club 57. One trio—two bankerish guys, one in black tie and one in white tie, who looked like they had been to somebody's memorial service, and a stringy blonde in nasty red pumps, who *looked as though she was about due for her own—had been dancing to save the dolphins and they were complaining about how boring it had been, which was really funny, because they were really boring. The lingua franca was English, though the German boy spoke it sulkily.*

Cissy and the roué inhaled more blow.

Would she and he—who was trying to hide his annoyance when she chatted with richer men, meaning all the other men—sidle into the little bathroom with its tiles colored like mushroom soup, and fuck, with her bottom perched on the hand basin?

They did some more blow. They went into the bathroom. "It feels slimy," she complained, slipping off her knickers. Cold china always felt like that.

Disco records were being pushed out so quickly and so successfully, and not just by midcareer rockers like Rod Stewart, but by the likes of Dolly Parton and Frank Sinatra, that Herb Alpert had the brainwave of getting the great diva Ethel Merman to do a disco version of some of the Cole Porter and Irving Berlin numbers she had done on Broadway. The project was seen through by Alpert's manager, Kip Cohen, and by Peter Matz, an arranger and conductor who had worked with Streisand. "It was really wonderful. She did everything on one tape," Cohen says. "It was very danceable. But it was sort of a short-lived left-field phenomenon. I don't think it really appealed to a disco buyer. It was more of a culty and strange album for a theater aficionado. It seems not to exist much anymore."

The lead story in the November 1978 issue of *Life* magazine was "DISCO! Hottest Trend in Entertainment" by Albert Goldman. Goldman noted that "there are now more than 10,000 discothèques in the U.S: last year no less than 37 million Americans got out on the dance floor at least once. The total revenues of that first big season of operation were in excess of four billion dollars—equivalent to two thirds of the combined gross income of both the recording and movie industries . . . a large proportion of the entire top 40 list was either disco music or music that showed the influence of its beat and style."

Life is a national mag, so Goldman touched lightly upon such nouveaux palais-de-danse as Scandals in Los Angeles and Galaxy in Chicago, but soon reached his main course: Studio 54. This is his description of the Man in the Moon. "Once every night a surrealistically distended coke spoon is thrust under the Moon's limp schnozz. Cocaine represented by white bright bubbles goes racing up the elephantine proboscis . . . The dancers scream!" Goldman's description is so judgment-free as practically to constitute an endorsement.

This in an issue of *Life* magazine with Mickey Mouse on the cover. Such innocence would not endure for long.

THE OTHER

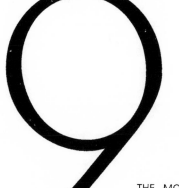

THE LIGHTS ARE MUCH BRIGHTER THERE
DOWNTOWN!

PETULA CLARK, 1965

THE MOST REMARKABLE NIGHTWORLD SCENE IN THE
years immediately before Studio had been Max's Kansas City. Max's was owned by Mickey Ruskin and it
was beloved by artists, in part because Ruskin condoned a certain forgetfulness where the tab was concerned. It had been a watering hole of Andy Warhol's
Factory crowd. Holly Woodlawn remembers Andrea
"Whips" Feldman jumping on tables there, screaming
"I am Andy Warhol's wife and it's show time!" She
would then pull up her dress. Robert Star, a Factory
worker, was in Max's when Feldman took a dive off a
nearby building. "She'd jumped from the fourteenth
floor with a can of Coca-Cola in her hand. She left a
note to the effect of This time, I'm going to hit the big
time," Star says. Studio didn't invent celeb mania.

There had, as it happened, been a disco in Max's.
It was run by Wayne County (who is now Jayne

County). "It opened at midnight and went till closing," said Sterling Morrison of the Velvet Underground. "If you called and asked about it, they denied that it existed. If you didn't know, then you weren't supposed to know." The Velvet Underground, which was Andy Warhol's house band for a while, and fronted by John Cale and Lou Reed, was a prime inspiration for disco's supposed arch-enemy, punk. The phantom disco in Max's would have hardly been a competitor with Studio 54 or Xenon. Still less, the club on the Bowery which was the main venue for punk and new wave, Hilly Kristal's CBGB.

Hurrah was something else.

Arthur Weinstein's Hurrah had been the fabulous people's boîte of choice before Studio. After his departure, the club had tried to revive itself by out-gaying its nemesis, and there were nightly performances by the drag empress Divine in *Neon Woman*. This didn't generate much business, though, so Hurrah switched to playing rock, but mainstream stuff, and the reception was still lukewarm. Hurrah, in short, remained nothing more than Studio roadkill.

One summer night in 1978 a guy named Jim Fouratt went to the club. Fouratt had spent two and half years as an actor and union activist in Los Angeles and had just arrived in New York. He was aggressively charming and well informed about both music and clubs. He was introduced to the owner, who made him manager on the spot. That's the way things *go*.

Fouratt brought in a British DJ, Shaun Cassette. "Everybody was told there's going to be a new sound," says Brad Balfour, a music writer who had recently arrived from Cincinnati. "I remember the first two records. I ran up to the booth to write them down." Both were British. Donny Miller's "Warm Leatherette" was one and the other was Bauhaus doing "Bela Lugosi's Dead." "That was the beginning of the counterculture to Studio," he says.

Why Hurrah, rather than Max's or CBGB? Partly because the older clubs had that Old World bohemian aesthetic, down to the smelly bathrooms with scribbled-upon walls—the taunts about Nancy Spungen, Sid Vicious's heart-throb, being supposedly by her own hand—whereas Hurrah had been a haunt of the fabulous, and had a pretty sleek look. Looks were at least as important to punk as to disco. There was also, of course, the fact that Max's had a worn-out feel, and that CBGB was a bare-bones framework for live bands, thus unsuitable for the ordinary business of socialization (who gets to go home with whom), whereas Hurrah was actually a disco, albeit a new wave one.

This last difference was soon erased, though. Studio had begun having occasional live performances, and Jim Fouratt turned Hurrah into a venue for bands like the Dead Kennedys, Urban Verbs, and the Feelies. It was also in Hurrah that Sid Vicious stuck a broken glass into the cheek of Patti Smith's brother, Todd. Hurrah became wildly successful, and it ended as club successes often do. The owners got greedy. Fouratt left after nine months. That's the way things go too.

Steve Maas has a head vaguely configured like a light bulb, hooded eyes, and a sleepy manner. He came from Georgia and had inherited a small ambulance service, so he was one of the rare people in the East Village with funds. He worked for a bit with Jack Smith, the experimental moviemaker, and became friendly with younger moviemakers, like Amos Poe. Maas and Poe started a company, Mud Films. "A critic had written that my films look like mud," Poe explains. It was Anya Phillips and Diego Cortez, two Lower East Side live wires, who urged Maas to open a punk club. Cortez talked Ross Bleckner, a young artist, into renting out the lower floors of 77 White Street, a building he owned two blocks south of Canal. Phillips and Cortez named the conceptual club the Molotov Cocktail Lounge, but it was Maas's dollar, so he got to pick the name he wanted: the Mudd Club.

Maas cobbled the Mudd together with stuff bought cheap from the surplus and discount outlets along Canal Street, a look that said: This isn't disco. It supposedly cost $15,000, the mighty amplifiers included. The club opened on Halloween 1978. "The rumor was that the opening was a party for Patti Smith. And there was another rumor that Brian Eno owned a part of it. It was 'Let's go to Eno's club,'" remembers the writer Glenn O'Brien. The party was actually for *Punk* magazine. "The punk awards had been held elsewhere," says Brad Balfour. "Everybody said, 'Oh, we're going to a new club.'"

Max's Kansas City and CBGB had been going strong, but downtown tends to be even more fickle than uptown—downtowners have, on the whole, rather less to do—and suddenly Mudd was It. Anita Sarko, a young DJ from Atlanta,

Georgia, a frazzle-haired blonde with a tongue sharp enough to carve meat, had come to New York with a friend. It never occurred to them to try Studio, but they couldn't even get into the Mudd. "The doorman didn't think we were cool enough," she says. "We waited until he would try to come on to a girl on the other side of the front door, and we would sneak in and run up the stairs." Upstairs was where the VIP Room was. "They thought it was hilarious. They would hide us under the pool table. I couldn't believe I was actually seeing my record sleeves walking around." A month later Sarko was Mudd's DJ.

Steve Maas was a doctrinaire stylist, but one whose doctrines could change direction on a dime. He was quite capable of the super Studio maneuver of renting limos with blackened windows to stand along White Street, lending the impression that potent individuals were in the club. "We were the joke on Studio 54. We were the antithesis," says Sarko. "The whole idea of Mudd Club was we went against anything anybody expected. We were *reactionaries*.

"Everybody would go to Fiorucci on weekends to get the punk look. So Steve Maas would go out in front—nobody knew what he looked like—and he would find the ugliest, nerdiest people, like people wearing plaid, and he would give them free passes. And he wouldn't let in any of the fabulous people. On weekends no fat people would be allowed in, because we could only fit four hundred people in the whole place. But he would go out in front and give out free passes.

"Because they were the antithesis of fabulous. But you'd get these nouvelle punks walking in, making faces. They'd dye their hair pink or something and they would wear a leather jacket, and they'd say, 'Why don't you play something hip? Why don't you play the Sex Pistols?' I'd say, 'I *am* playing the Sex Pistols, asshole.' Or else you'd get these people who were on their way to Studio. These uptowners, and they would be standing there, a lot of lockjaws. Right? They'd go . . . 'Wheah are the punks? Why ahhhn't the punks heah?' . . . I'd go, 'Hello! It's eleven o'clock. Our people don't come till two or three in the morning.' 'So wheah the puuuunks?' 'I don't know. They're out shooting up.' "

The speed with which punk was devoured by chic was rather shocking. As early as April 1977 a photo of Warholette Barbara Allen sporting a torn T-shirt as part of a breath-mint campaign had appeared in a society column. Things were racing. The Mudd was soon blazing hot. Sarko's favorites there were a bunch of kids, like Jean-Michel Basquiat and Michael Holman, who formed the art band Gray. But a lot of heavy hitters in rock began showing up. "You'd turn around and Bowie, Jagger, and Iggy would be in one corner, the Kinks would be in another, and Roxy Music would be in another," Sarko says. Where Studio was disco, coke, glam, multicolored, and polymorphous perversity, the Mudd was punk, heroin, glum, black leather, and—if a couple should actually manage to get it on—straight. If the body parts on display at Studio were the cute ass, the exposed nipple, the serrated nostril, the Mudd anatomy featured the sunken cheekbone, the unseeing eyeball, the perforated upper arm.

Appropriately, rather than velvet cord like at Studio, the Mudd had a metal chain. The Mudd also outdid the unisexual bathroom. It had a two-seater John. The singer Antonia de Portago recalls finding herself sitting alongside somebody she had been at school with in Paris. I regretted there were no photographs. "We can re-create it," she said.

"*Deux demoiselles faisant la toilette,*" I said, giving the picture a title.

"I didn't say we both were girls," de Portago said.

In certain ways Studio 54 and Mudd had parallel sensibilities, not least in the reverence of their inner core for excess. One of the Mudd's more admired regulars was a kid whose purchase on the upper slope of celebrity was that on a trip to Studio he had vomited copiously over Andy Warhol's shoes.

There was also a lighter pop/kitsch aspect to Mudd. Maas's affection for the B-52's, the kitschpop band from Athens, Georgia, reflected this. Maas asked Fred Schneider, the band's lead singer, to throw a party. He did so with a Hawaiian theme. This would be the first of the Mudd's offbeat "Theme" parties. These were the invention of Tina Lhotsky, who had actually had herself formally crowned Queen of the Mudd Club. The party to celebrate dead rock stars was one. It was attended by many individuals who would shortly be dead rock stars themselves.

Being DJ wasn't all roses. "You could always tell if Steve was on coke or on acid. He would walk over to the board—which, by the way, was designed by another treasure, Brian Eno. Urghhhh! Gahhh!—and if he was on coke, he would jack down the music. If he was on acid, he would jack up the music," Sarko says unforgivingly. "There would be nights I would walk in and there would be a short fat girl with big breasts standing there, trying to figure out how to put a record on. Steve had fucked her the night before and had decided she should be a DJ. He would scream that I was a piece of shit and I should leave. Of course, he would come crying the next day. For eight hours work he would give me forty dollars and take out taxes, which he wasn't paying, and give me thirty-four dollars a night in take-home pay."

The Mudd wasn't a Xenon, a mutated clone, let alone a Magique or a New York, New York. It was The Other. Naturally Rubell was fascinated, but perhaps the thought of being on the wrong side of somebody else's velvet Cord unnerved him, because he still hadn't been there when he and Ian were interviewed by the photographer Marcia Resnick and the writer Anne Bardach on March 29, 1979. Marcia Resnick was a punk archetype, the type that the writer Victor Bockris calls a "negative girl." Once married to Wayne Kramer, a guitarist for Detroit's power group, the MC5, Resnick was paper-white, had unruly black hair, dressed tip to toe in black leather, and was able to maintain a cold articulate chatter as nonstop as a newspaper office teletype machine. She was getting together a sequence of photographs called *Bad Boys,* for which she had already nabbed such aristocrats of the sneer and the snarl as Johnny Rotten, James Chance, and Richard Hell, and she wanted to add Schrager and Rubell. Anne Bardach, who was providing the text, had lugged along a tape recorder.

They talked in the club's cavernous interior in midafternoon. Rubell had no earth-shaking confidences, saying earnestly that "celebrities are very, very, very, very nice people." Ian Schrager was surprising though. Close-mouthed with reporters for newspapers and heavy-duty magazines, he chose to speak to a couple of females with a ramshackle nonassignment. "You know, I don't give interviews. Never give interviews. Because I'm a private person. Maybe I'm shy. But I don't give interviews, and you're *persevering*. But I don't give interviews. So what am I doing, giving an interview? All right?" Ian told the young women, almost as if he were questioning himself, and speaking in spritz and fizzes, like a shaken seltzer decanter. "When people think of Studio 54, they think of Steve. Which is perfect for me. Studio 54 is a twenty-four-hour job. It's my life. I'm a lawyer and I used to practice. I don't have the time now."

When they asked him how much he actually enjoyed it, Schrager said, "I wouldn't be here every night if I didn't have to." It was partly the puddle of limelight that bothered him. "I enjoy it in the shadows. I'm happier with myself. I guess I am the dark side of Steve. This parnership works because we have different roles and we like the jobs that we do. Steve loves people."

Did Schrager love people? "No," he admitted. "Not really."

The interview over, Steve Rubell grilled Marcia Resnick about the Mudd Club. "He knew a lot of people from Studio were going," Resnick says. He duly made his first visit there just one week later. A naked Victor Hugo, Halston's lover/window dresser, was performing in some sort of play, which seems to have been otherwise unmemorable, because Ben Brantley, now *The New York Times* theater critic who was present then, doesn't remember a thing about it. Resnick photographed Rubell, in a Quaalude nirvana, cuddling Roy Cohn on a sofa, alongside Halston and D. D. Ryan.

But actually very few uptowners had the inclination to become Mudd Club regulars. The clientele of the Mudd was too young, too straight, too threatening, too unnervingly poor. Studio 54 jauntees were much more inclined to make well-chaperoned visits to the hard-core sex clubs in the meat-packing district on East Twelfth Street, ogle the fist-fuckers and the Glory Holes, and then return to Xanadu.

In the winter of 1977, Ken Auletta, who had become a writer and was a contributing editor at *New York* magazine, went to the Christmas open house given by Warren Hoge of the *Times* and writer Charlie Michener in their apartment on Ninetieth Street and Riverside Drive. "They had this huge foyer and I was standing there. The door opened and I saw this little guy. I said, 'Steve!' I hadn't seen him in twelve years. We hugged each other," Auletta says.

Rubell told Auletta he had been following his career. "I said, 'So. What have you been doing?' " Auletta says, and reconstructs the dialogue.

"I own a nightclub."

"You do? What do you own?"

"Studio 54 . . ."

Auletta simply had not associated the club whiz he was constantly reading about with the tennis player he had known at Syracuse. "So *you're* Steve Rubell," Auletta said. They laughed. Auletta adds, "I was the only one in the room who had no idea who he was. Of course, all the people in the room were people who wanted to get into Studio 54."

Rubell invited Auletta, who went with his wife, Amanda Urban, and Richard Reeves, the political journalist. "Steve took us on a tour. It wasn't our scene so we didn't stay long," Auletta says. "We had a drink with Steve and we chatted. It was a real warm tour he took us on. He would introduce me as the guy who helped save him from trouble in college and stuff like that. We would hug."

Ken Auletta and his wife never came even within long-range distance of becoming regulars—"I was an old fogy when I was in my *twenties,*" Auletta says—but they would go from time to time, and would chat with Rubell. Then at the end of 1978 Auletta was assigned by Clay Felker, who was then at *Esquire,* to write a piece about Roy Cohn.

"So I went to Studio 54 one afternoon," Auletta says. "We sat on a platform by the dance floor at maybe three or four in the afternoon." Rubell was, as usual, jacketless. Auletta brought out his notebook and his tape recorder, and looked around the place which bore the usual aspect of a glamorous nightspot in the daytime, being at once forlorn and somewhat unsavory. There were people sweeping up, and workmen. Liquor was delivered, which made Steve Rubell vehement on the corruption of the booze business. "He was very funny, as always. He was very observant about Roy Cohn," Auletta says.

Rubell told Auletta about being attacked in California by the writer Lillian Hellman. "How can you have Roy Cohn represent you?" Hellman had said. "He ruined people's lives!" But Rubell explained away such inconvenient data as part and parcel of Roy Cohn's growing up. "Look, I did crazy things when I was fifteen years old," Rubell told Auletta. "He understood Roy Cohn very well, and what a killer he was. But he was *his* killer. So he felt secure with him," Ken Auletta says.

The meat and potatoes done with, Auletta asked Rubell about himself. "I said, 'How are you doing? Are you enjoying your life? Are you happy?' "

"Well, it's *complicated,*" Rubell told him.

"What do you mean complicated?"

"Yeah, you know, I have some troubles."

"What do you mean?"

"You know, this is a tough business, Ken. The liquor people, they sell you booze, and they want a kickback and . . . it's just a tough business. I'm not proud of the things that go on."

"I saw that he was looking up at the ceiling. I remember there were some open wires. He was looking up at the ceiling as if there was something there."

Rubell began talking intensely about "The cash in this business!" Ken Auletta says "He was talking and talking about the cash in this business. He was saying there was so much cash that floated around."

Auletta concedes it may be a trick of his imagination but something Rubell said has lodged in his memory bank, true or false. "I seem to remember him saying something like 'You could put cash in the walls!' I remember him looking up at the wall. He seemed depressed. He always seemed cheerful at Syracuse and the few times I had seen him subsequently. But he seemed *somber*. He seemed heavy. A weight. He was carrying some kind of weight. He was perceptive, about politics, and life, but he seemed jaded, not innocent. Cynical, not skeptical. He looked tired and pained.

"We hugged when I left. And I felt kind of sad, even though I was exhilarated by the interview. And then within a month he was busted. He was obviously in the middle of negotiations with law enforcement when he spoke to me. He was almost forewarning me but he was trying to hold it in."

The venue that would, in its goofy way, play Xenon to the Mudd Club was a church basement on Saint Marks Place. It was started by Tom Scully and Susan Hannaford, who were involved in new wave cinema, the end of the seventies being a period when everyone on the Lower East Side was either making a two-reel movie or playing in a punkish band. They took over the space to show ratty old horror movies, opened in May 1979, and had soon screened such rarities as *Invasion of the Bee Girls* and *Hercules in the Haunted World*. People took to hanging out after the screenings, and Scully decided to turn it into an impromptu club. A young actress, Ann Magnuson, was appointed manager. It was officially called the East Village Students Club—it was a young crowd—but it was known as Club 57.

It began with people sitting around making fun of these appalling movies, but soon special events were devised, and Ann Magnuson would distribute beautifully designed printouts on colored card giving details. Just one month, for instance, Club 57 showed *The Girl Can't Help It, The Blob,* and Russ Meyer's *Beyond the Valley of the Dolls.* There was also a "Punk Rock Game Show" and a "Ladies Only" lecture by the Ladies Auxiliary Gun Club, which was Ann Magnuson's downtown version of the Junior League.

The crowd at the Mudd was also an art/music crowd—a young artist, Keith Haring, did a stint on the door—but there was a sense of division too. "The people at Mudd had been around longer. They were more hard-core," says the galerist, Patti Astor. Steve Maas wasn't about to let the younger club enroach, either. Michael Holman approached Ann Magnuson with an idea for a Soul Party. "She said great," Holman says. "Somehow Steve Maas heard about it. He offered me a $10,000 budget to do the same show."

Holman took it to Mudd. Pyschedelic Day-Glo figures of characters in big afros going at it in various tantric positions were on the walls of the main room. "We had a Pimp's Bedroom in the back room," Holman says. "With a round bed and a disco globe. We went to Sylvia's in Harlem to get candied yams and black-eyed peas. We fed the first fifty people for free." Maas left the Soul Party trappings in situ for an unprecedented six months.

The Muddites, by and large, treated Club 57 with scorn. Jean-Michel Basquiat was friendly with the artist and Club 57 habitué, Kenny Scharf, but said "Aesthetically I really hated Club 57. I thought it was silly." Scharf says, "It was like two camps. We called ourselves the Groovy Camp, and they were the Cool. We were more like up. They were more cold. Heroin! It was basically heroin versus psychedelics. It was kind of like a big commune. We were in 57 day and night. Everybody was screwing everybody. It wasn't like a big orgy. But it was very, very incestuous."

In September 1979 Scharf had a show of paintings at 57. He gladly lent one to Xenon. "They borrowed it for a party. Somebody stole it. It was a painting of a big pink Cadillac," Scharf says glumly. "I wish I still had it."

In many ways, Club 57 *did* seem silly at the time, but it was ahead of the curve, the first of the art-driven clubs.

★　　★　　★

It was Shaun Cassette who introduced Jim Fouratt to Rudolf. "Why do you want to know me?" Fouratt asked. "He said, 'I want to know you because I want to know how you do things. Then I won't ever have to talk to you again.' He said it very nakedly, very openly. And I didn't hear it."

Rudolf had appeared in New York in 1978. Aged thirty-four, he flaunted a single name, politics of anarchistic cool and the retro-pop dress sense of Bryan Ferry of Roxy Music, but was born Rudolf Pieper, the son of a German diplomat. "He worked for who was in charge," Rudolf says dryly. Rudolf, who had grown up in Argentina, and told a girlfriend he had known the Mengele children there, got a Ph.D. in economics at Berlin University, and went to Brazil as an expert on stocks. A tall, fair-haired fellow, Rudolf played on the fact that he had the corroded good looks of somebody playing the torturous Nazi in a war movie, but he is actually laid-back, with an icy business brain, a subversive sense of humor, and he is a fanatic only about style.

He liked Brazil for its women, and the general Brazilian attitude, and he made a small fortune there starting a chain of Laundromats and a rock club. He says he was forced out of Brazil by the music, which he loathed, and the sun. "I was just too tan," he says. "I told people I was going to open a nightclub in New York. They said I was mad. I was going to be shot." He gives his high whinny of a laugh. *"Heh-heh!"*

It was 1977 and he went to Europe first, winding up in London. "I caught London at the right time. Punk was really happening on a tremendous scale. Incredible! You had punk armies, marching down the streets in London. People thought punk was becoming this neo-fascist movement. Which didn't happen. Then it happened more than ten years later."

Rudolf planned to open a boîte, possibly a combination nightclub/art gallery. Rudolf does not take nightclubs lightly. "The greatest ideas of this century began in nightclubs and bars," he says. "Dada began in the Cabaret Voltaire. The Russian revolution was dreamed up in the bars of Zurich." New York nightlife was, he soon saw, as revolutionary as he had imagined. Actually there were two revolutions, Studio and Mudd-ite. "There were two different lifestyles that shared one point. Hedonism! One was punk, one was disco, but full enjoyment of the senses was both," Rudolf says.

"So there were several things happening at that time. But uptown was

basically ignoring what was going on in the rest of the world." Uptown meaning, of course, much of the clientele of Studio. "There were not that many
ideas uptown. Uptown was oblivious to an entire art trend that was happening
in SoHo and the East Village, that was fun, and interesting, and that originated
at Club 57 on Saint Marks Place. That was the beginning of Ann Magnuson
and Kenny Scharf. And there were all these bands."

He became one of the very few Mudd regulars who would also frequent
Studio. Dressing in a way that would work in both venues was quite a trick.
"In New York you don't have a car, with a trunk where you can change your
clothes. So you have to dress in a way that is neutral, but at the same time
acceptable to both places. There were very few people that could do that,"
say Rudolf. Fortunately, he had been on a buying spree on King's Road while
he was in London. "Sort of upscale new wave. That was acceptable. The girls
at Studio 54 were obviously much better than the girls at the Mudd Club.
Healthier!" Another *"Heh-heh."* "Well. Not for long . . ."

Some time in 1980, Sarko walked out. Maas drove after her, talked her
into the car, and drove her back to Mudd. "He took me upstairs, which had
been under construction. He said, 'I did this for you.' He showed me a DJ
booth that was built totally out of Plexiglas. Because when people would get
upset at what I was playing they used to throw ashtrays and glasses and bottles. I was always ducking." She stayed. It wasn't the music. It was the attitude. Glenn O'Brien remembers an evening there with Anya Phillips, the
half-Chinese designer, who was one of the muses of the club. "She could be
mean," O'Brien says. "I saw her walk out onto the dance floor and punch
out a girl.

"I said, '*Why did you do that?*'

"She said, 'I didn't like the way she was dancing . . .' "

Sometimes the behavioral codes got rather jangled between Studio and
Mudd. John Scribner, an ingenuous young buck, remembers one particular
night at Studio. "I was standing with some friends at the back of the dance
floor. We were a little bored. It was early and the place wasn't hopping that
much," he says. "I saw this pretty girl dancing in a punk rock dress or whatnot."

He asked her for a dance. She said sure.

"We were dancing for a while. And I said, 'Could you give me a good-bye *punch* instead of a good-bye kiss?' It just seemed to fit her aura more. Next thing I had landed on the floor and I was seeing *total white lights*. She had socked me in the eye," Scribner says, sounding still bemused by the event.

ADDICTED TO THE NIGHT

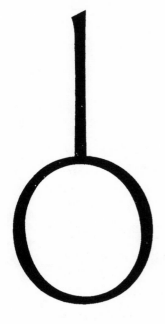

QUAALUDES OR NO, SHEER HYPER ANXIETY HAD MADE Steve Rubell lose twenty pounds in the first year of running Studio 54. Or so he told Henry Post. Why so hyper, the writer asked? "God," Rubell told him. "I made so many mistakes. Bad mistakes. Boy, it's not all roses and peaches and cream." As driven as ever, he and Ian Schrager set out to squash Xenon, as they had New York, New York. Joanne Horowitz was booking the *Superman* party for her new employer. "Ian and Steve couldn't stand to lose a big party," she says. "They wanted it so bad that Ian offered me double what Howard Stein was going to give me." Studio got the party and Horowitz took back her old job. She had been at Xenon only for a matter of months.

Four important New York politicians, including Carter Burden and Andy Stein, held fund-raisers at Studio in 1978. That August 6 the club threw a birthday party for Andy Warhol, during which a trash can filled with eight hundred-dollar bills was upended on the artist's head. Warhol, presumably fearful of the IRS, chose not to confide this to his diarist, Pat Hackett. Nor, more understandably, did he reveal another treat. Bill Hamilton, who was Steve Rubell's lover during the last years of his life, says that Warhol came over to Rubell's apartment on West Fifty-fifth and watched while the club owner hauled stacks and stacks of dollar bills from a hiding space behind the bookcase. "And for his birthday present Steve piled all the money in the living room. He left him with $800,000 or whatever amount it was. And he spent the afternoon looking at it," Bill Hamilton says.

Studio 54's 1977 tax report had declared a gross income of $1 million, plus or minus a buck or so, and a net taxable income of $47,000. Rubell and Schrager paid altogether $8,000 in taxes. Not a smart move, this.

There was a thorough redesign of the club for the second year. The courtyard was closed off so no more gate-crashers would be flattening themselves on the cement. The highlight of the reopening design was a moving bridge, and Egon von Furstenberg plus a clutch of A Listers were filmed aloft at the party. "Diana Ross loved the bridge. I remember being on it with Elton John and him thinking it was wonderful," says the architect Scott Bromley.

Not everybody thought it was wonderful, though. "It was a most peculiar thing, that bridge. It was like a project. You had to have two people on either side to stop it," Nikki Haskell says. Antonia de Portago performed up there with her band, the Operators. De Portago loathed disco but adored Studio, and she was one of the first performers to appear there live. "I was dressed as Marie Antoinette, as usual, but in a short short dress," she says. "I had a ghost onstage carrying a candelabra.

"It was very scary for me to be on that bridge, which was moving. I have always had a fear of heights. It was like a tree, unrooted, each time the bridge was moving. Uhhhh! I hated it."

Scott Bromley concurred that some were fearful of the device. "There was some trickiness. You couldn't get off the stairs unless the bridge was right there," he says. So in the third annual redo, the bridge became anchored, immobile. "It was getting to be too dangerous. And people were getting too wild," he says. "It was the drug era . . ."

Indeed. Studio *was* getting wilder. It wasn't just arbitrary rooting-tooting, snorting, underwear-shredding wildness either, though God knows there was plenty of that, but a wildness that seemed the working out of some inexorable process. "Studio gave license," Jim Fouratt says. "That was what the door policy was about more than anything else. It was to make you feel that if you got in, you were in a world that was completely safe for you to do whatever you wanted—that was the genius of that door policy."

The barmen could facilitate that license. "Being a Studio 54 bartender was like being in an elite military outfit, like the French Foreign Legion or something. We were all very close. We considered ourselves the lucky few," Chris Sullivan says.

Sometimes the luck was financial. Scotty Taylor would always wait on Tom Sullivan, a gangly Floridian, with blue eyes, pink skin, and longish fair hair, who was given the Studio nickname "Cowboy" because of his fondness for western gear. "He would come up to the bar. And he'd ask for a Jack Daniel's filled to the brim," Scotty Taylor says, "a seven-ounce glass. I would put it down. He'd take a hundred dollars, put it on the bar, and say thanks! So I always waited for Tom to come in. When Alan Finkelstein asked me what was the biggest tip I ever got, I said, 'Well, Tom Sullivan comes in every Sunday and leaves me a hundred dollars . . .' "

Finkelstein, who was then the constant companion of the model Esme, decided to outtip the Cowboy. "How would you like to go to Acapulco for ten days?" he asked. Taylor said he would like that just fine. "Anyway the limo picked me up at seven-thirty in the morning and we all met at the airport," he says. "Alan ordered fourteen first-class round-trip tickets. When the woman asked if that was a charge, he said, 'No, cash.' He got out a wad of hundreds and started peeling them off . . ."

It happens that I knew both Tom Sullivan and Alan Finkelstein slightly. I knew also that both were alleged to have been in the same trade: bulk importation of marijuana and/or hashish. (Finkelstein was arrested for narcotics smuggling. The case is discussed in *Bad Dreams,* a book of mine published in 1979. He was acquitted.)

Taylor was also invited to Halston's famous drag party. The invitation carried a picture of Victor Hugo in a fetal position. "All the other bartenders went to Halston and got $5,000 sequinned gowns," Taylor says. "I was the only straight guy and I wasn't going to be fitted. I got kind of nervous. So I had the coat check girls dress me as Pippi Longstocking. We put my hair in braids and makeup on my face, and they gave me this little dress.

"I was the first one there. I'm from Queens. What do I know about being fashionably late? The Chinese houseman opened the door . . . *'Awww! You are early.'* . . . Halston came down the staircase. He wore a black gown. Steve wore a black gown. Even Andy was in a gown. There were about seventy people. Of course, Bianca . . . Halston was a really sweet guy. It was great."

Steve Rubell was always ready to believe that the barmen were on the fiddle. "He brought in a spotting service," Scotty Taylor says. "Steve always thought everybody was stealing." Actually, he says, the worst they generally did was give out free drinks. Most of the time it was just Steve's friends. The spotters would see us giving David Geffen or Halston or someone that wasn't that recognizable free drinks. Or someone like Potassa. Potassa was a transvestite and thoroughly gorgeous. "Steve would love the fact that she would pick up on the Wall Street guys that didn't know she was a man. And she would take them upstairs to the balcony and give them blowjobs. Steve would always say, 'Give Potassa a bottle of champagne whenever she wants it!' "

Potassa was often part of the entourage of Salvador Dalí. If any "ism" ruled in Studio, it was voyeurism. Most went to see or be seen. Dalí, a veteran of the human gaze, would go with people he needed to impress. A man who liked a hectic sort of order, he would follow a routine, dining first—Trader Vic's was a favorite spot—with his considerable retinue of regulars before going on to the club. "There were always three or four transvestites," says Roger de Cabrol, a designer and regular himself. "Potassa. There was this French transvestite, very pretty, named Pascale. Then this American transvestite named Chrysis, who used to be, I think, a truck driver, and she had huge breasts, and she had a dress with hands on the breasts. You know, a print.

"Then he had this friend named Mrs. Kalashnikov. She was married, I believe, to the son of the inventor of the Kalashnikov machine gun. He used to call her Louis XIV, because we all had different names. Her hair was very high, and she always liked war."

Others in the Dalí entourage included a fierce woman, known only as "Le Notaire," (the Notary), and often a bevy of petite "bunheads," as young ballet dancers are called. "We would all go to Studio together," says Antonia de

Portago, who was a regular herself, in her very early twenties. "I would wear a little *bustier* with feathers and diamanté everywhere, and much before Madonna I was wearing those garter belts outside for an evening, and a fake fur, and I would open my fake fur, and I was half naked. I can't believe I was wearing things like that, but everyone was pushing the extreme. No?

"It was amazing the effect on people to see all that group with Dalí. I remember dancing with a very tall beautiful black woman. That night I had a black *bustier* from Saint Laurent and a red Fiorucci lace skirt that was transparent. And that girl danced with me like . . . it was amazing . . . and then she took my hands and put them . . . *right here. . . .*" De Portago gives a shrill French squeal, not quite of shock, a parody of shock. "I thought I was dancing with a woman! But why not at that time? It was so . . . she was adorable.

"And Dalí would say to the transvestites, 'Get up and dance, but show me your derrière . . . so I can see your *trou de balle*' . . . He was speaking French. *Trou de balle* means, like, in golf. You know, the hole when you play golf? It was so odd. They were darlings."

Most of what went on in Studio was pure—if "pure" is the appropriate word—fun. Bitten Knudsen, a seventeen-year-old model, had arrived from Denmark—"from a place so teeny it wasn't even a village"—and hit Manhattan in August 1977. She remembers the vogue for leaping from the balcony and grabbing hold of the illuminated gizmos that would rise and fall above the floor. "You had to do it and not have anybody see it," she says. "So that you did it and ended up on the dance floor. It's like what the young Brazilians do, surfing the subways, jumping on the top of trains." She loved the communality of the experience, the euphoria. Sexual possibility was remote from her mind. She remembers chattering politely with a man. A girlfriend told her later that it was O. J. Simpson, and that he had been hitting on her. "I didn't even notice," Bitten says.

The majority went to Studio to float around, looking, and to dance. "I just went there to dance and forget everything," says the photographer Francesco Scavullo. "I never took a camera there. I just let off a lot of steam. I wasn't involved in drugs or drinking, and I wasn't involved with the sex stuff downstairs. I just went there because I loved the music, and I thought it was good air, because it was so high and well-ventilated, and because I love to dance."

Howard Oxenberg, the Manhattan socialite, took Mary Tyler Moore to a party. "Somebody put a popper under my nose. I felt euphoric," he says. "Paloma Picasso lost a gigantic earring. A diamond? Next thing, we borrowed a dustpan and brush, and were dancing around, sweeping up anything shiny . . ."

Some early music videos were shot in Studio. Musique's first album, *Keep On Jumpin'*, for one. This included the group's first hit "In the Bush," with its pounding refrain "Push, push, in the bush." "I remember we had on tight red sequinned pants and tube tops," says Mary Seymour, one of the trio of singers in the group. "It was at the beginning of that whole video thing, so it wasn't very sophisticated. They did double impressions of our faces, going backward and forward. Certain stations wouldn't play the record. They thought it was a bit risqué. It really wasn't specifically meant to have the meaning that people assumed it did," She says. "But interpretations of music are wondrous . . ."

They were wondrous enough for the album to sell millions of copies worldwide, lustily crossing over between disco, pop, and R&B, and for Musique to be named Best Female Group by *Billboard* magazine.

Push, push, in the bush, indeed. Some had convoluted game plans at Studio 54. A model I shall call Mini, because she was ultra tall, a woman with china-blue eyes, a prickle of blue-black hair, and skin as white as white cheese, had a part-time job as "publicist" for an Asian magnate, who was notably model-friendly. She had fended him off on his yacht: "I told him I didn't feel well. I thought I had syphilis or gonorrhea or something," she says. It had worked, but she was now on permanent assignment to provide replacements, and Studio was her favorite hunting ground.

The conversations with her fellow models in Studio would usually be in the woozy early hours and it could be frustratingly hard to close the deal. "Why should I? I don't need the money," a model would say.

"Don't you want to meet one of the richest men in the world?" Mini would ask reasonably.

"Well. Uh . . ."

Mini would call the contact, who was some place like the Waldorf Towers, and the woman would be flown out to the yacht on a private plane. "They would get at least five grand," Mini says. "Some would get jewelry . . . watches . . . or a Christian Dior . . . I would brainwash them never to talk about it.

"It was like brokering a real estate deal, and getting a lot of pressure from both sides . . . 'Is she really great?' . . . 'She's wonderful.' . . . 'What's being taken from you? Were you a virgin?' . . .

"It was kind of hard to deal with if they got serious money. Like a hundred grand. And I was getting a thousand dollars. *But I would be there the next night.* It was a golden situation."

Other golden situations took place on the spot. Those who traversed the nooks and crannies of Studio are likely to have images burned on their brain, like outtakes from the hotel corridor sequence in *The Shining*. "It was the only club where you could have sex," Egon von Furstenberg told his wife, Lynn, and me over lunch. To her, he added, "I once had sex there with one of your best friends." She turned saucer-eyed with mock outrage.

"Halston was in the balcony the whole time. Nureyev too. My brother with him," says Richard, one of the twins known as the fake Duponts, who were part of the Warhol menagerie. Others have less merry memories. Jim Fouratt mentioned a supposedly straight magnate. "He is a closet homosexual but he would take boys up to the balcony for blowjobs, and *quite visibly,*" Fouratt said. "The fact that he would behave like that in a public place is symbolic of the way that a lot of people behaved." Fouratt was censorious only about the closet part.

For a few, there were always treats, from the silver packages of cocaine tucked into the ashtrays of the limousines that were sent to pick up special guests to pills and packages stuffed into favored pockets. "Steve was always slipping Quaaludes into my pockets," says Reinaldo Herrera. "Then he would forget, and put in some more. I would have to empty my pockets every night." Trusted employees were assigned to cover situations that Steve couldn't take care of personally. "For instance," says Richie Notar, "Steve would tell me, 'Mick's coming in tonight! I want you to stay with him all night, and make sure he gets whatever he needs.'

"Mick was with Jerry Hall . . . drinking tequila, champagne . . . I would be sitting there with them, filling their glasses. Just staying with him the whole night. Not bothering him, not intruding. I'd be in the balcony with them. Or if they wanted to go into one of the little private alcoves of Studio 54, which was like a maze of small offices, and underground cavernous areas. I mean, the place was *huge*."

By the second year Studio had become so stratified that there was both a private door, the Fifty-third Street entrance, and, indeed, a "private" Studio, the space behind a scrim on the dance floor, a scrim that would be lowered for special parties, and raised at midnight or so. This was the province of a young artist, Thierry, who had left an excellent art school with an award in 1977 and had worked as an assistant to one of the flaming art meteors of the period, but had been drawn from studio to Studio, as though by an electro-magnetic force.

"I started at the bar, but that wasn't very interesting," he says. Then Thierry, who is agile, landed a plum diplomatic assignment: taking care of the VIPs. "My job was to make sure that you were . . . all right. Once you got in. I didn't want to work the door. That wasn't interesting to me. I was working as a pseudo-bartender. If somebody wanted quote *something*, you know, I managed to find it for them.

"When an entourage would come, okay? Where were we going to bring them? Let's bring them to room three. Downstairs? Upstairs? At that time, everybody wanted coke. Everybody had to have sniff. Let's say I was brokering situations . . . 'Uh, you need this? Okay. Why don't you go to him and he'll take care of you. . . . Oh, thanks very much!'

"You have to remember I was eighteen years old. So all this was like a revelation to me."

He knew who could provide the necessary. "Oh yeah. That was evident. I mean, everybody knew who everybody was. Again, I am not talking about the dance floor. I'm not talking about the public space. I'm talking behind the scenes now. There were people let in because it was known what products they were pushing. That was very, very well curated. It was very clear what their function was and what the limits were. People who were ripping other people off were immediately tossed out of there. I have to say that was well curated, too.

"That's exactly the kind of thing I would look after. If I saw some nonsense going on, I would mention it to the doorpeople. And the people would be very discreetly taken out."

The central venue for the inner core was the basement, which had replaced Steve Rubell's first-floor office as the VIP Room. The basement was reached through a door in the wall behind the bar in the appropriate vicinity of the Man in the Moon and the spoon. You went down grungy cement stairs, holding on to a metal balustrade, and found yourself in an ominous wasteland as large as Studio itself, with spaces, and cubicles, and one more-or-less main room painted gray, with overhead piping hissing away. The spaces were divided by Cyclone fencing and furnished, if that is the word, with destroyed banquettes, rolls of carpeting, and leftover props—like the children's toys that had been used for a Truman Capote party, supposedly celebrating a face-lift. It was a bit like being in the bowels of a freighter, a feeling not lessened by the thrumming of the dancers overhead.

It was the height, or depth, of Reverse Chic, and it was hard to get there uninvited. Indeed, it was not unusual to chance upon security men with walkie-talkies roaming the basement's remoter reaches, to head off inquisitive outsiders, even though most of what went on in the basement actually was just sniffing, snorting, the passing around of vodka and champagne bottles, and increasingly fuddled socializing. Richard Dupont remembers being downstairs with various members of the Britpack for some anniversary or other. "There was a cake with tits," he says. "We did acid and heroin together. I was a mess. I fell into the cake." For those who could actually get it together, there was a small cubicle, furnished with mattresses. "There was this little room. I went there a lot with guys" Richard Dupont says.

Thierry's job also entailed occasional fringe benefits. He remembers vigorously mounting a star's wife, only to see, mid-performance, that the star in question was looking directly at them. A fraction of a second later, he realized from the man's unglued incomprehension that he might as well have been looking at a car wreck in a movie.

"Studio 54 really changed everybody's life in a substantial way," says Steven Gaines. "It changed eating habits, and sleeping habits, and drug habits. I mean, the Hamptons were empty on Sunday nights because Studio 54 was the most important place you could be. It was the center of the universe."

The heyday of Studio 54 was brief and luminous, and it is perhaps because of this brevity and brightness that former habitués of the club tend to describe it in peculiarly parallel ways, not as if Studio were comfortably sunk into the past, but as if it were almost unbearably of the present, a lost present, as though suspended in time. Visual memories—my own included—seem like so many photographs, thumbed and familiar, but as vivid as the moment they were taken, whereas sensual memories—my own, at any rate—are less of moments of physical pleasure than of a floating euphoria, a release of pressure, as though one had a watching brief on life, with no nagging censor on the shoulder.

Ian Schrager would sometimes roam Studio or look down on the dancers from the DJ booth, but he did so objectively, as though it was at once a theater production that required his detailed attention, a social experiment of which he was a disinterested observer, and a giant cash machine, stuttering out numbers. His main pleasure there was just leaning against a wall behind the bar or secreting himself in the DJ booth and playing with the lights. The VIP basement was alien territory to Ian Schrager.

For Steve Rubell, who had only come into the nightclub business on Schrager's urging, Studio 54 had become wholly consuming, as though it were an extension of himself, and vice versa. Fred Rothbell-Mista, a nightperson in the years to come, says, "Steve Rubell was a cut above the mentality of the other club owners. Everyone else's motivation was the money. His motivation was the party." The party was getting too fast, too furious, though. Steve Rubell was surrounded by famous, powerful friends, and, like so many of them, habituated to a massive intake of what were still believed to be non-addictive party drugs, and both he and Ian Schrager had come to feel they were inhabitants of that special zone where nothing much could touch them. So safe did Steve feel that Lenny, a young art student who worked as a busboy, was permitted to wander around taking photographs at will (the rawest were destroyed). Ian Schrager, who could switch between light and dark versions of reality in a Jekyll and Hyde fashion, was not immune to tremors of disquiet, but Steve Rubell felt blithely invulnerable, like an inflatable in an agreeably tossing sea.

Clubgoers, like Brian Saltern, who had met him in Hurrah's, noted not a cooling in his friendship, precisely, but a growing sense of distance. Myra Scheer remembers the night a Saudi prince, a brother to the king, came to the club. "Steve went up to him and said, 'Listen, I'd love to meet your brother. Next time he's in town, let's have dinner. I want peace. I'm Jewish, and I want peace!' He had world power. He was just this incredibly gifted person, who radiated this joy."

The joy could go into overdrive at such times as the artificial soapflake snowstorms that were one of the climactic moments of a night in the club. "Rubell would often get whatever celebrities were superbig on his list, and he would hustle them up to the DJ booth for when the snow came down," Baird Jones says, adding that there were always glasses on the ground around the dance floor and that many had taken off their shoes to dance. "Especially the girls. There was still this hippie transition," he says. Sooner or later, the vincible force would meet the movable object. "I would have to say it happened one out of three times," Baird Jones says. "When the snow came down, someone would then tread on a champagne glass. And he knew that. It was almost always going to be a woman. You would see this red pool that would expand on the perimeter of the dance floor. In all that white." Baird Jones says Rubell would never fail to point this out, with the gleeful, feckless cruelty of a child.

"There was always this, oh, wacky Steve! Having a great time and loving everyone," Jones says. "He would hug everyone like crazy, like a bouncing ball. But he did that because he forgot their names. He told me that. It was a stalling technique. It gave him time to try and remember."

Most of us categorize. So-and-so is exuberant and over the top, whereas so-and-so is calculating, an adding machine. This is a profoundly useless distinction in the case of Steve Rubell, who was both. Reinaldo Herrera remembers talking in the early hours on a Studio banquette with Catherine Guinness, a young gilded Brit who worked for Andy Warhol. Herrera, who is married to the couturier Carolina Herrera, is a social troubleshooter for *Vanity Fair,* and figures high on the world's party lists. The Herreras had met Rubell on one of his rare visits to London. Rubell had been diffident until Reinaldo Herrera had told him his favorite meal was a hamburger. The Herreras had enjoyed privileged status at Studio forever after. And they and Steve had become friends.

"Steve was on the floor. He had passed out," Herrera says. "He called the next day. He said, 'You and Catherine are so full of shit!' He had remembered every word."

"I'll tell you, the guy used to do drugs, and, oh man, nobody knew how he did it!" says Chris Sullivan. "We all thought he was going to drop." He vividly remembers one specific count-out. "All the bartenders would be finished and we would have to wait for the manager to bring us down to the basement, where we counted the money. I'm telling you, we made lots of money. I would make six or seven thousand dollars at my bar in one night. And that was just my bar. There were six, seven, eight bars on a Saturday night, plus the door.

"We'd all be down there, counting our money. Steve came down one night. He could hardly stand up. He was luded out of his mind. But the guy was amazing. He could add up all the figures. We had to write down each amount. They had a strange system. He was looking over my shoulder. I was sitting there, trying to add up twenties and crumpled-up ones, and stuff, and I was just about to add, and he said, 'Six thousand three hundred and twenty-two dollars and fifteen cents. Sullivan!'

"He was right on! And he was totally out of it, completely fucked up on whatever he was on. And then he went on. It made me realize, this guy doesn't miss a thing, no matter how high he is. You know, as free and chaotic as the place looked, there was nothing chaotic or free about the way he ran it. The guy didn't put up with any shit. He had an incredible sense of detail."

The staff were young and more than a bit naive. A lot just passed them by. The staffers didn't wonder, for instance why a paper shredder was sitting in Studio's main office, and only a very few like Richard de Courcey, the bookkeeper, were aware of the fact that, nightly, after the money and cash register tapes had been taken out of the cash registers in the bars, the takings from the coat check and cigarette concessions were added and everything was piled into bank bags, which were then packed into a beer crate. The skimmed cash was counted, split, and stowed in such hiding places as behind the ceiling panels in the basement. Did this seem a heinous sin to Steve Rubell and Ian Schrager? Why should it when skimming was as natural as breathing to New York's bar and nightclub culture? The skim at Studio was several digits greater than the norm, but was it not the most powerful and glamorous club in the world?

A world where power *is* glamour and glamour *is* power.

"You'd see wild Steve, and he would seem so high that he couldn't even stand up," Baird Jones says. "Then when it was four or five in the morning, he really changed. A complete transformation would take place. He would be out of view in the office, and he would have a chance to read the papers. He would sit there, chewing away at a bagel and reading the gossip columns to see if Studio 54 had been mentioned. All of a sudden, you realized, my God! This guy is a *thinking machine*."

Anybody who managed to find a reference to the club was rewarded. "He would give twenty-five dollars to anyone who found the name Studio 54 anywhere. I mean, it could be a giveaway. It could be the lowest level of publication, like a college newspaper. And he would give you twenty-five dollars if you brought that clipping. He was a maniac about publicity," Baird Jones says.

But then Steve Rubell, still craving his fix on people, would as likely as not, hit the Crisco Disco. The Crisco Disco, a boîte named for the cooking oil sometimes used as a lubricant in (mostly gay) lovemaking, was on Twelfth Street and the river. It was one of the after-hours joints that were springing up to sate the appetites that Studio was creating. Indeed, it was, in some respects, a parody Studio. "There was a VIP room on the second floor," says Fred Rothbell-Mista, who was a regular. "And to the right was the VVIP Room, for very, *very* important people. There were four leather couches there, and rubber plants.

"But this is where the insanity begins. Inside that VVIP Room was the MVIP Room, which was for more very important people. It was the smallest little closet. It held six chairs and a tiny table. Off-the-record people wanted to go in because this way they could do whatever they wanted to do." If more celebs wanted to get into the MVIP Room than the place held, Hank, the club operator, had a cruelly logical solution. "Hank would decide who was the bigger celebrity," Rothbell-Mista says. "If Liza Minnelli came, and Lorna Luft was there, he would get rid of Lorna for Liza.

"I saw Tanya Tucker there, doing an imitation of Joe Cocker high, and she was so high she didn't realize he was *there*, out of it, watching her." Still marveling, he said "It was unreal."

★   ★   ★

It was the recklessness that was extraordinary. It was astonishing when a New York politician, in office, would publicly boast of having bedded another pol's wife in the basement. It wasn't, perhaps, so remarkable that a crew of male staffers should cheerfully have an ejaculation contest in the same venue, prep school style, but it was astonishing that Steve Rubell should cheerfully tell Steven Gaines about it. Jack Martin, an imperturbable columnist then at the *New York Post,* having a drink with Steve Rubell in a booth, was startled one night. "It was about one o'clock," Martin says. "Suddenly he looked around and said, 'Where's the countess?' I said, 'Who?' He said, 'The countess . . . the countess . . . ' And he got very nervous and agitated. He ran over and there was a heated discussion with one of the topless good-looking bartenders. Steve went tearing off, and I waited, and waited, and waited.

"Finally he came back, sat down, and said, 'Well, I took care of that. Can you imagine?' " It turned out that the noblewoman in question, a boldface four-star, gossip column–ready noblewoman at that, had taken a fancy to the bartender. "So Steve arranged for them to have a rendezvous in the basement. They went down. He handcuffed her to a hot water pipe, at her request. They did their stuff. The bartender thought it was such a great experience. But when it was over he felt 'Oh my God! I've got to get back to the bar!' He sort of forgot about her. Steve found the countess in a state, I can tell you."

It is to the point that Steve Rubell would share this with a newspaperman with the certain knowledge that it would not appear in print. "There was a moment in history where everyone perceived that the law was not operable in certain environments. And Studio 54 was one of them. That whatever you did would not enter into the rest of your life," Don Rubell says.

I quoted the precept laid out in *Gargantua,* the sixteenth-century libertine masterpiece by François Rabelais, to him,

"En leur regle n'estoit que ceste clause: Fais ce que vouldras." (Do what you want shall be the whole of their law).

"Exactly. Perfect," says Don Rubell. "It was do what you will. And there was no concept of punishment. And no new morality that was in existence at that time. And it was really observed. The press was very good—or very bad— at never reporting any transgressions. They would say it was a wild party! A nice party. But there were no specifics.

"In today's climate that would be an impossibility. Was it abused? Yes. Were bad things done in the name of good? Yes. But it was a moment of ultimate freedom."

The moment was almost over. In June 1978, Henry Post published a feature in *Esquire* called "Sour Notes at the Hottest Disco." In this, he quoted a New York State Liquor Authority report upon Ian Schrager's father, Louis. This report, drawing on police records, stated that he was "a known associate of Meyer Lansky, and was second only to Herman Siegel in Lansky's loan-sharking and numbers racket." Organized crime, whatever that overly familiar phrase precisely means, is one of the biggest businesses in the United States. The Kennedys are just one family who bear out Honoré de Balzac's mordant aphorism that behind every great fortune is a crime, and the Kennedys, God knows, don't seem to labor under a burden on that account.

But Ian Schrager had been exceptionally close to his father. Louis's death in 1967 had profoundly affected him. Indeed, Ian once told a writer that he doubted if he would have gone into the club business at all had his father still been alive. Schrager, who had not become a lawyer by accident, was filled with rage and grief.

So Nightworld wasn't safe from the media, after all.

Far from it. RPM—Richard Manning—was patrolling Studio one night, and came across Margaret Trudeau. "She came in with Halston and Liza Minnelli's husband," RPM says. "She was luded out. She slid off the couch and her dress fell back."

Trudeau was wearing no underwear. "The picture appeared in the Canadian papers, with captions like The Beaver Will Never Die. Pierre Trudeau was running for reelection and she had left him with the kids, so it became a pretty hot item up there," RPM says.

Margaret Trudeau was actually in Studio on the night of May 22, 1979, when her husband lost to a conservative, Joe Clark. She had a ditsy dance with Jami Bernard, a female writer from the *New York Post*. But the *entente cordiale* between the media and celebrities that had made Studio 54 possible was over. It seemed unlikely to be renewed anytime soon.

IMPERIAL VISIONS

PERHAPS THE FIRST PERSON TO REALIZE THAT THE OVER-weening success of Studio 54 could be parlayed into something larger was the professional retailer, Jack Dushey. He says he was soon trying to persuade Rubell and Schrager to give up the Black Economy of the Skim, that they would be greater rewards in going legit. "It was something that really could have been exploited," Dushey says. His first notion was mundane. He approached his partners and proposed they lend their name to a line of T-shirts. "They spurned that," Dushey says.

Dushey swiftly saw that the instincts of his partners had been spot on. "To go with a line of T-shirts six months after you are open would really have been a tremendous mistake," he says. "Then I realized that what you really needed to do was build the quality of the name." Studio 54, in short, had the potential of becoming that most desirable of entities: a marquee. Those compact numerals would float free and join the universal vocabulary of negotiable class alongside the Ralph Lauren polo player, Tiffany blue, Picasso's signature, and the Gucci stripe. "We were going to be very, very selective. Very high-class. We wanted to change the image of just simply licensing out everything from T-shirts to sunglasses," Dushey says.

The clearest area for growth lay in the businesses they knew: restaurants and clubs. "At one point I had some friends who were very heavily involved with the World Trade Center," Ed Gifford says. "And they said, 'You know, we've got Windows on the World in one tower. And we've got this tower that's not being used in the other building. And boy! Those guys could probably do a hell of a job in the other tower. Why don't we schedule a meeting?' "

Ed and Michael Gifford set up the meeting. "We were all set to go up there and Schrager called me in the morning and said, 'Listen! You and Michael are not going to the meeting. Just me and Stevie.'

"I said, '*What?* We have a whole plan. It's a whole setup as to what we could do down there.' "

Gifford fell into a parody nasal-borough accent. "Nah! Me and Stevie . . ."

Later the Giffords asked their connections at the twin towers how the meeting had gone. "There were about thirty people from the World Trade Center in a huge conference room, all with notebooks and ideas and receptive to an unbelievable extent," Gifford says. "And Rubell showed up, still half awake, luded out of his skull. And Schrager showed up. And the two of them sat down. And they had a dumb meeting that went nowhere. And that was the end of it."

They were also approached by Mark Fleischman, a hotelier, who had just bought the Virgin Islands Hilton in St. Thomas. "It was a very lovely building," he says. "It was built by the same architect that built the Fontainebleau in Miami. Rum-running money." Fleischman, a genial curly-headed fellow of forty-two, had been dazzled by Studio and decided to reopen his hotel, plus a discothèque, affiliated with the hot spot. "It would be a scene. So I started talking to Steve and Ian about it. They would be hot on the deal— '*I love it! I love it! I love it!*'—and then all of a sudden they would completely forget about it. We met a few times and Ian went down to St. Thomas and we talked. But they couldn't focus," Fleischman says. New to nightlife, he was baffled by the stroboscopic on-off flicker of their dual attention span. "I didn't yet realize what the drug era does to you—what an active nightclub person really becomes after a few years," he says.

"Ian wouldn't fool around because he didn't do Quaaludes like Steven did. I remember Steven on five Quaaludes. He was spitting, staggering. It was unbelievable."

Some say they found it frustrating that the giddiness of their success was blinding Rubell and Schrager to a time of rare opportunity. "They could have had a record company . . . they could have had a film company . . . a television company. All sorts of people were always on the telephone to these guys, trying to put together joint ventures," Ed Gifford says. "They had the nub of an empire. Of an entertainment empire. *For several years.*"

Gifford remembers walking into Schrager's office one day. "He was sitting there, with his feet up on the desk, talking to Barry Diller or David Geffen in California . . . 'Oh yeah! Your name will be on the list. Twenty people? No problem' . . . I look at this guy and I said, 'Put a thousand days up on your wall. And every day you come in, scratch a day off. Because that's all you've got under any circumstances in this town. You have a phenomenon going. You'll last a thousand days and no longer.' "

Actually, intoxicated though they might be with success and the things that lubricated success, Rubell and Schrager were not letting things slide. They talked of getting into the movie business. Plans were on the table for a Studio 54 in Los Angeles. In the summer of 1978 it was announced that Studio had teamed up with Hardwicke, an entertainment miniconglomerate that operated restaurants, resorts, and animal parks. It was claimed that a Studio 54 would definitely be opening in London and that other Studios would be located in Tokyo and Munich. Also they accepted a first merchandising deal. It came from a fuddy-duddy Boston clothing wholesaler, Landlubber. Landlubber saw the designer jeans business going supernova and wished to follow in the footsteps of Gloria Vanderbilt and Brooke Shields. Schrager, always alert to the taste of the moment, called the adman Peter Rogers.

"I was kinda hot at the time," Rogers says. Indeed. His clients included Bulgari, Bottega Veneta, Vidal Sassoon, Bill Blass, the cosmetics outfit, La Prairie, and a line of fairly inexpensive fur coats, Blackglama. "Copy was over at the time," Rogers says. "People were not reading reams of copy. I became known for one-liners." The one for Vidal Sassoon, for instance, was "If you don't look good, we don't look good." Bottega Veneta claimed "When Your Own Initials Are Enough" and La Prairie, which he shot using society women as models, was burnished with "Beauty's Not Only Skin Deep." But Black-glama was Peter Rogers's finest moment, a celebrity sell, which became one of the few campaigns to become sufficiently embedded in the psychocultural circumambient goo to enter commercial folklore: "What Becomes A Legend Most."

Rogers happened to be at a shoot when Schrager called. It was in the studio of Gordon Munro, a photographer with whom he worked regularly. It happened that Rogers had never been to Studio, but he had his instinct for myth, and he and Munro were batting ideas around, and then the killer line hit. "Bong!" Rogers says. "Now Everybody Can Get Into Studio 54!" Munro instantly called a favorite model, Maaret Halinen. Halinen, a Finn, and one of the stars of the seventies, was tall and slim with hair the color of Sancerre that always looked as if she had taken it off the ironing board moments before, had never had the remotest problem getting into Studio 54.

Halinen came over straightaway. "I shot a dummy shot to show to the clients," Munro says. "And that's actually the picture they used. It was her, nude, pulling on a pair of jeans. It's done in such a way that you see it's a beautiful nude but you don't really see anything. Then I shot the commercial which was nothing more than the still picture come to life. You saw Maaret from the side . . . stepping into the jeans . . . pulling them up. And the camera sort of faded away before you would see something . . . descriptive. You heard the zip of a zipper. And then a voice said, 'Now you can get into Studio 54!' "

A similar shoot was done with a male model and a hefty campaign was planned, with the pictures running on bus shelters and the sides of buses, and in such venues as *The New York Times* and *New York* magazine. Then the *Times* and *New York* both turned the campaign down flat.

This, it should be said, was an interesting moment for sex and the media. Feminism was newly powerful and in rather a steely mode. *New York* magazine was still reeling from an unexpected furor over a photograph of Warhol superstar Ultraviolet merely showing a nipple. Guy Bourdin, the maestro of Paris *Vogue,* a photographer with an unequaled capacity for injecting a vivid, mostly sexy dream pathology into commercial work, had just produced a lingerie catalogue for Bloomingdale's, *Sighs and Whispers,* which had caused another almighty fuss.

But Peter Rogers was dumbfounded over the reaction to the Maaret shot.

"I didn't think of it as erotic. I thought of it as sculptural and beautiful," he says. "At the time I had a lot of clout. I went all the way to Sydney Gruson at the *Times* with these ads. And he absolutely was shocked. He said, 'We can't run that. The breast is showing!'

"I said, 'You've *got* to run this ad.' He said, 'If you remove the breast, I will run the ad.' "

New York magazine's publisher Catherine Black came by Rogers's office with the magazine's fashion editor, John Duka, who loved the ads. But Black was even more adamant than the *Times*. The Studio 54 jeans ads never ran in *New York* but did run in the *Times* after some fastidious retouching. Elsewhere the campaign was massive. The goods were trucked into the stores.

The TV ads were ten-second spots. Even before release they were so admired that they were put up for the ad business's Oscars, the Clio Awards. The campaign that was to rocket Studio 54 jeans into the sky was set to go.

THE BUST

12

IT HAS ALWAYS BEEN ASSUMED THAT IT WAS DAN DORF-man's article that so enraged the feds that they moved in on Studio, but this was not so according to Peter Sudler, the assistant U.S. attorney who handled the investigation. Sudler, the scion of a New Jersey real estate family, says. "The Dorfman article was salt in the wound, but the wound was already there. Donald Moon had already approached us."

Donald Moon, a good-looking fellow with long fair hair, had originally been hired by Richard de Courcey at Enchanted Garden and then had come to Studio. "I was amazed when I heard he was the guy that snitched on them," Joanne Horowitz says. "He seemed as loyal as Michael Overington." But Moon had fallen afoul of Steve Rubell soon after the move to Manhattan. "Steve wasn't very tactful about getting rid of people," Jack Dushey says. "He fired him. The guy didn't like it." He disliked it enough to call the feds. Peter Sudler met with Moon after the approved film noir fashion in the Federal Reserve Building on Wall Street.

Moon's only motivation seems to have been burning rage. He did not ask for bounty, for instance, as was his entitlement under Section 7623 of the Internal Revenue Code. All he asked for was to disappear—to vanish into the federal witness program. This was granted. He told Sudler about the secret safe with the double set of books. He told him about the treasure in the Hefty bags in the gap between the hard and drop ceilings in the basement. He *told*.

Sudler started organizing his pieces on the board. "The IRS do not like giving out search warrants. They think it's rather heavy-handed," Sudler says. "So I made out a search warrant and found a judge who signed it."

He showed the document to a counsel at the IRS, who looked it over gloomily. "No judge in the world would sign this," the IRS man told Sudler.

"I *got* a judge to sign it."

Reluctantly the IRS acceded. "I knew we had to go in right away," Sudler says. One whisper, a single tremor, and the cobwebbing of data that would ensnare Studio would be brushed into nonexistence. "That would be the ultimate egg on my face," he said. Speedily, he put his task force together.

Bohdan Huzar, an IRS agent, had actually rather wanted to go to Studio 54 for some time. Indeed, he had gone along with half a dozen buddies from the agency before his wedding, which was on November 13, 1978. "We were going to have my bachelor party there," he says. Marc Benecke had taken one look at these single guys. Forget it!

"I didn't have a problem getting in on my second visit," Huzar says dryly. Because he was with Sudler's task force. This included some fifty agents of the IRS Criminal Investigation Division, led by Frank Frajolillio, backed up by a contingency from the Drug Enforcement Agency. The first group of raiders arrived at 9:30 in the morning of Thursday, December 14, and went straight down to the basement and homed in on the metal safe with the real books. The Studio staff were reluctant to open it at first. The IRS said, "Fine. Don't open it. We'll take it along with us."

The staff opened the safe. The safe gave up books, envelopes, lists. "They were arrogant and stupid," Sudler told me later. "If they had been smart they would have destroyed the records." The feds had the works.

The agents found the Hefty bags filled with cash in the walls, behind the pipes, up in the roof, nearly a million dollars' worth, and scooped up all and any documentation. "That night I saw myself on TV carrying out a file cabinet," Huzar says. Steve Rubell was collared in his Mercedes and a further $100,000 was found in the trunk. Other agents went around to his apartment and grabbed the cash in the secret compartment behind the bookshelves in the main room. Sudler's face was egg-free.

There were three interruptions to the raid: an annoyance, a bonus, and an annoyance. The first annoyance was that a TV crew, who just happened to have been a block away, heard about the excitement and hurried over. So the media, as usual with Studio 54, were there well in advance of reality.

The bonus was that Ian Schrager showed up in Studio, carrying some books and papers. Sudler surmises that he was "startled to see fifty or so IRS agents searching the place" and put the books on the floor. "They were now on the premises and entitled to be searched," Sudler says. Five packets of white powder were found tucked coyly between the leaves. The agents called Sudler, who said, "Okay. Tell everyone to stand still." Then, he says, "I called DEA on Fifty-seventh Street. They shot over there. They were there in fifteen minutes."

The powder field-tested positive for cocaine. "So I told them to arrest Mr. Schrager." Ian Schrager was charged with possession with intent to distribute, and then released on $50,000 bail.

The other annoyance was Roy Cohn, who was swiftly on the scene and putting on one of his bravura Rod Steiger performances. "He was throwing desks over," Sudler says. "He called the press in and said, 'Look what these Nazis are doing!'" Cohn, the former counsel to Senator Joseph McCarthy, also said, with the splendid shamelessness of the culture that Studio 54 was ushering in, "I've never seen McCarthyism practiced this way!"

Cohn got a federal judge to order the agents out by ten that night. A private party was canceled but Studio valiantly opened that night anyway. "When you are in the public eye, you expect to be harassed," Steve Rubell told *The Washington Post* with a game show of sangfroid. He let it be known that Friday night had been the biggest weekday turnout in the club's history.

Arrests can't often seem splendidly timed, at least for those arrested. That said, the timing of the arrests of Rubell, Schrager, and Jack Dushey seems particularly unhappy. Jack Dushey says he had been hammering away at his partners for months. "I can't tell you how long I was trying to convince them to go straight and turn this thing into a worldwide entity," he says.

Ian Schrager had come around to this thinking. "You get intoxicated with your success," he told a friend. "We had gone wrong. But we were trying to get ourselves straight."

What Schrager and Rubell were trying to do was buy Emerson's, a restaurant chain with a lot of outlets, which had recently gone belly-up, incurring a tempting tax loss. "That would have sheltered all the income we had. And we would have cleaned everything up," Schrager told his friend. "As a matter of fact, when we got raided that morning I had all the 10Ks and prospectuses on me. And we probably would have closed that deal in a couple of days. So we were in the process." They were working with Alan N. Cohen, an investor and a tax lawyer with Paul, Weiss Rifkind. "Just as I had put it together, the raid happened," Cohen told a reporter. He remembers that before the raid Rubell had told him, "There are some other things I have to talk to you about."

Schrager would later say: "We had realized it was ridiculous. We were on a self-destruction course. It just came down at the wrong time. So the same good luck we had with Studio, the same bad luck we had at the other end of it."

In the aftermath of the bust, Steve and Ian's relations with Jack Dushey seemed fine at first. Their principal focus was simply keeping Studio afloat. "The federal government had taken every stitch of paper out of the place. I mean, the *telephone books*," Dushey says. "There wasn't a filing cabinet left. We had no idea who was coming, how to handle everything."

Steve had brought in Roy Cohn, reflexively, as you might release a pit bull on intruders. Dushey, though, decided a pit bull was not what was needed. He talked to Schrager and thought that they were agreed that what they needed was credibility, a quality that was not quite in Cohn's gift. "That's when we went to Paul, Weiss Rifkind," Dushey says. They were working up a defense in which chaotic bookkeeping would figure rather than downright villainy, and Dushey was going to say it had happened on his watch.

"I was willing to take the fall," he says. "The idea was to keep Steve going in the nightclub and to keep Ian from losing his bar association license. It didn't bother me so much. I'm in retail and real estate. I knew it was either all three of us or one of us. And I was willing to do it."

Rubell and Schrager let Sudler know that they wanted to cut a deal. Convention dictates what happens here. "Law enforcement says to a defendant, 'Okay, you come in . . . tell us the truth, answer all of our questions . . . we'll agree not to use those statements against you if you decide to go to trial,'" Sudler says.

Rubell and Schrager duly came in. "At our first debriefing I asked Steve Rubell, 'Would I get into Studio 54?'" remembers Sudler, a hefty figure of a man. "He looked at me. He had this little smile. He said, 'No. You're one of the gray people.' I was in my office. I thought the agents were going to fall on the floor. I thought this is unbelievable. What chutzpah! The balls on this guy."

The fed "debriefings" deteriorated. "They came up with all these crazy stories—really cockamamy stories—to explain the money and the second set of books. They came up with this story that they had been hoarding to pay for renovations," Sudler says. They claimed that the bagfuls of cash had been untouched. This yarn lasted until the IRS found detailed records of the split, along with $900,000 cash, in a safe-deposit box at the Citibank at 640 Fifth Avenue.

Rubell and Schrager—and this was not Roy Cohn's doing, oddly, but the brainwave of one of their Washington lawyers—also came up with something in the "national interest": the name of President Carter's chief of staff, Hamilton Jordan. Rubell claimed that Jordan had obtained cocaine in his presence in Studio on an April evening in 1978. The origin of this was one of the more bizarre inhabitants of the Celebrity Culture, Barry Landau, a self-described "enigma." Landau was a political groupie, who had been a bipartisan intern in Washington under LBJ, worked with the press office under Nixon, and in protocol under Jerry Ford. He had also taken Steve Rubell on his first trip to Washington. "We stayed with Jamie Auchincloss, Jackie's half-brother," he says. "I introduced Steve to Elizabeth Taylor."

One night, Landau says, he had gone to Studio after Roy Cohn's July Fourth party in Greenwich. He was with a group when Hamilton Jordan came up. Landau remembers that he asked, "Where's your friend, Vitas Gerulaitis?" and says that he demanded cocaine and champagne. Landau, who insists he never saw the aide indulging in the former, gossiped about it, naturally. One of the people he had told was Steve Rubell.

★   ★   ★

Real estate is also part of the story of Nightworld. Infinity was less chic than it had been but was still doing a roaring trade. "The landlord tried to sell the building to us for nothing—$225,000 for the whole building! Everyone I knew that was smart said why buy the building? You have such a long lease at a low rent? Why buy it?" Brahms says. His tone was dolorous. The numbers betrayed him. His smart friends were dumb.

"He sold it to another landlord in the area who had had a building that burned down by accident," Brahms says. The new landlord called and said he was interested in buying out their lease. Could they talk about it? Brahms said sure. For whatever reason, the talk never took place.

"Two weeks after that, we caught fire in the basement. There were some rags that were soaked in oil. We thought it was just a disgruntled person," Brahms says. "Two weeks after that, it burned down. From the top. Professional job. It went inside of eight minutes. The whole building was burned. The sprinklers were turned off."

This was February 14, 1979. Valentine's Day. Nobody died, but "almost. Two girls were trapped at the top. From what I understand the landlord never got the insurance money. He never pushed for it. Do you know what a J51 is? At the time you took an old building, and if you kept the facade and renovated it, you didn't pay taxes for ten years. A tax abatement for ten years! He sold it, I think, to NYU. He sold it inside of six months after he bought it for five or six times his money. At least a million dollars."

Studio fever was unabated, regardless of the bust. Rubell was on the cover of *Interview* that February, and the club was so busy that Shay Knuth, the party planner, a blonde from Milwaukee, was going crazy. She told Rubell and Schrager she needed an assistant, and she recommended a friend, Myra Scheer. Actually Scheer, a lush young woman from Atlanta, a graduate in public relations from the University of Georgia, already had plans. "I was going to move to L.A. and work for Denny Cordell, who was opening a roller rink down there called Flipper's," Scheer says. But she went to the Studio offices without expectations anyway.

She was surprised. "I had been intimidated," she says. "Steve was this powerful person that rejected people. That was the image. But his mother was sitting on the couch with him, and I saw this warmth. And Ian seemed familiar. I relaxed right away." Scheer was hired as Steve's assistant. She was in her early twenties. "And that was old. Everybody was kids there," she says.

It was early 1979. For the first six months, Scheer spent some time on the door and she saw how Rubell could be both funny and brutal. "I remember one guy who would wait every day. For *months*. He was wearing one of those fishnet kind of things they wear in Brooklyn, which are not acceptable. The man was imploring, 'Steve . . . Steve . . . What can I do? How can I get in?' Rubell finally looked him over. 'Why don't you go to Europe for six months?' he offered."

Scheer began to find her own power disorienting. "A man offered me five hundred dollars to get his son in. I just couldn't do that," she says. "Marvin Mitchelson offered me a free divorce to get his agent's son in."

Within the club, she worked on public relations. It was her first job in PR. "Can you imagine?" she says. "I never had to pitch. I had to *screen*. Who was legit and who wasn't. People would write letters . . . 'I am going blind' . . . 'I am dying of leukemia' . . . 'Get me into Studio 54!' "

This was, Myra Scheer realized, more than a burning desire to get into a hot nightspot. This was more even than celebrity spotting outside the Grammys or the Oscars. Myra Scheer says, "I realized that people thought they were going to find Paradise!"

She also worked on the parties. "The parties Shay worked on were the parties where people paid to rent," she says. "Like Monday was the dark night and that was when they made money." (In clubs, as in theaters, "dark" means closed; to the public anyway.) "Again, not anybody could rent it. You had to be approved. Let's say it was a hair show. They would pay out a lot of money to rent out Studio. And then sometimes during the day you could have a cocktail party there. Stuff like that."

Myra was also working on the private parties, the ones behind the scrim, and she swiftly found that Manhattan grandees were as eager for a summons as the unfortunates on the wrong side of the velvet cord. "Steve gave me the call list. I had to call the people on the list and invite them to the next party. I was very new to New York and I enjoyed that. I'd be on the telephone and I would say"—she mimicked a breathy squeak—" 'Hi! May I speak to Andy Warhol?'

If I said I was calling from Steve he would get on the phone right away. Whenever I phoned."

She worked on the Valentine's party, the Halloween party, the Broadway openings, and the party for Michael Chow. There was still a giddiness about Rubell, a refusal to contemplate what lay ahead. Discussions were under way with Neil Bogart of Casablanca concerning a Studio 54 album. Landlubber executives were preparing for the launch of Studio 54 jeans. And the other, embryonic Studio 54s in London, Munich, Tokyo, and Los Angeles were being nudged toward a conceptual start line.

Steve Rubell, who disliked leaving New York, even went to Los Angeles. He turned up for the opening of Flipper's, where Scheer introduced him to the owners, three young Brits in the music business, Denny Cordell, Nick Cowan, and the eponymous Ian "Flipper" Ross. They were aces on the music front—their artists included Tom Petty and Leon Russell—but hadn't quite thought Nightworld through. "It was a great idea. On paper," Scheer says. "But liquor and roller skating don't mix."

"What was the difference between Flipper's and the *Titanic*?" Cowan asked a friend later. . . . "The *Titanic* was full when it went down."

Flipper, an Etonian, took a highly paid job as a butler in Los Angeles. He is now a writer and lives in Wales.

In the early summer of 1979, discomania approached an apogee. It was announced that *Got Tu Go Disco,* a $2 million musical, would be opening at the Minskoff Theatre on Broadway. Marc Benecke was hired to appear as the "doorman." Great. Or fairly great. The producer, whom I had known since coming to New York, was the son, by his account, of a "Jewish housewife and a Puerto Rican numbers man who operated in Harlem." His name was Jerry Brandt, and again by his own account, he was "the greatest promoter in the world." A hyperkinetic straight, Brandt was certainly one of the first promoters of gay.

Jerry Brandt knew the . . . parameters. In 1966 he and a partner took over an East Village boîte, the Dom, where the Velvet Underground and Nico had played, and reopened it as the Electric Circus. "There was no alcohol served.

I was afraid, because everybody was doing LSD," Brandt says. "Ivan Chermayeff designed it. Then I redid it two years later and Charles Gwathmey did it." Robert Stern, the architect, says mordantly "Gwathmey did the design that closed them down, basically."

Certainly, with its light shows, face painting, onsite drugs, and pulsating sexuality, the Electric Circus had been an avatar for Studio. "Steve Rubell and Ian Schrager asked me to write a presentation about what Studio 54 should be. They were just starting construction," he says. "They stiffed me. I think they gave me a thousand dollars. It didn't bother me."

Jerry Brandt had been chucked out of the Electric Circus by his partner, though, after being nabbed for marijuana possession at Toronto airport. Brandt's wife left him. Depressed, he followed her to Los Angeles. He opened a club there, the Paradise Ballroom, with money from Bernie Cornfeld, and revived the dance marathon. "Our very first contest was won by two guys," he told the writer Jean Vallely. The club was soon kaput. In 1973, however, Brandt discovered a young male singer, improbably named Jobriath, whom he decided to promote as upping the ante on David Bowie. "It's gay time and I think the world is ready for a true fairy," Brandt told Vallely. "The only thing that's keeping us alive is sex. I'm selling sex. Sex and professionalism."

David Geffen, then the president of Elektra/Asylum, came up with some dough for the prodigy. A first album tanked. Brandt took Jobriath to London. "He went into the studio. I hired the London Symphony Orchestra. He wrote this entire symphony. And he recorded this song called 'Scumbag.'

"My God! How am I going to tell Geffen this? We just spent fifty thousand dollars to record a song called 'Scumbag!' One song!

"I called. I said, 'David, I'm sixteen feet above the pool on the high-diving board. There's no ladder down and no water. And I gotta jump! You've got the water. I'll see you tomorrow.' "

Brandt flew to Los Angeles. Geffen's secretary announced that he was out. "I said, 'Don't get involved,' " Brandt says. " 'Either buzz me into his office or I'm going to break the door down.' That's how desperate I was. You don't stiff the London Symphony Orchestra. You're finished!" He was almost rolling on the floor of the Bowery Bar with mirth at the memory.

"She buzzed me in. I didn't find him. But I'd been in that office. I knew the doors." Brandt located the evasive mogul. Geffen agreed to sign a check under one condition. . . . "You sign a letter saying you're not going to ask for any more money."

"I said, '*That's it?*' . . . 'Yeah!' . . ."

Brandt penned the letter, got the check. Jobriath had yet to mount a serious threat to David Bowie, but Jerry Brandt still thought his time would come. "Glam Rock. In a few years," he guessed.

In the summer of 1975 Brandt announced another plan. He was going to reopen a famous nightclub, the Diamond Horseshoe on West Forty-sixth Street. His partners were a young couple from Long Island, named Jerry and Reva Hart. This never happened. There is more than one version of what *did* happen next. This is Jerry Brandt's: "I'm in St. Tropez. I'm on the balls of my ass. I'm having coffee and I see these great *pants* walk by."

The pants were local jeans, and everybody looked wondrous in them. "The fat ones look skinny. The skinny ones look great. The short ones look great. So now I'm checking labels, and I keep seeing this one, McKeens. It had an English flag on the label." He tracked down the source. A store in an alley off the port. The jeans were made by Moroccan Jews. "I sit there on the curb. There's this young lady sitting out there. She hands me a pipe. We're smoking hashish. I said, '*Look at these pants.*'

"She said, 'They're not pants.'

" 'What is it?'

" 'It's a *cosmetic.*'

" 'It's a cosmetic? Brilliant!' "

Brandt raised $50,000 by calling a friend in New York, then walked into the store. "I put a big bag of cash on the table. I said, 'Pack up the jeans.' " Brandt opened up the French Jeans Store on East Sixtieth Street alongside Serendipity in partnership with the Harts, who have claimed that the whole thing was their idea, not Brandt's, and they had the notion in California.

These are not trivial matters. Arguably, cheap, durable trousers deserve a place with movies and motorcars as America's contribution to world culture. "They were the first designer jeans." Jerry Brandt insists. "I sold the patterns to Calvin Klein, to Jordache, to Sasson at fifty thousand bucks a pop." But he left the company shortly thereafter.

Then came *Got Tu Go Disco*. This actually began as *Gotta Dance*, and it was originally to be a musical à clef about Studio 54. The seed financing came from the owners of Spring Records, a neighbor on West Fifty-fourth Street; the designer was Joe Eula, and the first writer approached was Steven Gaines, whose novel *The Club,* likewise about Studio, was to come out that fall.

It was Joe Eula who introduced Brandt to Alan Finkelstein, the Studio regular who had ferried a planeful of guests including Scotty Taylor to Acapulco. Finkelstein, a dark, thin-faced young man, with long black hair and moustache in the Frank Zappa manner, came up with major, major money. It wasn't much of a secret where the money came from either. He was the owner of Insport, a sportswear store on Madison, but had made his dough from major, major marijuana smuggles. "They were bringing in the money in A&P bags," Brandt recalls. "Number ten, I used to call it.

"Another number ten bag! Another hundred thousand. *Cash.* I would say, 'What am I going to do with this? I can't go on Broadway and pay cash. I have to deposit it.' And I did.

"Then I fired some PR person. She got pissed off and said, '*It's all pot money!*' And that's how it leaked out . . ."

It would have leaked out anyway. On the night of April 23, Alan Finkelstein went to a birthday party that Joe Eula was giving in his apartment for Halston. Among those attending the revels were Barbara Allen, William Paley, Andy Warhol, Jerry Brandt, and Steve Rubell. Finkelstein was arrested early the following morning. So were fifteen others, in different locations, accused of running an aggregate $200 million worth of pot and hash through Kennedy Airport.

Cast changes and script changes zapped around like tracer fire. Steven Gaines, who had learned he had been fired only from reading *The New York Times,* wrote a not-unfriendly piece on Brandt nonetheless. It was published in *New York* just before the boffo opening and in it Brandt showed how Steve Rubell was the target to aim for in Nightworld. It was for this reason that he hired the guardian of the gate, Marc Benecke.

About a show biz career beckoning, Benecke said, "Everything has been going well for you, you think sure! Why not? There's a certain naïveté . . ."

Brandt told Gaines magnificently, "What do I want? I want to be the grand man. I have to wear spats and a top hat and be the *grand man.* And you know who can give that to me? Not Steve Rubell. Only the public can give that to me." He ended, "Some people fall off the curb. Now that's *embarrassing*. At least when I fall, I fall from a high wire with no net. Now that's a *show!*"

The critics fell on *Got Tu Go Disco* like hounds on a lame fox. "I forced it to stay open for nine days," Brandt says. He went on a morning show with the famously acerbic critic, John Simon. "He's ripping me apart! I said, 'Wait a minute. The only people that can tell me if it sucks are the audience.'

"So I stood up in front of the camera, and said, 'Tomorrow's free! Everybody come. And *then* we vote.' "

Brandt thought that was a shrewd way off the hook. The theater owner felt differently. "Jerry Minskoff called me, and says who's buying the tickets? Because the union controlled the box office. I said, 'Boy! I didn't think of that.' So I went to the box office and took out my American Express card and bought a hundred tickets.

"Then I had someone distract the guy, and I took a stack of tickets that big, and I put it in my jacket. I bought a hundred and I took five hundred. Okay?"

The free audience trooped in. Irene Cara, the lead, did not appear. "She didn't show up. From the reviews. She got devastated," Brandt says. But there was this terrific understudy. Brandt leaned over to pick up a dropped program or something and straightened up. "She was gone. The lead singer had gone. *She fell into the pit.* So that was how it went, you understand.

"But I had a great time. And as I was leaving the theater on the last day, and I was watching them take down the marquee, and my name, and tears were rolling out of my eyes, I put my hand in my pocket, and I had sixty-four cents to my name.

"I looked at the sign, and I said, 'Ah, fuck it!' And I threw it onto Broadway. And I had to walk home. And six months later, I opened the Ritz . . ."

The Ritz was another Nightworld contender, but The Ritz likewise failed to transform Jerry Brandt into the Grand Man.

Marc Benecke was back at Studio. Backstage tensions were mounting, particularly between Dushey and Rubell. "Steve was up to his old ways. I mean, here we were under investigation. They had everything, and we were about to be convicted or at least indicted," Dushey says. "And Steve is at the door, doing drugs and taking cash. Again." One evening he was due to join Steve and Ian in a meeting with Roy Cohn, and he called Steve that afternoon. Steve told him the meeting was off. "Oh okay," Dushey said.

That evening, he called Steve at Studio. Steve's secretary told him that Steve had gone to see Roy Cohn. "I drove over to Roy Cohn's," Dushey says. He saw both Rubell's and Schrager's cars parked outside. "I started shaking," he says. "That's when I went out and hired my own attorney." In late spring 1979 Dushey approached the feds. In mid-June, he pleaded guilty to a single count of tax evasion.

Rubell and Schrager had been plea-bargaining for several months. At the end of June they and Richard de Courcey were charged with skimming $2.5 million. The *New York Post* quoted "sources familiar with the case" to the effect that "possible ties to racketeering and drugs were being investigated."

The impact of the charges was swift. Ed and Michael Gifford had stuck with Studio through the bust. "Then a court reporter slipped me the indictment," Ed Gifford says. "Michael and I sat down and read it. We got sick to our stomachs. It was the enormous haul of cash that these guys had dragged in. The fact that they had made a guilty plea, and had gone ahead, and were still hiding money. And got caught. At which point I just said, 'Jesus! These two boys are terrible. Let's get out of this!'" Roy Cohn begged them to stay on until he had given a press conference on June 28. They did so, and resigned later that day.

The Studio 54 jeans ads had been due to air. Landlubber canceled. "I'm as proud of these ads as of anything I ever did," mourns Peter Rogers. "The whole thing was a fiasco. We sold a lot of *posters*."

Maaret Halinen kept a poster. When asked if she kept the Studio 54 jeans, she laughed throatily. "Did I keep a pair of jeans? Are you kidding? They had too small a pair. I literally could not get into them." So Maaret Halinen actually at that moment had not been able to get into Studio 54. And the poster? She had it on the wall of her apartment for the longest while, she says. "It's so weird," she says. "I don't know what happened to it. Next thing I knew, it was gone." Gone, along with Ian and Steve's dream of a Studio 54 empire.

★　　★　　★

The Hamilton Jordan story wasn't going to fly. "Steve asked me to recant my testimony. But it was too late," Landau says. It had a ruinous effect on him. "I was a leper. A social outcast. I became the piranha," he says. Perhaps he meant pariah. "It was like being at a Mad Hatter's Tea Party. Roy believed that there was no such thing as bad publicity. He said everybody will know who you are. I didn't *want* everybody to know who I was.

"It was sheer hell. I didn't trust anybody. But I found out who my real friends were. Who knows how long that would have taken me in the delusionary world of Studio 54?"

In the first week of November 1979 Studio 54's defense collapsed. On November 12, 1979, Henry Post published a cover story in *New York* magazine; its headline: STUDIO 54: THE PARTY'S OVER. In this story he published for the first time details of what would become infamous, the list of "party favors." This detailed all those little presents, mostly cocaine or poppers, slipped into the palms or pockets of Steve's celebrated friends, with the monetary value of the freebie alongside. Post, who maintained a tone of high, clerical indignation throughout, also took note of the shock of the famous at finding themselves on a list, which was less at seeing their habits exposed than at finding themselves treated as business expenses.

There was worse. Post also wrote that "alleged Queens-Williamsburg loan-sharking king and racketeer Sam Jacobson was a frequent Studio 54 visitor during both business and disco hours. . . . The IRS inventory of documents confiscated from Studio 54 included a five-column accounting sheet headed 'Steve Rubell–Sam Jacobson,' with weekly dates and dollar amounts ranging from $2,500 to $25,000."

The fact was that, going into the investigation, the feds had thought it highly likely that Studio was, if not a mob front, thoroughly connected. A painstaking investigation of several months had negated this assumption. In this regard, Rubell and Schrager had come up squeaky-clean. The mob connection had vanished like mist, and Peter Sudler now theorizes that Sam Jacobson was not so much a dark presence as a useful person to have around to discourage the sorts of fellows who had called on Yoram Polany. Ian Schrager has said Jacobson was an infrequent visitor to the club and that Henry Post's reporting was an "outrage." Indeed, even Post's colleagues would speculate why he was taking a meat-ax to what were, after all, just operators of a fancy nightclub. "He loved the tension of going to the same parties as them. The deliciousness of it," believes his editor at *New York,* Craig Unger.

Post's first feature for *Esquire* had been bad enough. This was devastating. Steve made an anguished call to Jim Fouratt, a Nightworlder who was simultaneously active—indeed, at times, combative—in nightclubs, "advanced" rock, and radical politics. "Henry had been very, very kind to me in print. Henry was one of the people who helped my career. He liked it that I was openly gay," Fouratt says. "Steve called me up, saying, 'How could Henry have done this?' "

"But he was not angry. He was hurt. He considered Henry a friend. In many ways Henry was all those things that Steve would have loved to have been. A golden boy! Attractive, a good family, all that kind of stuff. Henry was the kind of person Steve liked to have around."

And now this. *Wasp honor.* "He broke perhaps the code. But you allowed him to see all this. And he really hasn't said anything that isn't true," Jim Fouratt told him.

Myra Scheer says that Steve took off for a weekend, and then got over it. Steve Rubell was nothing if not resilient.

Rubell and Schrager approached Peter Sudler through Roy Cohn. They agreed to plead guilty and that they would cooperate. The cooperation would consist of information against other potential targets. Together they compiled a list of people who had been paid off the books. The main targets, though, were to be their former partners and current rivals, particularly John Addison and Maurice Brahms.

It was simple enough to the feds. "What was curious about Studio 54 was the size of the money they took. They were really greedy," Peter Sudler says. "Normally, if people skim from a cash business, they'll skim ten percent, or fifteen percent, or twenty-five percent at the most. These guys skimmed five million dollars in one year. Probably eighty percent of their gross. It was ridiculous, what they did."

The guidelines at the time had been that nobody was prosecuted for less than three years of tax evasion, but there was a frontier of the permissible, even in this shadowy terrain. Rubell and Schrager had bounded over it, and would be punished. For the first months after the bust neither Rubell, Schrager, or their lawyers had thought prison a likely option. Steve Rubell, in particular, was in cloud cuckoo-land. It barely penetrated when Arthur Liman, one of the heavyweights among their fifteen lawyers, called them into his office and warned them they would be going to jail. "I didn't grasp the problem," he said later. "When Jimmy Carter called me a liar I was insulted."

Rubell and Schrager appeared in front of U.S. District Judge Richard Owen for sentencing on January 18, 1980. The judge blitzed them for their "tremendous arrogance." Rubell later described his inner turmoil thus: "When the judge said I was arrogant, I thought What's he talking about? I still go visit my parents on Sunday. I never thought about these things! Suddenly I was with Liz Taylor, and going to London, and having lunch with Princess Margaret, and going to Mustique. Who was even thinking? I was like a kid at FAO Schwarz!"

Among the spectators who watched Judge Owen give Ian and Steve three and a half years apiece was Ed Gifford. To him, Ian Schrager and Steve Rubell looked shamefaced, like schoolkids called to the principal's office, feeding off each other's emotions. Owen observed that the two had said they had cooperated in a federal investigation, and noted that this could lead to a reduction in their sentences. Even Peter Sudler thought it was rather a stiff sentence.

It is hard not to sympathize with Steve Rubell and Ian Schrager at this juncture. Sure, they had been over the top, greedy and arrogant, but it was the gluttonous arrogance of kids, as if Steve Rubell had rolled over the law in his red toy car. The trial had been the media-culture's version of the Moscow's Show Trials in the Stalin era. It was, as much as the Leona Helmsley trial, a celebrity sentencing. Rubell, Schrager, and the Nightworld they had created had been squashed. Or so it seemed.

In their last days of freedom Rubell convened a final meeting with some core staff. It was in his office on the first floor. Among those present were Chris Williamson, the night manager, Michael Overington, Roger Parenti, and a couple of the coat check girls including Lisa. Ian Schrager was his usual phantomlike background presence. Steve, his manner an odd mixture of the buoyant and the rueful, told them what they knew already, that he and Ian would be away for a while. Then he introduced John Kadama, a Japanese American who had been at Syracuse with them, and said that he would be running things in their absence. Rubell also regretted that the club would not be able to keep everybody on. Roger Parenti assumed it would be Benecke who got to keep the door.

Then came the Rubell touch, which was typical in that it was off the wall but bang on target. It related to a notion he had played with at the beginning. "They had this idea of setting up holograms. Back when it was becoming voguish to think about laser beams projecting real people," Chris Williamson remembers. "The whole idea was to have him hologrammed in from jail. We thought it would be an incredibly wonderful joke." Parenti adds, "He was going to host a party from the center of the dance floor. As a hologram."

The meeting broke up in excellent humor. Rubell scuttled around over the next few days with increasing energy. Williamson ran into him in a hallway on the last day. "He gave me a big hug," Williamson says. "He said 'You've done good! I know I can count on you.' " It was the first time he had been so effusive.

The final party was emotional, and fairly small, nothing like the rambunctious affairs on Halloween and New Year's Eve. A lot of old Studio hands who hadn't been around much in a while, people like Lester Persky, put in an appearance.

Steve Rubell and Diana Ross went up to control central, the DJ booth, and a bunch of his closer friends jammed themselves into the booth behind him, including Ian Schrager, trying, as usual to mingle with the shadows in the background. Diana Ross began to sing out over the crowd. "She was blitzed. Totally trashed," Chris Williamson says. Reinaldo Herrera, who was there with Carolina, says, "It was rather moving. Touching. Steve had this passion for Diana. He had every single song in his car."

Ross prodded an even more trashed Rubell into singing himself. He launched into an enthusiastic rendition of "I Did It My Way." A bit too enthusiastic, in fact. "He basically fell over the thing at one point," Roger Parenti says. "We had him by the ankles. He was hanging off the DJ booth. He could have killed himself . . ."

Most were moved. A few found it maudlin. One who was there remembers

David Geffen reproving Rubell. "He said, 'Stop with this "My Way" stuff and grow up already,' " the friend remembers.

The crowd started thinning fairly early. Diana Ross, who had lost a shoe, searched for it fretfully, told Chris Williamson about it, then she left too. Rubell was not abandoned, though, because gossip columnist Jack Martin arrived with Lorna Luft, the actress sister of Liza Minnelli, and Luft's then husband. Jack Martin, who had a whole page at the *New York Post*, was a Studio regular. "Nothing happened at Studio until after midnight. So I would go out to dinner, go to the theater, take a nap, whatever. But I always wound up at Studio," he says. "I would stay until three or four. Then I would walk home. I lived at Sixty-second and Fifth. I don't know if people still walk through the streets of Manhattan at four in the morning." No, Jack. "By that time, I was tired. I would go to bed. Then I would get up and start writing my column."

With regular nutritious items from Studio, of course. But this was the end of it. "We arrived late. We had been some place else. The festivities were over," Martin says. "Steve was sort of alone. There was nobody else with him but us for the next four, five, six hours—however long we sat with him. He was sort of spaced-out. He had accepted it. It was a sad going-away party but we were laughing and having fun. We were with him literally until he took a car to go home and meet the authorities." It was over.

Williamson did find Diana Ross's missing shoe. She came by and picked it up soon after.

It would come to pass that after Steve and Ian had been released from prison, Ed Gifford paid a visit to Studio 54. "I went to have one last drink in the club. And sure enough, there he was! I can see it now," Gifford says.

Rubell was with Calvin Klein. Gifford mimed Steve's excitable nasal bleat: " 'Calvin! Calvin! C'mere! I want you to meet Ed Gifford. C'mere!

" 'Ed! Ed Gifford! I loved you. And I hated you. I hated you and I loved you. Why were you there for the sentencing? I saw you sitting there for the sentencing and I could never understand that. Why did you do that to me?' "

"I said, 'Well, Steve, I did that because that was one of the most interesting periods of my life, those years at Studio 54. It was sort of a Greek tragedy. I had to come and see the machine come down from the gods. I had to see it reach its climax. I was there for the denouement. I thought it was important for me to be there. I wasn't there for any petty, vindictive reasons.'

"So he went, 'C'mon, Calvin!' And off he went to some other place."

Studio's liquor license expired on February 28, 1980. It appeared that the club had died by celebrity as it had lived by it, and it was printed that Sylvester Stallone had bought the last legal drink. "Studio closed in March," Marc Benecke says. "Howard and Peppo opened Rock Lounge. I worked for them for a while. Big mistake on my part. That was a weird place. I did that strictly to be employed again. But I did that with total disregard of loyalty to Ian and Steve. It was a mistake and something I wouldn't do now."

That was then, though. Marc Benecke had suddenly toppled from a prominence of Nightworld. "It was kind of like being on tour with the Rolling Stones for three years straight. And then it was . . . *over*. There was this great whirlwind, and it just stopped. It was very difficult. I went through a terrible period of self-doubt, of wondering where I was headed.

"And then you find out who your friends really are. The invitations stop coming or don't come as often. You get a lot less cards at Christmas. Stuff like that. But being so young, you really have to get to understand that. And I'm glad I learned that lesson at that very early age."

DISCO SUCKS!

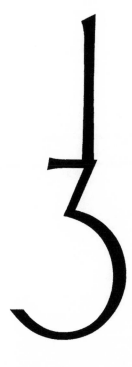

THE KILL DISCO MOVEMENT HAD STRENGTHENED EVEN AS Studio 54 was moving toward its zenith. Chicago radio jock, Stephen Dahl, organized a bonfire of disco albums in Comiskey Park. "He burned my record first. Then he started a movement called Disco Sucks, based on my song. I feel sorry for the Bee Gees, because he and a couple of other guys on the show would do impressions of the Bee Gees," Rick Dees said. *"And they would all inhale helium first!"* Dees, compassion short-lived, gave an explosive giggle. "Isn't that great?" he said.

Joyce Bogart is still astonished by the rapid withering of disco. It happened she says almost immediately after Casablanca put out Donna Summer's album *Bad Girls*. She noticed it first at a disco convention. It was as much fun as a museum after closing time. "It was like one of those things when you know a person is going, but when they go, you're still surprised."

What killed disco? Not punk. In fact, Debbie Harry of Blondie scored a major disco hit with

"Heart of Glass"—admittedly, it had been intended to be a parody—and Glenn O'Brien, who used to DJ on the first floor of the Mudd Club on Mondays, would spin disco he favored, like "Disco Inferno" by Trammps and "Funky-town" by Lipps Inc.

Frankie Crocker, New York's most powerful radio DJ at the time, says disco got samey. "Everybody was cloning the same sounds. They weren't branching out and changing," he says. "But where was disco going to go?" Giorgio Moroder, the producer, blames the death of disco on disco itself. "Certainly disco killed itself," he says. "And there was a terrible backlash. Too many products, too many people, too many records companies jumping on this kind of music. A lot of bad records came out. I guess it was overkill. Everybody started to come out with disco and it became . . . what's the word? A cuss-word."

"The amazing end of it all!" Joyce Bogart marvels in her crisp snap, crackle, and pop way. "How Middle America rose up, Cleveland and Detroit and all those, and said 'Death to Disco!' Because it had taken over the culture. When you got the sixty-year-olds in the disco collars and chains doing the bump and grind on the dance floor, that's when the younger generation said, 'That's enough of this!' And once you lose your base, it's over. It died an incredibly quick death. Recordwise. It took us all by surprise."

Another reading is that disco didn't just kill itself, it helped cripple the record industry too. "*Fever* was as good as gold. In other words, there was no such thing as an unsold record," Fred Gershon says. That brought in the mob. The mob had gone into the bootleg business before when there had been monster hits, but the double success of *Saturday Night Fever* and *Grease* inspired them to set up a major pressing operation, and a superb one, to boot.

"We met with the FBI," Gershon says. "We couldn't even identify the bootlegs. The artwork was fabulous. Under a spectroscope you could see the quality of the vinyl, which was cheaper than our vinyl. Ours was more flexible. Otherwise, you could not tell.

"*Fever* and *Grease* helped destroy the business. People began to think aha! You could go platinum times ten, platinum times twenty, if you hit the right one. The expectations of every record company became totally demented and deluded because they all saw that little RSO Records was able to become a half-billion-dollar-a-year company. From nothing."

RSO's next move was *Sgt. Pepper's Lonely Hearts Club Band,* with Peter Frampton and the Bee Gees. George Martin, the Beatles arranger, had been brought in to produce. The assumption was that it would be another whammo and Stigwood sent out three million albums. "We shipped triple platinum. That was unheard of," Gershon says. "Lo and behold! The movie stiffed. The album stiffed."

The mob had a pressing operation in the Midwest, and were moving the albums out. "The FBI told us that the word got out to the guys driving a convoy of trucks that the *Pepper's* were valueless. They found them all dumped on the side of some road in Southern California.

"We sent out three million albums. And we probably had to take back more than four million returns. It was the beginning of the end. Robert said we're a small record company. Why bother staying in a business that is no longer very profitable?" He closed down RSO Records shortly after.

Gloria Gaynor was a diva, the "Queen of Disco," according to a poll of DJs, who crowned her in Le Jardin. "It was quite a big affair. So many people showed up," she says. In 1978, she was asked what she would like to record as the B side of a single. Her mother had just died, and she herself had had back surgery, so she decided to deal with that. The result was "I Will Survive." She recorded it wearing a brace. "It was broken out in Studio 54," Gaynor says.

"I Will Survive" became an anthem. Then Gaynor went through changes. Her father was a musician, and she had grown up listening to jazz. "I never was what is called religious," she says. "My grandmother was very religious and inundated my mother with church, so my mother decided if she had children she would never make them go to church. There was a Bible in the house, but my mother read it as if it was a novel. I read it when I was in trouble. Like so many of us do."

She returned to it at the height of her success. "What happened was that I didn't like the shenanigans going on in the music business. I was constantly struggling with that."

Gaynor worked her way through Scientology, transcendental meditation, and Buddhism. "Then I sat down with my Bible. And I called out to God. And He spoke to me. And I was what you call Born Again," she says.

Donna Summer, who became outspoken about a religion from which she had never really strayed, would have harsh words about, for instance, gays. Gloria Gaynor was more tranquil. "My positive view of it is that beyond the sex and drugs, there was a camaraderie," she says. "People in the business and the clubs recognizing that they weren't the only ones on the planet . . ."

But disco was dead for both divas. For the time being.

There is another reading to the death of disco. It never actually happened! The clutter—the disco shirts, disco chains, and disco balls—went into thrift shops. The tattier discos folded. But the music simply mutated; indeed, triumphed as dance music. "There's a lot of disco in new wave and rap," says Michael Zilkha, a spry Briton who came to New York in 1976 and founded a record label, Ze.

Ze was ground-breaking in its signing of new wave and punk performers, like Kid Creole, Lydia Lunch, Teenage Jesus and the Jerks.

Soon Zilkha turned his attention to disco. "What I figured out was if you had a disco beat, which was the right relationship of the bass to the drums, the weirder the stuff you put it over, the more it would sustain repeated listening," he says. "If you had a disco beat, you could have really depressing material."

He made a terrific move in the summer of 1978, signing up the Contortions to do a disco album. James Chance and the Contortions were one of the ultra-punkest of the New York bands. "They used to beat up their fans," Zilkha says. They made the disco album under another name, James White and the Blacks. "They did a concert at Irving Plaza, miming to their music, which nobody did then, and got covers of the *Soho Weekly News* and *The Village Voice*."

That winter Zilkha had his then wife, Cristina Monet-Palaci, make a single, "Disco Clone." It was produced by John Cale formerly of the Velvet Underground. It was Cale's one and only venture into disco, but he has a certain abstract enthusiasm for the form. "It was a search for perfection," he says. "It was in admiration of James Brown's demanding precision. He would say, 'If you play the wrong note I'm going to dock your pay a hundred dollars!' There was a kind of mentality of absolute exactitude. The electric metronome came in and it would not change by one iota. It was rigid all the way through."

"Disco Clone" was a witty piece of fluff in which Monet is backed by a male voice intoning lyrics like

WENT DOWN TO THE DISCO LAST SATURDAY NIGHT
LOOKING FOR ACTION AND FEELING ALRIGHT
ONE LADY DANCING WAS SUCH A DELIGHT

The first person hired was Tony de Portago, the son of an iconic jet setter of the fifties, who killed himself in one of the fast set's most reliable modes of self-destruction, pre–hard drugs: a car wreck. Tony, who was the former husband of Antonia de Portago, was deleted as sounding "too foreign." The next male backup hired was myself. A long overdue stab at stardom, I decided.

I, too, was deleted. I was told I sounded "too mature." The third person hired was an unknown actor. In my irritation, I hoped he would remain unknown. His name was Kevin Kline. Apparently the single did rather well in Germany.

Neil Bogart sold Casablanca Records to Polygram in 1980. He had talked with Rubell and Schrager about buying Studio. "Neil was close with Steve, but he was *very* close with Ian. Their minds worked alike in creating visions for people to have fun in," Joyce Bogart says. "Ian was really the person who structured everything." The talks came to nothing, though. Too much was going on. Too much success. Too much cocaine. Too much muchness.

Bogart was diagnosed as suffering from a cancer in 1981. "He got a transfusion. At Cedars," Joyce Bogart says in her telegraphic manner. "Nobody thought twice about it. It was before we knew about the blood supply." Neil died later that year.

People felt differently about the safety of the blood supply scant months later.

*　　*　　*

Billy Idol, who would be an avatar of punk-disco crossover, and one of the first Brit punks to move to the U.S., happened to spend his early childhood in New York State. His father, who had married an American Irish woman, ran a laundry in Patchogue, Long Island. The family returned to England, and Idol grew up in Worthing, a resort on the south coast of England. Great timing. He was right on to catch one of the last great style wars, the mods versus the rockers. "They used to come down the High Street and take all the windows out like marauding bands. That was brilliant," he says. "When you're really young you ought to believe in chaos." The first high-energy rock band he saw was the Detroit band, MC5. It was at Fun City, a free festival outside Worthing. "I was twelve and a half, smoking hash," he says. "They got me because they were dressed in spangled suits. They made a show. Everybody else was hippie."

But, elephantiasis struck British rock. "It all got further and further away and bigger and bigger," Billy says. "The bands became so massive that they didn't play clubs anymore. Then everybody went to America or whatever. We felt very left high and dry by our own music.

"There was this massive kind of hole. And it was then that disco came thrashing through."

Disco grew quickly to be huge in Britain in the early seventies, especially in the London suburbs, such as Bromley, where Billy was then living. Proto-punks despised it. "Going down to the Wine Bar, dancing to disco, knowing you had to have a Ford Cortina," Billy says. "It was music that meant you had a job and you danced on Friday. We called it the 'weekend generation.'

"There were cool things about disco. I wouldn't say we didn't like some of it. It wasn't like we were in a little shell of a world where you wouldn't use disco ideas once you started to understand them. But our basic blast was to blow that out of the water. We liked David Bowie and Marc Bolan and people like that, the glam side of things, as a reaction to disco. But even so disco hung on. Until punk rock put a nail through it. For a few years . . ."

Billy joined a band. It was called Chelsea. "The whole thing was centered on the Kings Road. Because of Malcolm McLaren's shop," he says. (This was the boutique, called Sex, where McLaren and his partner, Vivienne Westwood, sold such *haut punk* attire as rubber T-shirts.) Their music was transformed when they heard New York punk, specifically the first Ramones record. "We were still doing things at normal speed," he says. "For instance, the Sex Pistols never got faster. They stayed a midpace band, which was probably a good idea.

"But when we all got the Ramones record, it sent us and the Clash and everyone into the whirlwind music. We just embraced it completely. You had to be out of it, crazy, to love this music."

They changed their name to Generation X, a borrowing from the title to a book of pop sociology. He changed his name in 1976. At first, he was going to take the name "Idle" because he had been so described in a school report card, but Eric Idle, one of the Monty Python crew, seemed to have nailed that down. "Then it hit me like a ton of bricks," he says. "I'm not idle, like lazy. It's more like a rock idol. Like the fifties. That's what we felt we were bringing back after disco had really created this wasteland. Of nothingness!

"There was a massive polarization at first. Because part of what we wanted to do with punk rock was to attack. And so at first we were most definitely trying to do music that had nothing to do with disco music. We wanted music that was wild, crazy, chaotic. Nothing to do with steady beats and stuff. You had this belief that it could only make its mark. There was no way that people could stop this aggression."

Idol arrived in New York in 1978 on a PR tour for Generation X. He was instantly taken to Studio 54. "Most people, even in New York, didn't understand about punk that much. So the first thing they thought to do was take you to a disco. Then you had to find your own way down to the Mudd Club," he said.

A young Englishwoman Perri Lister was also in New York. She was a dancer with Hot Gossip, a dance troupe whose energetically sexy routines had made them wildly popular with the British TV audience. "We were six white girls and three black guys. Mary Whitehouse tried to have us banned," says Lister. Whitehouse was the voice of British morality at the time, so naturally her exertions generated more attention for Hot Gossip. This attention got them the movie contract that brought them to New York to appear in a disco movie, *Can't Stop the Music,* produced by the flamboyant and overweight Allan Carr, still trailing clouds of glory as the co-producer of *Grease* with Robert Stigwood.

"We were filming in the Village that summer," Lister says. Another movie was being filmed in the Village, as it happened, *Cruising.* It had become known that this movie, in which Al Pacino played a cop, was about a sequence of murders in the gay bar scene. "There were these big signs all over saying STOP THE MOVIE 'CRUISING.'

"One day we were filming on the street. Allan Carr was just standing there, and this guy came up with a baseball bat, and just whacked him! And he fell over. And, you know, he's so rotund he couldn't get up. He hit him across the back, not on the skull or anything, and he's rolling, and we're laughing hysterically. Suddenly the Village People come running out of their trailer, going, 'We're not filming *Cruising*! We're the Village People!' So, of course, these people felt awful. But they were arrested anyway. I mean, it was a terrible thing to do. To anybody."

The shenanigans in the street over *Cruising* were not an anomaly. Gay assertiveness was on the rise, and in Nightworld too. Gay clubs, like the Flamingo and Le Jardin, had always had women and straight hipsters among their clientele—cheerfully, at Michael Fesco's club, a mite icily at John Addison's—but every night was gay night at the grandest new addition to the nightlife, the Saint.

The Saint opened in 1980 in what had once been Bill Graham's Fillmore East. It was started by Bruce Mailman, a short man with the pursed-up look of a loan officer. No alcohol was served in the Saint. It was about music, and drugs, and sex, all in settings of splendid theatricality. "The Saint was spectacular," Michael Fesco of the Flamingo says.

"I had thought we would survive," he added wistfully. "But with a gay crowd, if you feel like you're not in the place that's *in* right now, you don't feel you're in the right place. The thing I forgot was how fickle people are. No matter how much people say they love your club and everything . . ."

The Flamingo closed in February 1981. There are devotees who will tell you to this day that it was the best nightclub of all.

The single that Generation X's label put out in the United States was accompanied by a photograph of Billy Idol with a punk hairdo. This proved to be a poor marketing decision. The single died. Idol returned to England. Perri Lister concluded the New York shooting and wrapped in L.A. Then she went back to England, too. "That's when I met Billy," she says. "I was performing at Caesar's Palace, Luton. Which is about as much like Caesars Palace as a hamster's cage."

The two became an item. *Can't Stop the Music* did not, except as a famous flop.

CLUB FED

14

STEVE RUBELL WOULD LATER TELL DAVID KNAPP, HIS driver in the Palladium days, about his first tussle in the Metropolitan Correction Center. He was asked, according to the standard practice, to surrender his belt. The belt had been a present. " 'Why?' he said. 'I like this belt. I would like to keep it.'

"They said, 'No. You can't. You might hang yourself with it.'

"Steve said, 'Why would I ever consider hanging myself? You must be out of your mind!' "

His first day in the slammer was the worst. The MCC, a bleak brutalist building downtown abutting Police Plaza, is supposedly for felons on their way to other prisons elsewhere. Rubell walked into the recreation room. There was a Spanish-language program on the TV. The czar of Studio 54 switched the channel.

Error.

"Next thing I knew I was outside, hanging from a hook," Rubell told me soon after his release. A group of inmates had strung him up by the neck of his drab army shirt on a nail in the wall outside the workout area. Rubell fell into a sort of a void, aware of nothing. "Except it was a freezing February day," he said. "Nobody was doing weights. I lost any sense of time. I didn't know if I would ever be found."

He was found and unhooked and he was smart enough to keep his mouth shut. Bill Hamilton remembers making some idle joke or other, long after Rubell's release, about the prison sentence handed out to Leona Helmsley, the hotel magnate's wife, the infamous Queen of Mean. Rubell had been upset by Hamilton's joke. "He said prison was the worst experience of his life. It was just a very, very bad time. You're Jewish, you're a criminal. You hear that cell door slam behind you," Hamilton says. "Both he and Ian felt that they would never wish it upon anybody, no matter how mean they were or how wrong they were."

Steven Rubell called Halston on Valentine's Day a couple of weeks after their arrival. "Diana Ross got on the phone. They were all going to Studio after. I got so depressed," Rubell told the writer Jesse Kornbluth.

The Hamilton Jordan investigation had been taken over by a special prosecutor. Peter Sudler, who had been much more interested in general malfeasance in Nightworld than in the dabblings of a particular pol, had Steve and Ian hauled over to the U.S. Attorney's Office, which is alongside the MCC. Sudler is canny. "They absolutely hated the food in the detention center," he said. "They give you a slice of baloney on white bread.

"I waited until about two o'clock in the afternoon. We went out and ordered a gigantic meal in Chinatown. We had all this great Chinese food sitting there. And they went absolutely bananas when they saw all this food. I said, 'Jesus! We'd love to share our lunch. But you're not on the team. . . . '"

Sudler remembers that they broke that day. He had his list of wants.

Together they compiled a list of people who had been paid off the books. The main targets, though, were their former partners and current rivals, John Addison and Maurice Brahms. Turning people in has become standard operation procedure in the criminal justice system. It is indeed one of that system's main motors, but it was not a process either Rubell or Schrager relished. "They put records in front of us and asked us what they meant," Ian Schrager later told writer Michael Gross. "They said, 'Either you play along or you keep breaking the law.' We played along. We had no choice actually." The Feds can squeeze until bones are pulp.

Steve Rubell, the people person, did what he could to have a good time in prison. Ian Schrager, the introvert, settled into intensive reading. He read biographies of "great men," in particular, and was particularly impressed by a book on media moguls by David Halberstam. "That's what got me out of the doldrums. All those guys had interludes, and consolidated," he told a reporter later. "Granted, they didn't go to jail. Mine and Steve's interlude was a forced one. Bill Paley's interlude was to be a war correspondent. He came out and decided to do CBS. Chandler came out and decided to take the *LA Times*."

If Steve Rubell was consummately the Late 20th Century man, there is something nineteenth century, indeed Dickensian, what with his fierce belief in privacy and learning from hard knocks, about Ian Schrager. After seven months in the MCC Rubell and Schrager were transferred. They were to spend their last six months on Maxwell Air Force Base in Montgomery, Alabama. Meanwhile, of course, Rubell and Schrager's night kingdom was up for grabs. John Addison and Maurice Brahms, ignorant that wheels were turning, were doing the grabbing.

"Here's what happened," Arthur Weinstein says. "I had a bug up my ass to bury Studio 54. Because they buried me. I was a kid." Steve Rubell and Ian Schrager hadn't yet gone to jail when he chanced on Bond's, a defunct clothing store in Times Square. "I got in there. I've got photographs," he says. It was a block-long colossus designed by Donald Deckie, who later designed the Radio City Music Hall. "I got *obsessed* with it. It was all I could think about," Weinstein says. "U.S. Steel owned the building. Where was I going to get the money? I put a proposal together and went to Robert Stigwood's pad. The guy at the door said, 'Go fuck yourself, Mr. Stigwood ain't seeing nobody.'

"After that, I went to see John Addison. He told me I was crazy. I mean, no, it wasn't too enormous. No! Nine thousand square feet of open space!" Weinstein hammered and hammered away. "We had married. Our daughter, Dahlia, was just born. We didn't have a quarter. Because all I was doing was trying to get this place together. Dealing an ounce of pot here and there. We hardly had money for diapers. Two lean years followed."

Addison affected disinterest. Briefly, some entrepreneur from Long Island horned in with the notion of transforming the place into a dance palace with an Egyptian motif. He faded. Then Addison called Weinstein. "We got it!" he announced. "It was all your idea. We're going to kill him! Because he wanted to bury Rubell too. Guess what!" Weinstein dissolved in mirth. *"We never heard another word!"* Weinstein was out. This was standard operating procedure in Nightworld.

Maurice Brahms was the official owner, because Addison couldn't get a license. In actuality, Addison and Brahms went in as partners. They put over a million and a half dollars into the place—"more than had ever been spent on a Manhattan nightclub," Brahms says. Maurice Brahms hired Baird Jones to make parties there. "Maurice gave me a tennis ball and said I'll give you ten bucks if you can throw this across the dance floor. My wind-up took me halfway across the dance floor. And I couldn't make it," Jones says. Its hugeness was overwhelming. "There was another floor downstairs," Jones says. "There was an above floor with five or six VIP rooms that were as big as nightclubs are today. I said, 'Maurice, I can't fill this club!' " He took the job nonetheless.

Bond's International Casino opened its tremendous doors in July 1980. A sort of a limp zeppelin bobbed languidly around the club's roof and there were fountains from *The Liberace Show* on the floor. It began consciously as a post-disco. "We play all sorts of music, from 'The Blue Danube' to new wave like the B-52's and Blondie, and then conventional disco," Addison told the photographer Jill Lynne. He exulted over the musical staircase and the fountains, which were usually filled with near-naked men. "We've even had incidents of people jumping in fully clothed," Addison boasted.

Addison was finally prevailed upon to let Arthur Weinstein do a party there to make himself some dough. Joey Hunter, who ran the male division at Ford Models, was friendly with Weinstein from his days as a photographer, and agreed to let Ford men be the lure on the invitation. The party was a smash. "There was such a crowd they broke the fucking doors," Weinstein says. "Maurice was running around like a lunatic. Like his suit was on fire. There had to be six thousand people in the place.

"I said, 'Maurice, do you think I could have $300?' He gave it so quick.

It was like I didn't even blink. Sure, you can have $300. I should have got $3,000. I was a kid then." Studio 54 was about to be pulverized.

Plato's Retreat was in fine fettle, as a straight version of the thriving hard-core gay clubs.

The government, of course, was keeping a beady eye on its finances. In mid-1979 a couple of IRS inspectors went in to conduct an audit. "Plato's accountant got sick halfway through," Peter Sudler says. "They asked the secretary for the books."

It is possible that the secretary had been chosen for, say, grooming, rather than rapier wits. "She said, 'Do you want the second set too?'

"Yeah . . ."

The second set were a bit different. The IRS men called Sudler from a telephone kiosk on the corner.

Good morning, Judge. Larry Levenson got six years. Hi Gordon got the same.

Maurice Brahms was living with his family in Harrison, New York. John Addison was sharing an apartment with Fifi Nicholas on West Fifty-seventh Street just over the road from Carnegie Hall. Early in the morning of August 4, 1980, each dwelling received a shock: a visit from agents of the Criminal Investigation Division of the IRS. Addison had the luck of living in a doorman building. "John was fortunate," Brahms says. "He threw a lot of the information they were looking for out of the window. It fell into an alleyway."

But the feds got quite a haul from each place anyway. Brahms hired James La Rosa to be his attorney and Roy Cohn offered to put together a joint defense for Addison and Fifi Nicholas. Shortly thereafter Brahms got hold of the documentation that had papered the raid and found the source of his woes. Not only had Schrager and Rubell given the feds information but they had used Honey Aldrich, a Studio loyalist, to put pressure on her friend, a cashier at New York, New York, named Liane Jensen. "Steve and Ian got her to turn me in. That was how they got the search warrants," Brahms says. "Without Liane, all they had was hearsay. But Liane had real information. Liane could tell how John came in and took out $20,000. She could tell how I called every night."

Brahms saw Roy Cohn's fingerprints all over the deal and told Addison that the lawyer was a traitor. "He's my friend. He's my ex-lover," Addison protested. But Brahms went with La Rosa and confronted Roy Cohn in his office. Cohn acted the innocent, saying of Rubell and Schrager, "Our friendship is over. They're rats."

"You're a lying coward," Brahms said.

Cohn thumped the table with his fist. "It's Roy Cohn you're talking to," he bawled.

La Rosa separated them and went with Cohn into another room. Cohn came back and was cordial. "I understand that you're upset, Maurice," he said. "And I want you to know that I'll do what I can."

"I looked into his eyes. I could see he was lying," Brahms says. "I shook his hand. I said, 'Thanks, Roy, I'll call if something comes up.'"

Brahms was, and remains, white-hot. "You couldn't believe that somebody as charming as Rubell could be so treacherous," he says. "He was a devil. He and Roy Cohn were the two most evil people I have ever met. Schrager was quiet and laid-back, and he wasn't as dangerous. But he would never say no to Rubell. Even when it came to turning people in, he never said no."

A whole slew of people who had been paid off the books were named in the indictment, but the no longer low-profile Maurice Brahms got the attention. "Roy Cohn made up a story that I had threatened their lives," he says. "That I had threatened to kill them. All right? And he put it in the newspaper . . . 'Rumor has it that Maurice Brahms has threatened the lives of Rubell and Schrager' . . . It was terrifying. My kids were being teased at school. My wife said, 'What's happening? Everyone thinks we're gangsters! That we're Mafia!'"

Addison and Brahms were both pressured to plead guilty. "They terrified me. That if I challenged them, he would come after me with everything. For the rest of your life. It's awesome to have a prosecutor say that. And your lawyer says the prosecutor's angry. What did you do to him?" Brahms adds dismally. "I shouldn't have pleaded guilty. I would have beaten it."

They pleaded guilty.

The legal documentation is fastidious. It relates how

DURING 1974 AND 1975 THEY [RUBELL AND SCHRAGER] WERE PARTNERS WITH AD-
DISON AND NICHOLAS IN SEVERAL DISCOTHÈQUES. . . . ADDISON TAUGHT RUBELL AND
SCHRAGER HOW TO SKIM CASH RECEIPTS, HOW TO HIDE THESE SKIMMED RECEIPTS
FROM DETECTION BY THE GOVERNMENT AND ALSO THE ART OF "LAUNDERING" THE
CASH. WHEN THE FOUR OPENED "15 LANSDOWNE STREET," RUBELL LAUNDERED
$100,000 IN CASH BELONGING TO ADDISON AND NICHOLAS THROUGH HIS STEAK LOFT
RESTAURANTS.

This, incidentally, was so as to disguise Addison's interest in the place—
the cash was hidden in the meat bill—because Addison had been deemed by
the SLA an "unfit person" to hold a liquor license on account of his criminal
record, and this taint might have attached itself to Schrager and Rubell.

Even after the downfall of their students, Rubell and Schrager, Addison
and Brahms had merrily kept on skimming. One document makes the acerbic
point: "Apparently the only lesson learned by the defendants from seeing their
former partners, Steven Rubell and Ian Schrager, get incarcerated for 3½ years
for skimming from 'Studio 54,' was don't keep the second set of books at the
discothèque, keep them at home instead."

A footnote to the document begins: "Rather than feel remorse for the
crimes which he committed, Brahms' sole preoccupation since his criminality
has been discovered concerns taking revenge against Steven Rubell and Ian
Schrager, the persons he blames for his present predicament."

Maurice Brahms and John Addison were put under intense pressure to help
New York police the wildness of Nightworld. Brahms wouldn't cave in. He
recalls one time Sudler was giving him a hard time in his office. "I said, 'Why
do you make me the bad guy and them the good guys?' " he remembers.
"They've suffered enough. Ian has had a breakdown. Give them a break!"
Sudler told him.

John Addison buckled under the strain and turned in a man who had been
laundering money for him. That man fled the country. "I told him he was no
better than Rubell and Schrager. He got a three-month sentence and he cried
every day," says Maurice Brahms.

Brahms was obdurate with Sudler and on December 12, 1980, the prosecutor made his presentencing report. "Brahms has refused to cooperate with

the Government in any respect. His cooperating could have been extremely valuable had he chosen to give it," he wrote. His recommendation: "Under no circumstances should Brahms EVER be paroled." "Al Capone maybe gets a report like that," Brahms says. He was sentenced to three years and went into Allenwood Federal Penitentiary on January 5, 1981.

The Clash, the British group anointed to be saviors of rock and roll, played Bond's while Addison was in the joint. "Do you think John would have been hip enough to book them?" Arthur Weinstein asked. They filled the colossal club for three nights. It was glorious, but it was the glory of the sunset, at least for the notion that clubs could grow forever bigger, like trees reaching the sky. "That was the end. Clubs couldn't sustain that. They needed to shrink," says the pop archivist, Brad Balfour.

Rudolf Pieper, a fledgling Nightbird, ran into Addison soon after his release. The club by this stage had no noticeable door policy whatsoever, so you had to be careful whose toes you trod on. "John would sell his soul to fill the place," says Blue Flettrich. But it was degenerating into a huge nothing of a club. Rudolf describes Addison as a broken man. "He wasn't angry with Steve and Ian. He was sad," Rudolf says. "I think he went to Florida quite soon."

Maurice Brahms remained in Allenwood the customary two thirds of his sentence. "I had been flying high. I had three successful clubs. It was over," he mourns. Ian Schrager's and Steve Rubell's jail terms began melting like ice cubes in a pitcher of warm wine.

It was not, of course, over for Brahms at all. The feisty clubman would never forgive Addison for cooperating with the feds, and the cousins never spoke again. Florida wasn't Manhattan, but John Addison's activities were pretty colorful, according to Baird Jones, who kept in touch, at least via gossip. "John Addison—I call him 'Uncle John,' by the way—started these underage strip joints, where all the people have to be underage to come in," Jones says. "They have like these sixteen-year-old girls doing topless. They proof them to get into the club. You have to prove you're under eighteen. And it's a runaway success."

Baird was out of date. I traced Addison back into his very first profession.

He had a plant business called the Rebel Nursery in Loxahatchee, near West Palm. He sold out in about 1995, according to another nurseryman, and died of AIDS shortly thereafter.

Mark Fleischman had seen his opportunity. He had realized Rubell and Schrager were bound to lose their liquor license as soon as they had been sentenced. "Liquor licenses in those days had to be renewed every March 1. They went to jail on February 1. On February 28, they wouldn't renew and there was no liquor. Steve and Ian had tried to put a phony board together—a bunch of fancy names—and say it was the new owners of Studio 54. But the liquor authorities wouldn't go with that." Neil Bogart had talked with Steve and Ian about buying Studio, but disco was dead, and soon Casablanca would belly-up with it. Dick Clark, the veteran of rock and roll television, had also fashioned a bid. So Mark Fleischman made his move.

"I knew Roy Cohn through negotiating with them earlier," Fleischman says. Cohn began slipping him in on visits to MCC in March under the pretense that he was an attorney. The visits continued after the pair had gone to Alabama.

Secrets are hard to keep in Nightworld. One evening Fleischman had run into Maurice Brahms in Bond's. "It was just before he was going to jail, and he was very, very upset. I could understand it. He knew I was negotiating with Steve and Ian. He looked me in the eye. He said: *'Don't buy Studio 54!'*

"I said, 'Well. I've already signed the agreement.' He said, 'This is very bad! This is a very bad buy! This is very bad karma!' I mean, it was like a curse he was putting on me for touching Studio 54."

It had been a complex deal. The feds and the state had a $3 million lien on the building, which was what they estimated Steve and Ian owed in back taxes. Fleischman agreed that he and his backers, primarily Stanley Tate, would assume this lien. He agreed to make the state and the feds a down payment of $500,000, and said he would pay them a chunk of the weekly gross.

Mark Fleischman was to pay Steve and Ian several million dollars, which would instantly go to the taxman, and a further $2,500 weekly, for "consultancy." They made an undertaking not to compete in the nightclub business for eighteen months. There was also a lump sum for the two and until it had been fully paid, Fleischman agreed he would do nothing to tarnish the name of Studio 54, and that Steve and Ian would have control over the aesthetic policy, and the staff.

Fleischman had assumed getting a liquor license would be easy. "I had been to the Cornell School of Hotel Administration. I had run officers' clubs as a lieutenant in the navy. I had a lot of liquor licenses in the state of New York. Clean. No problems. I had to have a liquor license. I had a right! But it's a very arbitrary agency. They hated Steve and Ian so much that it took eighteen months. By that time, the place had gotten very cold. People said disco is dead. It's over!"

It wasn't dead at the Virgin Islands Hilton in St. Thomas, though. Fleischman took a whole bunch of Studio 54 hands there, including Michael Overington and Marc Benecke, and set up a disco, with Marc at the door. "St. Thomas was *raging*," Fleischman says. "But I didn't realize the islands were such a pain in the neck. There's crime. There're things going on that really kill you." Literally, almost. "Somebody threatened Marc with a gun. And something snapped in his head. He didn't want to be a doorman anymore. He was right. He had a way of really infuriating people. And one day someone would have got him."

Mark Fleischman's sweet Caribbean dreams curdled.

Thus it went until Fleischman *did* get a license. It was September 1981. One of the conditions was telling: No VIP Room with decadent doings in the basement. "I had to sign a piece of paper with the State Liquor Authorities agreeing not to run a basement operation. That was the condition," Mark Fleischman said. He chuckled richly. "Of course, we went upstairs. The offices replaced the basement . . ." He was beginning to really get into the Nightworld.

Rubell's and Schrager's first job at Maxwell Air Force Base was to cut two miles of grass beneath a chain-link fence, for which they were each issued a pair of scissors. They shared a room for a while, Schrager won the toss, but let Rubell sleep in the bottom bunk. He joked later that this was better than having to listen to him complain for the rest of their time. "Jail made our friendship more intense," Schrager said later, but acknowledged that their prison careers had rather different arcs. The tainted reputation of Max Schrager had always haunted his son. Going to prison and losing his lawyer's license was just about as ugly a thing as Ian Schrager could imagine. He came near a breakdown. He felt like a failure. A low-life. "I had a harder time in jail," Schrager told Jesse Kornbluth later, with characteristic knottedness. "Steve was still around people. I found no consolation."

"Give me a tree and I'm okay," Rubell had concurred blithely. Certainly, Rubell had fewer inner demons. Sometimes to the point of sappiness. "I used to have dinner at my parents' house every week," he said later of that time when Studio was burning bright. "I thought I was the same old guy. I didn't realize I had lost my way. I never thought I was hurting anybody. I enjoyed it so much. Every day I looked forward to the night. But I was like a permissive parent. I let everybody do what they wanted. And I paid the price."

In jail, too, the Nightworld king showed a noonday personality. "He said he was in charge of organizing prisoners' birthday parties. And that they threw some good parties in prison," David Knapp says. Ian Schrager has described Steve as the mayor in prison much as he had been in Studio. "He would play handball and racquetball against the other inmates," Bill Hamilton says. "Ian was telling him, 'Knock it off. These guys will kill you! Over winning a game. Lose!' " Rubell would go ahead and beat them anyway.

Ian Schrager was made a busboy. Steve Rubell became the superintendent's driver. They talked interminably about their rise and their fall. "Things don't just happen," Rubell later told the writer Michael Daly. "It had to be a major problem, a weakness in character. Greed and stupidity." The two were targets of some free-floating hostility, based on the fact that they were (formerly) rich and famous and that they were going to be out in a matter of months; there were inmates there looking at great lengths of years. "I guess there were a couple of black guys that were picking on him," Hamilton says.

Steve Rubell had his own way of dealing with that. A woman telephoned. "She said 'Is Steve Rubell there?' " Hamilton says. "They said, 'Yeah. Who's calling?' "

" 'Diana Ross.' " *Diana Ross!*

Rubell's brush with racial problems in the federal system vanished.

Ian Schrager didn't expect to hear from many people. Why should he? He had always been background. But Steve needed people. Roy Cohn became the middleman. Cohn said in a conversation taped by his longtime telephone switchboard operator Chris Seymour:

WHEN HE AND IAN WERE IN JAIL, STEVE WOULD CALL ME AT HOME, COLLECT, AND SINCE I HAD A CONFERENCE PHONE—I REALLY HAD TWO OF THEM—I WOULD CONNECT STEVE TO WHOEVER HE WANTED TO TALK TO.

ONCE HE CALLED LIZA MINNELLI—WHO WAS STAYING AT HALSTON'S HOUSE OUT ON LONG ISLAND—AND THEY WERE TALKING ABOUT HER SONG "NEW YORK, NEW YORK," AND HOW SHE WAS FURIOUS WITH FRANK SINATRA—HAVING THE SAME SONG. "MINE IS SO MUCH BETTER. FRANK IS SUCH A PISTOL." BUT SHE NEVER SAID THAT IN PUBLIC.

WITH STEVE CALLING ME EVERY NIGHT, I REALLY HAD TO LAUGH, BECAUSE AT THE TIME THERE WAS AN ARTICLE IN *NEW YORK* MAGAZINE ABOUT STEVE CALLING PEOPLE, AND THE A, B, AND C LISTS. WHICH LIST WAS EVERYONE ON? I CERTAINLY WAS ON THE A LIST—I CONNECTED HIM TO THESE PEOPLE.

Well, to some of these people. Many were loyal. Claudia Cohen. Bianca Jagger. Others, including a great many who had enjoyed his hospitality nightly, were proving oddly elusive. Jim Fouratt said that, judging by his conversations with Rubell later, it wasn't jail itself that was so terrible. "He felt abandoned . . . so lonely . . . he really was hurt by that."

But if the outside world wasn't checking in, Rubell could still check it out. The hotel business was on his mind, but that was virgin territory where Rubell and Schrager were concerned, and Steve, in particular, was keeping a weather eye on clubland. Nightworld, he realized, was again undergoing a metamorphosis. "One thing he felt had changed was that the *Saturday Night Fever* thing was no longer there. The dancing mania had completely evaporated," Baird Jones says. As a jungle animal can sniff information on a breeze, Rubell had a good reporter's instinct for rootling clues out of anecdotes, gossip columns, and glimmery-papered magazines, even from behind prison walls. He was telephoning Arthur and Colleen Weinstein, for instance, a couple of times a week. "He became convinced that new wave was where it was at . . ." Baird Jones says.

"Steve called me from jail," Jim Fouratt says. Fouratt was now running Manhattan's hottest joint, Danceteria, with Rudolf, who'd become distinctly higher profile, partly because of his consort. This was Dianne Brill, a young woman from Florida with the burstingly ripe shape of an old-fashioned pin-up, which she would clothe in outfits of her own design in striking materials, like rubber.

"Steve said that he had had to sell Studio, but that he and Ian would still be controlling it." He told Fouratt that what he and Rudolf were doing was the first new thing in Nightworld since Studio itself. Rubell also said he wanted Fouratt to get involved with Studio. Fouratt said fine.

Fouratt asked, "Do we need Rudolf?"

"Yes," said Rubell.

Should Fouratt and Rudolf visit. *No!* Steve and Ian were getting out. Then they and Jim and Rudolf would *talk*.

Steve Rubell and Ian Schrager were released on the morning of January 21, 1981. Rubell had spent much of his last few days giving himself a tan by holding a sheet of silver foil beneath his chin on the jail's baseball field. "I didn't want people to say, 'He looks beaten,' " he later said.

Honey Aldrich picked them up at the airport. Rubell was garrulous, Schrager withdrawn. Aldrich gave them each a pair of striped pajamas and dropped them off at their halfway house on Columbus and Seventy-fourth Street, where theoretically they had an eleven o'clock curfew. It took an hour to check themselves in. It was a sunny day in Manhattan and Rubell treated himself to a walk through Central Park. "I think that was the happiest time of my life," Rubell told me. That day Bianca Jagger gave him a Cartier watch and told him that now was the time to start all over again. He was forty, slightly balding, as energetic as ever.

GOBLIN
BETWEEN THE ACTS: I
MARKET

BACKWARDS UP THE MOSSY GLEN
TURNED AND TROOPED THE GOBLIN MEN,
WITH THEIR SHRILL REPEATED CRY,
"COME BUY, COME BUY."

CHRISTINA ROSSETTI

KIDS, WHICH IS TO SAY, RICH KIDS, or attractive kids, or kids coming from some place interesting, had been prized elements in
Steve Rubell's salad—the baby lettuce, say, or the spring onions—
from the beginning. It was a favorite venue for the black-tie high
school prom–type bashes, which were a phenomenon of the late
seventies, and at which the nursery dowager was Cornelia Guest,
then still in ninth grade, somewhat before she turned being deb
of the year into a hardy perennial.

Brooke Shields, who had just become Calvin Klein's pubescent jeans model, likewise went to Studio regularly. "You could
just dance and sweat and have a good time, and you supposedly
were cool because that supposedly was the place everybody
wanted to go," she says. "I had my friends at school come with
me. I was always able to have fun."

Asked if the spectacle of bizarrely dressed folks, making out
near-naked hadn't been worrying, she said, "I wasn't interested
in them. I wanted to meet Jimmy McNichol. I was fourteen." As
some will recall, Jimmy McNichol was a teen idol of the time.

Brooke Shields, anyway, was practically a senior compared to
some of the kids vying to outdo the grownups in and around
Studio. The model Bitten Knudsen, herself then just seventeen,
remembers running into a covey of what looked like eleven-year-
olds by the entrance. "Their clothes had hangers in them. They
were hooked up," Bitten says. "I said, 'Well, what are you guys
doing?'

"A little girl said, 'I'm so happy someone's asking. We're
hanging out!' She was so dying to say it, and nobody had asked
her."

Elyn Wollensky, a writer, remembers a young cousin baby-
sitting her while her parents were away and her brother and sister were at boarding school. "He came over and said, 'Put on
your funkiest clothing. We're going out!' I put on the most ridiculous makeup you can imagine. Blue eye shadow I had stolen

from my grandmother, and a really thick blush, Estee Lauder goop. And I put on this little outfit I used to wear to parties. It was a mix between a Lilly Pulitzer school print and a sort of a plaid dress with crinolines. A red plaid with puffy sleeves and a little bow in the back.''

Off they went. She had been ecstatic when her cousin said they were going to Studio 54. *''There was this big article in Newsweek about the movers and shakers of Studio. And I wanted to go there. I wanted to be with them!'' she says. ''I remember thinking I don't want to go to boarding school. I want to go to Studio!''*

She had been eight when she read the article. She was now ten.

About getting in, *''they didn't ask questions,''* Wollensky says. *''They thought I was funky. I had on my sister's heels, Ferragamo pumps. I guess they thought I was trying to look young.''*

About any specific recollections of the evening, well yes. Somehow she and her cousin had found their way into one of the VIP cubicles. *''It was a man,''* Wollensky says. *''I swear to God, he was jumping around on the table with just chicken feathers on his arms and a G-string. It was just too much. He was hopping around, and screaming 'I am nouveau art! I am nouveau art!' I wanted to go home. But I got really drunk and when I did get home, I threw up. When my parents heard about that, I was grounded until I was about twelve.''*

That was Kids' World in Studio 54, Act I. It had been accidental. Kids' World in Studio, Act II, was a program.

Bea Breuer also first got into Studio at fourteen. *''I went with a girl in my class's older brother. I went to Benetton and I bought a bright blue wool dress. I was paranoid that I would walk in and somebody would stab me with a heroin needle. I kid*

you not. That was 1981,'' she says. Soon Breuer, who lived in
her mother's apartment in the Sixties between Park and Lexing-
ton, was lying about her nocturnal whereabouts and heading to
Studio four nights a week with her crowd. ''I've often wondered
where I got the money. We didn't pay an entrance fee. But we
took taxis back and forth,'' she says.

There was a reason for the allure of Studio 54, and it was
not directly to do with Halston, Andy, and People magazine. Bea
Breuer was pretty and smart. Her family was blue book and well-
to-do, and she was at the upper echelon of a set: rich kids.
There had always been rich kids, but the parameters of their
lives were changing with disconcerting speed. ''The generation
before us had something called Bandwagon,'' Breuer says.
''Bandwagon was a town house between Madison and Park on
the Upper East Side where people would go and there would be
Kool-Aid and stuff. I think it was actually sponsored by the
Young Republican Club. Before me, that was where they all
went.''

Bandwagon had faded however. Hence Studio. ''Even though
it was a nightclub, where there were drugs everywhere, and per-
verted people, and bizarre things happening,'' Bea Breuer says,
''that was the playground for myself, and so many friends. That
was our Bandwagon.''

Michael Stone, the writer, was commissioned to write about
what he called the ''socialettes'' by Clay Felker who was then at
the East Side Express. Stone arranged to meet a clump of them
in the winter season of 1983. He notes that in his generation
kids would have suggested a get-together in the corner coffee
shop. The meeting was, at their suggestion, in McMullen's, a res-
taurant on Third Avenue, and he found them in possession of the
grandest table.

It was an eye-opener. ''There was this number of kids who
had no place to socialize because of their group ethic,'' he says.

Manhattan apartment buildings do not have rec rooms in the basement. Cruising the strip isn't much of a local option. Stone says, ''There were no nonalcohol clubs or meeting places where kids could specifically gather, and the schools had stopped organizing events because so many New York kids, being as precocious as they are, wanted to smoke and drink and make out.'' Alcohol had replaced soporifics, like pot. ''None of the parents would let them have parties because they would give a party for twelve and two hundred would crash, and junk the place.''

When there were parents, that is. Breuer recalls that she was the first kid in her class whose parents divorced. ''By the time I was fourteen everyone's parents were divorced,'' she says. ''It was really a new thing. They were two-income families. But no one was there. We were at people's houses till five in the morning, six in the morning, then going on to the Crisco Disco, Save the Robots, and this club, and that one. It got boring.''

When Breuer relives the beginning of the eighties among her set, a single insistent thought nags. ''No one was looking,'' she says, wonderingly. ''There was no one watching. That, combined with the teenager dynamic. I think, where was everyone? Where were everyone's parents?''

What Michael Stone found so astounding was the mingled ignorance and indifference of the adult world. ''The most ignorant people were the parents and the second most ignorant were the teachers.'' No matter. Nightworld was there, an enveloping, if not necessarily sheltering, presence.

Baird Jones was the first to organize this fresh, attractive market, so he put together lists of pupils from private schools and posh functions like the Gold and Silver Ball. ''His agenda was simply to liven up Studio 54,'' Stone says. ''The kids came en masse and for the first couple of months there was the golden time when they were admitted free. Their names were on lists, and they were sent invitations to special events, and they all showed up. All these kids from the single-sex schools came together and coalesced as one big citywide social group," Baird Jones says. "It got incredibly young. There were a lot of ninth, tenth, and eleventh graders."

It was then that the culling took place. The culling was partly an organic process, the end result of a process of clumping among the kids themselves. It was the coming together of an inner core among the mass of prep. That core, as is the way of things, was made up of kids who were particularly attractive, or whose parents were rich or famous. They were, in short, a junior division of the lists of Carmen D'Alessio and the promoters, a permanent pubescent A List. There were about two hundred of them. They had clout.

At that stage, the other kids began to be asked to pay. The whole thing was skillfully worked out. There were elements of it most nights, but Friday was the big kid night. "At ten twenty-five they would let in a hundred kids from the line. That was to take the pressure off," Jones explains. The distributors of invitations, the list makers, the moles in the schools and colleges also got in free, but everybody else—"usually a good fifteen hundred adolescents"—had to fork over the eighteen-dollar entrance fee.

That was not the end of the ignominy. "The other kids had to wait in line while the cool kids were let in free," Stone says. "The cool kids would get free drink tickets. The others would have to pay going rates." The cool kids, moreover, were allowed into the VIP Room. This wasn't one of the old discreet VIP areas, down in the basement or up in the offices. There was actually a roped-off area on the main floor of the club. It was about as discreet as a first-class carriage with no walls.

"I've been here a lot of times, and I've seen classmates of mine, just hanging around," one of the A Listers told Michael Stone when he was writing his piece. "I mean, they'd be like two feet away, just a rope between us, and they'd pretend it didn't make a bit of difference, but we all knew it did.''

In October 1983 People ran a story about a ''Second Generation'' party that ended up with an ''all-night revel at Studio 54.'' It was given by Victoria Leacock and Frazer Pennebaker, son of the documentary filmmaker, D. A. Pennebaker. A full-page picture included a bunch of the partygoers, including Gwynne Rivers and Amy Lumet. Gwynne Rivers told the reporter: ''Finally, here's a way to get away from just saying, 'Hi, I'm so-and-so's daughter.' '' The magazine did not exactly help her make her point by headlining the piece: AT THIS STUDIO 54 BASH, THE RIGHT NAMES TO DROP BELONGED TO THE PARENTS.

This sense of being the second generation of fun was debilitating. ''We were the second wave,'' Breuer says. ''Before Steve Rubell and Ian Schrager went to jail, there was the supercool wave. Now instead of Calvin Klein, there was Marcy Klein. There was a huge difference. We were aware of that.''

They grew up in traditional fashion. ''Me and my friends, we all became drunks,'' Elyn Wollensky says. ''We used to go between Dorian's and Studio, and we were all very underage, and nobody cared. It was really okay to do as many drugs as you wanted because all the adults were doing it, and it was okay to drink as much as you wanted, and to have sex with whoever you wanted to, because the adults were doing it. I was being fed free drink, and drugs, and whatever I wanted.''

Under the circumstances, it is surprising that Studio didn't generate a darker folklore than it did. There were a few horrors. A young woman went to Studio at fifteen and got into a conversation with a grandfatherly man, who kindly drove her to his apartment on Fifty-seventh Street to show her photographs of himself with Jimmy Carter. It seems that he then may have slipped her a Mickey Finn. At any rate, she let herself be photographed in various naked poses. Then he raped her. ''That must have been his MO,'' I was told. But exploitation of innocence is as old as time. Studio 54 merely offered an old perve the opportunity. Anyway, such squalid stories prove to be—surprisingly, perhaps—few. Almost all the Studio kids look back on such tales as anomalies, the kind of stuff that might happen any place.

Wrongly, in the eyes of some parents. ''It was a hellhole! A hellhole!'' says Gail Lumet, whose daughters Jenny and Amy were starry A Listers. ''I used to have a letter up on my bulletin board from a kid who said it was the worst experience of his life. I used to see seventh graders there. Let's say twelve-year-old girls from Spence. I think it was a hotbed of drugs and pedophiles and everything else. I mean . . . I hated everything about that place!''

A father and mother went at their daughter's invitation one night. ''It was 1983. We went to a party she and a bunch of her friends were involved in,'' the father says. ''We saw incredibly young people. Possibly eighth graders. We left. I said to a cop something like 'I've just seen four hundred violations!'

''He shrugged and said, 'Roy Cohn! What can you do?' ''

But the posh club kids tend to look back on those days as a time of vivid, exciting innocence. Certainly, compared with what came swiftly, a bit later.

Pierre Prudhomme adores the memory of Studio 54 to this day, despite the ''balcony flight.'' Prudhomme, the much-liked manager of a highly fashionable bar-restaurant, where the patrons were generous—''I didn't take tips,'' he says. ''But the tips I was given were in drug form. I mean, at the end of a Sunday brunch, if I think about it, I probably had two thousand dollars' worth of cocaine.'' He would invariably move on to Studio after closing up his own place. ''I'd go to Studio every night. First you'd spend a few minutes with the guys out there. 'How yah

doing? Why don't you come by the restaurant?' " he remembers.
"Then you'd walk into that wide hallway . . . You heard the music . . . Your mood just got better and better." He liked the
sweep of the main spaces. The VIP basement bored him. "Who
cares about doing coke with a movie star with this great thundering herd of hooves overhead?" he says.

That particular night Pierre was on ludes. His date was a celebrity's daughter. He has no memory of actually climbing up
onto the balcony, nor of toppling over. "And luckily—because
otherwise I would have crushed several people—I was tangled up
with one of the speakers. People pulled me back up. I was wearing baggy corduroy trousers. You know, the kind you get in
Brooks Brothers? I looked down and the seams were ripping at
the knee. That's how quickly my knee blew up."

Pierre wound up wearing a metal brace for six months. Did
this slow him up? No sir. Buying in Studio was easy, even for the
proles, and Prudhomme was no prole. There was a guy named
Dr. Moon, just for one. "He had a van outside. You know, one
of those vans that surfers have," Paul remembers. "He sold
Quaaludes, coke, acid. And don't forget amyl nitrites. The dance
floor drug. Perfect strangers would pass you these bottles or
these things."

These were just aperitifs. "I had a lot of English friends.
Soon I started getting heroin," Pierre says. Cocaine is "foreign"
so far as the British are concerned, whereas the heroin poppy is
a British Imperial crop. One of his English friends was a young
woman, just arrived in Manhattan, the daughter of a magnate.
Call her Perdita. Her first night in town they went to Studio.
Where else? He saw her gabbling in a corner with some scums-
ter, then he lost her. Totally.

The following night he went to a dinner in Perdita's honor. It
was in the Fifth Avenue apartment of a Manhattan hostess, a
stone's throw from the Metropolitan Museum. "I was told to

come at seven-thirty,'' Pierre says. ''I arrived. It was a very grand apartment. Only the guest of honor wasn't there. She was upstairs in bed. I was told to go upstairs to see her. She was as white as a sheet, she couldn't move. It was so . . . peculiar.''

Smack was still peculiar then to Pierre Prudhomme. It would not be so for long.

We agreed to meet in Danceteria because the Private Dealer spent a good deal of time in nightclubs and Rudolf's Danceteria was then where the nocturnal pixiedust was glimmering. The Rich Boy and the Party Girl, who were to effect the introduction, patrolled the upper floor. Antonia de Portago was to perform, so there were fashionable uptown faces coursing among such downtown presences as John Lydon, the former Johnny Rotten, in a white coat, a PiL T-shirt, a black hat. We found the Private Dealer on the ground floor, sitting motionless and alone, at the hem of the stage. He was gaunt, with a beaky nose and intent blue eyes, and his skin had the greenish pallor of flesh seen underwater. He was carrying a Nikon and whenever something caught his attention—a hairy man swaddled in transparent polyethylene, wearing a bird's crest—he would get to his feet and get off a couple of shots.

It was past midnight. De Portago was being conventionally late. We fetched drinks, but the thudding of taped music would have made small talk painful, and anyway, the Private Dealer was clearly getting twitchy. We left. The Rich Boy and I climbed into the Party Girl's Mercedes, brand-new, but dented and squelched here and there by sloppy roadwork. She followed the Private Dealer as he gunned through the traffic in a bright red Maserati.

His apartment was in a run-down building on the fringe of the Upper East Side. It was small, tidy. A TV was on. No sound. There was a lot of expensive camera equipment lying around and a few magazines, but not a single book. The only decorative touch was provided by a couple of plastic Oriental masks. We seated ourselves opposite the Private Dealer who sat stiff-backed behind an oblong desk. To his left were a telephone and a grinder. To his right, like a table setting, were a dessert spoon, an artist's palette, knife and an oblong of plastic. To his front were a square of mirror, a white-enameled scale accurate to a hundredth of a gram, receptacles for Quaaludes and hashish, and a nine-inch glass vial holding half an ounce of white heroin. For this, the Private Dealer had paid one of his own suppliers $4,500. This might last three days.

"You want coke?" the Private Dealer asked us. The Rich Boy and the Party Girl muttered to each other. She shook her head petulantly. "Downtown," the Rich Boy said. They concluded the transaction and sidled off into a corner. Soon their heads were lowered, their backs carefully turned, as though what they were doing was a bit risqué, like leafing through a porn magazine in school. The Private Dealer, less encumbered by protocol, took off his jacket and spectacles. Working quickly and precisely he filled the dessert spoon with a mixture of heroin and cocaine, liquefied it with Poland water, heated the spoon, and drew the liquid up into a hypodermic syringe. "I have a very strong notion of right and wrong. And that has not been touched one drop," he said as he rolled up his sleeves, exposing veins that looked like burned-out electrical circuitry, and stuck the syringe into his left forearm, mechanically, like a heavy smoker lighting up one more cigarette.

Only the constant telephone calls interrupted his conversational flow. "It is the beginning only between you and me. We start only now to relate to each other," he told one client. "If we cannot adjust to each other, we split. No hard feelings."

The Private Dealer is a European, who describes his paternal line as "old aristocracy." He was thirty-six and had been in prison twice for short periods, each time in Europe. He had set up in Manhattan just seven years before and was grossing $500,000 a year. "I have in mind to have a serious figure when I finish," he said. Dealers frequently justify their ways to themselves by adopting roles. Some see themselves as dashing, piratical. The Private Dealer sees himself as a philosopher. The Rich Boy calls him "my guru," only half ironically. The Private Dealer does not return the compliment. "For me there are two basic categories. You have human beings and you have humanoids," he said. Junkies being the latter, of course. "I am in a position where I can see a lot of the true personality of people. And I cannot accept their scale of value. It revolts me to see human beings so fucking low. So low, man." His voice was now slurry.

Nonetheless, he took some pride in his client list. "It is like a private club," he said. "It's like a barrier has been put down. Respectable people are doing it. It happened very recently and it has been quite, quite sudden." He added, "I do not deal with people who are not implicated already. It is a principle of mine."

The Rich Boy and the Party Girl floated toward a sofa, giggling, she a bit unsteady, so I wondered if she was going to throw up. The Private Dealer chose a vein and shot up another speedball, the third since our arrival. "You seem to be doing it every twenty minutes," I observed.

"Yes. I shoot up too much," he agreed. His speech rhythms had altered again. He now sounded crisp, neutral, businesslike.

"Always speedballs?"

"Constantly."

"How much?"

"A gram a day. That would cost me twenty-five thousand dollars a month, retail. I am a real junkie. I was always very fragmentary. With smack I feel like I'm normal. I no longer get plea-

*sure from it. I am not happy, I am not unhappy. It is a necessity.
To feel normal.''*

''How are your veins?''

*''Terrible.'' He kneaded his upper arm, as dispassionately
as a shopper judging the ripeness of an avocado. ''They collapse.'' He sometimes shoots in the legs, he said, but had so
far avoided such extreme measures as shooting in the neck,
the penis, the artery in the rectum, or close to the eye. ''I
should quit fairly soon,'' he added.*

''In how long?''

*''A year is too long. I do not want to continue longer than
six months. Otherwise I will lose.''*

*Losing. He used the word constantly, but imprecisely. It
emerged that he wasn't talking about death, or not right away,
but about falling totally under the drug's control. His voice had
undergone another tonal shift and was high and squeaky, like
somebody doing Mickey Mouse.*

*There was a knock on the door. I motioned toward my note-
book, my tape recorder. He gave a wave of nonchalant uncon-
cern, got up, and let in a young woman. She was an actress. I
knew her. She didn't seem surprised to see me. She paid $160.
For cocaine, I think.*

*The three of us got up to leave as the Private Dealer was pre-
paring another fix. ''Why the stuffed penguin?'' I asked at the
door.*

*''It is my mascot,'' he said, an unexpected flicker of humor in
his pale eyes. ''It is like me. Harmless.''*

In December 1982 there were a couple of arrests at the JFK airport. On
December 8, Peter Madok, once a lawyer for the Who, was picked up with
over four pounds of Brazilian cocaine. Twelve days later a woman was arrested
with roughly the same weight of Indian heroin. Working on intelligence derived from these arrests, the New York bureau of the Drug Enforcement Ad-

ministration set an investigation in motion. Over the next few months the DEA covertly recorded thirty-five hundred telephone calls.

On May 19, 1983, they raided a town house on the West Side that belonged to Nik Cohn, the author of *Rock from the Beginning, Rock Dreams,* and some vivid novels, but best known for the *New York* magazine feature that was to become *Saturday Night Fever,* that inarguable motor of the disco years. Nik Cohn was arrested. So were fifteen others, including a woman, Frin Mullen, and two Englishmen, Lord Jermyn, heir to the Marquis of Bristol, and Ben Brierley, a record producer whose marriage to Marianne Faithfull had recently ended.

The federal case was of classic dumbness. One call that had been recorded and to which the feds had devoted great ingenuity in decoding was actually the ordering in of a Chinese dinner. Nik Cohn, John Jermyn, and Ben Brierley were recreational users only. Cohn pleaded guilty to a lesser charge and got a $5,000 fine and probation.

It was Pierre Prudhomme who introduced me to Anglo-American sisters, Erica and Dodo. Erica, the older, was twenty-six; pale, with straight brown hair, she was beautiful, a beauty set off by a scar on her left temple, the consequence of what she called "her accident." They came recommended as expert guides through a scenery in which cocaine might be a jagged peak, heroin a deep gulch, but all around rolled the hills and valleys of narcosis, fashioned from pills, poppers, and old-fangled hard alcohol; the drug landscape of Nightworld.

Erica's grandfather was a shipping magnate. Her father was English; her mother was remarried to an effete American preppy. Schooled in Connecticut, Erica had first seen somebody shoot up when she was sixteen. "A friend of mine and I used to be very involved with the music scene," she told me in her sweetly prissy way. "We'd go to parties. Basically, in retrospect, we were just sexual toys.

"My friend was going out with this roadie. He had this dumpy apartment on Jane Street. And he had five Dobermans because of the drugs. He had this bed with manacles, an S&M room I never went into. Anyway there was a party after a show and this roadie had no veins left. So he jerked himself off and shot up in his penis. And the blood spattered on the walls and I was appalled. I was only snorting. Plus, I preferred amphetamines."

At another revel in the same venue Erica notched up a further first. She saw a man, sitting quietly, not participating in the fun. A closer look showed that his fun days were over. "I was amazed at the blasé way people reacted," she says. " 'He's dead? Uh-huh. Hey, don't interrupt the party. We'll call the cops later.' "

At eighteen she abandoned Manhattan in favor of Miami Beach. "Not that I ever saw the beach," she says. "We used to go to parties in Coral Gables. I came to at one and there was blood all over the place. It wasn't my blood. It wasn't the guy I was living with's blood. But there was *an awful lot of blood.* I decided it was probably time to leave Florida."

She returned to New York and began going to a college upstate. She was seeing a psychiatrist but found him ineffectual. "He would just sit there, going *'unhhh! unnnnh!'* I was basically being a pimp and a drug dealer. I had a photographer friend in New York. He would give me drugs which I would go to school and sell. So these preppy young girls from Texas and wherever would get very interested, and all hooked up on Quaaludes, and he would send the limousine, and they would do beaver shots in their lynx coats."

There were many, many disco nights, but things were getting too swimmy, too blurry. She made a run for home. Her grandfather, the patriarch of the clan, was fond of her, and incurious about her habits. Erica behaved like a lady while she was close to her money, so much so that her grandfather had her preside over the launching of a new ship.

She was shooting up that same evening. Her mother confronted her after dinner. Erica permitted herself to be flown out to Minneapolis, where she checked herself into a three-thousand-dollars-a-week rehab, St. Mary's. This was in 1981. It was there that she was later joined by her sister, Dodo.

Dodo was twenty-one, a few years younger than Erica. She was pretty, with tender, heavy-lidded eyes, and she was as vague as a guess. She had first done smack in London, snorting once, then smoking it—"chasing the dragon's tail"—at a dance in the country. This had been attended by two members of the royal family and you couldn't get into the upstairs bathrooms for the groupuscules doing coke and smack.

Dodo returned to Manhattan and got a job with a theatrical agent. One evening she was in Mortimer's with a cheerful crowd, including a wry young medical man who, because of his nifty ways with hard drugs, rejoiced in the nickname "Doctor Death." They zoomed on to Xenon. Dodo found Doctor

Death attractive. For that reason or for whatever reason—"I am still blocking so much," she told me—she took him aside as they were sitting down at one of the posh tables to the left of the dance floor. "I really want to try it with you," she said. He told her he would make a house call the following evening.

Dodo was supposed to go to a party with a roommate that night but dawdled, saying she would be along later. Doctor Death arrived at half past ten, bearing a black Gladstone bag, which he took into the bathroom with him. "He seemed to be there forever," she said. He came out at last, and opened the bag. The interior shone with stacked syringes. He turned off the main light, draped her pretty pink slip over the bedside lamp, and bent to his task.

Dodo's progress was quick. Soon she was shooting up daily and had moved in with a young junkie who would send her off to score in vicious neighborhoods. She grew sallow, and pumped so much money into her body that she started kiting checks. Her mother threatened to send in the cops and the young junkie quickly threw her out. She scored one last time and took the Long Island Railroad to her home, where her mother told her she would be joining her sister in St. Mary's.

The following morning was tranquil and sunny. "Dodo! There's a telephone call," her mother shouted. "Don't disturb me," Dodo bawled back. "I'm trying to get a hit. I keep *missing*."

She was in a high good humor on the flight to Minneapolis though, literally, because she had shot the last bag in the plane's lavatory. "You know all I had packed?" she says. "Evening dresses. I thought I was going to clean up a bit, come back, and start all over again."

There was a banner slung across one of the thoroughfares of the Lower East Side. It read "This Land Is Our Land" and was doubtless the leavings of some street fair or other but it seemed loaded with special meaning. We got out of the cab at Twelfth Street and Avenue D and walked past the town houses of Tompkins Square, handsome once, now fallen into decrepitude, with beer bottles and busted household appliances on the steps. It was early evening. We trod a bit more quickly as we got closer to the block where Erica and Jeff meant to score. "Actually, I do get nervous over this," Erica confided. After a pause, she added, "The danger is half the rush."

A van was at the end of the street, rhythmically flashing its lights. It was marked MORTUARY DIVISION. A passerby told us somebody had been shot dead a couple of hours ago. A few cops had come and gone. Rosita's was eighty yards away. Rosita had a sound reputation, for both dealing in quality goods and maintaining decorum, but this evening there was something about the demeanor of some of the people huddling outside that Jeff found bothersome. "These guys aren't dealers, they aren't buyers," he muttered, hunching into his blue cashmere. "I don't like this. Let's get done and get out. Shit!"

We joined the short line just as a college kid came out. He trotted jubilantly across the street and climbed into an automobile filled with whooping girls. New Jersey plates. Some young guys were just standing there, eyes darting, light on the balls of their feet. "Shit!" Jeff repeated. He had been robbed half a block from here three weeks ago. His neck had been cut, but lightly, and he had lost little blood.

A black man, dapper in a leather flying jacket, confronted us in Rosita's tiled hallway. "Show me your tracks," he instructed me passionlessly, as though asking for my ticket for a ride. "I'm with her," I said quickly. Erica was waving her arms around as though signaling for help. Her milky underarm was marbled with blue-black veins like a Stilton cheese. The man stuck out his palm, saying, "I'll go and get you some." Thirty bucks changed hands.

The modus operandi of scoring shifts constantly, according to street rivalries and the ebb and flow of law enforcement. In one venue the dealers have grown so nervous that they lower a basket from a high window. The customer pops in his or her dough, watches as the basket whisks skyward, and hopes it will return with the correct number of nickel or dime bags. Rosita's was more placid. The guy returned, handed over some Chiclet-sized oblongs of folded yellow legal paper, and was off.

Moments later, a young woman walked in off the street. Rosita. She glimpsed Erica's purchases and bubbled with scorn. "Shit!" she said. "Ain't I told you never deal with *nobody* but me? That stuff's no good. Look!"

She fished out her own oblongs. The differences were plain, in size, and in style. We sheepishly shelled out another forty dollars. Outside, the gauntlet of darting eyes seemed less menacing. "We need works," Erica decided. We walked past vendors of Toilet, where the sachets of heroin are stamped with an image of a lavatory, and sellers of Smiley, where the trademark is a smiley face, stopping outside a convenience store. A small group was homed in on us. "Works?" they said. "Works . . . works . . ." I went into the store, picked a pack of cashews. "Something tells me you just looking to make change" the storekeeper said cheerfully, breaking a twenty.

A muscular bearded fellow approached us outside. His price was three dollars. Another rip-off? We dithered. "I'm here all the time," he said irritably. "I do *business* here."

He took the money, slipped off, returned with a surgically packaged syringe tip. "Where's the rest of it?" Erica asked.

"You only said the point."

"The *works*."

The man produced the plastic body of a syringe from his pocket. It was unwrapped. "This has been used," Erica said petulantly, but accepted it anyway. That was back *then*.

In the studio she poured a Baggie of heroin into a spoon, bent so that the bowl would sit flat on the table. I inhaled two lines, then watched carefully as she poured water into the bowl of the spoon, then heated it with an eighteenth-century silver candlestick, one of her few belongings of value not to have been stolen by Dodo. "You have to be careful about getting fiber into the system," she said, holding a wad of cotton and drawing the stuff into the hypodermic. "You can get a disease. Cotton Fever."

She tied up her arm with a piece of rubber tubing and looked for a place to shoot. "I don't have any veins left," she complained. "Now I find myself looking at other people's. It's rather a nasty habit."

The needle slid in. "Shit! I skin-popped," she said. But blood began welling out, dribbling over a copy of *Bazaar*. "I must have hit something," she said more happily.

Jeff shot up.

I, until then a needle virgin, did likewise. The bluish tip slipped in like a sharp fruit knife into a peach. The liquid went pink, and red. Erica swabbed the puncture with isoproypyl and cotton. I felt no emotion whatsoever; neither fear, nor anticipation, nor regret, not even curiosity.

"Should we go dancing?" Erica said suddenly.

"Dancing?"

"You can do whatever you want. It adapts."

I sat down. Somehow a great warmth was stirring inside, a friendly beast, nuzzling, like a puppy. "It may or may not grow up to be a Doberman pinscher," I said very clearly, but to myself, and smiled at my acuteness. I began feeling a tremulousness, a shortness of breath. This seemed strangely momentous. I imagined expelling my soul through my mouth, and watching it float up up and away, a puff of blue cloud.

"Are you having a good time?" Erica asked a few seconds or maybe an hour later in her society voice.

Why? Did I look unhappy? Surely I was a porcupine, bristling with light. Erica looked clear, but distant. It was like looking at her through thick glass. "Fine," I said, and meant it. Not terrific, fine. I did not have a halo. I did not have horns. The surprise was there was no surprise. I began scribbling notes to myself. They were fearfully important.

"I know Jeff and I are going to stop," Erica said suddenly.

Jeff bestrirred himself for the first time. "Do you know that?" he asked.

"I'm going to stop out of boredom," she said. "Being a junkie is like having a nine-to-five *job*."

Much later, I reread the brilliant notes.

They went:

A WARM WIND I BLOWING THROUGH MY HEAD.

I CAN HEAR HER WALK.

TEETH . . . RECEDING

GOLDEN HEDGEHOG

From this high point, they lapsed into incoherence.

Amazingly, we did go dancing. At Xenon. I still have a Polaroid taken of me that night, at my own request, as a document. My eyes are dead in my head. They look like wet black stones.

I have learned to recognize such eyes.

★   ★   ★

An entry in *The Andy Warhol Diaries* for January 9, 1978, set in Halston's town house, reads:

THEN PETER BEARD CAME IN WITH A GUY WHO HAD A BEAUTIFUL GLOVE ON AND A BOTTLE OF COKE IN THE OTHER HAND, AND THEN LATER HE SHOWED US HIS HAND WHICH WAS A STUMP, IT LOOKED LIKE IN THE MOVIES WHEN THEY SHOW THE FIENDISH GHOUL—HE LOST IT IN A PLANE CRASH, HIS THIRD PLANE CRASH, A DC-10 THAT HE OWNS. HE PASSED THE BOTTLE OF COKE AROUND.

The man was Tom Sullivan, and he was from Tampa, Florida. Beard, a photographer and socialite, had been introduced to him by the tennis player Vitas Gerulaitis. Sullivan looked like a charming rube, and a former football player, which he was. What with his leather clothes, his western hat, he also looked like a country rocker in a sixties band. Sullivan, in brief, might have seemed an unlikely addition to the inner core of the club, except that he always seemed to have amazing quantities of both drugs and money, so the core swiftly enfolded Sullivan in their embrace.

In the diaries, Warhol voyeuristically picks over Sullivan's affairs with the Anglo-Irish heiress Catherine Guinness, and Margaret Trudeau. Sullivan was mysterious about the source of his wealth, but was not above dropping hints. Andy Warhol, for whom he bought elephant hide cowboy boots, and who entertained him at a lunch for Isabella Rossellini, where his fellow guests were a potpourri that included Bianca Jagger, Claus von Bulow, and Picasso biographer, John Richardson, confided to his amanuensis, Pat Hackett, his impression that Sullivan was a cocaine smuggler.

This was not quite so. Tom Sullivan was indeed legendary in the fraternity of heavy-duty smugglers, but it was as a bulk smuggler of marijuana and hashish. In the words of another smuggler, "He took it off wheels and put wings on it." The late Albert Goldman, who knew Sullivan, reconstructed a particularly ominous mission in a piece he wrote for the narcotics industry magazine, *High Times*. Goldman's focus was on Tom Forcade, the founder of the magazine and a political activist given to such hectic overreaching that he was suspected for a while by Jerry Rubin and Abbie Hoffman of being an agent provocateur for the CIA.

Forcade had also done some smuggles. In the spring of 1978, Forcade and his closest friend, one Jack Coombs, decided to fly in a load. Coombs, a beginner at the controls, and another more experienced pilot were to fly to Colombia and pick up a load of marijuana. They would fly it back and drop it in secluded terrain in Florida. A waiting crew would run the pot to a safe house in Atlanta. Forcade and Coombs agreed that Forcade would go up in another plane and guide Coombs's returning twin-engine plane to the drop zone. Goldman describes this in-air rendezvous as "wholly unnecessary." Forcade's partner in the enterprise was Tom Sullivan. "Forcade liked Sullivan quite a bit," Lech Kowalski, a moviemaker and a friend of Forcade, says. "We had a few meetings at night where money was counted and certain things went down. Sullivan was in the fast lane then."

The day of the flight, Tom Sullivan was in a duplex penthouse in Atlanta's Peachtree Plaza. He was called from Colombia at one in the afternoon. The plane had left. A Southerner, Joe, who was Sullivan's lieutenant, had been at the loading site. Joe was close to Sullivan, indeed lived with his sister. He, too, had taken the plane. Sullivan, according to Goldman, was in a particularly high state of excitement because a shrimp boat loaded with pot was scheduled to dock in Louisiana that same evening. Tom Sullivan's reputation among his fellow smugglers would acquire new luster.

At midnight the telephone rang with somber news. The in-air rendezvous had, indeed, been effected but Forcade had kept ordering the smuggler plane to fly lower, lower, lower. It had presumably hit a tree. Forcade had seen the fireball that had lit up the sky. Nobody had survived. That was Albert Goldman's version, as told to him by Tom Forcade. What Forcade told Lech Kowalski was darker. "He was set up," Forcade had said, opaquely.

Tom Forcade and Tom Sullivan were both devastated. Forcade abandoned smuggling, and started a film company with Lech Kowalski. "We produced a film called *D.O.A.* At one point we needed money and Tommy Sullivan helped us get financing," Kowalski says. *D.O.A.*, which stands for Dead on Arrival, was the superb rockudrama on the Sex Pistols' American, and last, tour. Kowalski also reedited a drug-oriented movie that Forcade had bought down south.

Forcade also wanted to make a movie centered on some of Sullivan's experiences in the traffic. He passed on any involvement in Sullivan's own movie, though. This oddity was shot on the Montauk estate of Andy Warhol that he had rented for the season. The name star was Jack Palance, whose career had been in the basement for some years. The real agenda, though, was to turn Tom Sullivan into the superstar that he already was in his own imagining. He played a rock and roller who smuggled between gigs and Forcade claimed he had made the movie for a million dollars. "It was a pretty dreadful film," Kowalksi says. Warhol appears in a cameo. "Andy *had* to appear in the movie. It was one of the terms of the lease," says Paul Morrissey, who had made films with Warhol and owned part of the Montauk property. "We increased the rent."

Tom Forcade committed suicide in 1979. Kowalski says he had a melange of motives: a Quaalude habit, a busted-up marriage, and guilt over the crash. Albert Goldman wrote that Forcade's suicide was "emblematic of the final failure of adaptation by the hippies to the alien climate of the 70s."

Tom Sullivan was still cutting a swath in Studio 54.

On April 3, 1978, Warhol noted that Tom Sullivan, Margaret Trudeau, Catherine Guinness, and he went together to the Oscars party that he and Truman Capote were hosting at Studio. Warhol loathed the party but was advised by Bob Colacello that "all the people who counted were down in the basement—Halston and Appollonia and Tom Sullivan and Margaret and Barbara Allen with Ryan O'Neal," et cetera. On January 23, 1979, Warhol described Sullivan as acting strangely, and offering to give him a quarter of his business. "But what is his business?" Warhol wonders, petulantly. Was that, perhaps, just because the diaries were, after all, intended for the eyes of the feds, in the shape of the IRS? "We all knew," Fred Hughes, Warhol's lieutenant, told me, years later.

The fact was, though, that Sullivan actually was going to pieces. Neither he nor Forcade had been happy at the way the happy-go-lucky smuggling adventure was changing from the hippie phenomenon it had been from the late sixties through much of the seventies, a mixture of entrepreneurial zeal and a kind of goofy idealism. "You trusted a guy, you gave him cash. Guys were buying DC-3s, they were buying tractor trailers. It was pretty cool," Kowalski says. "And Tommy Sullivan enjoyed the speakeasy kind of situation. There would be these places you would go." Studio 54 was perhaps also his last speakeasy.

Cocaine smuggling was a more feral business, though, low on hippie ca-maraderie. Sentences were getting stiffer. In consequence, when traffickers were caught, it became commonplace for them to rat on their associates. "Sullivan, in the end, it was the same thing that happened to Forcade," Kowalski says. "They ran out of room to deal in. The feds were breathing down their necks. They couldn't really function. They burned a lot of bridges. And a lot of people died. Suicides. I know of a few possible setups. Maybe murders. People that were on the inside were being snuffed out or going to jail. The industry was changing. It wasn't that much fun." He added that Sullivan was "sort of pushed out of it."

Nor did it help that Tom Sullivan got hooked on heroin. In this, he became as one with the chic Brits in Studio 54. He was buying from a well-connected dealer, who operated not far from Studio. Sullivan married Winnie, a very beautiful Dutch girl, a former Miss Holland, and they lived in a midtown hotel, but it was a volatile, violent relationship. On July 6, 1980, Warhol records that he was avoiding Sullivan's calls. Sullivan had been saying that he had friends in the hospital and needed a few dollars. Warhol shrewdly speculated that he had blown his stack on *Cocaine Cowboys*. Kowalski saw him in a drug dealer's apartment midtown in the summer of 1981. "He looked really awful," he says. Sullivan died on June 17. Warhol says his heart stopped, Kowalski that it was pneumonia. He was twenty-four.

ACT 2

: NIGHTCLUBBING

THE SHUNNING

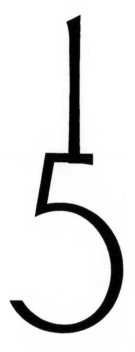

LISA WRIGHT, ONETIME GOOD SOLDIER OF THE STUDIO 54 coat check operation, had been apartment sitting for Steve Rubell. A knock on the door indicated that he was back. She cooked him a chicken dinner and stayed on as his roommate for the next four years. Ian Schrager, who had been living with Norma Kamali, preferred solitude. "I needed to be alone. I felt insecure," he says. Returning to an early passion, he stocked up weekly with architecture and design books from Rizzoli.

There was also the matter of earning a living. Everybody just *knew* that Steve Rubell and Ian Schrager had salted millions away. Everybody was wrong. The lawyers and the government had taken almost the whole caboodle. Paul, Weiss Rifkind alone had been paid $2 million. "We should have pleaded guilty," Rubell would say.

The reaction of Steve Rubell's host of friends to the melting away of his money, his drugs, his power, was interesting. It was true that some actually had been upset about the Cocaine Favors List. Diane von

Furstenberg, for instance, and Andy Warhol (who usually in his diaries refers to Rubell as "Stevie" before prison and "Stephen" after). Some came through, like David Geffen, and Calvin Klein, who gave the pair a blank check. But many others chose to turn moralist, sometimes improbably. What followed shocked both Ian Schrager and Steve Rubell: The Shunning.

"Nobody wanted to know Rubell when he got out of jail," says the writer Dotson Rader. Rader's first après-penitentiary sighting of Rubell was at the open-air restaurant outside the Pier House Hotel in Key West. He was with Tennessee Williams, another playwright Jose Quintero, Quintero's boyfriend, and Victor Hugo. The formerly gregarious clubman, who had been released only some weeks before, was standing by himself at the bar. He seemed lost, lonely, out of place. "He looked terrible," Rader says. "He was wearing tan slacks, a beige windbreaker, and a canvas hat with flaps, the kind of hat Woody Allen wears. And it was *eighty degrees*."

Rader said, "Look, Tennessee! It's Steve Rubell." The playwright made no comment. A while later, Rader went across to the bar to say hello, and returned to the table. In due course, Steve drifted over and stood beside an empty chair. Rader asked him to sit down.

"Baby, that seat is taken," Williams said to Dotson Rader, not looking at Rubell.

"It is not!"

"That seat is *occupied!*" Tennessee Williams said with finality.

After the discomfited New Yorker had beaten his retreat, Rader got a few more drinks under his belt, then tackled Williams. "You know what we're going to do, Tennessee? We're going to have Steve Rubell to dinner at the house tomorrow night," he said.

Under no circumstances, Williams said. "I don't want to sit down with a *jailbird*."

Dotson Rader was thunderstruck. "I was thinking how lucky Tennessee and I were that we weren't jailbirds ourselves," he says.

Peter Stringfellow, a London club owner, saw Rubell not long after his release at the fashionable downtown restaurant Indochine. "It was a sad sight," Stringfellow says. "It was as if all of a sudden everyone moved away from his table. I went over and sat and had a chat with him. He was absolutely alone."

Jim Fouratt believes that a sort of belated *post coital tristia,* mostly gay, was a factor in this. "A lot of people with the social lubricant of Studio 54, and the safety, and the drugs, behaved in ways that were not part of their identity. It was completely safe.

"Then they got straitlaced. They walked away."

Ian Schrager described Rubell as feeling so uncomfortable on Columbus Avenue, close to their halfway house, that he froze. This was no place he knew. Being recognized was a trial too. When some people he knew came over to say hello in Charivari, he fled the store. Rubell would later tell Jesse Kornbluth, "You get out. You're elated. You feel you've paid the price. A few weeks later, you realize you have to start all over again. People have grown in different ways. And you're alone. I went into a four-month depression. Coming home was harder than being *there.*"

"It's never over," Schrager agreed. "Steve said it's like having a bad disease. You're cured, but there's a scar."

Steve Rubell and Ian Schrager earned their weekly $2,500 from Studio 54. "They acted like they didn't have any money at all. They really needed it. There was no question about that," Fleischman says. But so, come to that, did Mark Fleischman need *them.* Rubell especially. "Steve guided me. In the beginning. You walk into a *huge empty room* that's been empty for a year and a half. You're supposed to fill it every night of the week and you need three thousand people. Steve was a good trainer. There are certain *knacks.*"

Steven Rubell's knack was for people, the menagerie of Manhattan à la mode. Manhattan had changed, and in ways that had nothing to do with the Shunning. It had something to do with Ed Gifford's notion of the Thousand-Day Chic, but it went far deeper than that. Change is swift in Nightworld, and not always subtle, because Nightworlders are peculiarly quick to pick up on changes in the lives of cities, which they then present in caricature version. So changes in Nightworld, frivolous in themselves, can indicate changes in the whole culture, as much as the twitches and squeaks of tectonic plates may predict the rise and fall of the landmass.

Studio 54 had been both an implosion and an explosion, the culmination of some very 1960s notions of freedom, openness, giddy display, hope. Sex was good for you and more sex was better, and, as for drugs, well, cocaine had been inhaled by Sigmund Freud and used as a punch line by Cole Porter. It was believed to be a nonaddictive pick-me-up, much easier on the system than Dom Pérignon or Jack Daniel's.

The innocence was gone. The new Nightworld was more knowing, and this was one of the legacies of Studio 54. Another was that nightlife had, in itself, become an addiction, so much so that for a growing number going to bed at two seemed ridiculous; three, or four, or five acceptable. There had always been after-hours joints, of course, but they had been frequented by a handful of souls with inhumane schedules—whores, musicians, newspapermen on the lobster shift—and the ambience of these boîtes tended to be slovenly, melancholic, and dim. Now there was a whole fancy community aching to colonize the night. Crisco had been the forerunner. A new sort of after-hours joints were springing fitfully to life. Downtown. Naturally.

Rudolf had made one of the earlier moves. He located a building on Crosby Street on the margin of Little Italy in 1979. He didn't know many downtowners and asked Jim Fouratt to go in with him. It was to be an experimental venue, presenting performance art, fashion, video et cetera. Rudolf put $150,000 into it. At Fouratt's suggestion, they called it Pravda, which is, of course, Russian for "truth."

Pravda opened with a glorious party. It was sponsored by Fiorucci in aid of the fashiony avant-garde *Wet Magazine* and the revels included a Betsey Johnson fashion show. The police closed it down on the morning after for want of the correct papers.

"It was a great club, a Bauhaus statement. But the neighborhood went bananas against it and managed to close it down," Rudolf says. Fouratt's more acerbic recollection is that Rudolf's contractor threatened to punch out a neighbor who was opposing their liquor license. "She was a good old dyke. I knew her. That was it," he says.

Wet Magazine, incidentally, folded not long after. Fiorucci whooshed into nonexistence as a Manhattan presence in the mid-eighties. Fabulosity is so fleeting.

★   ★   ★

Jim Fouratt and Rudolf's next space was at 252 West Thirty-seventh Street. "It was a club called Armageddon that opened and closed. The guy that was in charge offered it to me and Jim," Rudolf says. Rudolf had suggested profiting from the resonances his background evoked by calling it "the Bunker" but they settled on Fouratt's more American name, Danceteria. The duo, who now operated under the name Average Normal, Inc., did a $25,000 make-over and got the place open in a couple of weeks.

The timing was fortuitous. It was March 1980. Steve Rubell and Ian Schrager had gone to the slammer and Studio was no competition. Indeed, Jim Fouratt has a dream-vivid memory of a post-Pravda and pre–Mark Fleischman trip to Studio 54. Michael Overington, acting as Schrager/Rubell viceroy, had been leasing it out to different black promoters on Friday and Saturday nights for parties that were, at least theoretically, alcohol-free. At one such party, a guest remembers, a bowl of "nonalcoholic" punch was overturned and the juice ate through a carpet. "The place had run down physically. But they would fill it," Fouratt says. "It was a cash cow."

Fouratt took Abbie Hoffman there for a safe night out while the yippie was still on the lam but on the verge of resurfacing. The almost entirely black crowd were making a night of it, not making the revolution. "We were talking a lot about cultural politics. Why I was doing nightclubs, what that was all about from a political point of view. I had it all worked out. We were standing on the balcony, looking down, and talking about Gramsci. Needless to say, this conversation was taking place at four or five in the morning . . ." It was the Sixties Meet the Eighties, Act One.

Danceteria was the next phase. "Danceteria was like an after-hours place that presented live music," Rudolf says. "It was basically a step in between the Mudd Club and Studio. It was between uptown and downtown.

"Although it was more directed to rock and new wave, it was the same principle of sex and drugs that worked so well at Studio 54. But, contrary to Studio and contrary to the Mudd Club, Danceteria was egalitarian. The concept was that we're all the same. Let's dance! So I remember that Scavullo and all those Studio people were there, because they had to be there, because it was the trendy place to be, but at the same time not entirely *happy* to be there."

That whole summer Danceteria blazed away, with Devo, the Gang of

Four, Sun Ra, Pere Ubu, and Tito Puente all playing there. Danceteria played an important part in the growth of the alternative music world. But the usual furies of clubland—angry neighbors, jealous rivals, and, finally, sluggish officials—were soon riding the nightwinds and Fouratt and Rudolf arrived one night in time to witness a spectacular police raid. They were charged with breaking the liquor laws. There were twenty arrests. "We had no licenses whatsoever. Not a single license!" Rudolf exults.

Jim Fouratt was now approached by Frank Roccio, a nightperson with connections in all the right and some of the wrong places. While Roccio was still a partner in Club 57, a relative of his second wife had directed his attention to a place on West Forty-fifth. It had recently housed G. G. Barnum's, a glitzy club known for transvestites and circus acts which had folded its big top because "there had been two murders there. They were about to lose their liquor license," Fouratt says. Fouratt happened to know that it had once been the site of the Peppermint Lounge, a joint still revered by Nightworlders. He went into the basement and was enchanted to find photographs of the old place. There were pink-and-white candy canes, photos of Jayne Mansfield. He called Rudolf in high excitement.

Fouratt also happened to know that it was a mob-connected joint. So what? He felt the two of them could handle *that*.

Rudolf tried to cry off, saying he was exhausted. All he wanted was a holiday. Jim Fouratt talked him into it. They made an agreement with the construction company that owned the premises on behalf of whomsoever. They were to have complete aesthetic control. "And the mob was to be kept outside. Rudolf's job was to talk to them and make business deals with them. There were no written agreements. Which was how we could walk."

How does one keep the mob outside, especially in a place they have money in? "Every club I was ever involved with, they were kept out," says Fouratt. If you make them money. They're interested in *cash*. You let them have the liquor, you let them have the napkins, you let them have the garbage carting. All the businesses that they have. It's a cash flow thing."

The Peppermint Lounge was duly reborn. It was a smash. The mob, of course, kept an eye on things. "They had a spotter," continues Fouratt. "They always have a spotter. The spotter would sit at the bar. It's like the lowest level of the Mafia. Steve Rubell would always recognize these people. They would watch the bartenders. Watch how many drinks they were giving away." But the spotters caused no problem at the bar. Nor at the door. "I never had any trouble at the door. How many people were let in and not let in, that kind of stuff."

Unbeknown to Fouratt or Rudolf, the Elf Queen was approached and offered the drug concession. The Elf Queen, a former flower child, ran a salon and narcotics distribution network to the upper classes from a gothic building on Central Park West. Something about the place caused her nostrils to flare and she turned the proposition down. For Rudolf and Fouratt, the problem came when the owners tried to bring in a mob aesthetic. To wit, a transvestite performer from a spot called the Gilded Grape. "I said to Rudolf we're outta here!" Fouratt says. "Rudolf had a discussion with them. They threatened him. Rudolf had never been threatened. He came back and said we're going *now*."

Fouratt's most vivid memory is that one of his former employers told him, in friendly fashion, "You're a good kid, Jimmy. I'm going to have to kill you but I want you to know that it's not personal."

What followed was Blitz. Blitz was named for a club in London's Shepherds Market run by Stephen Strange, a leader of the "New Romantics." Fouratt and Rudolf put on a succession of nightclubs on Long Island, a populist-minded attempt to show that clubs could rock even when they were across the bridges and through the tunnels. This lasted four months. Rudolf and Fouratt then refocused on Manhattan, where two new clubs were vying for the hole in the night that Studio had left: Bond's and the Underground, which was owned by Maurice Brahms.

John Addison had, in fact, talked to Fouratt about coming to Bond's. "John was calculating . . . withholding . . . but charming. Absolutely charming. But I have to feel that I can trust somebody," Fouratt says. Instead, he and Rudolf began Modern Classix, a series of nights at Underground. They opened with the American launch of one of the direst acts in rock history, Spandau Ballet, and a "New Romantics" fashion show from London. "People were dressed like Captain Kirk. It was a very brief trend but very fun," Rudolf says. But while they were at Underground, Rudolf and Jim Fouratt were sitting down with the newly released Ian Schrager and Steve Rubell.

It was characteristic that Rubell and Schrager should not instantly cement their relationship with Rudolf and Jim Fouratt. For one thing, they were impressed by a wholly illegal after-hours club that had just been started by two young Californians, Shawn Hausman and Eric Goode. Both were junior veterans of Studio 54. "We lived there," Goode says. As it happened Hausman's father had produced *Saturday Night Fever,* and both had worked on the movie. "You see Shawn getting a blowjob," Goode says.

Their club was quite unlike Studio. "It was really a club with no name," Eric Goode says. "It was on a second floor on Fourteenth Street. It was about ten or twelve thousand square feet. It was big, but it was raw. We would change it every week." A visitor remembers one metamorphosis keenly. "There was a long coffin in front of you, filled with rows of candles, and pig's feet," he says. "And there were thousands of chains, hanging down in the dark, and hanging motorcycles, and things. There was a glass cabinet with snakes in it for the bar.

"And there was a constant shower of leaves all evening, just falling. And there were hard-core sex films projected onto the walls. Women with animals. It was the first time I had been to a club that was more than just *disks.*"

Goode's club-with-no-name was open only about three nights a week and it lasted for only a couple of summer months. It impressed what Goode calls "a bunch of sleazy guys from Germany," though. It impressed them enough that they offered to back Goode and Hausman in a bigger club. It also impressed Rubell and Schrager. "Steve and Ian would come there after they got out of jail. They took Shawn and me over to Studio. We were going to help them with the reopening of Studio. We did a couple of installations. We didn't do much," Eric Goode says. "That was before Rudolf and Jim got involved."

Rudolf had begun seeing Steve and Ian downtown. He had been suprised, partly because they were still, officially, in the halfway house and partly because downtown had never been their milieu. "They were being shunned uptown. Because they were convicted felons, I suppose," he says. "All the doors were being closed in their faces. So they were going downtown. To the artists' places. I saw the two of them, sitting in an S&M club." He also saw them in Arthur Weinstein's after-hours club, the Jefferson. "It was five in the morning. They should have been in the halfway house. And even there, which was a strange mixture of everybody, they were sitting alone. Some were shunning them because downtown has a lot of bad feeling. 'I don't agree with you ideologically—therefore I am not going to talk to you.' Attitude.

"But others, I'm sure, were too shy to talk to them. Because they were Sacred Monsters!"

Rudolf sat and talked to them. "The strange thing was that I realized that Steve and Ian had absolutely no idea about the outside world whatsoever," he says. "Anything out of Studio 54! It was as if nothing else existed. I took them both to their first exhibitions in SoHo. They went through these art galleries in a daze. It was sort of like *wow, man!*

"Ian was the most impressed. In the car back, he said, 'Well, this is a whole new world.' He caught on, and became a person that's very interested in the arts. He always made very complicated questions. 'Is this art? I think it's art.' Before jail, he had no idea."

Fouratt and Rudolf duly set to work reopening Studio. "We were very well paid," Fouratt says. "We got three thousand dollars a week. We weren't just going to do Studio 54 as it was." The Man in the Moon was a speedy casualty. "Ian was very attached to it. He liked the look. But I thought it was a very late seventies symbol. It had to go. That was part of our deal," Fouratt says. "We supervised all the staffing. We brought in women as bartenders. And there were a couple of women at the door. Because we had done that at Peppermint. It was little things like that that kind of brought it up to date."

He remembers Steve Rubell's reaction when he proposed the woman bartenders: "Really?" A thoughtful pause. "Will they take their tops off?"

The casting call for the bar people was melodramatic. "Rudolf and I were doing the selecting. Fleischman was just sitting there. He was kind of floating. I was polite to him. I don't think Rudolf ever talked to him. Steve and Ian were behind a black curtain. They could see but you couldn't see them." The women were not asked to take their tops off.

Marc Benecke returned from Los Angeles in July. "I was liking my life there," he says. "But I owed Steve and Ian a lot." Studio finally reopened on a Tuesday night, September 15. It was an invitations only, but some twelve thousand had been mailed, as insurance. Unnecessarily. The reopening proved to be a mob scene that rivaled the opening. New gizmos within included screens that dropped onto the side walls with visuals that simulated a moonwalk, a desertscape, an opera house, and thunder and lightning. Brooke Shields was at an upstairs party thrown by Calvin Klein. The crowd included Jack Nicholson, Ryan O'Neal, Paul Simon, and John Belushi, and, of course, Andy Warhol, who had been at a dinner given by, of course, Halston.

Steve Rubell and Ian Schrager were likewise there, but for once Rubell stayed in Schrager's preferred milieu, the shadows, allowing Mark Fleischman to wallow in the media attention. The staff were dressed as ballerinas, jesters, and queens and at one juncture some forty cowgirls did a faux Rockettes number. An equally large crowd, mostly invited, waited outside, also in thunder and lightning, but not simulated. Within, the snow fell at 2:30.

The following night Andy Warhol gave a party for the writer Fran Liebowitz. It was going to be just like old times, wasn't it? No. Not really.

Rudolf and Jim Fouratt's Modern Classix nights were Wednesdays and Sundays. Steve Rubell, who cordially disliked avant-garde rock, endured the likes of Lena Lovich and Nina Hagen. It was somehow inevitable that Malcolm McLaren, the creator of the Sex Pistols and director of *The Great Rock 'n' Roll Swindle* should be roped in. Actually the Pistols had self-destructed by the time McLaren came to Studio. He brought one of the last live groups he handled, Bow Wow Wow. The lead singer was Annabella, a fourteen-year-old. "I don't know why they wanted them. They were only on the verge. But they were culty and quite fashionable," McLaren says.

McLaren marked the occasion by making a special record. "I personally pressed two or three thousand copies," he says. "It was a forty-five called 'The Mile High Club.' The label had an airplane on it and it said 'For Studio 54.' I think they were actually sent out as invitations. It was about that fantasy notion of people fucking, high in the sky. I just thought it was very applicable at that time to Studio 54."

McLaren duly took Bow Wow Wow to Studio. They set up and played. When asked how it had gone down, "I think we were a bit too loud for Steven. He kept complaining," McLaren said with relish.

Downtown did, finally, begin frequenting Studio. Fouratt and Rudolf even brought a downtown doorman, Chuck X, who knew who was who. Live music was a risky strategy. A concert with Kid Creole and the Coconuts cost the club $50,000. Not all the risk was financial. Brad Balfour, a music writer, remembers being involved with bringing an event to Studio. It was a party celebrating the First New York Noise Fest, which had featured New York's three extremist bands of the time, Live Skull, Swans, and Sonic Youth. The party, which was supposed to wind up long before midnight, the Studio's real witching hour, began with Eric Bogosian doing stand-up, and featured a West Coast band called Flipper.

Flipper—no relation to the roller disco—was the band that pioneered the habit of having fans slamming off the stage into a roiling mosh pit. "They were really dirty . . . grungy . . . *angry* . . . wow!" Balfour says enthusiastically. "You had all these downtown people. And waiting outside was the Studio 54 crowd. The Beautiful People! The models and the gays. Everything got going late. I remember Flipper going onstage . . . the Studio 54 management flipping out— literally flipping out!—at this music. And the Flipper people were all heroin addicts at the time. So they didn't give two fucks about anybody.

"Wow! They were abrasive. After four songs the Studio people took the music off. They cut the power and they cut the lights. *And Flipper flipped out.*"

Balfour got into the middle of the fray as a security guy was about to go for a band member, and they were all hustled out of there. That was uptown meets downtown with a vengeance.

This lasted three months. Good months. Fouratt and Rudolf both saw Steve Rubell as one of the ultimates in Nightworld, a construct that both men take extremely seriously. Nightpeople, as depicted in the movies, are customarily heavy-lidded, if men, mask-faced, if women, variously slimeballs or hard hearts. Actually, nightpeople are fervid. True believers.

Rudolf pooh-poohs the notion that Steve Rubell had overreached and been thwarted in building a mighty entertainment empire. "I am a club owner too," he says. "When you're a club owner it's just some kind of quirk that bites you. You cannot let go! Sure, who doesn't want to be a movie producer or whatever. But the public adoration that movie executives get is very indirect. It is through the press. You don't see a director or a producer with thousands of people that are cheering him, that know him personally.

"No! While the club owner—like Steve Rubell and others—you go to your own club, and you see thousands of people, and they want *you*. They love you or they hate you . . . they want to shake your hand . . . they want to drink with you . . . they want to give you drugs . . . they want to be your friend . . . that's something that very few other jobs in life give you. And it's an easy job. Right? You have no hours. You don't have to work that much. Let's face it."

Both Rudolf and Jim Fouratt also very much liked Steve Rubell personally. "I loved him. Absolutely loved him," Rudolf says. "Have you ever found anybody who didn't love Steve Rubell? I loved Stevie," Fouratt said. "My career has been up and it's been down, and up and down, but he always treated me the same way from the first time I met him to the last. He was a very loyal person.

"He was *amazed* I wouldn't do drugs. He would call me in the middle of the night and say"—Fouratt mimed a silly, sloppy ludedness—"*'You really don't do drugs? You don't use any drugs?'* He was trying not to use as much."

It was a tough love, though, in both cases. "He was a strange character," Rudolf muses. "Like a dangerous character that you had to sort of basically follow a certain procedure with and not get on his wrong side. Because he could get very mean and revengeful. He had the job of an authoritarian that was capable of great kindness and great cruelty." Both describe Rubell's sex life as for the main part brusque and commercial. "He couldn't fit anything other than a trick into the picture because he was far too busy," Fouratt says.

Neither man knew Ian Schrager nearly as well. Jim Fouratt speaks of Ian's "Machiavellian overview." He says that Ian and Steve were like Rudolf and him. That Ian, like Rudolf, was the killer businessman. He added, "And I was the charming little fag."

Rudolf vividly remembers a specific conversation with Ian. It was during the rebuilding of Studio and it was striking because Ian had touched upon a sensitive subject, his feelings in prison. "Ian was very affected by his time in jail. Especially because of his father," Rudolf says. "He had a paranoia that he had been going to die in jail." Schrager's melancholy mood had extended to Studio 54 itself. "He said, 'You know, this place really exploded,'" Rudolf remembers. "'It was like a meteor that just crossed the sky. But it has a curse. Because it crashed. It takes with it everybody that is involved with it. We are doomed.'"

He gave a thoughtful *heh-heh-heh* and said, "I thought it was a very important sentence. That is why I still remember it. It is not entirely true, but interesting."

It ended, though. "After three months, Mark Fleischman began deciding that really he *was* the owner," Jim Fouratt says. Fleischman began flexing his muscles. Also downtown showed no signs of taking to Studio, nor the Studio crowd to downtown acts. The concerts often lost money. It was then that an overture was made to Fouratt by a tough-guy realtor who owned a failing club, Interferon. Fouratt and Rudolf departed to reopen it as—what else?—Danceteria.

APRÈS DISCO

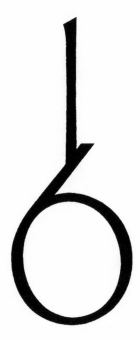

IN THE EARLY EIGHTIES MICHAEL ZILKHA OF ZE RECORDS shepherded a small group, myself among them, to Staten Island to listen to his new pick, a pale young blonde chanteuse. Zilkha introduced us after the set, and he asked for our verdict on the drive back. Mine was ho-hum. She had, I said, rather a light voice. "She's going to be tremendous," Zilkha said simply.

This was Madonna.

"How can anyone say disco died when disco's biggest star didn't put out a record until November 1982?" Zilkha asks. The record was *Madonna* and Zilkha signed up her cowriter.

One might call what was going on disco post-disco, and there was a club that was one of its incubators. The Paradise Garage had opened at the end of the seventies in a huge, raw space, a cast-concrete garage for heavy-duty industrial vehicles down by the docks. It was like the ominously spare space used for the concluding sequence—when the budget had run out—of *The Incredible Shrinking Man*. Don Was, the Detroit musician, a co-founder of the group, Was

(Not Was), which recorded with Ze, played the Paradise Garage in 1980 and 1981. "I felt we were on the cusp of this thing. A few people, myself included, had started listening to Jamaican dub reggae," Was says. The result was "a different kind of disco. It wasn't this happy kind of thing.

"I think maybe the drugs changed. The first time I went to the Paradise Garage I was high on mushrooms. Which is distinctly different from going to Studio and doing a bunch of blow. It's a very different kind of experience. It was enormous. *Man, it felt like the speakers were five storys high!* The place took on a really dark monolithic feel. And it wasn't like . . . happy. It was more trance. People were dancing in a trance."

Was instances "You're the One for Me," which was remixed for D Train Records by Francois Kevorkian. "That was the paradigm of the Paradise Garage," he says. "It might have been the nature of the instruments that were available. A new generation of synthesizers had come into prominence. You got this really dirty dark bass sound."

This was actually the second incarnation of the Paradise Garage—which had previously been the Chameleon—and the club's moving spirit was Larry Levan, the DJ. It is doubtful whether many habitués of Studio 54 could have named the club DJ, Richie Kaczor. Levan, a gay black man, was probably the first DJ to be recognized not as a "star" precisely—that would come soon with Jellybean Benitez—but as a creative force in making the music. Chris Blackwell, founder of Island Records, says, "You couldn't buy the music. It wasn't purchasable. You'd think you'd been there one hour. And it would be four."

"I've never seen anything quite like it, to tell you the truth," Don Was says. "I've seen places that tried to get that vibe, maybe that had primarily a black gay clientele. But Larry Levan was It. The power of the club was incredible." Larry Levan broke a single of theirs, "Tell Me That I'm Dreaming." "Frankie Crocker used to come in and sit upstairs. Larry would hit that record four or five times a night. Frankie Crocker started playing it. Larry really made it happen.

"I would notice that there would be more and more record companies coming and promoters coming to the visiting area of Larry's booth because they knew I came down on a Friday or a Saturday," says Frankie Crocker, a friend of Levan. The radio jocks knew the game. "We knew we were being manipulated. But that was the business."

The dub music to which Don Was had been listening was made by a handful of Jamaican musicians just using tape. It was hard to find outside London, Canada, and Jamaica itself. Billy Idol, who moved to New York with Perri Lister in 1981, was listening to it too. He, like John Lydon, the former Johnny Rotten, was moving on beyond punk to techno, but making stuff that was danceable. "Punk rock you could pogo to, but it wasn't sexy. It wasn't like you could fuck a chick to it," Idol says reasonably.

Disco lived. It was just that it was now called Dance music. The disco bonfire in Chicago hadn't consumed disco after all. "After that, we started our own music," says Rachel Cain, a young woman from that city. It began in clubs that were old warehouses, so it was soon called "House" music, and Ms. Cain, aka "Screamin' Rachel," likes to refer to herself as the "Queen of House." But House is itself pure dance music. Essentially, it was stripped-down disco. So disco lived there too.

What was not sexy was the increasing violence in Nightworld. Nobody had thought twice about walking home from Studio. Bill Avery, a publicist, was a discothèque junkie. "Studio 54 was my first experience in the nightlife," he says. He helped with some parties there, and earned Rubell's trust. "Steve would say you can take in eighty people free. No more! Eighty," he remembers. "I just went every night and stayed out until four in the morning. I slept there in a tuxedo after a charity ball and woke up at seven o'clock when they were vacuuming next to me. I just got addicted to that world.

"I was a heavy drinker, a *heavy* drinker, and I used cocaine a lot, but it was all in discothèques. I never sat down and did anything. Everything was always in motion. I kept on drinking, and doing things, and moving, and then I'd go to bed, and wake up, and be out again. It was really extraordinary. I was a voyeur," he says. Halston would sometimes invite him to parties at the house. He would never go. His main addiction was not sex, or drugs, but just floating around within the discothèques themselves, dancing, or on perpetual enthralled watch.

On September 3, 1982, Avery went to Xenon. His next conscious memory was finding himself in bed. "My head had a big gash and I was all bloody. I had a concussion. I have no idea who did it to this day. So I wasn't too thrilled to go to discothèques anymore. I stopped going out."

Predators were moving in on Nightworld. It was becoming a dangerous place.

Mark Fleischman became very much the foreground figure at Studio after the departure of Rudolf and Jim Fouratt. So, too, did one of his partners, a businessman from Florida, Stanley Tate. Earle Mack of the New Jersey real estate family had met Tate in 1973 when the Mack company bought a real estate investment trust that he was running. They had left him in charge. "He was a tough businessman. He wore suits. Married, with kids," Mack says.

Years later, Mack went to Studio. "Earle! Earle!" he heard.

He turned but saw nobody he knew.

"It's me. Stanley. I used to work for you."

Stanley Tate was in jeans and a T-shirt. He looked buff. He had a cutie pie on each arm. They greeted each other, and Earle asked how he was doing. "Making *tons of money*," Tate said, gleaming.

Earle took him aside for a moment. "Stanley . . . the wife . . . the kids . . ." he said.

"I, uh, got divorced," Stanley Tate said.

Tate, incidentally, was proposed as head of a powerful government agency, the Resolution Trust Corp., the federal government's instrument for cleaning up the savings and loans mess, but the proposal ran into flak and was dropped. Tate had simply been too outspoken, according to Mack.

Steve Rubell had never been merely interested in goings-on of the famous. He was an addict of news and information generally. It was part of an appetite for life. CNN was always playing in the background on his enormous screen on East Fifty-fifth Street. It was natural that he should be curious about a sickness that barely yet had an agreed-upon name. Jim Fouratt was active in gay politics and Rubell discussed it with him more frankly than most. "We talked about it in the early Eighties when a whole lot wasn't known about the disease, when there was both denial and discussion," Jim Fouratt says. Rubell was particularly concerned because he and an inner core at Studio had been as incestuous in their sociosexual lives as any close highly charged group. "All of those people shared the same type of boy—the hustler type, the bodybuilder— so Steve was very concerned that sex might have something to do with AIDS," Fouratt says.

It was a time when information, misinformation, rumor, and theory abounded—I remember being authoritatively told that the breakdown in immune systems was occurring because Americans were too sanitized, too unused to dirt—and the lineaments of the plague were still indistinct, like a dark rockface in a mist. Baird Jones remembers that Eddie Newberg, whose job was handing out free-drink tickets to the deserving at the Sunday night parties, was required to put on gloves in about 1982. "He had the gay cancer. At this point they were calling it GRID," Jones says. "There was some sense that it could be communicated by hand. And he would wear white gloves."

Henry Post was at *New York* magazine when Anna Wintour was appointed fashion editor. "He took me up right at the beginning. He was very helpful and gave me the dope on everything," Wintour says. He gave her a back issue and insisted she read an article about the newly diagnosed "gay cancer" or Kaposi's sarcoma. Wintour and Post became friendly, and they worked on a couple of stories together. "But he was bitter," she says. "Henry was so weird, you know. I never thought he was telling you the truth about his life. I think there were a lot of things he was a bit embarrassed about. But he was terribly proud of that article he wrote about Studio 54. He thought that was quintessential. He really did."

On April 4, 1982, Wintour gave a party for Post and for the artist he lived with at the Broadway loft she shared with Michael Stone. I remember being interested to see that the guests included Steve Rubell. That wasn't the half of it. Andy Warhol wrote of this party in his diaries: "Steve Rubell was there. But the strangest thing is that he was with the prosecutor who sent him to jail! And I think Henry—who actually wrote the article that started all the trouble— I think Henry got them together."

What Warhol didn't know was that Sudler had come to like both Rubell and Schrager and that he very much liked Post, though he was baffled by what he calls Post's "love-hate relationship" with Steve Rubell.

It wasn't long after this party that Post called and asked Sudler to do his will. Post was young and seemed fit. Why, Sudler asked, perplexed?

"Haven't you heard of gay cancer?" Post said.

Sudler has doctors in his family. "Cancer is treatable," he said.

"Not this cancer," Post said. He explained about the immune thing. Sudler says he was "stoic."

It was, I think, June when I heard Henry Post was sick. I telephoned. I wanted to drop by with fruit or magazines, the way one does. I never got to speak with him and was told he didn't want visitors. I found this odd.

Craig Unger called Post in early July. Unger had written a feature for *New York* about the emergence of what was not yet called the post-modernist sensibility. It was to be published later that month. "He was going to read the first draft," Unger says. "I called him. I called and called. And then he died. I was quite stunned by the whole thing. I thought you just had to take some pills. The idea that this could be fatal was beyond me."

Henry was the first person Anna Wintour, Craig Unger, or I knew to die of what was still not yet called AIDS. His memorial service was at a Quaker place near Gramercy Park. Steve Rubell and Peter Sudler were among the mourners.

A small group of people were in a Manhattan apartment sometime in 1981. They included Richard Neville, the Australian writer, and myself. Malcolm McLaren came by. McLaren, who was in recovery from the splintering of the Sex Pistols, and who was opening a branch of his punk boutique downtown, tried to coax us into accompanying him to the West Bronx. He was going to listen to a new sort of music he called "scratch."

We were saying, well, Malcolm, that sounds just great. But perhaps some other time. Right? None of us went with him.

McLaren was taken on his first visit to the scratch venue by Michael Holman, who had played with Jean-Michel Basquiat in Gray. "McLaren was dressed as a pirate. It was the New Romantic theme. He had a frilly shirt. He was a target," says Michael Holman. McLaren remembers, "There was this huge waste ground between two fired-out condominiums, with a few burnt-out cars. There were about five hundred black guys, a gigantic group of very volatile people. There were tall guys holding torches, and then suddenly characters would bounce on their heads, and do these amazing acrobatic dances. Fights would keep breaking out and I would keep as close as possible to this guy Afrika Bambaataa behind this trestle table in order not to get a whack. They had set up a couple of trestle tables. A few amplifiers, a couple of big speakers. It was pretty do-it-yourself.

"They were making music out of old records. I thought it was extraordinary. It was really deconstruction! And they were talking over the music. People running up to the tables and grabbing hold of the mike. And meanwhile they would be scratching Gary Numan's 'Cars,' and mixing it with some Supremes record on another deck, and somehow concocting this rhythmic sound. It sounded very much like the terrain one was looking at."

What Malcolm McLaren was listening to was what would become *Planet Rock,* which has been called the first hip-hop album. Afrika Bambaataa, the still little-known focus, was from the Bronx. This was not, of course, the birth of hip-hop—that is credited to the legendary Herc in the mid-seventies—but it showed hip-hop getting ready to take control.

McLaren and Holman put together a package, Bambaataa included, to open for Bow Wow Wow, at Jerry Brandt's club, the Ritz. This performance was seen by a young Briton, fresh to town, Ruza Blue. Ruza Blue—"that's the name on my passport," she says elliptically—was from Peterborough in the British flatlands. She had studied mime in London, had come to New York in 1981 for "a two-week break," but had taken a job in McLaren's store. She was twenty-one, blue-eyed, had a Punkish bristle of hair, and was as pale as a glass of milk. Her night at the Ritz decided her on her next move. "That was it," she says. "I knew what I wanted to do."

Blue approached Afrika Bambaataa and asked if he would be the presiding DJ at a weekly night if she could find a club. Bambaataa asked the waif if money was likely to be forthcoming. "I told him yes and he agreed," she says.

She found a boutique-size club, Negril, on Second Avenue. He began doing Thursday parties, which effectively introduced hip-hop to Manhattan. Blue called the nights Wheels of Steel and had elegantly stark black-and-white fliers designed by the old-style graffiti writer Phase 2.

In the summer of 1982 Blue, who had been having increasing problems fitting her operation into Negril's small size, moved to Roxy, the grandiose roller disco, which had fallen on hard times. Wheels of Steel, which ironically was the only night upon which roller skating was not permitted, opened on Friday, June 18. Included on the bill were DJ Afrika Bambaataa; the rap group Soulsonic Force; the Mac'D Double Dutch Girls, who skipped rope; the break-dancers, the Rock Steady Crew; and graffiti writers who spray-painted back-grounds while the furiously energetic proceedings were under way.

Soon Ruza Blue's Fridays were the most profitable night of Roxy's week. They were a breakthrough, too, in being parties at which straight whites and blacks partied together, with, mostly, an excellent vibe. Blue decided this was just the beginning, signed with European promoters, and took the whole she-bang to the South of France. "Blue took the whole Roxy rap package on tour," Futura 2000 says. "Bambaataa and Rammellzee and myself and Dondi . . . the Rock Steady Crew . . . the Double Dutch Girls . . .

"In a sense, it was a little laughable. I thought wow! Damn. It's kind of cheap in a way, to import these girls to jump rope. But I guess it was cool. Because that one tour sparked a lot of stuff in Europe. And then Japan."

Blue, unfortunately, would not be part of it much longer. The very sweet-ness of this success made the owner of Roxy act according to the less savory mores of Nightworld. "He decided to take over what I had created" Blue says.

She found herself teamed with a local, Vito Bruno. Bruno, a soft-spoken and magesterially overweight figure, had begun in the nightlife as a security guard at 2001 Odyssey. He had indeed been there for the shooting of *Saturday Night Fever*. He had segued into Manhattan in the late seventies, bringing a mobile disco—with speakers, a hang-it-yourself disco ball, the whole thing—into New York's Statler Hilton, of all places. It had not gone down well with all the hotel guests, who didn't particularly *want* a mobile disco or its habitués. "People would come into the lobby painted gold . . . half naked," Bruno says. "Every night the general manager would say, 'You've gotta lower the sound.' They were not happy campers." That venture was short-lived.

Ruza Blue was not a happy camper either, and soon departed, leaving Bruno in control at the Roxy. The Wheels of Steel lost their spin. Roxy itself began to get an ugly reputation for violence. "After that I went low-key and underground for a while. Because it really messed me up for a bit," Ruza Blue says. "She was screwed," Vito Bruno says. "We were all screwed in the end."

Blue remains in music and dance—she still manages the Rock Steady Crew—but has lost her innocence about Nightworld.

WILD & FREE

1

MAURICE BRAHMS HAS HIS CANDIDATE FOR WHO KILLED
nightlife. It is his usual candidate for whatever is
wrong in Nightworld: Steve Rubell. "We didn't have
any such thing as free at Infinity," he says. It's one of
his favorite refrains: *Everybody paid.* But Steve Rubell
had intuitively understood that few things more
delight the rich and famous, and their courtiers, including the press, than getting something free. Rubell
paid his A Listers through the nose, so to speak, because he liked them to like him, and because their
presence attracted media attention, and that attention
attracted the horde of spenders. Full disclosure: In all
my many, many, many nights at Studio 54, Xenon,
and a host of subsequent clubs, I seldom actually laid
out more than a few bucks in actual folding money.

Rubell couldn't then have cared less that he was
implanting in an already privileged group a huge sense
of entitlement. It wasn't just that they disliked dipping
into their pockets (though it *was* that, too; the lousiest
coke being more expensive than, say, even the best

claret). There was the feeling that if you were asked to pay, you were reduced to the level of the plebeians, the hopeless, the losers. Access to freebies meant you were free and brave. Also, the bigger the freebies, the more important the recipient. It was a bit like handing out titles of nobility in early Europe, except disco titles changed more quickly.

Mark Fleischman took over Rubell's amazing celebrity-power cash machine in rather different times. "In the early days of disco, it was such a drug-oriented thing," Fleischman says. "People were just going to discos because there were drugs there. I think that started to slow down. For one thing, the law wasn't tolerating it. It became harder to actually get people to go out every single night of the week the way they used to in the late seventies. All of a sudden some people were beginning to clean up their acts. They just weren't going out to do coke every night. I started to feel this in 1982, 1983. That's when I started to bring in the promoters . . ."

Promoters! It is widely accepted that it has been the promoters who have throttled nightlife—especially by the promoters themselves—but it is worth establishing how they were able to seize power. Carmen D'Alessio, who had learned the cash value of a famous face at Valentino, was paid a flat fee at Studio, and a modest slice of the gate. Then Nikki Haskell upped the ante, both for the clubs and the promoters.

Haskell happened to be in Los Angeles when Xenon opened, but was introduced to Howard Stein upon her return. Haskell was going out with Didier Milinaire, son of the Duke of Bedford. The designer suggested that Xenon let Haskell throw a party for fifty for a beau and give them some free champagne. Howard Stein, who was no visionary of the free list in the Steve Rubell mold, agreed, a bit grudgingly.

"The fifty ended up as two hundred people and Howard went crazy. He was just berserk!" Haskell says. "But it became a very heavy-duty party. *Women's Wear Daily* wrote it up, and everything. A month later the Duke and Duchess of Bedford were coming. So I went to Howard and said I'd like to give them a sit-down dinner. He said, 'Okay. I'll give you the room for free and I'll give you the rentals.' I sent out all the invitations . . ."

There was then an ugly moment. "I realized that Howard was not going to pay for this dinner. But *New York* magazine had a big spread on caterers.

And they showed this one caterer who did the thing with pheasant and quails. I called them on the phone out of nowhere and I convinced them that it was in their *best interest* to give this party.

"Urgggh! It was the whole damn floor of Xenon. So it had to be two hundred people. That's how the whole thing started with the parties. Okay?"

Nikki Haskell hadn't figured out yet how to spin a career out of this. That would come.

Gwynne Rivers, the daughter of the artist, Larry Rivers, first went to Studio at sixteen. Her father had a show at Marlborough Gallery and Myra Scheer roped her in to help with the party. Gwynne's mother, Clarice, was a great party giver, so she knew the drill. It was a good party. "Mick Jagger arrived and it immediately got into the press," she says. "There was a picture. 'Sultry Gwynne Rivers, Rolling Along with Rolling Stone, Mick Jagger. Jerry Hall Nowhere to Be Seen.' Something like that. Of course, it was silly. It was literally him putting his drunken arm around me for a second.

"And, because of that, Mark Fleischman said, 'I would really like you to work here, so we'll pay you off the books.'" Her work was in the daylight hours. She was attending a tutorial school which had elastic hours. Mark Fleischman would drop by at about one in the afternoon in his limousine and pick her up, rather to the amazement of her schoolfellows. He would have the tabloids in the limo. They would check to see whether Studio had been mentioned as they drove to the club. Then she would set to work.

Gwynne Rivers was preppy-connected and worked the preppy parties. "I would pick out the ten big social people from Brown and put them all on a committee," she says. "They would invite everybody from Brown. I had a party for the polo club, the thousand-dollar Piaget cup. I rented polo mallets and covered the bar with them.

"Mark paid me anything between five and eight hundred dollars for a party. Then I got a little something here and there for hanging out in the office and making calls. I would do things like call Celebrity Service to find out if so-and-so was in town. I was always looking for a reason for a party. I would see a show was opening and I would call the theater and say do you want to have your opening party at Studio 54? Nine times out of ten they would say . . . *yeah!*"

She also became, as was natural, a habitué by night. It was stunning. "You're between childhood and adulthood," she says. "I think a lot of people, even if they were adults, were going through their second adolescence in Studio 54. You came in out of ordinary life, which was buildings and streets and arguments, and you walked into this . . . glitz.

"The lights were flashing . . . it was a bit smoky . . . you were in a daze . . . the environment immediately took over. In a funny way you didn't have to worry about *doing* anything because the environment was so overwhelming that it took you out of yourself. The flashing lights, and everybody dancing."

Gwynne Rivers was aware that there were dark aspects to the goings-on in Nightworld. Some were thrilling, like the catacombs in the basement, with itsy-bitsy cubicles filled with adults doing exotica. Some were, well, *educational,* like the time Gwynne and a best friend were leaving Xenon. A limo hove up alongside, the window open. "Do you want to get into the car?" asked a famous TV person. "I was a little bit hesitant," Gwynne says. Her friend was "more adventurous. So we jumped into the limousine. He had two friends in the back. They were having cocktails." She added, "I was sixteen. I wouldn't do it now."

They all jumped out at Studio. He was famous. She was disco-famous. Marc, who was standing on the standpipe, motioned them in through a convulsive spasm of mob worship, and they all went straight up to the balcony. "He did a line of coke," she says. "Then I felt kind of . . . movement. I looked over. A woman, plain as day, was giving this guy head. She was oblivious and really did not care that we were sitting about a foot away from her.

"It was like . . ." Gwynne Rivers did a convincing replay of the bug-eyed cartoon animal routine with which mid-teens indicate a fused light bulb of a mind.

There was worse. Gwynne Rivers was a friend of Alison Gertz and met Alison's one-night fling of a bartender boyfriend. She didn't know about AIDS, but she knew something bad was happening out there. Somehow or other, it was to do with bisexuals. "I knew he was bi. He scared me," she says. Alison Gertz was one of the first middle-class women to come out as being HIV positive. She died of AIDS in August 1992.

It was for such reasons that Gwynne Rivers, who usually went to Studio with a girl friend, preferred the Gay Sundays. "You felt safe, because you were a young girl, and they weren't going to bother you. Because at that age a lot of guys are bothering you. It was very liberating for a young woman. You could dance and you could practically undress."

She added swiftly. "I never did that. There was a very open atmosphere. It was the whole coming-out-of-the-closet thing. It was fascinating to see so many beautiful men but to feel at the same time so safe. A lot of them were doing poppers and stuff, so it would be fun. You'd be on the dance floor and somebody would offer you a popper or something. It wasn't my favorite thing but maybe once in a while I'd do that and then it was like . . . phewwwww! You'd be totally gaga.

"Studio was a fantasyland. A playland for grown-ups. It really was."

It was also a playland for the staff. Gregory Gunsch, one of the straight barmen, would arrange to meet some eager creature at the door that led down to the VIP basement, where he had favorite nooks and crannies. "There were four or five rooms down there. One had beds in it. One just had pieces of foam," he says. "That was half the guys. We would cover for each other . . . 'Okay, you'll go next, and I'm going next' . . . 'Which one do you want?' . . . 'Okay, I'll take that one' . . . Boom, boom! Away we'd go! We'd come in . . . have fun . . . get drunk, get laid!"

I asked how often this might be expected to happen. "Oh, pretty much every night for some people." Sometimes three times a night, which could make things complicated. "You'd come back up. She stays at the bar. You say to another guy, 'Switch sides with me. This wacko won't leave me alone!' You're working on another one, and she's watching, and she gets pissed off and—yi, yi, yi!

"There was a few nights we wouldn't. I wasn't feeling well. Or I'd get too whacked or something. Usually we'd come in . . . have fun . . . get drunk, get laid! What the hell! It was perfect."

Studio's week was constantly sliced and resliced. At the re-opening, Wednesdays and Sundays were given to Rudolf and Jim Fouratt. Then Steve Rubell suggested making Sunday gay. Michael Fesco, late of Flamingo, was brought in. "Steve was great," Fesco says. "He said whatever Michael wants, he gets.

"I did the white parties and the black parties. I did A Night Aboard the Titanic. This was a twenty-minute production. I built the big bow of a boat up on the bridge. It hit the iceberg. The ship opened up and va-woom! There was Eartha Kitt in white fox, singing *I Want to Be Evil*! The audience went crazy!"

Why did the gay crowd get off so on black divas? "Oh, they associated with them so much. Gay men couldn't associate very much with male singers. Not even Johnny Mathis. At Studio we got all the female names. The only person ever to break that image was Sylvester. We had great times with Sylvester. One time he came down from the wings on a swing. He said, 'Never again, Michael! Never again!' " Gay Sundays took off like a rocket.

Monday nights, the club was dark. Tuesdays were given to Marc Benecke, who had lost his taste for the door. He denies Fleischman's tale that he had been menaced by guns in the Virgin Islands. It was just that dealing with preppy hordes had little allure. "It just wasn't as compelling as it used to be. It wasn't as *lofty*," Benecke says. The time when the doorman at Studio was the keeper of the gate, the warden of the marches, was over. Benecke adds that "it wasn't monetary. I was on a salary."

"Marc organized a group of kids we called the 'Harvard Boys.' A very cool night, with young preppy boys and beautiful blonde girls," Fleischman says. And Wednesdays? "Wednesday was an open hole." Until, that is, Fleischman went to one of Jerry Rubin's networking salons.

It was disconcerting to see the preppies, baying en masse, but there always had been preppies in Studio; the cucumber slices in Steve Rubell's salad. There were now concerted efforts to attract the very customers that Rubell and Benecke had been most keen to keep out. Even now it seems remarkable that one of Studio 54's most intensive party givers was none other than the sometime revolutionary, member of the Chicago Seven, Jerry Rubin, and that his fiefdom should have been the equivalents of junior Kiwanis, Elks, and Lions.

There had been a time when Jerry Rubin had been best known for wearing fierce tribal face paint, advising his coevals not to trust anybody over thirty, and helping bring down capitalism by showering the New York Stock Exchange floor with dollar bills. Indeed, I first met him in London at the zenith of his bandanna-at-the-barricades days. Some time at the end of the sixties I was in a car stuck in traffic in Kensington High Street, with Rubin, Abbie Hoffman, and some people from *Oz* magazine, including Richard Neville. Rubin gesticulated in the direction of a comfy old department store, Derry & Toms, and said, if memory serves, that it would be "groovy" to see it in flames.

I had demurred, pointing out that my great-aunt sometimes had had tea there. The *Oz* people let it slide but the Americans acted as if they knew a class enemy when they saw one. I got on better terms with Jerry in San Francisco in the early seventies. I would see him here and there: in New York, for instance, at the party in his apartment (which had been formerly occupied by the singer Phil Ochs) during the Nixon-McGovern election. McGovern was being eviscerated on TV. A few people—Allen Ginsberg, Dave Dellinger of the Chicago Seven, and Julian Beck of the Living Theatre—were watching dejectedly but most guests ignored the screen. Ed Sanders of the Fugs left early. John Lennon was there, noisily, as were Claes Oldenburg (briefly), a couple of Black Panthers, Dotson Rader, and a quorum of Hells Angels. I watched the screen with Rubin for a while. "It's not going to change the way we live. Is it?" he asked.

Obviously, he felt not. So perhaps I was less surprised than many at the later trajectory of the radical ideologue's career. But, since Jerry Rubin was killed jaywalking in Los Angeles in 1994, I think the tale of his Second Coming—how he turned the disco world to gold—should come from his former wife, Mimi, formerly Mimi Leonard. "I came from a very lefty background," she says. "My father, George Leonard, coined the phrase 'Human Potential Movement.' Daddy was one of the founders of Esalen Institute." She had been in Haight-Ashbury in 1967. "I was seventeen. I was as much of a hippie as anyone was ever a hippie," she says. By the time she met Jerry Rubin nine years later, though, she was a senior market analyst in new product introductions at the ad agency BBD&0.

They started living together in 1977 and married the following year. Jerry was by then making his radical celebrity pay by speaking countrywide about his new (nonradical) "goals," and making $30,000 to 50,000 a year doing it. His agency was New Line Presentations, later to become New Line Cinema, of which an owner was Mark Fleischman.

In 1980 Mimi went to Wall Street and started trading commodities. "Then

Jerry got jealous of how much fun I was having and he went down and got a job with Ray Dirks as a marketing director. He was never a stockbroker as they reported," Mimi says. They felt such a buzz that they wrote "this really wonderful piece." It was published in the *Times*. The gist was that Jerry Rubin was proud of everything he had done as a radical, but clearly capitalism was the best system in the world. It ended: *"I am going to Wall Street and yay for Capitalism!"*

Mimi and Jerry were startled by the response. "It was the entire op-ed page. There wasn't anything on it, except this *hideous picture* of Jerry in a tribesman outfit, and about thirty letters, each of which was more scathing than the last," Mimi says. "Turncoat. Duhduhduh! There was no germ of forgiveness, and consciousness that Jerry had changed."

Mimi left Jerry anyway. "Jerry was devastated. Beyond belief," she says. Adding, with the airy capitals that the human potential movement somehow creates, "And he, in a very Positive-Thinking kind of way, a Taking-Action kind of way, decided to meet every beautiful woman in New York." His way was to give parties in his apartment. Ray Dirks, a whiz kid du jour with a fondness for media, ponied up to the tune of $1,000 a week. Rubin's first party was in April 1981. "It was supposedly—well, actually—for stockbrokers to meet clients," Mimi says. "He took the term 'networking,' which had always been a feminist term—it was always women networking with each other— and said it's business networking, and he asked everyone to give a business card at the door.

"So all my friends called me and said Jerry is so gross! I cannot believe that guy! How could he do something so repulsive? And, of course, within months they're not calling me, they're going to the parties."

I attended a couple of Jerry Rubin's salons, and, I suppose, networked there myself. Next, though, Ray Dirks went belly-up financially. Mimi and Jerry were together again, but broke. They had about $500. Mimi's commodities trading was barely ticking over. "We had been used to all these book advances and everything," she says. These, too, had dried up.

It was then that a director of the disco Underground suggested to Rubin that he throw his networking salon on the premises. "It seemed a contradiction in terms," Rubin mused on the printed invitation. "Who talks at a disco? Who meets people in a disco? Who parties at a disco before 11 P.M.?" But he ended,

"Do invite your most attractive and respected friends and associates . . ." Four thousand invitations were dispatched. "More people than had ever come to Underground came. All beautifully dressed elegant people rushed there," Mimi says. He gave three parties at Underground. But Mark Fleischman, Jerry's old lecture organizer, was quickly on the telephone. "Studio 54 was so hot. Studio 54 was so cool. There was no question but that we were going to go to Studio," Mimi says.

Jerry Rubin kicked off in March 1982. A letter explained: "After work and early in the evening every Wednesday, Studio 54 will become a salon. The music will be soft and classical, and serve only as a background to encourage lively conversation and business interactions. There will be no dancing music or flashing lights." The hours would be five to ten. "Imagine 500 animated conversations taking place on what is usually a frenetic dance floor!"

What kind of people went? Mimi pondered. "It was probably people that couldn't get into Studio otherwise," she said with admirable honesty. "Ninety percent of them. Or were afraid to try. It was a crowd that couldn't even really *imagine* starting an evening at ten o'clock at night."

At this juncture, any zeitgeist hound should have spotted that nomenclature was in order. It happened that Bob Greene, a Chicago columnist, who had known Jerry since 1968, the Democratic Convention, and the trial of "the Seven," was in town working on *Nightline*. "I was in a bar on Columbus taking a break from editing," he says. He overheard some people joking, the joke being that Rubin had gone from being the head of the yippies, the Youth International Party, to the head of the Young Urban Professionals, yuppies. "I put it in a piece. I used the phrase 'Observers have said' as euphemism for 'I overheard this somewhere,' " Greene says. "I think the headline was FROM YIPPIE TO YUPPIE. It got picked up on syndication and all of a sudden people started using the phrase." The yuppie sprang to life.

So staggeringly successful were Rubin's nights that soon he was doing Sundays too. "Jerry Rubin's was the ball game that succeeded. Other than Rubin, everything was a tremendous fiasco," Baird Jones says. "They would pay five dollars to get in, and he would get the door. He would get it all. Oh my God, it was incredible! He once made thirty-five-thousand dollars in one night. He had so much money stuffed in his pockets—because he got paid in cash and it was in low denominations—that he looked like the Michelin Man.

He looked like he had tires around him. He had this stuff in his socks, in his pockets, everywhere. He had two shopping bags.

"I remember him diving into a cab with lots of money falling over the place, just to get away. And he would badger the club, saying he wanted the coat check as well as the door. He started to get fifty percent of the coat check. And he was pushing them for his expenses."

It so happened that meantime Abbie Hoffman had been preparing to reappear. He had remained close to Jerry while he was on the lam. "It was like we were his troops. And he was the general," Mimi says. "It was call these people . . . arrange this . . . make a telephone call to this agent. And he was in charge. He was such a hero when he was underground.

"So when he came out from underground, suddenly he was like a regular person that had to make a living. And capitalism, we felt, came into play. We had had a very successful year at Studio 54. We had had about two thousand or twenty-five hundred people a week for a year. It was a phenomenon. We had this huge list, about forty thousand people, or whatever it was at that point. *And Abbie wanted our list.*"

Abbie Hoffman wanted the list because he wanted to give a benefit at Studio 54 for a radio station. It was, Mimi says, so that he could land a job. "Because Abbie was such a hustler, in a way," she says. "In a *good* way. You know? There was always an angle."

Jerry and Mimi decided against it. "Hey! We've worked so hard to build this list up," they told Hoffman. "It's all we have, is this!"

"The gloves are off!" Hoffman told them, ominously.

Mark Fleischman did give Abbie a party at Studio. Hoffman gave Fleischman an inscribed copy of his sixties classic, *Steal This Book*. But Abbie Hoffman failed to land a job at the radio station. "Abbie never made it. He never could make it," Mimi says. "There was no growth." Jerry Rubin saw what a success Timothy Leary and G. Gordon Liddy were having as a touring double act and approached Hoffman. They did likewise, billed as Yippie Versus Yuppie. It was a big success. But their friendship or alliance essentially was over.

For the twinkling of an eye it seemed Steve Rubell's tossed salad had been the principal dish in town. "You knew that at midnight everybody you wanted to see would be *right there,*" R. Couri Hay, a flamboyant columnist for *The National Enquirer,* says. "I think that was the beauty of it. You didn't have to go to five restaurants, and three clubs, and six parties. It was midnight. And everybody was there."

The promoters had changed all that. Nightworld was being furiously niche-marketed, what with the gay nights, preppy nights, yuppie nights. Fesco's gay night at Studio, for instance, had fierce competition. "The gay clone crowd had shifted over to the Saint. And the gay clone crowd was really tight. They knew the whole ball game" says Baird Jones. Annoyingly to Fesco, some of the competition came from within Studio itself. Fleischman brought in a friend of his, John Blair, to do Thursdays.

Fesco argued. "I said you can only do one gay night a week," he says. "John said, 'Oh, I have different crowd.' " Fleischman says that Blair "created a real cool gay night, not a gay gay night. A lot of models. Gay guys and beautiful women. And a lot of photographers." Fesco says, "It didn't work out that way. It split up the crowd completely. It was only a matter of time before Studio closed."

In 1981 Baird Jones had got a letter from Maurice Brahms in Allenwood, the federal pen, asking him to do parties at Underground on Fridays and in Bond's on Saturdays. Brahms, not one to let a little thing like being in the slammer get him down, had delightful visions of each club filling with preppies caterwauling for booze. He had an even more delightful vision of this cutting Studio 54 off at the knees, separating Rubell and Schrager from any hope of seeing whatever monies they might have been promised. Then even the air in Allenwood would smell sweet.

Baird Jones, whose sister worked with the D.A.'s office, decided that, yes, Brahms was serving everybody else's time. Baird had duly done some nights at the elephantine Bond's, but in due course went over to Studio to do society nights. Soon his ingenuous preppy-from-hell weirdness had enabled him to take over half the week. His co-hosts were disco-surreal in their social mix. They included, for instance, George Plimpton, the ubiquitous writer and editor of the *Paris Review,* socialite paparazzo George Whipple III, and Carolina Somoza, the daughter of the Nicaraguan dictator, Anastasio Somoza. "She was very social at that time," Baird Jones says. "I got paid four thousand dollars a party. I was making twelve thousand dollars a week. Eleven thousand dollars' profit. Because my expenses were virtually mimimal."

Nonetheless this was the silver age of Studio, and it was very different, but not everybody picked up on the sea change. Manhattan was filled with former Studio celebs going through acute cases of limelight deprivation, if not freebie withdrawal. "People like Bianca Jagger just didn't get it," Baird Jones says. "They kept showing up and what they were like was *beached sea monsters*, and the tide had run out, and they looked *so peculiar*. They would always go downstairs to the basement first, and the basement wasn't happening, so then they would come around to the office.

"This was constantly happening. Johnny Carson would come, and Sun Yung Moon—you know, the Moonies—came to one of the events, and Schwarzenegger. There were people that would show up, and Marc Benecke would be apologizing, telling them they were making a big mistake. They were walking right into a party where the average age was eighteen.

"People like Leroy Neiman would be coming to Jerry Rubin's parties. They just didn't know any better."

EUROTRASH EPIPHANIES

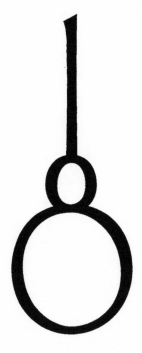

IT WAS CRYSTAL CLEAR THERE WAS MONEY TO BE MADE by anybody who could identify a fresh pool of partygoers, particularly if they were the sort of partygoers the gossip pages would love, and that club owners would cut deals to have on the premises. Ludovic Autet and Marc de Gontaut Biron, two Frenchmen, did just that.

Autet, who was born in Algiers, had set his sights on Manhattan since childhood. "It was a mission. To come to New York," he says. He arrived in 1972. He was married. "My wife hated it. Because it was not jet set," he says. In 1975 he started a restaurant, Le Coup de Fusil, with a Frenchwoman, Marina de Brantes. It was nouvelle cuisine, one of the peculiar horrors of that time, and so became wildly fashionable. Steve Rubell, the meat-and-potatoes man par excellence, was often there with Ron Ferri, being willing to endure the tiny quantities of food prettily displayed on a plate so long as it was in a hot spot in Manhattan. Autet sold out to de Brantes, and started a PR agency. One client was Regine's. Regine asked him to get the jeunesse dorée in to her joint. She promised a temptingly cut-price meal.

There is some slight disagreement as to just how the Junior International Club was born. Autet says, "The concept came to my mind at one of Baird Jones's parties in Studio 54. I thought, my God! All these young people are in New York." Marc Biron sees it a bit differently. Biron had come to Manhattan in 1978 with the ambition of becoming a movie director, but was supporting himself as a housepainter. He was staying with a crowd of fellow Euros. "They were fascinated by Studio 54. They were trying to get in, but they were never invited," he says. Biron, though, quickly learned how to crack the social codes. "I went out every night," he says. "Even though I was a housepainter, I went everywhere." Sensing that there was a future in this, he approached Ludovic Autet.

At any rate, Biron and Autet agreed to organize. In 1982 they founded the Junior International Club. "My concept was to have a club within a club," Autet explains. "Then I created the charter [read: free] membership." Charter members included the princes Albert of Monaco and Jean of Luxembourg and such young Americans as Harry Tower. The first charter membership lunch was at Quo Vadis. The JIC was a splendid engine, for attracting new (read: paying) members, for getting column ink, and for prying hefty discounts out of restaurants and clubs. Indeed, soon Moët & Chandon guaranteed to provide all JIC events with champagne at 30 percent off.

What about Carmen D'Alessio? Wasn't this trespassing on to her turf? Not exactly. D'Alessio's cronies were from the early wave of IWT, International White Trash. They were grandees, high-profile nomads on the Paris-Rome-London-Marbella-Gstaad circuit, whose names had been bold-face on the gossip pages long before they had come to Manhattan to escape socialism, the taxman, and guerrilla groups like the Red Brigades, the Baader Meinhoff gang, and the Montoneros. "Carmen used to have one prince. A party for just one prince," Biron says. "But there are also ordinary princes, you know. At my parties with Ludovic we used to have six princes on an invitation." Biron's princes were *working* princes. Little princes. This was the aperçu that had created the Junior International Club: the realization that there had been a whole incursion of well-heeled foreigners who were younger than D'Alessio's crowd. They were polite, low-key, with no high-style *nostalgie de la boue*. They were simply in Manhattan to find a home for flight capital or to put in a three-year stint at a bank, and they were delighted to get into Manhattan clubs where they were unknown and to meet young Americans of similar tastes. "It was a lifestyle. It was clean. It wasn't about drugs and sex. Well, maybe sex a little," Autet says.

Biron and Autet were unalike. Marc Biron is an elongated fellow, with a high laugh and sometimes skittish thought processes. (Once, sitting alongside him on the Hampton jitney, I said I wanted to read, rather than discuss the party of the night before. "You are so boring," he complained. "You have no conversation." This was only partly a joke.) He bears the title of count, and his family, which comes from Périgord and can trace a pedigree of a thousand years plus, includes four marshals of France, including one who lost his head trying for the crown. Biron is a disarmingly unapologetic snob. Ludovic Autet is a thruster from a middle-class family. It was, in Euro terms, the preppy and the yuppie, and a psychologically precarious union from the start.

JIC invitations boasted a coat of arms, a shield supported by a pair of what were supposed to be lions but resembled foxes, wolves, or possibly jackals. Club dues were $300. Soon there were several hundred actual members, and probably an equally great number of unpaid-up satellites. Most of these were rich brat Americans, with the sort of names that used to be made sport of in Marx Brothers movies. The JIC, whose members were soon being cooed over by the gossip columns, cheerfully played Studio, Xenon, Visage, Club A, and other contenders off against each other. These were among the hosts on JIC invitations in 1983:

PRINCE JEAN OF LUXEMBOURG	LEONARDO FERRAGAMO
AND PHILLIPPE A. BIGAR	AVERELL MORTIMER
LIBBY PIERPONT AND ANTON ROJAS	CLAUDIA OLIVIERI
ARCHDUKE SIMEON OF AUSTRIA	ANNE EISENHOWER
MARGO DONAHUE	THE EARL JERMYN
ROBERT L. SOLLEY	PRINCE KIKO HOHENLOHE
ANGELA HO	FABRIZIA BUCCI CASARI
PETER CHAPMAN	JACK KEEFE
DIANA CLARKE	SEBASTIEN DE GANAY
PRINCE LAURENCE PONIATOWSKI	PRINCE SERGÉ OF YUGOSLAVIA

An invitation for an event at Studio 54 featured

PRINCE PIERRE D'ARENBERG	LIZA OESTREICH
JENNIFER BANCROFT	CHRISTINA GALESI
CORNELIA GRASSI	BEATRICE DE CASTELLANE
PRISCILLA WOOLWORTH	

Some New Yorkers, it has to be said, took a certain unholy glee in poking fun at the JIC. It was noted that some of their regulars, while clearly posh, were hardly sparklers, like Albert of Monaco, and that among the social stars of the set were Angela Somoza, daughter of one despot, and Mimi Trujillo (a fledgling designer, whose invitation to a party bore a handwritten instruction Eurostyle: "*Tango look de rigueur*"), the niece of another.

Wholly phony titles could not easily withstand the JIC vetting procedures, but European titles, apart from those grand enough to get into the *Almanach da Gotha*, are far less easy to check than British ones. Italian custom, say, allows considerable leeway, with numbers of family members—often quite remote family members—flaunting the same title. Certainly, there were suddenly a lot of titles floating around Manhattan. Taki Theodoracopoulos, the columnist, called a friend whose name had just appeared in *Interview* with a newly minted ancient title attached. "Everybody's doing it," he was told. Biron and Autet did sometimes over-egg the pudding. "The JIC had one party in which there were just too many titles on the invitation," Biron told a reporter at the time. "We had like ten princes, and a lot of Americans thought: Are they trying to tell us they are aristocrats or what?"

But with the Eurotrash flooding in, the future of the JIC looked sunny, except for stresses within the partnership of Biron and Autet. "We got an office . . . secretaries . . . mailings. It became very complicated when it was very simple," Biron says. "We had an argument about that. We started fighting." He sighed. "Like everybody fights with each other."

Steve Rubell and Ian Schrager were receding from Studio 54, like stars departing a darkening galaxy. The last authentic Rubell/Schrager event was a Halloween party. The paintings of Hieronymous Bosch had been the visual inspiration but the mood was flat. "It had no passion," Ian Schrager admitted at the time. Steve would talk with Rudolf and Jim Fouratt, but to new promoters, like Mimi and Jerry Rubin, they were background figures. She and Jerry never even met them.

It mattered little to Rubell and Schrager, who had picked a different comeback trail. In his disastrous interview with Dan Dorfman, Steve had confided that he fancied owning a hotel on the East Side of Manhattan one day. The hotel business, insofar as it has to do with keeping a lot of transient people happy, has many areas of overlap with the club business. There had been a spurt of hotel building in New York. Donald Trump had opened the Grand Hyatt, and one of Rubell and Schrager's first sorties after their release had been a look at the Helmsley Palace, Harry Helmsley's recently opened grand hotel on Madison. Indeed, the duo had first imagined they could get back on top in a matter of months by creating a grand hotel according to the exacting standards of Studio 54. "When I came out of prison, I stayed in hotels for a week," Rubell told me. "I felt like an out-of-towner. Everywhere from the Hyatt to the Mayfair-Regent. None of them was my style." Rubell even went to London to check out the Savoy.

Although the pair were looking at places in the $80 million category, they had little money—they never did fill in Calvin Klein's check—and less clout. Even their office, a one-bedroom apartment on West Fifty-fifth Street, was leased in the name of Honey Aldrich, and Rubell had to put up a $2,000 bond before he was allowed as much as a credit card. Neither was allowed to open a checking account at Citibank. They had to go out to a Long Island bank where nobody knew who they were. They were, after all, a couple of near-broke released felons. Jesse Kornbluth asked if they were insecure about deals. "About *deals*? How about walking into a room?" Rubell said gloomily.

They set their sights on a particular hotel, the Hyde Park on Madison and Seventy-seventh Street. "We had about twenty meetings. We went over every little thing," the owner, Bill Judson, says, who now believes that this was purely an information-gathering exercise. "It still irritates me," he says. In fact, Clifton Harrison, a Texan realtor, tried to get them investors from Argentina for the Hyde Park deal. No soap. Harrison, a genial fellow, with a fondess for shetland sweaters and pretty women, advised them to find something smaller. And, preferably, a single backer.

But, time and again, potential backers would tell them they weren't interested in a hotel deal. "Nobody wanted to back us in anything but a nightclub," Schrager said. Both were skittish about clubs, though. "A club is a moment in time and that moment was over," as Schrager put it. Then along came Alan Cohen, who had been their lawyer at Paul, Weiss Rifkind, and was a former president of Madison Square Garden. He, and an associate, Peter Frankel, offered to finance them in a club in Europe.

Rubell and Schrager visited Dusseldorf and Paris. Ian Schrager actually contemplated running a Paris nightclub, the El Dorado in Les Halles. The notion of leaving New York appalled Steve, of course. "We decided we didn't want to live in France," Steve told me at the time. Fortunately, the dollar capsized against the franc. Alan Cohen asked the pair to be consultants on a club in New York.

Rubell and Schrager began that venerable Nightworld routine: looking for a venue. They were shown the former opera house on Fourteenth Street—Howard Stein's quondam Academy of Music—early. They turned it down. It had high ceilings, and zoning, and it was a fabulous building, but it also had *resonances.* "We didn't want another theater. We didn't want to be compared with 54," Schrager has said. They checked out the bus garages on Ninth Avenue, the East Sixtieth Street heliport, the disused train station under the Waldorf-Astoria, and the Cloud Club in the Chrysler Building. They tried to sweet-talk the president of a savings bank on West Thirty-sixth Street and Sixth Avenue into parting with the premises. "He said he didn't know if the board would go for it," Rubell remembered later. In the end, they returned to the opera house on Fourteenth Street for lack of anything better.

Their search for a hotel also continued. It was Mark Fleischman who said, "Why don't you buy *my* hotel?" This was the Executive on Madison and Thirty-eighth Street, alongside the Pierpont Morgan Library. Fleischman, who actually only had a minority holding, had a handsome duplex there, but the place was not anybody's dream except in an Alice-in-Wonderlandish way, because it only had 154 poky rooms, some so small that the beds would have to be six inches lower than the norm and the bathrooms would need the sort of sinks with which Rubell and Schrager were hauntingly familiar, being that they were of the dimensions as those used by the prison service. Rubell described it to me as a "fleabag." But Ian Schrager's prison reading had included stuff about the new micro deluxe hotels which were all the rage in Europe. A precursor had been L'Hôtel in Paris, but the famous current exemplar, Blake's

Hotel, which had been started by the actress Anoushka Hempel in a not wildly fashionable part of London, with rooms like velvet-lined shoe boxes, was ragingly expensive and incredibly modish.

The price of the Executive was $6.2 million. "That was the exact right price in 1983," Fleischman says. Ian and Steve had just $60,000 cash between them. It was a small sum compared with their grandiose plans upon leaving jail but they had spent six depressing months failing to find backers. New Year's Eve, 1983, was a nadir for the two men. Ian again contemplated leaving New York. "Here it was, New Year's Eve and we had nothing to celebrate," he says. "I thought 'Maybe it won't work.' I thought 'Maybe we won't get back together again.' "

It was then that Ian thought of the man who had bought up the Studio 54 real estate and done well out of it, Philip Pilevsky. Pilevsky was an odd fish, an academic who had taken to real estate development almost as a lucrative hobby. He swapped his flair and his ability to weave connections for a slice of any deal. Without putting in a cent of his own, he was well on his way to putting together a conceptual real estate imperium with a solid value of $1 billion.

Philip Pilevsky looked at the deal. He noted that, by virtue of an unusual clause, any bank that loaned money would be in line for repayment before the Fleischman group. This meant that Steve and Ian could borrow using the actual building as collateral. He said he would get them their dough for half of the deal. With this credibility, they got a bank loan of $2.5 million. The Executive became theirs in July 1983.

Work began. André Putnam, the Parisian battle-ax of rococo minimalism, was signed up as designer. It was agreed that Mark Fleischman could sit it out in his duplex until they were done. It took fifteen months, with Rubell and Schrager working fourteen-hour days. I made a couple of visits to the reborn hotel, which was now called Morgans, after the adjoining Pierpont Morgan Library, because I was working on a magazine piece. Rubell would cheerfully show off such designy touches as the all-but-nonexistent lobby, the walls that were not covered with wallpaper of fabric in the usual way but speckled with paint, like polychrome caviar, and the bus shelter walls installed in the showers. The photographs commissioned from Robert Mapplethorpe were not yet on the bedroom walls.

Steve Rubell's social life was still constrained. He told me about a dinner party at which he had been seated near the rumpled pit bull of the CIA, William Casey, and various other heavy lifters. He had been appalled. "These are day-time people. They're no fun," he told me.

If Ian Schrager was content to put the glory nights of the club behind them, for Steve Rubell it was a wrench. Neil Travis had been close to Steve when he was the editor of the *New York Post's* "Page Six," but had left the city to write a book. In May 1984, he returned to New York with his wife, Connie. He called Steve, who picked them up at the Plaza. "He'd let his chauffeur off for the night. He picked us up in this huge Mercedes 600. It was pissing down with rain," Neil says.

"He was sweeping down Broadway at sixty miles an hour. Steve's wearing that goddam hat. It's the one the boatmen used to wear in Nantucket. It's got flaps and a visor and things, and it's slipping down over his head and over his eyes, and we both swear we're going to die. And we go down to the Empire Diner."

"Everyone in the restaurant was on some form of drugs or whatever. I felt totally out of place," Connie says. "Then we went somewhere and got Quaaludes or something. And I'd never done a drug in my life. But I thought I might as well join them as not join them. Because I was just totally left out."

Neil says, "Then it was back up to Studio. We were up in the sound booth with him, and it was KC and the Sunshine Band! Alive onstage. And we were all sitting there with him, luded out, after a mad drive through the night. *So, suddenly, for one minute it was as if nothing had ever changed!*"

Things had changed, of course, for Rubell and Schrager. "Studio 54 was the moment of youth. This was their magic moment," Don Rubell says. "The rest was to prove that they could enter the system—that they could become a version of Corporate America." But the night owl was hard to kill in Steve Rubell and one day I spotted an architectural model in his office at Morgans. It was huge, chalk-white, a delicate invention, like the exoskeleton of some form of marine life. The model was by Arata Isozaki.

"It's a new club. I'm just advising on it," Rubell confided. "I don't know how it will be different from Studio 54. But Studio was seventies. This is eighties. I don't want to talk about it yet, really. All that is ahead of me."

Some of Morgans's features proved gamy. Stephen Quinn, who had been hired from the Carlyle to be general manager, noted to *New York* magazine's Michael Daly that "a lot of rooms turned over six, seven times a night." One whore smashed a bottle over her escort's head in the lobby. The john riposted by punching her in the mouth. A couple of guests on the sixth floor had put their own locks on the door. Rubell and Schrager discovered they were FBI.

"I went, 'Oh no!' " Rubell told me. It turned out they were merely bugging the nearby Polish consulate.

All of such problems had to be dealt with. Some proved tougher than others. Among the more intractable had been Mark Fleischman.

Mark Fleischman had merely been a dabbler. "I was a casual user of light drugs. Like everybody," he says. "Then all of a sudden I was in this place where people were doing things beyond anything I had ever imagined. I used to go to Studio 54. *But I had never been in the basement!*

"What happens when you do it every night of the week, you just get into it. The most famous people in the world say, 'Mark! Do you want to do this?' " More intensely. "You've got to understand, people would come from California, well-known stars, and say, 'Do you have any coke?'

"What do you say? No?

" 'Okay! I'll go some place else. I'll go to Howard Stein's place. . . . ' For the first of my Studio 54 years I was high and happy every night. That's the way it works. You think it's the greatest thing in the world. You function, and you're wonderful! My goodness, I'm a superhuman! I can work thirty-eight hours a day!"

After work, there were the after-hours joints. And there were women, lots of women, sometimes by twos and threes. True, Fleischman was married, and to a strikingly attractive woman, but the powder can work its magic ways on marriage vows. "It was so heavy and wild," says Milan, the party promoter, who maintained office space in the duplex in Morgans. "Like when you would go to Crisco after Studio closed. There was this whole group of people who were addicted to going to Studio, just like they were addicted to coke.

"Or even worse. And this huge group of people had to go out at night. *They had to keep going.* It got pretty twisted."

Nor was Fleischman's duplex big on discipline as a work environment, and Mark's assistants and/or associates were frequently as hopped up as he was. Victoria Leacock, who had dropped out of Adelphi College at eighteen and a bit, was recommended as a replacement by Gwynne Rivers. "I had been going to Studio since I was fourteen. It was my home," she says. But Mark Fleischman took so long to get around to seeing Leacock that she accepted four other positions the same day, including one where she was supposed to try out cosmetics on her own skin.

But Fleischman did hire her. Leacock duly showed up at the duplex, where a first vivid vignette was seeing another assistant, with her face pressed onto the floor. "She was snorting the carpet, muttering *Is this dust or coke?*" Leacock says. Leacock was soon helping herself to an endless sluice of white wine spritzers from the open fridge. "Fran was the first person to tell me I was an alcoholic," she says of another assistant, Fran Boyer.

Work was, of course, parties, and it was agreeable. "Mark taught me to spell everybody's name right and pronounce everybody's name right. That was important," she says.

Her second vivid vignette on the job was the attempted eviction of Fleischman by Schrager and Rubell. Mark Fleischman's own memory is a bit blurry. "They didn't have any trouble getting me out," he says. He had got a new apartment but it wasn't completely ready. "They were saying you gotta move! I said, 'Fuck you. I'll move when I can move.' "

Victoria Leacock remembers it a bit differently. Rubell and Schrager suddenly just appeared. "I was on the telephone taking names for a guest list," she said. "It was about eleven in the morning. Steve and Ian must have got in with their own keys.

"Mark came blasting through the bedroom door with this big gun. It was like Li'l Abner. Steve and Ian ran for the elevator. Then they shouted obscenities from the hallway. But they were talking on the telephone later that day."

Victoria Leacock lasted a couple more months, but left Studio before she was twenty. "After nine months, it was too grim," she says. "Everybody was a mess. Everybody was too much drugs or alcohol." It had lost its magic for her. She was replaced by a pretty and bubbly English blonde, Hilary Clarke. Who just happened to be in love with Ian Schrager.

They were all out of there in time for the official Morgans's opening in early October.

★   ★   ★

Cocaine had stopped being so good to Mark Fleischman in the second year. "It sort of levels off, and you have to take more and more just to feel the way you are," he says. "Then after that it depresses you. By my third year I was feeling depressed. Not depressed, just not feeling good about the place or me.

"Things weren't right. Your body starts to feel bad. And then your head starts to feel bad. I wasn't the same as I am or who I was. It distorts your personality. Finally I wasn't having a good time anymore. If you don't have a good time in this business, it's terrible. *I didn't want to be there!"*

Mark was burning out fast and knew it, so he was receptive when he was approached with an offer to buy. "It was late 1984," he says. "It's funny. It was doing very well." The club's turnover was about $8 million a year, and $1 million of that was profit. The new owners, a fellow called Frank Cashman, who owned a gay club in Fort Lauderdale, and a Boston group that ran a number of clubs, assumed the $3 million lien which the feds assumed was what Rubell and Schrager owed in back taxes. They paid Fleischman $700,000 down, with two more annual payments to come.

Not all of the Fleischman team took to Frank Cashman. "He was a pock-marked bald greasy fat faggot who had the Backstreet," says Milan, who left swiftly, complaining of sexual harassment. Nor was Fleischman delighted when the new team had made no bones about letting him know that they could make a better job of running the place than he had been doing. "They saw it was always jammed every night," Fleischman says. "They said, 'It's only making a million dollars? You're giving away free champagne and you're letting all these people in for free?' They didn't understand that there are people and then there are . . . people." Still appalled at the idiocy, Fleischman says, *"They went and cut the comp!*

"They decided to make everybody pay. I turned over to Cashman a vibrant club that was doing great business. He stopped giving out drink tickets. He stopped booking free parties. The reality is that the parties and the celebrities—the *right* celebrities, the Couri Hays of the world, and the Nikki Haskells—they make the night scene.

"Because unless you've got all of the right people, or some of the right people, you don't even get the *wrong* people. Within one year, the business went from eight million to four million. Just like that!"

Cashman and the Bostonians paid the second year's owings, but reneged on the third. So Studio was again Mark Fleischman's. But it was a ruin.

Arthur Weinstein had let Robert Boykin buy him out of Hurrah after Studio 54 exploded. It turned from a disco to a live music venue under the direction of Jim Fouratt. "And it was better. If I'd had any brains I would have stayed around. But I was headstrong," Arthur says.

"Miserable times." he says, "Studio 54 was like unstoppable. They had three of the greatest years you can imagine. They made so much money. They had so many great people. So many great times. So really nothing else could exist alongside it. It just dwarfed everything."

He and Colleen and their daughter Dahlia were living at 200 East Fifty-eighth Street, a building where fellow tenants included Debbie Harry, lead singer of Blondie, and the designer Stephen Sprouse. Arthur had teamed up with Scotty Taylor, who had quit Studio, partly because Rubell had been chilly, and partly because his bartending career had slumped. "Instead of making $300 a night I was making $150 a night. I thought that was horrible. Later I didn't think that was so horrible when I was making nothing."

They remained friendly with John Addison. "He would say, 'Take Dahlia. We're going to a Rolling Stones concert.'" Colleen remembers. "I would say great. Then I would find out the concert was in Boston. He'd say, 'Hurry up! The plane is waiting . . .'"

Every day Weinstein and Taylor were out, pounding the pavements, looking for premises and financing. Scotty remembers a lunch with a prospect in the Russian Tea Room. "Art and I didn't have a cent in our pockets. He told this guy, 'Don't even hand me the menu if you don't have a million dollars!'" He was handed the menu, but nothing even cohered.

Arthur was making ends meet by doing something he didn't much care for, promoting parties in clubs that belonged to other people. "Some people can do it. I can't," he says. At a party he was giving at Magique for Kid Creole and the Coconuts he was alerted by Errol Wetson to the existence of a defunct theater, the Jefferson on Fourteenth Street. The timing was propitious. Studio

54 was no longer impregnable. There was a thundering great hole to fill in Nightworld. Arthur made a deal with the theater's owner.

It ended in an ugly fashion as Nightworld deals so often do. In this case the owner had conniptions over the vaulting expenses. "The scumbag just stopped work and fired everybody. End of story." Except it wasn't, because Arthur, who had labored on the project for six months, had managed to get hold of the lease of the loft on top of the theater. He, Colleen, Dahlia, Scotty Taylor, and their respective dogs moved in. Scotty Taylor got a job tending bar at the Ritz.

One night Arthur was giving a birthday do in his loft, for Paul Garcia, with whom he had become friendly since the end of Garcia's fling with Colleen. Paul Garcia, incidentally, had become a mini-celebrity of a darkly comic sort. He had been cover boy for the herpes issue of *Newsweek* during the brief period when herpes inspired dread as an incurable sexually communicated disease: Proof that sometimes farce comes first, tragedy after. Anyway, Garcia, who swears he does not suffer from the complaint, had not found the publicity had done much for his love life.

Arthur remembers looking around the party. The party was—well, it had that magic feel, like the opening of Studio. "I thought to myself: Fuck it! I'm going to open the space!" he says.

He needed money and would visit Scotty at the bar. "I'd say fork it over!" Arthur says. "He was so scared. I would say, 'Do it! Don't worry about it!' He would glom one hundred, two hundred at the most. And that was how we funded the Jefferson. Until Garcia came along and gave us a whopping ten thousand bucks."

At the notion of ripping off Brandt, Arthur gave a mirthful bark. "Please! Nightclub owners are the biggest thieves on earth!"

Jerry Brandt later told me sunnily, something hardly news, "All barmen steal."

Arthur began buying stuff and Colleen started to decorate, as she thought, their home. It was only when Arthur started building a bar, though, that she got the picture. "Art," she said. "We *live* here."

Arthur remembers that his argument ran: You mean you don't want a nightclub in your apartment?

Arthur let word about his club slip out here and there in Nightworld. The

Jefferson opened its completely illegal doors on New Year's Eve, 1981, which happened to be almost simultaneously with Eric Goode's club-with-no-name. Colleen had given the Jefferson a dandy look: all retro, plastic and leopardette, cheap glam, a pulp fictive Lolita sunglasses milieu. It was a sardonic take on the sleaze that had characterized after-hours clubs pre-Jefferson. "Arthur was downstairs," Scotty says. "Colleen was at the door. I was at the bar." There was a protracted moment of nothingness. "Then a couple of people arrived. Arthur said that'll be ten dollars . . . they paid . . . they came upstairs and went to the bar . . . I said that'll be six-fifty . . . they said fine . . ." Among the first customers was the model Christie Brinkley. "She didn't like it but she paid," Arthur says.

Soon the Jefferson was burning bright. It was suddenly the time for after-hours clubs. Vito Bruno had opened AM/PM on Murray Street. "In AM/PM everybody was somebody," Bruno exults. Everybody who was somebody was sometimes wired, too. That exclusive dealer the Elf Queen remembers spilling a gram of cocaine on the stinky lavatory floor. "Suddenly the Rock Hall of Fame were on their knees," she says. Billy Idol and others recognized that the Jefferson was the jewel. It was soon as hot as a white coal. Arthur says, "It was largely because the Ritz was going well and Jim and Rudolf were doing parties at Underground. And we were right there. It was the first time anyone had opened an after-hours club for nice people, not scum. We had a *door policy*." He laughed. "The only thing was—it got *out of control*."

The Jefferson was open only on Fridays and Saturdays but upon those long nights and early mornings—nights and mornings of which my own memories are alternately sharp and smudgy—hundreds were passing through the small space. Hard-core celebs of the David Bowie sort got goodies for free, of course, but most were happy to pay; and, with the take on a good night running to $8,000, Colleen would sometimes cart Dahlia off to the Gramercy Park Hotel for a night's peace and quiet, but Arthur would always be there, patrolling his Nightworld kingdom, usually with allies Scotty Taylor and Paul Garcia. Or sometimes with a new player, Frank Roccio.

Frank Roccio, a dashing man with fine long gray hair when I met him in 1984, was born in the mid-forties in the Bronx. He grew up a paradigmatic hippie. "I was in the 1963 March on Washington," he says. "I got married in

People's Park in San Francisco, wearing black Vietcong pajamas and daisies in my hair. Tim [Leary] blessed our baby." He was in Chicago for the 1968 Democratic party convention—"It seemed that all we did that weekend was run"—and came to live in New York.

Unsatisfactory time had passed, along with Roccio's first marriage, when he saw an ad for a new wave band he admired in the *Voice*. "I'd seen the sixties come and go and never made a quarter. The seventies were going and suddenly we were thirty. We were smugglers and junkies and suddenly we were grown up. We were good boys—we didn't want to hurt or steal—but we couldn't go nine to five." He talked himself into being the band's manager and signed them up for a gig at Club 57. "It was ice-cold. There were only eighty people there. But it was . . . *magic*." Roccio became a convert to Nightworld.

He was soon a partner in Club 57 itself. Then, with Jim Fouratt and Rudolph Pieper he had opened the old G. G. Barnum's as the Peppermint Lounge and it was hugely successful.

Roccio went to the Jefferson's opening and couldn't believe it. There was a dark-haired fellow standing there. Roccio walked up to him. "Have we ever met before?" he asked.

"No," the man said. He spoke, according to Roccio, with lots of attitude, even for a New Yorker.

"I'm Frank Roccio. I own the Peppermint Lounge."

"I'm Arthur Weinstein. I own this place. I've heard of you. And I don't know if I like what I've heard," Arthur said.

Frank Roccio says, "This was our Bogie and Claude Rains scene. We became the closest of friends. We said, 'Let's do something together.' "

The Jefferson had four great months of glory. "Then Public Morals came down and busted us. It was like they were busting John Dillinger," says Arthur. Colleen and Dahlia were in the Gramercy. "Luckily I was outside on the back fire escape. It was pretty warm. It was when the first *Columbia* went up. It was April eleventh, I think." He made himself scarce.

"They waited for me. They waited, and waited, and left. They even cleaned up. We opened a few more times after that. But it just wasn't the same. But we knew we *had* something."

⋆   ⋆   ⋆

After-hours clubs were suddenly The Joints. They seemed a scouring of the nocturnal palate after the huge clubs, and, more important, they separated the sheep from the real night goats, the hard livers who would keep blazing way until they met the workaday world, getting up at breakfast time. They included the Red Parrot, which was such a favorite of old Studio hands that Steve Rubell was once found blurrily offering free drink tickets there. There was also AM/PM. Its VIP holy-of-holies was a painfully bright basement, where the primary seating consisted of beer cartons. Steve Rubell looked at AM/PM, and *learned*.

AM/PM was quasi-legitimate in that Bruno had shelled out $25,000 for a sprinkler system so as to conform to the "Blue Angel" law so named for a lethal fire in a club a couple of years before. A host of others were wholly illegal. "I couldn't believe it!" says Billy Idol. "It was a rebellious, piratical kind of thing. You could go to five different clubs every night of the week and never go to the same one twice! And all you did was go." A whole community adjusted their schedules in accordance. One young woman told me she would go to bed at eight or nine and catch a few hours sleep so as to be fresh for the Wit & Wisdom or After Hours.

Perri Lister has surprisingly keen memories of a place on Third Avenue and Eleventh Street which had a menu with gold-leafed pages listing uppers, downers, hallucinogenics, and so on, ending with hypnotics. "Hypnotics? I thought that sounded very interesting. I had a few of those," she says. "They were called Rohypnol. That was their real name. We called them forget-me-nots, because you could not remember anything you'd done.

"We dropped them in the Dug-Out. A real alcoholics' bar. Then I re-member going up the steps of the Dug-Out. That was my last memory. Then I was in the Continental, with my ass sticking out from under a couch. I woke up in this gorgeous apartment, a leopard-skin print apartment with a dentist's chair. I was thinking, oh my God! Where the hell was I? I looked next to me and all my clothes were neatly folded in a pile. So I was thinking would a guy rape you and then fold your clothes? I don't think so! I was safe."

The Continental was the Weinsteins' next after-hours. It was in a building more or less next door to the one that had housed Goode's club-with-no-name on West Twenty-fifth and Hudson. It had been a garage and they had put whatever money they had into doing it up. They then ran out. This is one of the leitmotifs of Nightworld, the way that all those falry profits just wink into nothingness in the daylight. They borrowed a bit from Frank Roccio and they were loaned $25,000 by Vadim Semov, an émigré from what was still Leningrad, who had been in New York a decade dabbling in real estate.

The Continental opened in the fall about five months after the Jefferson had closed. Colleen had got the place looking like the cheesiest of bad dream motel suites with violently clashing wallpapers that perfectly caught the post-apocalyptic look of the art that was bubbling and frothing in the East Village. It was a hit.

One evening a foursome arrived. A couple of men in too-tight suits and their dates. "Hey!" one of the men asked. "*Am I here?*"

Arthur Weinstein, who can be as naïve as only the cynical know how, looked at him, puzzled. "Of course, you're here," he said.

They returned the following evening. Paul Garcia, who was on duty, got the message, and barred their entrance. "He had balls," Arthur says. Garcia, whose ownership of another joint, the Munson Diner, made him a serious player, attended a meeting with the Mafia family concerned.

The would-be partners did not return.

The Continental was written about. It was famous. It was illegal, but never caught the attention of the NYPD's Public Morals Squad, who clearly had other stuff on their plate. It did well enough for the Weinsteins to repay their debts but Arthur closed it after a year. "Hey! It was tired," he says.

Arthur had two other projects. One was small. Just another after-hours joint to bring in ready dough. He took on a partner to develop it, a Leningrad buddy of Vadim Semov. He was named Victor Malinsky and had once been chauffeur to Robert Stigwood. "He wore all this leather. A real cowboy," Scotty Taylor recalls. Characters from different parts of what was still the Soviet Union were beginning to surface, and to play an increasing part, in Nightworld.

Arthur's other project was grandiose. He had come across a capacious building, a former Polish wedding chapel on Second and Avenue C. This was in the ramshackle Alphabet City, as Manhattanites call that part of town where streets have letters rather than numbers, a place of bodega storefronts and heroin dealers but also with an upsurge of small art galleries, and the Lower East Side seemed to Arthur a locale of radiant possibility. He brought in partners: Frank Roccio, who put up $8,000 without even seeing the place; and Steve Maas, who, as owner of the Mudd Club, had all the needful licenses. This wedding chapel, Arthur sensed, would be the next big thing.

Steve Rubell came down to check it out and was enthusiastic. "I would love to have a club this big," he told Arthur. Things were looking great. And then came to pass the events nightpeople still call Arthurgate.

Maurice Brahms remains convinced that it was Steve Rubell who gave up Arthur Weinstein to the feds. But Arthur tells it this way. Shortly after the Jefferson opened Jerry Brandt advised him that he "should meet with these people who would smooth things over." He paused bleakly. "I met 'em." The people were cops from the 10th Precinct. "They told me what it was going to cost. And that was basically it.

"Five hundred a week. But then it got bigger as more people came." Another pause. "And I had the *great luck* to have the fucking FBI for some unknown reason watching these two guys."

One, a sergeant, was nabbed. "He blurted out the whole story. And he wore a wire against the whole goddam 10th Precinct. It was a joke. The guy that first approached me, he suddenly decided to go honest. After fifteen years on the force, stealing! He brought down the whole house. That guy had a lot of nerve. He wouldn't move out of his own house. They were sending him fishes in the mail. He refused to move. The son of a bitch had balls. He really did."

The upshot was inevitable and Arthur details it with the tough guy cadences of a private-eye movie. "There was the proverbial knock on the door . . . six guys . . . they took me downtown to meet a guy I knew I didn't want to meet. I had two FBI agents on either side of me. All of them large and none of them smiling. They took me down to a building next to the MCC and through a door marked STRIKE FORCE."

Behind the door was the scourge of Nightworld, Peter Sudler. "He said, 'Arthur, you have a decision to make. You have been paying a police sergeant. I think you had better tell me who it is.'

"They talked about back taxes. They told me they could put me away for six years, just for paying a cop. All eyes were upon me. I had a white shirt on. I think my skin was whiter than the white shirt. It was a nightmare. Anyway, I told them his name. Believe me, when the feds squeeze, you dance."

Arthur was fitted with a wire and wore it half a dozen times while paying off three or four of the cops. The grand jury was being formed while Arthur was putting together his third after-hours place, Le Pop. His partners were Paul Garcia and the Leningrad Cowboy, Victor Malinsky, neither of whom knew of his predicament. The club was on West Twenty-seventh and Colleen had done it up in a cheery and minimalist sixties fashion. "It was pop not hippie," she explains.

On January 20, 1983, twenty-six New York city cops, some active, some retired, were subpoenaed to appear in front of the grand jury.

Le Pop opened on February 5, 1983. At three in the morning there was a telephone call for Malinsky. He left for a rendezvous.

This rendezvous seems to have taken place. Two and a half hours later Malinsky was found in a doorway a block from the club with a bullet in the brain. The murderer was never found, but there was no shortage of suspects because the Leningrad Cowboy, an avatar of the Russian mob, had been dealing significant weights of cocaine; owned a slice of another after-hours joint; and, perhaps most significantly, was tied in with a ring of Russian counterfeiters of such expertise that they could get $10,000 genuine for $50,000 fake, all in fifties. Malinsky, who had been going to testify against the ring, had been due to take the stand in a couple of days. He had changed his mind about ratting. Possibly, too late. Le Pop, like Fouratt and Rudolf's Pravda before it, closed its doors on its second night, but this was not the end of Arthur's troubles. On the morning of February 22, Frank Roccio called Weinstein. "Congratulations," he said. "You're a star!"

There was a story in that morning's *New York Times* by reporter Howard Blum. Its headline was F.B.I. INQUIRY ON AFTER-HOURS CLUBS STRAINS LINKS WITH POLICE. It began:

AT 4 A.M., THE GROUND FLOOR OF THE WAREHOUSE WAS TRANSFORMED INTO A CAVE OF FANTASTIC SHADOWS; AN ALL-NIGHT CROWD SPURRED ON BY FLASHING LIGHTS, MUSIC, LIQUOR AND A LITTLE COCAINE.

STANDING ON THE LOADING DOCK IN FRONT OF THE AFTER-HOURS CLUB, THE
CONTINENTAL ON WEST 25TH STREET, WAS ARTHUR WEINSTEIN, THE CO-OWNER.
HIS HAIR WAS SLICKED BACK 50S-STYLE AND HE WORE A WHITE DINNER JACKET
WITH A JET-BLACK CUMMERBUND. UNDERNEATH HIS EVENING CLOTHES WAS A
TRANSMITTER THAT ALLOWED THE F.B.I TO MONITOR EVERY WORD HE SAID.

Vito Bruno of AM/PM was quoted in a letter that he too had given Christmas presents to the cops. Presents of more than $100? "Let's say a lot more," Bruno said.

The cops were vengeful. The weekend after Blum's story ran, AM/PM was, as the columnist Stephen Saban observed in *Details*, not so much late as late lamented. "We got busted. We didn't close by choice," Bruno says. Other after-hours joints, Berlin, Elan, and Pink Cadillac closed down likewise. The move by the feds against a few greedy cops had quick results in Nightworld. Entrepreneurs stopped putting their risk capital into after-hours joints and turned their attention back to the big venues.

Concerning Arthur Weinstein and the Continental, the authorities had leaked like a shotgunned bucket. Especially concerning the wire. Arthur's wire sounded as bad as Steve Rubell's "little list." Worse. It was like discovering that the Studio balconies had been on video. Stephen Saban hit off the downtown reaction: "One's heart stopped. At least the hearts of those who had ever spoken with Arthur, had ever lifted a spoon with him. And they were legion."

It had been a slipshod leak, though. "That was total bullshit," Arthur says. "What for? I wore it only to meetings with policemen that the FBI set up. It was a joke." Not a funny joke, given the heavy dudes who frequented Arthur's clubs and some of the goings-on in nooks and crannies. Arthur, who had quailed in the face of the feds, had now to confront more menacing demons. "My strategy was to go out and explain to each and every person what really happened. And, believe me, it wasn't easy," he said. "People kept on coming up and saying, 'Why aren't you dead? Why aren't you in Brazil? Do you need money to go away? Where do you want to go?' "

Nor were things hunky-dory with Arthur's partners. He, Maas, and the others had given an exploratory Halloween party in their cavernous building on the Lower East Side which they had named The World. It had been for the German rocker, Nina Hagen, and it had been a wow. Garcia and Roccio were comfortable with Arthur's tale of the wire, but not Steve Maas. "Steve

Maas went berserk. Anybody would have. In the end I let him buy me out," Arthur says. "I went home with fifteen thousand dollars in my pocket," he says. "We hadn't had enough money to eat. But when Colleen heard I had let myself be bought out, she wept. I felt like shit."

Downtown paranoia—*Which button do you want me to talk into, Art?*— subsided but not the paranoia of the Weinsteins themselves. Any kid in any club might decide to act the hero. Worse. The cops were convicted. Four were jailed. "You think they're smiling?" Arthur asked me at the time. "You think they mightn't be just a little bit *unhappy?*"

In 1983 Barbara Carrera was in Hamburg, promoting the movie *Never Say Never Again*, in which she played one of the tastier Bond girls, Fatima Blush. It was some years since her divorce from Uva Hardin, the progenitor of Studio 54. "I was in the Atlantic Hotel," Carrera says. "I had an interview of some sort, a press conference. And as I was on my way back to my quarters I saw a very young Uva.

"It was a most extraordinary thing. He came up to me and said, 'Barbara,' the same way Uva speaks. I almost fainted. It was Uva's son, whom I had never met. And he was the one who told me about Uva's death."

Sidney Beer had been among the very last of Uva's friends to see him. Uva had gotten into trouble in both France and Germany, Beer says, and had wound up renting an apartment in Athens. Beer had flown out to Greece. "He looked terrible," he says. He told Uva that he would send him a ticket back to Manhattan if he lost thirty-five pounds. Uva called some months later. "I've lost thirty-five pounds," he claimed. Beer told him to come up with the date he wanted to return to New York and promised the ticket.

Two weeks later Uva's son, Kai, called him. "He said, 'My father committed suicide,'" Beer remembers. "Some days later I got a collect call from Uva Hardin. What the fuck was this? I took the call." It was a woman.

"She said, 'I can't afford to make the call. I was living with Uva.' She told me she went on a booking for two days. She came back. He was dead in her bed. He had drunk two bottles of vodka and swallowed a load of pills." With that angry affection, and a note of wonderment, he added, "I never thought he had the guts to kill himself."

UPTOWN, DOWNTOWN

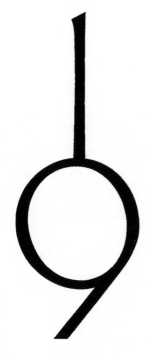

THE NOTION THAT PARTIES CAN BE WORKS OF ART, THAT partygoers are players, and that the long night itself can be considered as a raw art material would be no news at a Jacobean masque or in sixteenth-century Venice. It is certainly as old as organized nightlife itself. Steve Rubell and Ian Schrager made a conceptual advance when they applied the idea to clubland, actually putting the partygoers onstage in Studio 54. It was a further development when performance art was incorporated into the "theme" parties at Mudd and Club 57. Since the experiment with the club-with-no-name, Eric Goode had been determined to take the notion to a giddy limit.

The Goodes and the other Californians spent a couple of years and $250,000 on the project. Ian Schrager helped out, writing a letter on the Studio 54 letterhead. It was dated January 19, 1982, addressed To Whom It May Concern, and praised the club-with-no-name thusly:

I FOUND THE EVENTS CREATED LAST SPRING AT 516 WEST 25TH THE MOST INSPIRING NEW DEVELOPMENT IN NIGHT LIFE FOR SOME TIME. THIS GROUP OF ENTREPRENEURS, INCLUDING SHAWN HAUSMAN, ERIC GOODE AND DARIUS AZARI, HAVE IMPRESSED ME WITH A BROAD SUPPLY OF INNOVATIVE AND TRULY AVANT GARDE IDEAS. THROUGH 25TH STREET AND THEIR INSTALLATION AT STUDIO 54 THEY HAVE PROVEN THE CAPACITY TO EXECUTE THESE IDEAS IN A POLISHED AND EXPEDIENT FASHION WITH ATTENTION TO DETAIL

The property they alit upon was downtown, way downtown, 157 Hudson, and it had a history. Its owner, Howard Rower, who has a pigtail and a pouchy, professorial face, is a successful hippie entrepreneur, who, among other activities, had begun a macrobiotics food business in the sixties, importing seaweed from Japan, brown rice from California, and fifty-gallon drums of pesticide-free peanut butter from Greek rancheros in Argentina. His fist premises were on Duane. He moved to Hudson when the business grew.

"In 1976 I had to decide between the food business and real estate," says Rower, who had been buying buildings in Manhattan's TriBeCa area and turning them into loft space for artists. He decided to get out of food, which left a big empty building on his hands. He rented the ground floor to some guys who turned it into an after-hours joint called Feel the Heat. "You got bikers there and wet T-shirt contests," he says sourly. It briefly became Rock City, but was just as unloved by its landlord. "I turned them out," Rower says. They did not go quietly. "My life was threatened . . ."

He depressurized the place by renting it to an outfit that transported art-works in and out of the city for museum shows and needed a place to stow the crates. After two years, Rower turned them out too, raised the rates, and put it on the rental market, which was when the Goode team showed up. "They did not tell the complete truth," Rower says. "They said they wanted to open an art gallery there . . . they said they would have openings and serve champagne . . . they said they were going to maybe play a little music . . ."

The Goodes brought up the subject of a liquor license. Rower reassured them. "I said they wouldn't need a liquor license. That was the caterers' responsibility," Rower says. "They said it would probably be better if they got their own liquor license . . ."

The inner core of Nightworlders in due course were sent square boxes covered in black velvet and holding a blue capsule. A printed note within instructed recipients to drop the pill in water. Thereupon an invitation floated niftily to the surface. The opening was on September 13, 1983, and you could see Area was going to be different as soon as you walked in and spotted a fellow holding a blade to a whirling whetstone among showers of sparks. It was as though one had wandered into Marie Antoinette's fake farm, Le Petit Trianon. Other enigmatic objects and Performance pieces loomed up here and there around the club's handsome spaces. "In a way, it really was an art gallery where they played music," the duped landlord, Howard Rower, says handsomely enough.

The bathroom in Area was hugely important, an extension of Studio and Mudd. Indeed, at the beginning, drinks were served there, but this kind of minimalism proved unappealing and was dropped. The ruling gimmick, though, was the fact that "themes" were constantly changing Area into a different club. The opening theme, which was "indeterminate," in Eric Goode's phrase, lasted six weeks or so. Other short-lived themes followed, some more determinate than others, like "Faith," "Gnarly," "Light," and "Body Oddities." These themes were carried off in a way that was at once offbeat and finely tuned, free of art school pop or commercial surrealism. Anyway, because of, or despite the themes, Area was a wow. Although it had no VIP Room—another risky innovation—it was The Joint. And, as had been the case with Studio 54, you saw no particular reason why its time shouldn't last for ever.

Eric Goode, who was the Steve Rubell of the operation, the Mr. Outside, took care that an Area archive was kept up as meticulously as any gallery. Much later, he had a series of interviews conducted that convey something of Area's shrewd madness. Here Jennifer Goode, Eric's sister, is talking to "Little Mike," namely, Michael Anderson, an exceedingly short person from Colorado who had been hired on the spot while dropping into Area soon after his arrival in New York.

For his first theme, "Carnival," Little Mike remembered, he had been dressed as an elf. He was in a booth selling T-shirts and chili during "Gnarly." Cher bought some T-shirts from him and was strolling off. "I said, 'Cher!' and she stopped and turned around," he told Goode. "I said, 'I love you.' She just smiled and walked away. It was fun." On Valentine's Day, he was dressed as an angel, and put on a swing. On Halloween, he was a devil. "I must have been a good devil, because all the gigs I had after that were devils," he told Goode. "Area launched my career. That's all I can say. Since then, it's taken off."

"Some people have said Area exploited people. Did you ever get that feeling?" asked Goode.

"In America," Little Mike shrewdly observed, you are "better off being exploited than not being exploited . . . I came to New York to attract attention. And here was a place someone was hiring me to attract attention. So I went right after it."

Other memories were more lurid. Chi Chi Valenti, the chanteuse and paramour of DJ Johnny Dynell, had a fruity encounter in Area with a groupie. The groupie "had been doing nipple worship of Johnny and kind of just like bothering him," Chi Chi told Jennifer Goode. "So Johnny warned her and said, 'My wife is a bodybuilder and she's gonna come and beat you up.' But that just made it worse. Some people will stop and some will get more obsessed."

Chi Chi and a bunch of female friends were in the DJ's booth at Area while Dynell was spinning one Thursday when the groupie came in. "She came in and slid her hand onto his nipple. I just went for a TKO," Chi Chi said, meaning a technical knockout. "She went falling down the stairs. But Bob Gruen was walking into the DJ booth at that exact minute with Yoko Ono's two Hungarian chefs that had just come from behind the Iron Curtain to cook for Yoko . . . They were going like, wow! America is really a great place. People really fight for what they believe in here!"

There was even an addition to the archive from Archbishop O'Connor, New York's senior Catholic prelate, who had been asked to the opening of the "Religion" theme, the invitation was declined by his secretary, graciously: "Archbishop O'Connor regrets that he was unable to attend the opening of AREA. The concept of finding the divine within the sphere of the secular is indeed the beginning of holiness and peace. Please be assured of the Archbishop's best wishes on your endeavor."

Only Rudolf was sourish. "What do you think Area's vibe was?" he was asked. "What was the thing you got from it?"

"I think it was the first one of the real posing, drink-holding establishments," he said. "I think aesthetically no club would ever be like it. On the fun department, I know that a lot of people liked it. It's not my type of fun that was given there. I thought it was too static, a little bit contrived. I don't think that it was really a great dance space. It never got any notoriety because of its DJs or live shows, and I don't think it was such a great place to get laid either." It is typical of Eric Goode's fastidious cool that this was in the Area archive too.

Maurice Brahms has many sterling virtues. Forgetting wrongs is not necessarily one of them. When rumors began circulating about Roy Cohn's health, he telephoned three men that he knew had been sleeping with the lawyer. "I think you should know Roy Cohn has AIDS" he told each of them.

"Who *is* this?" each responded.

"A friend," Brahms said, and hung up.

When Cohn went to Washington, D.C., for the inauguration of Reagan's second term, Brahms learned that Cohn was going to a restaurant with a group of heavyweight pols and Beltway types, including Roger Stone. He called the restaurant. "I'm sorry. We have to cancel. Mr Cohn is deathly sick. He has AIDS," he told them.

He heard that Cohn had been "totally freaked," he says, adding, "but he never found out who it was to his dying day." Roy Cohn, after all, was not short of enemies.

Area's best defined opponent was uptown. What Sid Vicious and Johnny Rotten were to punk, the four Beavers brothers—Wick, Toby, Angus, and Nick—were, in differently nuanced ways, to prep. The Beavers brothers had every attribute, from a sinewy blond mother, who supported them, to a hard-drinking philanderer of a father, who was hard on them. Charles Beavers, Jr., customarily called Budzo, owned a machine tool business, the Brubacker Tool Corporation, and, of course, expected his sons to join him at the family firm. Times were changing though. Toby was the only brother to sign on at Brubacker, and only briefly, giving it up to work the door at an Upper East Side bar. One day in the late fall of 1983 he was sitting around, getting stoned with his brother Angus. The brothers, who share an abrasive sense of humor and the brutal air of well-being that suggests a life spent with horse, rod, or gun, were actually talking about—well, what else?—Nightworld. Specifically, they discovered the fact that there was no boîte for people like themselves, who had no interest in being disco flamboyances, but were a cut above Jerry Rubin's nerd horde.

"We decided we should open a bar for the yupsters," Angus says. "The preppies. Our friends, that Studio treated like shit. They had wads of cash. They may be in suits because they came straight from Goldman Sachs, and they're treated like shit by a bunch of dudes from Brooklyn who spend their days in the gym. And unless you were a star, or were painted gold, or had nothing on but a tutu, those were the arbiters of who got in."

The older Beavers brother, Wick, was off sailing around the world. Nick, the youngest, was promoting parties for Mark Fleischman. Toby and Angus started putting heel to pavement the very next day. Toby was twenty-eight and Angus twenty-two, and neither knew a thing about zoning or real estate, but they knew where they wanted to open. "When I was a kid you really wouldn't walk east of Lexington because that was where your doormen came from," Angus Beavers says. Now, though, young brokers and bankers had been settling the far East Side en masse.

They lucked into a place pretty quickly, a former carpentry shop on East Ninety-first and York Avenue. "Fortunately, it was in the proper zoning, C8, dash 4. There are only about eight blocks on the Upper East Side that have that," Angus says. "There had been a vinegar factory there that had been a front for the mob. They brewed beer there in the thirties." Toby and Angus fixed it up for about $150,000, borrowing a lot of stuff from their country place in Watch Hill, Rhode Island, including a slew of old surfboards. They decided to call their place the Surf Club.

Toby and Angus saw Area, rather than senescent Studio, as the Surf's defining rival. They had scoped out Area. Angus had chatted with Eric Goode. Achieving startling liftoff from Joe Prep, he started hewing Nightworld theory out of Friedrich Nietzsche. "There's two aspects of theater, the Dionysan and the Apollonian," he told me. "One is spectacle and the other is content-driven."

Area, Angus decided, was the ultimate, inspired Apollonian club. "It was really the logical conclusion of what all those other clubs were heading toward," he says. From the Electric Circus on, through Flamingo and Le Jardin, culminating in Studio—and taking in Xenon, with that flightless dodo of a Mothership—spectacle had ruled in the best clubs, and spectacle had culminated in Area.

This, of course, left an opening. There was room for the kind of club that a John O'Hara might have hung out in, a hard-drinking, rooter-tooting, rakehell kind of a place, heir to the sort of saloon that used to have spittoons and sawdust on the floor to soak up the beer and the blood. "At the Surf Club, all we gave a shit about was the content," Angus says. "We were Dionysian. We were going to fuck trends. We just wanted a place where the yuppies could go because they were treated like shit downtown."

The Surf opened its doors on December 20, 1983. "So it was just on the cusp of 1984. We timed it perfectly. Not knowing it, of course. But all of a sudden there was the leveraged buy-out boom and every preppy who got out of college was making seventy thousand dollars," Angus says. On Christmas Eve the Surf Club sold more champagne than any other club or bar in Manhattan.

Eric Goode never bothered to go and check out the Surf, but it was a blast. As were the Beavers brothers. Indeed. I remember leaving a party with Toby. The men were all in black tie, Anglo style, with buttons on their shirts, not ostentatious studs. Indeed, the only ostentatious touch of color among the sober black and white was the crimson blood trickling from Toby's nose. He dabbed it away in cavalier fashion with a white napkin.

That was overdoing it the way things should be overdone. Different times.

In October 1983 Steve Maas was himself busted. He was accused of offering a city auditor a $9,000 bribe to cut his sales tax on the Mudd Club. Maas, beset, decided to rid himself of the building on Avenue C. "The thing with Maas had left a bad taste in my mouth. But Paul insisted I take another look at the place," Arthur says. He was instantly as keen as ever. He promised to show me the place. It was February 18, 1984, a sunny afternoon, not that you would have known in the Weinsteins' dim loft on Fourteenth Street. It was filled with Burmese cats, seven salukis and a collection of ovoid and amoeboid 1950s furnishings, mostly by Finnish designers with a lot of As in their names. Occasionally there would be not particularly good vibrations from the upstairs and downstairs neighbors, a judo class, and a setup called the Drummers' Collective. "Funny to see people breathing this time of day," Arthur said as we walked down to the club.

The World had become The World/El Mundo. It was surrounded by busy bodegas and by brownstones with tinned-over windows and walls that bore graffiti reading "Toxic Junkie" and "SDP," this standing not for Social Democratic Party but sexual deviate perverts. A crutch stuck out of an oil drum beside the World's front door. "I love Alphabet City," Arthur said, walking in.

Con Ed happened not to be supplying current just then but dusty sunlight played on gold-flecked mirrors and crystal chandeliers. Within minutes a potential investor showed up, August Darnell, the lead singer of Kid Creole and the Coconuts, with his red-headed Coconut wife, Adriana. "There's a bad vibe when there's no light," Arthur apologized. "I kind of like it," Darnell said.

They looked around. "You can do this two ways," Darnell said finally. "You can spend a million dollars and devote a year of your life to it. And you could really open! A gorilla twirling a piano . . . show girls everywhere . . . a parade." He sounded entranced, but not too entranced, and reversed, midflow. "Or else just do it," he said. "Open the doors. Start the cash flow. Call it Arthur's World!"

"Arthur's World?" It wasn't often that Arthur Weinstein sounded flummoxed.

"Either that or the Stool Pigeon. But I tried that on a few people and they didn't think it was so funny."

"They don't have our sense of humor," Arthur said.

"What's the door policy?" Darnell asked.

"You pay ten bucks. If you look good, you get in. But we want New Yorkers."

Darnell said, "The doormen must be *friendly*. They've got to be kind. There's not enough kindness in this city."

Outside the club a man was standing beside a flaming car, aghast. A cop car hove into view at the end of the street. "They won't do nothin'. They'll drive off in another direction," a stout bystander predicted. He was right. We found a taxi that had passed a street fight just two blocks away. "I really like your neighborhood," August Darnell said genially. But he came up with

$35,000 anyway, which took care of the rent. Now for the permits. Meanwhile, though, a brand-new club was readying itself to open.

Palladium. Steve and Ian were back in the frame.

Did New York really have room for another club? "Don't worry about a thing," Arthur Weinstein said.

"*But where is the mermaid?*" *a woman was asking hectoringly.* "*There was supposed to be a mermaid.*" *She spun on her heel and marched away from the waterless pool. This was the opening of Visage in May 1984. It was a sort of a neo-Regine's. No artiness, no downtown nastiness, just the heavenly smell of freshly cooking money. Visage occupied a former stable and ran the length of a city block, Fifty-fifth to Fifty-sixth Street, between avenues Eleven and Twelve.* "*Ciao! Big kiss!*" *said the rich, the famous, and the arrant con artists, many of whom had not seen each other for as much as three nights, as they streamed toward the VIP enclave, which was in full view, but behind velvet cords, and guarded by a bouncer the size of a longhorn steer.*

Above the dance floor reared a translucent ziggurat within which pulsed lights like fireflies in Lucite. "*State-of-the-art. Fiber optics. Same as the things a doctor sticks down your throat,*" *an architect said approvingly. This we were told. The make-over had cost $10 million. The owner, or one of them, was Frank Lynch, a Scotsman, based in Miami. Lynch had been managing director of a British company that once ran fourteen clubs. One of these was in Glasgow, a city with some reputation—Glaswegians have been nicknamed* "*the men wi' iron teeth*"—*so Lynch presumably felt ready for whatever New York might throw at him.*

Elsewhere in the jungle, Infinity, Panache, Bond's, and the Savoy were gone, and the Roxy was now described as "*chain-snatchers' heaven,*" *but Xenon survived, as did Studio, Regine's, and Limelight, where, a few days later, I was at an event for new wave designers from the United Kingdom. There was a sign above the sacristy door reading* BUYERS & CELEBS *and the spot where the altar had been wont to stand was occupied by six giant hands of Fatima, fabricated from light projectors.*

The models descended from where the rood screen is normally found. They had feral snarls and strong makeup, like chocolate-cherry mouths and eyebrows like Hitler's mustache. "*Oh dear,*" *a fashion person asked me.* "*Are the British angry about something?*"

A male model appeared. He was wearing a suit of purple leather. "*He usually strips, this one,*" *the fashion person said.*

Music pounded, lights smoked, a female model gyrated. She was standing on what looked like a gravestone, embedded in the floor. Around her neck was a tubular device. "A vomit bag?" speculated the fashion person.

The next model wore a similar accessory, but in gold.

"An evening vomit bag," the fashion person said triumphantly. So onto Studio 54 where there were rehearsals for another event for another British designer, Arabella Pollen. Truly, the music was never going to stop, ever.

HEARTS OF DARKNESS

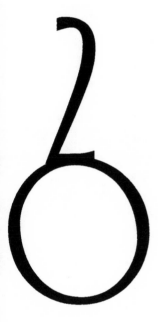

THE PREVIOUSLY MENTIONED LIMELIGHT WAS THE EN-
terprise of a newcomer to New York, Peter Gatien,
who has always seemed a dark horse, even in a
Nightworld that is traditionally home to dark horses.
Indeed, John Addison was a blabbermouth and Ian
Schrager a party animal alongside Peter Gatien, a
Canadian entrepreneur with tousled hair and a manner at once tough and carefully wooden, like a private eye in a B movie from the 1950s, who opened
Limelight in the former Church of the Holy Com-
munion at Sixth Avenue and Twentieth Street. Peter Gatien, who was thirty-one, and had bought the
building from Odyssey House, the drug rehab, says
he expected no problems from the choice of venue.
"If people go to pray in a building, it's a church."
he told me years later. "It's what you do in a building
that dictates what it is. I was brought up very
staunchly as a Catholic. There are cermonies of de-
consecration. If the pope and the hierachy are satisfied with those ceremonies, who am I to question
them?"

This dryly ordinary remark was pure Peter Gatien. Claire O'Connor, who was to become the director and resident goddess of Limelight, says, "Peter is very ordinary. That's his secret. I understand it. My father was an electrician. I'm ordinary, too." Gatien was born in Cornwall, Ontario, the third of five sons of a postman. "It was an industrial town of forty-thousand people, where your career opportunities, to say the least, were limited," he says. "If you graduated from high school, you could work at the local mill. If you graduated from the local university, you could become a doctor, a teacher, or a lawyer. Those were pretty well the only careers." Then something out of the ordinary happened. Gatien lost an eye playing hockey. He has sometimes implied that he was on the brink of a serious sports career. O'Connor doubts this. Gatien tried an artifical eye, found it uncomfortable, and has worn a dashing black eyepatch ever since. Also, though still in his teens, Gaiten took his disability payoff of $17,000 and decided to become extraordinarily rich.

Gatien's first venture was a jeans store in his hometown. He prospered, but got fidgety, and turned his hungry attention to another segment of the youth culture, the club business. People get involved in the nightlife for a variety of reasons, from the easy camaraderie of being a host to the promise of a more varied sex life. Peter Gatien claims it was the basic math. "In my mind, the bar business appeared really lucrative. You bought a pint of beer for twenty-five cents and sold it for a dollar twenty-five," he says. "I bought a dilapidated country and western hotel slash tavern," he said. "It was called the Lafayette House. I changed it to the Aardvark Hotel. That was 1972. I opened as a rock and roll club, and six months to a year later, I changed it to a discothèque.

"I was nineteen and, quite frankly, I thought I had the world by the balls. I was making great money for a small town. I thought this was as much as one could ever want from life."

In 1974 he made a visit to New York to attend the world's first disco conference, which had been organized by *Billboard* magazine at the Roosevelt Hotel. "I was looking into *The New York Times* and I saw a business opportunity ad," he says. It was offering a disco near Miami for sale. "It's describing a $500,000 light system . . . two-thousand capacity . . . this, that, whatever . . . selling price $400,000. Anybody reading that ad would have said: 'There's something wrong with his picture!'

"But I guess naïveté has always been my best quality. I flew down. The place was in Chapter Eleven. I didn't know what Chapter Eleven *meant*. I negotiated a deal. I was twenty-one, and I had bought one of the largest clubs in America, almost by default." He called it the Limelight. "I did the glitz, the spinning wheels, the neon," he says. The manager wore a white suit, Tony Manero style.

John Carmen, a New York publicist, met Gatien in Florida while he was booking a show for his client, then and now, Grace Jones, and the two entered into a working relationship. Three and half years later, Gatien sold up for a $600,000 profit. He and Carmen built an extravagant disco with a thirty-five hundred capacity in Atlanta, Georgia. The space under the glass dance floor was filled with sharks for a while, then drained, and filled with tigers. There was a movie theater in the complex and every few weeks there would be a party for some visiting celeb, like Ann-Margret or Ali McGraw. "What we were doing in Atlanta was sort of like what Studio 54 was doing," Gatien says. Plus a heavy *Saturday Night Fever* inflection.

But Gatien was chafing. He felt ready for Manhattan. Studio's fires were burning low. There was a hole. "When I arrived here and was looking around in the early eighties, I knew that to make an impact on the city I couldn't do another theater," Gatien says. "It wasn't like I could walk in and do a larger Studio with more spinning lights. It would have been laughted at. It's as simple as that.

"And the warehouse concept had been done here also. I felt that something using art and architecture was the way to travel in the eighties. Preferably a church, though I wasn't limiting myself to that. But that was my first choice." John Carmen says that he stumbled on the church on Twentieth Street almost literally, being on a daytime drinking bout. He telephoned as soon as his head cleared. He had found Limelight III.

The Church was an 1842 chunk of darksome Gothic Revival. Gatien painstakingly had it restored to augment such ecclesiatical features as the pulpit overlooking the disco room, the Tiffany stained-glass windows, the regilded pipe organ, and the memorial plaques in the walls. One of the bars was made from disassembled pews. All that Limelight lacked was gravestones on the dance floor. He never imagined he would offend churchgoers. Right. John Carmen was an obvious hire. With Carmen came Claire O'Connor. Fred Rothbell-

Mista, and addict of Nightworld, was hired to run the door. All three formed intense relationships with the Canadian. "What we had was like a love affair. But without the sex," Claire O'Connor says. It was, of course, based on the wielding of power. Power beat sex anytime, for Peter Gatien.

O'Connor also notes that Gatien was "quite naive. He was what the Canadians called a Newfie," she says. Other Nightworlders were swift to sniff opportunity. "Maurice Brahms called. He said he wanted to get involved," O'Connor says. "He said he wanted to bury Schrager and Rubell. John Addison called that same week. He wanted to take over a couple of nights." Gatien conferred with O'Connor. "I said you don't need those guys" she said. "He didn't even want to talk to them. I made him." Brahms and Addison were politely told to shove off.

Eric Goode paid the place a visit while it was being done up and worried that it would present Area with a serious challenge. "It was such a great building," he said. It opened on Wednesday November 9, 1983, with a thrash for *Interview* magazine, billed by Andy Warhol as "the party of the year." Several punks wore crucifixes, and one reveler arrived on a cross, got off, and dragged it around the dance floor. The Rt. Rev. Paul Moore, the Episcopal Bishop of New York, and a notably liberal cleric—he lent the Cathedral of St. John to the Black Panthers in the sixties—said, "We are horrified."

He was not the only one. Even Francesco Scavullo, the photographer best known for his bosomy covers for *Cosmopolitan,* asked, anxiously, "Is this consecrated ground?" Starting a nightclub in a church in increasingly conservative times might be construed as lusting after trouble. "Peter loves trouble," Claire O'Connor says.

In Nightworld, as elsewhere, action breeds equal and opposite reaction. Few, perhaps, would have pegged Vito Bruno as an agent of change. In 1980, when he started the after-hours place AM/PM on Murray Street it was, after all, just another club. "We didn't open till two," Bruno says. "We got Jagger . . . Bowie . . . David Byrne . . . Keith Haring . . . there were more celebrities per square foot in AM/PM than anywhere. More than Studio."

AM/PM folded in 1982, high-celeb quotient or no, and Bruno was hauled in to work with Ruza Blue, which led to Blue's aforementioned departure. As Roxy floundered, Vito Bruno began trying to make parties in other clubs. But the racial mix that had been one of Roxy's strengths in its good times was not a high priority elsewhere. "We were known for black and Spanish promoters," Bruno says. "We couldn't get rooms to work in. Then Michael Musto planted a seed in my brain." This germinated into the Outlaw Parties.

The Outlaw Parties were held at short notice in public or derelict spaces. "No one paid anything," Bruno says. "We charged a dollar for the liquor, which would cover the costs. Nobody made any money. We had a street gang, Can't Be Stopped, CBS, and it was those kids throwing it. Those kids were not allowed in any of the clubs. Yet all the fabulous people would come to *them.*"

The first Outlaw Party, which was in 1985, was in the Twenty-third Street subway station. The homeless people who normally use the space were taken to a shelter in advance and set up for the night. The next was on the West Side Highway, close to the moored battleship, the *Intrepid*. "We hand-delivered invitations all over the city," Bruno says. A birthday party was given for Annie Flanders, editor of *Details*, on the Brooklyn Bridge. "Steve Rubell came. Every fabulous person you can think of was there." Urban Fright, a Halloween party, was given in a destroyed space on the Lower East Side. "The invitations were each burned by hand. There were bricks with holes in them, and thousands of candles," Bruno says. "That was a great one."

There were also Outlaw Parties on the *River Rat*. "That was the second oldest riveted-steel-hulled tugboat in existence," Bruno says. "Susan Williams and I were promoting one night a week on the boat," says Victoria Leacock. "At that time Susan was called Candy. She had been a receptionist at Area and she was dating John Krevey, who owned the tug.

"The problem was that every week John and Vito would move the goddamn boat. One week it was here, one week it was there. So it was very difficult for our guests."

The boat was to be on the Hudson at North Moore Street for a barbecue, and Leacock, who was working at a magazine, went there with a checklist on her lunch break that day. "I was just about to cross the West Side Highway. *And there was no boat there,*" Leacock says. "I start cursing to myself. Those morons! Now I would have to write a hundred things . . . to make a hundred arrows.

"And when I got to the middle of the highway I noticed there was a lump in the water. A strange . . . *lump*. Some guys were on a raft, looking down into the water. I went, 'Oh no!' "

She got to the edge of the quay. Vito Bruno was standing there. "Yep! Your party's canceled," he told her.

Bruno explains. Nobody had been aware that the tug had been moored above some underwater pilings. There had been a party there the night before. "With the weight of the people, the boat got pieced," Bruno says. "We had four pilings coming through." The pump was set to work—it takes more than onrushing river water to stop a New York party—and Krevey tried to get the boat clear with a bulldozer the next day. "It ripped like a tin can. It went to the bottom in two minutes," Bruno says.

Victoria Leacock had found them puzzling out how to retrieve the safe from the river bottom.

"I don't recall," Vito Bruno says pensively whether they got the safe out. Meantime, the Outlaw Parties went on their merry way.

"Art" was the Area theme in May 1985. Eric Goode says, judiciously, "Curatorially, it was a weak theme. But it was as good as any museum show. Sol LeWitt did the whole entrance . . . Michael Heizer had these enormous sculptures, they were like meteorites . . . Sandro Chia had one of the best pieces I have ever seen of his . . . Clemente did a tattoo on Johnny Dynell . . ."

Among younger contributors were Keith Haring, who had become furiously modish, and who made a gigantic painting. Haring had been showing in discos since he had organized a "black light" art show in Club 57. "I was showing in discos because I was working in a disco," he told me later. "I was a busboy at the first Danceteria. And I worked at the Mudd Club too. When the work got accepted, it seemed like it was a responsibility to continue instead of saying 'I'm a gallery artist. I just want to sell paintings for a lot of money.' "

Andy Warhol did an elegant piece, which has been inadequately documented, for understandable reasons. It was a sculpture that wasn't there. He was given an alcove and if he was in the club, he might stand in it for a bit. Otherwise it was an invisible sculpture. Another sculpture on view already had a history. Patti Astor of the East Village's Fun Gallery had given a show of Jean-Michel Basquiat. It was around Thanksgiving, and Astor asked several artists to a pumpkin-carving party in the gallery beforehand. The artists, including Kenny Scharf, Keith Haring, and Basquiat himself, were all carving when Julian Schnabel arrived. "He said, 'Oh, this is stupid,' but then he sat down and carved this pumpkin, and he was so proud of it, he wanted to have it cast *in bronze*," Astor says.

The pumpkins went into the Fun window. Whereupon the Schnabel pumpkin disappeared. The artist was . . . indignant. "It became the most famous pumpkin in town," Astor says.

Jean-Michel Basquiat was the perp.

The remains of the vegetable went into a wooden box, covered with paintings, drawings, and an enigmatic inscription, "Vagina Water." This was Basquiat's contribution to Area's "Art" theme. Julian Schnabel himself refused to contribute. Characteristically, though, he somehow managed to get himself into Michael Halsband's group photograph commemorating the event. "He was so pretentious . . . so out of control," Eric Goode says.

It happened that Palladium opened on May 14 while Area's "Art" theme was still in situ. Palladium's opening plans were well known—"Steve went to Area every fucking night," Eric Goode says—and it was particularly well known that Palladium was going to be making a big deal of the new art stars. So Area's "Art" theme was widely seen as a shrewd preemptive strike. Eric Goode is insistent that this was not the case.

Jennifer Goode, Eric's sister, had a slightly different take. "It was a competitive move on our part," she said in an interview. At any rate, battle was joined.

Steve Rubell and Ian Schrager had lived close to the brink. They had seen others fall, and the fear of falling was on them now. Morgans Hotel opened on October 1, 1984, but it could be years before it moved into the black. Both Steve and Ian looked upon their tenure at Palladium as an interlude, a source of day-to-day financing; but neither wanted the club to be a lame second act to Studio 54. "Nobody knows what it's like unless they've been to jail," Rubell said later. "When you come out, you really feel like a piece of shit. So you're out to do something. You really want to top yourself."

That it was going to look good at least, they knew. Arata Isozaki had flown in from Japan. The architect toured Area and Studio 54 with Ian Schrager. His ultimate solution was a cubic grid, three stories high. "It can all be taken out and it can be turned back into an opera house," Rubell said.

With Alan Cohen approving all major expenditures—or sometimes disapproving of them, as in the case of Steve Rubell's 54ish notion of bringing in Coney Island bumper cars—the exhausting process of fine tuning began. And of making crucial hires. Since Area was The Joint at the beginning of 1985 it was standard operating procedure that Steve and Ian should offer Eric Goode a job at the Palladium. "They were really going to pay me a good amount of money," Goode says. He declined. They hired Rudolf.

Rubell's energy was particularly remarkable because he was under a medical gun, and knew it. Goode remembers a dinner with Steve, Andy Warhol, and the curator Henry Geldzahler while work on Palladium was under way. "He was just losing his hair and he was telling us why he was sick," Goode says. "He said he'd been with a hustler in a Greyhound bus station, and he had got syphilis."

Rubell had further confided that he hadn't wanted to go to a doctor, and hadn't done so until the disease was well advanced, but that now he was getting treatment and he was optimistic about a full recovery. "Later on that evening he drove Andy and me and I think Henry Geldzahler came with us, and Francesco Clemente, and gave us a tour of the whole club," Goode says. Steve Rubell was not one to play the blues.

Although it was Ian Schrager who had by far the keener interest in design, since Steve Rubell's brother and sister-in-law were significant collectors of leading-edge contemporary art, Steve was not short of information. "Artists are the new stars for the eighties," Rubell proclaimed. David Knapp, Steve's chauffeur, says, "Ian was very big into conceptualizing stuff and dealing with the architects. But Steve was a very social fellow and he knew the artists, and he could get them to do stuff."

Keith Haring painted a backdrop for the dance floor, but was under no illusions about the depth of Rubell's commitment. "There was never any competition in terms of quality," he told Jennifer Goode later. It was well done, though. Above Haring's piece were two nine-thousand-pound banks of monitors for which Eric Fischl, Laurie Anderson, and David Salle had been commissioned to make videos. Kenny Scharf was asked to "customize" the bathrooms and telephones, just as he had done at the 1985 Whitney Biennial, and he did so with lurid fake fur and kitsch figurines.

Francesco Clemente agreed to paint frescoes, and chose what has been described as "a tiny, innocuous hallway." The paintings that Clemente made on the ceiling would be Steve Rubell's favorite pieces in the club. He asked Jean-Michel Basquiat, who had just appeared on the cover of *The New York Times Magazine,* to paint some murals too. Basquiat, cagier than Clemente, said he would paint a couple of—removable—canvases instead. "I offered them to Steve for $50,000 each," Basquiat told me later. "I had no idea what I was going to make or how big they were going to be. And he didn't take it."

"He said he needed the money," Rubell told me years later in the Canal Bar when Basquiat prices were rocketing. He added dolefully, "I should have bought them."

Music was crucial. John "Jellybean" Benitez, who had been the DJ at Xenon, had moved to California. He had just produced a record for Madonna. "I was called and told it had gone to number one," he says. "That same day, Ian called and said, 'We want you to play opening night. Come back to New York and play on Thursdays.' I came back and worked on the sound system. It was incredible. The energy in that room."

That took care of the huge "public" part of the club. There were other spaces. Anita Sarko, the former DJ at Mudd, had first met Rubell in the club Chase Park, where she had done an occasional gig. "I went over to him. He'd just got out of jail," she says. "I said, 'Hi! My name's Anita Sarko and I'm the disc jockey here.' He looked at me and turned his back. Wouldn't talk to me."

She next saw him at Area. "Somebody said why don't you just go over to him and ask if he's looking for a DJ. I said fine. I went over and said, 'Hi! My name is Anita Sarko. I'm a disc—' He said, 'Yeah. I've heard of you.' And he walked away from me. Fine. That was it. I had tried."

Sarko was telephoned a month before the opening. "All of a sudden, out of nowhere, I get a call from Steve Rubell," she says. "He walked me up and up, all these stairs, and into this room that was total mayhem. I was looking around, and it just came out of my mouth. 'My God! What I could do with this room!'

"He said, 'It's so funny you say that. It's yours if you want it.' This was the person who had snubbed me twice. He said he knew this place was a wreck. I said, 'No, no, no. My father is a builder. I grew up in unfinished buildings. I know exactly what this room is going to be. And I know that I can make it talk.'

"He said, 'Do you know who Michael Todd was?' I said, 'Yeah. He was married to Elizabeth Taylor. He produced *Around the World in Eighty Days.*' He said, 'This used to be his screening room. We're going to open up this place in a month.' But I wanted my own room. I wanted a room that was just mine. And he told me, 'You've got it, baby.' He didn't care I wasn't fabulous. Immediately, the two of us just clicked. Steve Rubell had one of the purest creative minds you could meet in your entire fucking life." Rubell took Sarko downstairs to meet Schrager, and that was that.

The door was crucial, too. Haoui Montaug, who was close to Sarko, and had worked both at the Mudd Club and at Howard Stein's short-lived downtown club, the Rock Lounge, came aboard. They agreed they should have a woman on the door too. At this stage, Ian Schrager's longtime woman friend, the designer Norma Kamali, telephoned. She suggested he see one of her salesgirls. She was in her mid-twenties and her name was Sally Randall.

Sally Randall comes from a well-to-do town in upstate New York, Rye. Her father was a financial analyst with Chrysler, her mother had been trained in opera singing. It happened that Sally had sipped her "first cocktails" going with her girlfriends to a steakhouse of Rubell's in Mamaroneck, using fake ID when she was "fourteen or fifteen." She moved to New York in 1977 to study art at the School of Visual Arts, where she had become friendly with Kenny Scharf. She was just eighteen, a prudent brunette, living on Sixth Street. Nightworld was still another country.

One night, she decided she was being ridiculously guarded. "I said it's about time I went out and found the rest of the world," she says. "I walked down the block to a little club I knew was there, called CBGB. It was eight dollars at the door because there was a double bill. Well, eight dollars was all I had. So I gave them my holy eight dollars and walked in and sat up on a speaker, because if I had sat at a table I would have had to have a drink. The double bill was the Ramones and the Dead Boys. Talk about a first club!

"I was still a conservative little Rye girl, wearing gray corduroy Levis' and little tortoiseshell headbands. My wardrobe went through a drastic change over a period of about a week. I streaked my hair blue and pink and chopped all these bits out of it, so some parts stuck out and other bits hung down. That was how I showed up at the front door for Thanksgiving. My mother said, 'Sorry! You can't sit at my table looking like that . . . ' "

Randall quickly segued from punk into new wave, adopting looks like a red kilt held together by a colossal safety pin. She graduated in 1981 and landed a job as an assistant to Diane von Furstenberg. It was von Furstenberg who took her on her first visit to Studio 54 as part of a little group that included the screenwriter Paul Schrader and the model/actress Marisa Berenson. "I just remember the shock of going in there with those people," she says.

Randall became friendly with two art writers she profoundly admired, Rene Ricard and Edit DeAk. It was DeAk especially who introduced her to the world of downtown clubs. "They were these wonderful meeting places where people could get together after painting all day or writing all day," she says. Randall had begun making installations in clubs like Danceteria when she heard that there was an opening in the production design department at Paramount Pictures. She flew out to Los Angeles and met with a man from the studio. It was agreed they would meet again ten days later. It was the summer of 1983.

"I found myself an apartment after two days," she says. She flung herself into L.A.'s Nightworld, which consisted at the time of clubs like Zero and Club Lingerie, where a young singer, Jane Cantillon, would sing in her, yes, lingerie. The experience quite naturally decided Sally Randall to go blond. She forgot quite how blond she had become when she went for her second meeting with the guy from Paramount. "There was no way he could have recognized me. And I couldn't recognize him. We never ran into each other. Suddenly, without a job and having bills to pay, I had to rethink a lot of things."

Buying bits and pieces from the Pasadena thrift shops that sell off old movie wardrobes, she began putting together a spectacularly show-offy wardrobe, little-girl style. "It was freedom . . . and having the guts to do it. Then I began noticing people were treating me differently," she told writer Dinah Prince. Her shyness disappeared in disguise.

Randall was back in Manhattan that winter. "I knew it would be different," she said. Indeed, she was duly made fashion editor of the *East Village Eye* and began contributing a gossip column, first to that paper, then to *New York Talk*. She remained rather a Rye girl at heart, all the same. "I remained extremely naive about a lot of things," she says. "Extremely naive. I had friends who were junkies, and I had no idea. They would be nodding out and I would think they were *overtired.*"

Randall took an uptown job, as a salesgirl with Norma Kamali, and, by day at least, went into camouflage, trim suits and a dark brown page boy. Kamali was better informed, though. "She said I know you're putting on these wild outfits and going out to clubs. And that's basically what you want," Kamali told her, adding that she had set up a meeting with Ian Schrager. "I went in to see Ian. Ian handed me off to Steve. Steve walked me around. It was still under construction," Randall says. "He was asking me all kinds of questions. But he knew all about me." Rubell even knew about Randall's visit to Studio 54 with Diane von Furstenberg. She got the job.

A stream of people showed up as Palladium neared completion, Peter Sudler among them. "This time don't fuck it up," he told Rubell.

The opening was May 14. Jean-Michel Basquiat was still finishing his canvas, actually in the Mike Todd Room. "The last minute before opening, he was trying to get it done. And then they just hung it up," David Knapp says.

The invitations to the opening had not been the lavish geegaws of yore but simple white cards and the velvet cords in front were black. One by one, or two by two, the faces checked in . . . Halston . . . Calvin Klein . . . Boy George and Marilyn . . . Grace Jones . . . Bianca Jagger, assuring a *People* reporter that her Studio days were over.

Steve Rubell was all over the place, at first in an Armani tuxedo, which he quickly shed in favor of chinos. Andy Warhol was hanging over the balcony shooting Polaroids. Ian Schrager, of course, spent much of the night out of sight, lurking in the DJ booth with Norma Kamali.

There was a lot of Nightworld scoffing at the timing. You don't open a club just before the summer. Everybody knew *that.*

Rubell and Schrager's lavishness paid off. Palladium was instantly The Joint. "We had been doing two thousand admissions every Friday and Saturday," says Limelight's Claire O'Connor. "With only fifteen or twenty comps. How could we compete with all those free admissions and an open bar? Peter hated Steve Rubell. He hated him very much."

Downtown was blasting away full-throttle when Palladium opened, but the epoch when its denizens were wowed by the sight of fluffy debutantes cruising hard-core clubs seemed pretty much over. "Uptown is uptown and downtown is downtown," said Stephen Saban, then a columnist for *Details.* "It's a sort of voluntary apartheid." *Details* was just one magazine that covered the downtown waterfront. Also on the case were *The East Village Eye, New York Talk, Paper,* and the *Daily News,* where Dinah Prince wrote a daily social column called, of course, "Downtown."

Area remained a source of endless admiring copy, and elsewhere there was a blooming of cabaret, both undecorously gay or just over-the-top polymorphous perversity. Gabriel Rotello's "Downtown Dukes and Divas" at Peter Gatien's—now livelier—Limelight presented the likes of Dean Johnson, a bald six-foot-plus drag queen rock and roller, and Karen Finlay, whose high-pitched performance art would, in due course, make her an anti-poster girl for the Moral Majority.

Trey Speegle, whose daytime job was in the art department at *Vanity Fair,* had launched his career as an impressario at the Pyramid in 1984. "We did Sunday nights. We turned it into a gay cabaret night," he says. It was called Straight from Hell. Speegle says, "During the first six weeks we had Quentin Crisp . . . Fran Liebowitz got up and talked for half an hour . . . Kenneth Anger bought *Scorpio Rising,* and we showed it . . . I hosted nights with John Sex and Ethyl Eichelberger."

Speegle moved to Danceteria and did a gay night called Bad Boys on the club's fourth floor, which was called Congo Bill. "We made it into like a private party," he says. "With male strippers and porno movies, which is commonplace now in gay clubs, but which was not commonplace then. It was bringing the seedier atmosphere of Times Square into the downtown nightclub scene, and that was incredibly popular.

"It was funny. I was organizing it, so it was never that seedy to me. People would tell me they would see people having sex in the bathroom and stuff like that, but I was trying to get a show on. And trying to organize the pop charts with the DJs, who now handle RuPaul's career. There was an unwritten law of No Girls. It was a private party, so we could do that."

New places were opening, too. A couple of French guys had started up a place in a storefront on Eighth Street and Avenue A, giving it the early sci-fi name, Save the Robots. Scotty Taylor, who was not involved with the troubled birth of the World, was partner in a thriving after-hours joint, the Valentine Room. Early one morning, a middle-aged man with short hair and a sensible suit tried to get admittance. "Aleph, the doorman, wouldn't let him in," Scotty Taylor says. The man waited, watched the comings and goings, and took off. He returned, wearing a leather vest, and got in with no trouble.

Upstairs Taylor asked what he wanted. "Rémy is my drink," he said. There being none, Taylor poured some less celebrated firewater and pushed it over. "Why aren't you charging me? Everybody else is paying," the man asked.

"I don't want to be offensive. But are you a cop?" Scotty Taylor asked.

"I'm a successful businessman who has the luxury of not getting up until two," the man said, his tone authentically aggrieved. His name was Jack Lesco. He was a designer, who had won awards for a meat cleaver and—"the thing I'll never live down"—a lavatory seat, but he had become a successful realtor.

Lesco became a regular at the Valentine Room and Taylor made sure a bottle of Rémy Martin was always on hand. Then the building that housed the place went into Chapter 11. Taylor had been running a hot place for months and was stone-broke. Nightworld. He was in Area one night and needed five bucks to get home. He says, "I saw Jack. He seemed very happy to see me. I thought maybe I'll get twenty . . ."

Lesco was happy because he had just bought a building and had decided to turn the basement into a club. "I asked Scotty how he would like to go into business with me? Naturally he didn't refuse," he says.

And the five bucks? "I walked home," Taylor says.

★   ★   ★

David Knapp was a fledgling playwright in search of a paycheck when he went to Palladium for an interview in April 1985. It was an open call and he was hired as a waiter. Not long after his arrival, Steve Rubell fired his driver. "Something happened," Knapp says. He thought the driver had been caught dealing drugs on the side. Rubell needed a replacement and Knapp was brought in by the manager. "Steve said, 'Yeah, I've seen you. I know you. I'll need you for a week until I find someone permanent.' "

Knapp, who was in jeans and a leather jacket, asked what he should wear. "Just wear what you're wearing," Steve Rubell said. Even in the mid-eighties he remained immune to the Versailles Syndrome of the New Tycoonery. His car at the time was a rented Oldsmobile. "It was a piece of crap," Knapp says. "One of the windows kept falling down."

A routine was established. Knapp would show up at the club at ten at night. "My duties were to take care of any friends of his who came by. And any celebrities. I would give tours," he says. He would dole them out drink tickets from the wedge of up to a hundred he would customarily carry. And before Steve arrived he would be in charge of hosting the Mike Todd Room.

When Steve finally arrived, David Knapp would give him a status report as to the famous faces in the club. No matter the state of Steve's clarity, he would focus on the numbers. Anita Sarko would see him scribbling, alongside the telephone, never content until he knew they were floating above the waterline that night. He would usually stay till the very end. As in Studio, he would often be there for the count-out.

Sally Randall and Haoui Montaug had a simple nocturnal routine. "We would meet around eight-thirty and have a Japanese dinner on Ninth Street," Randall says. "Then we would go off to the club. As soon as we got to the door, somebody would thrust a clipboard in your hand, telling you what was happening. Five minutes later, the doors would open. And you were there for the night."

Breaks were few. "Steve would take me off the floor sometimes to baby-sit," she says. "Which meant a star would come in and I would take them up to Michael Todd and hand them off to Anita. And Anita would entertain them from there unless she was busy with some other . . . *fantastic celebrities*. And I would have to stay for a little while and make sure they were okay."

It was rare she got onto the main dance floor. "That was where the paying customers went. I loved it," she says. "Steve and I went down one night with two other people and square-danced in front of everybody. Everyone seemed to know who Steve was and who I was, and they cheered. It was the strangest thing."

Her liking for Steve Rubell was this side of idolatry, though. "Actually, I preferred Ian's personality to Steve's," she says. "You know the joke about Steve? You can always tell if someone knew Steve or not. If someone goes, 'Oh, Steve Rubell! I miss him so much, he was such a sweetie'—*They didn't know him!*

"If they say, 'I miss him so much. He was such a sweetie, that lying double-crosser!' That's how you knew someone knew him.

"He was such a double-crosser. He turned Anita Sarko and me against each other by telling us each something the other had said. Which was a lie. It took ages to sort it out and realize neither of us had said anything of the sort. He loved to see people . . . change."

This was just one pressure. The cheering on the dance floor had been a manifestation of another. Suddenly Sally Randall was famous. One of the most famous young women in New York, and some of the elements of that fame disturbed her. "Little blurbs were written," she says. "Oh, she's seeing so-and-so. A couple of times I found my name associated with some hot young actor. It was absurd. You expect that if you're a star. But for having a job standing on the door? It was all so damned ridiculous.

"I can't tell you how often I would see people refer to me as sexual. I thought that was really amusing. Because from the outside it may seem easy to see somebody that way. But if you're spending that much time putting on makeup and getting dressed every night, when can you find time for *sex*?

"What happened was that everything became public domain. All the privacy was gone. It took all the charm of a nightclub away."

Sally Randall went with the stupendous flow for a while. "A bunch of us were on *Oprah Winfrey*," she remembers. "Oprah asked, 'What do you do in your spare time?' And Elizabeth Saltzman said, 'Oh, we sit around and read articles about ourselves.' She meant it as a joke, but there was a grain of truth in it. It's wonderful to have an ego trip for a while. The problem is when you start needing it. It becomes really detrimental."

On July 10, Palladium threw a birthday party for Randall and photographer Patrick McMullan. Nine thousand well-wishers showed up. In August, she turned her thoughts to recording some pop music. She told Dinah Prince, who was profiling her for *New York,* that she was at "the Manhattan University of Life. I'm getting my M.A. in fame, and I'll be getting my Ph.D. in money."

Randall was in Los Angeles, celebrating at a Halloween party, when the *New York* profile came out.

"It was this huge, eight-page article. It talked about . . . things I did, what I wore to events, how I made an entrance to a room. I hadn't lived long enough to have one page written about me. But it was. And I didn't like it.

"When I got back to New York, I immediately quit. It was too much. Steve and Ian were fine. But everybody else saw me as this ungrateful child.

"I was famous! But for all the wrong reasons. I'll tell you something. There are people who know how to get famous for one teeny little thing and they know exactly how to parlay it into what they want. I didn't have the wisdom or experience. So the only thing I could do was walk away."

Randall painted and wrote, and continued to take paying jobs in clubs. She was an ex-icon, but she had survived her icon-hood.

Not so, Tinkerbelle. Tinkerbelle had been born Jeri Lee Visser, a woman I knew, and liked. She was a tart-tongued, thin-faced blonde, who had turned herself into an underground celebrity. A disco addict in the sixties, she had written for *Interview* and starred on cable TV, but it was as an acidly witty denizen of the nightlife that she had excelled. "Tink's whole life revolved around the clubs," says Steven Gaines. "It was performance art for her. She loved to be witty, and mean, and wild. She had just lived at Studio. The whole day revolved around it. And then she turned forty and the club scene was changing. The worst was when she couldn't get into Palladium."

Haoui Montaug, normally one of the less autocratic doormen, simply wouldn't let her in. "That was such an enormous blow to her," Gaines says. "She talked about it for weeks and weeks and weeks, and didn't let up, and went back to it, and niggled away. It just devastated her. It blew her ego away."

On January 22, 1986, Tinkerbelle leapt to her death from a fifth-story window.

★   ★   ★

Rubell and Schrager remained ferociously competitive with other clubs. R. Couri Hay was giving a dinner party for three hundred in his garden apartment on the West Side to celebrate the birthday of Boy George. The British singer, whose given name was George O'Dowd, a drag queen with an amazing voice, was then at the zenith of his popularity, and he had become a fixture of Manhattan's Nightworld. He was usually in the company of Marilyn, another British drag queen with a somewhat less amazing voice, and New York's perennial deb of the year, Cornelia Guest, who was then dating Eric Goode.

Couri Hay had agreed to let Palladium throw an after-dinner birthday party for the singer. Eric Goode asked whether Area couldn't do something for Boy George too. Couri Hay explains what happened next, his speech so constructed of emphases, flowery italics, exclamation points, and triple underlining as to constitute the spoken equivalent of a ransom note or an enraged letter to the editor: "We acquiesced and said, 'Okay, *Breakfast in Bed with Boy George at 4* AM' . . . When Steve Rubell and Ian Schrager found out about this, they both went ballistic. They flipped! And they threatened to cancel the party.

"I said fine! Go right ahead. Dinner at the house is what I'm doing. I have only added this party at Palladium for you, really. I'm not getting anything out of it. They said at that point what do you want? I said, oh, send me some champagne. Send me a dozen cases of champagne. Thinking Cristal or Dom, you know. They sent me six cases of California Chandon.

"I never used it. I sent it back to Steve, with a note saying I only drink French champagne. And I was rather *annoyed* at that. Considering that I probably made him a hundred thousand dollars that night. He was so mad that I did give a party at competing Area, even though it was at four in the morning, and Palladium had to close. It was this jealous kind of insane politics, which I came to understand."

The incident spotlighted two processes. "I remember being surprised when Palladium affected Area," Eric Goode says. He, his brother, Shawn Hausman, and Darius Azeri were tired, though. "The problem with Area was it took a lot of effort. We took all the money we made and we spent it on these thematic changes. It never stopped.

"We would spend endless time arguing and fighting about what we would do every time. We had a whole floor above where we were building things and we had a full-time staff of people working. It never ended. After two and a half years of that, we were just burned. I ended up going to Palladium *a lot*." The pixiedust began whooshing away from Area. It turned into a gray zone with dispiriting speed.

The increase in the powers of the party promoters was dispiriting too. Couri Hay soon became a promoter of club events himself, in cahoots with a new arrival to town, Scott Currie. "We had a flat fee," he says. "I got $3,000 a night to walk into a room. I gave him half. I never invited more than two dozen people. Anywhere. Never, never. I didn't have these *vast lists*." The point being, though, that Couri Hay's two dozen would be magnets for hot type, like Jay McInerney, Tama Janowitz, Boy George, Cornelia Guest.

Couri Hay became known for giving lavish openings for new clubs, which would become briefly modish, then die like fish in a contaminated pool. "I bankrupted everybody," he says. "You name it. They all went out of business. I spent $35,000 to open the Red Zone. An *unheard of sum* at that time." The Red Zone was Maurice Brahms's attempt to detach a segment of Palladium's business. "The party was fabulous! The press was fabulous! Poor Maurice thought he would be busy ever after.

"What he came to realize, and what I came to realize, was *nobody ever came back!* They would come to the opening night and that was it."

Club owners began resorting to ever more febrile measures, but still saw the promoters as the cure rather than the disease. "Then we took the idea of incorporating other promoters," Couri Hay says. "The idea of more than one promoter a night came into play. You had to book one to three parties a night five or six nights a week to fill what was considered a *big club*." His private agenda was to learn the business, then start a hot place of his own. "I thought let's lose everybody else's money. Let's bankrupt everyone first. And I'll learn all these lessons. And then I'll make a fortune.

"Of course, that never quite happened. You can make a success. Making a fortune seems to be *a whole lot* more difficult."

★   ★   ★

One lesson was that loyalty had become history. Another was the vanishing of the celebs. In Studio times, famous faces had drifted around the public spaces. Many had danced. At Xenon and Area, likewise. But the free-floatingness of the disco years finally dissipated in Palladium. The fact was that Palladium was simply too big for quality control of the sort Rubell had required. He capitulated, hired Jerry Rubin away from Studio, and networking yuppies swarmed in.

Steve Rubell had been ubiquitously visible in Studio. It became rare to spot him in the more public parts of Palladium. "If it was a big event that was happening downstairs, he would do it," Knapp says. "Or if he was with bankers or clients who were interested in the big disco scene. Then he would hang out down there. Otherwise he said the only reason he was there was for the Mike Todd Room. Because it was special. He had basically graduated into this more intimate scene."

It was, though, a dilution of the notion of a VIP room, because even the Mike Todd Room was gigantic. Indeed, with its capacity of some seven hundred, it dwarfed most after-hours clubs. The disease bred its own vaccine. Within the Michael Todd Room there were two further VIP rooms, and they were as private as they were uncomfortable. It may say something about these VIP rooms that they had acquired the in-house nicknames of Betty Ford In-Patients and Betty Ford Out-Patients.

Betty Ford In-Patients, which was the most frequented, was a bare box-room, lit by naked bulbs. The crème de la crème who frequented it would sit on the single chair or on liquor crates. "That was Steve's big joke because everybody looked like such shit in there," Anita Sarko says. "They spent $28 million and we all ended up in a closet," agrees Reinaldo Herrera. This was just the sort of *faux pauvre* minimalism that well-heeled elites enjoy, because it distinguishes those who have been through the rigors of private schools from soft and vulgar plutes. Compared to the two Betty Fords, Howard Stein's dreary little office in Xenon seemed in memory as luxurious as Cleopatra's barge. Not that they were wholly without creature comforts, of course. Drink orders were regularly taken in the Betty Fords and there were sporadic visits from the Elf Queen, dispensing those little delicacies to be found listed in governmental bulletins of defeat in the War on Drugs. Few habitués of either Betty Ford, of course, spent any more time in the vastness of the outer club than they would in Grand Central station. Even so far as Steve Rubell was concerned, the giant club was just business. Other people's clubs were pleasure, and as soon as he could, he would then have Knapp drive him out into the night. Area, first, Save the Robots, the World, and most especially, a new little joint, Scotty Taylor's Milkbar.

"DEATH OF DOWNTOWN"

2

SCOTTY TAYLOR AND JACK LESCO OPENED THE MILKBAR on November 7, 1985. This was just one week after the opening of what Scotty calls their "sister club," the World. Going legit can be a maddeningly slow process and a hefty wedge of paperwork records the inching of the World toward respectability. It had taken legal action to stir the State Liquor Authority into granting a license to one of the partners, Paul Garcia. Arthur Weinstein, Garcia, and Frank Roccio reopened the club as the World/El Mundo on October 30, 1985, although such crucial permits as a cabaret license were still lacking. There were images of dinosaurs on the invitation to the opening party. The partners began booking private parties, scuffling, waiting for the good times to roll.

The Milkbar had no such growing pains. It occupied a small assymetrical space, a basement on Seventh Avenue South, and had been done up by Colleen Weinstein. It had been painted to a pure white glimmer, with fluorescent panels in the walls that glowed lavender, digital green, rose, and X-ray blue, and it was furnished with bits and pieces from the early sixties, like Saarinen and Alvar Aalto chairs. It had a space age igloo look that suggested Courrèges jumpsuits and movies like *A Clockwork Orange,* from which the Milkbar had borrowed its name. It was a proper setting for basic downtown black.

The Milkbar, which opened with that fashionable accessory, an unlisted telephone number, was soon really hot. It became a dropping-in place for curious uptown socialites, who came to such events as Tama Janowitz's party for *Slaves of New York*. One such debutante was asked where she lived. "Avenue P," she said firmly. Her questioner drifted off, Park Avenue not being part of his geography.

For several months, Steve Rubell had Knapp drive him to the Milkbar every night. Scotty Taylor says that Steve had told him that, before he had opened the Milkbar, they had been thinking of giving him part of the Palladium to run as a bar, perhaps the pool hall. "Ian paid me the best compliment," Taylor says.

"One day he said, 'You know, you really hurt us at Palladium.' I said what? Are you kidding?"

Schrager told him that there were two hundred people that they wanted in the Mike Todd Room. And that a hundred and twenty-five of them would be in the Milkbar every night. "Including Steve and him actually," Scotty says.

In fact, keeping Palladium's ball bouncing was proving arduous. In 1986 Rubell called Arthur Weinstein. "I was waiting for my permits for the World," Weinstein says. "Steve said honestly we want to hire you. But we *gotta* have Frank." Rubell knew that Frank Roccio's wife, Lauren Goldman, was personal travel agent to the stars. "She was hooked up to Eddie Murphy and a lot of other big acts as a travel agent. So Frank had access to a lot of good parties," Weinstein says. Roccio and Weinstein duly joined the team. "We had Wednesday nights. We did Eddie Murphy. We did the Eurhythmics. We did Phil Collins. The only problem was that Frank had to do all the work. For once I got over on him." Weinstein's own favorite coup was a jaunt to London whereon he secured the services of the briefly fashionable Haircut Band, Sigue Sigue Sputnik, for Halloween.

The best music night ever, according to Glenn O'Brien, was the night when Einstürzende Neubauten were playing. This is a German noise band, who used machinery rather than conventional instruments. "Instead of a drummer, they had a guy hammering a sheet of metal," O'Brien says. "After the set, they got out these painter's trays, filled them with lighter fluid, and lit them.

"The club security went berserk and stormed the stage. They got into a fistfight with the band. Security tried to bring down this steel gate and the band were holding it up. The fans joined in. It was great."

Typically, neither Steve nor Ian was there. The end of the stint at Palladium was approaching, and they could contemplate the end of the giant clubs with some equanimity. Scotty Taylor remembers one morning in early 1986. It was early, really early, and he was sitting with Steve Rubell on the stairway that led up from the Milkbar to his own apartment. "We were polluted out of our senses," Scotty says. "His hair had started to grow back. He had plugs put in. Plugs were in vogue. Elton John had plugs put in at the same time. They would both come in with their hats on. Steve wore that painter's hat all the time. He was always conscious about his appearance because he felt he didn't have one."

Taylor says that Steve Rubell was spitting and sputtering like a damp firework, but suddenly started making sense. "He told me that he had just done his will. He said that he couldn't believe it. He was worth fifty million dollars!

"That he could now afford to get an *airplane*. Or anything he wanted to. And he still felt like he was a kid. That was for, you know, adults. He would be embarrassed. But everyone was telling him that that was what he should do, or get a yacht or something. And it was slowly starting to sound good to him. He went, 'I'm worth fifty million. But I'm a pauper compared to Ian!'

"He told me, 'I'm not a player, though. *To be a player you have to have a hundred million.* If you have a hundred million, then you're a player. Calvin is a player.'"

"Player" was the appropriate word. Steve Rubell, the man who liked driving a toy car across Studio 54's dance floor and wearing funny hats, liked his toys. Money was the biggest toy of all. "Steve's greatest pride now was that he was really, really rich. He was becoming as rich as one of the people he looked up to as being rich," Annie Flanders, then the editor of *Details*, has told a writer. "At this point in his life, he was becoming richer than those people. He was really proud of that."

★   ★   ★

Rubell and Schrager were sufficiently players to acquire a beach house on an oceanside road, not far from Southampton Village. It had been owned by the Finks, who supply much of the region with bread, but Rubell and Schrager first rented it in the mid-eighties from Joe Hanna, an advertising executive. David Knapp, who was appointed a sort of majordomo, had to put the house back together again at the season's end. "Then the second summer they bought it, so we didn't have to deal with him again," says Knapp with satisfaction.

Steve Rubell loved the country. He would settle down, get through the papers, and perhaps a popular biography, like the latest offering about the Kennedy clan. "They would come to the house and veg out," Knapp says. "Rent stacks of videos . . . hang out by the pool . . . eat a lot . . . sleep a lot, because basically they were tired, and wanted to rest. There were a couple of parties. But nothing too crazy."

So far as his public emotional life went, Steve Rubell had never been wholly out, at least in the straight world. He was "guarded," says David Knapp. "Specially with bankers and business people, it was nice to have Heather along as Steve's girlfriend." There had even been speculation that Steve and the young woman in question, Heather Schiff, might marry. Suddenly, though, Heather just wasn't there. "He just said it was over!" Knapp says. "That was it! We never saw her again." Steve had a few other close female friends. Anita Sarko, for instance, and the dancer, Stella, whom he would take nightclubbing. "He just needed a companion. It was very hard for him to wind down. He couldn't just go home after the club," Stella says. "Sometimes I would go and sleep over with him at Morgan's. And just tuck him into bed and give him a massage. He was like a little boy."

As for his love or, rather, sex life, this had been on the fly, like that of many entrepreneurs, straight or gay. He had had enduring liaisons, one with a fellow whose brush with fame had been appearing in a photograph advertising a health club, but they had been few. Soon after the breakup with Heather, Steve was dining in the Canal Bar with Reinaldo and Carolina Herrera. They were talking about relationships. "Everybody needs somebody to be close to. That is being happy," Reinaldo Herrera said.

"I've never been happy," Steve said. He paused, and confided, "I'm gay."

"Steve. We *knew*." Reinaldo said sunnily.

Steve also had bleak tidings. "Ian and I got tested," he told Reinaldo suddenly, while they were sitting in the car. "Ian's okay." Reinaldo Herrera concluded that this was Steve Rubell's oblique way of saying that he was H.I.V.–positive.

Soon after, he indicated to the Herreras that he wanted monogamy. The young man who had caught his eye, Bill Hamilton, was not, by any standards, part of the scene. Indeed, he worked for Carolina. Rubell had met him only briefly, and in company, but knew that the Herreras took a quasi-parental interest in Hamilton. Steve Rubell tiptoed toward the situation in a manner less reminiscent of the new decadence than a mid-nineteenth-century swain, albeit a swain on knee-buckling drugs.

"He wanted to ask me out on a date. He was petrified that I would say no," Hamilton says. Bill Hamilton was not an urban youth. Tall, with regular features and the taut springiness of a whip, Hamilton was the twenty-four-year-old son of an executive with National Cash Register, the technical equipment company, and he commuted daily to Greenwich, Connecticut. "My life consisted of working for Carolina, jumping on a 5:10 train, and going out to my horses," he says. Hamilton cared nothing for disco. His passion was three-day eventing. So Rubell made an approach, not directly, but to Carolina Herrera. When she advised Hamilton of Rubell's interest, Hamilton said yes, by all means, Rubell should feel free to call.

Rubell didn't actually get around to calling until half past three in the morning. Well, it wasn't Rubell. It was another man. "Hi! You don't know me. But do you know Steve Rubell?" he asked. Hamilton said that he did. "Well, he's here right now and he has a question to ask you, but he really can't talk. So we're calling you," the man said. "He wants to invite you out to dinner."

Rubell was put on the line and mumbled a few words, sounding as if his tongue was stuck in glue. They hung up. Now Hamilton was concerned that Rubell might be abandoned in a stupor. He ascertained that the call had come from Morgans and called back. He was reassured. Rubell was with a couple, old friends. "We're going to spend the night with him. He'll be fine," Hamilton was told.

It was arranged that Rubell would pick Bill Hamilton up that Wednesday evening. He was staying on Cornelia and West Fourth streets, in the West Village. He got a phone call at half past seven, saying that Rubell was downstairs. "There was a huge bodyguard. There was a crowd around him in the street," Hamilton says. "People were basically looking for free admission to the Palladium . . . the World . . . places to go."

They drove to Chinatown. "We ate in this remote family-owned restaurant. Sitting at a table in the back," Hamilton says. "And that's when I realized he wasn't really 'out' in a sense, that he had his image to protect. That we were on an official date. And he had never dated."

When asked how he knew it was a serious date, Hamilton says, "Because of Reinaldo and Carolina. They are like parents to me."

Rubell also told Hamilton that he and Ian had both been tested, and that he was H.I.V.–positive.

Their second date was at Wally & Joseph's, a steak house on Forty-ninth Street. "He was a meat-and-potatoes normal all-American," Hamilton says. "His nightmare would be having to put a suit on and go out to a fancy restaurant where the food tried too hard."

They started seeing more of each other. Then the oddest thing happened. Steve Rubell started to get jealous of the horses. Certainly Hamilton was having to shoehorn a lot into his day. "I would ride in the morning," he says. "Come to work. Grab a bite to eat with him. Go home later. Ride early Saturday morning. Come in at noon. Spend the afternoons with him. Go back home, et cetera. But Steve didn't like the idea that he was not at the center of my life. He finally said, 'Would you want to move into Morgans with me? And live with me?' "

Bill Hamilton loved Steve Rubell and thought that this could be, in some regards, a wonderful scenario. He is a practical man, though. "What if something happened and we broke up the following week?" he wondered. "I would be stuck, without my haven, living in New York, which had no interest for me whatsoever."

The solution was simple. Hamilton took over Rubell's old apartment on West Fifty-fifth. This had been rented to a couple of Columbia students, football players, who had totally demolished it. "They tore walls down. Just stupid college kids," he says. The place was a wasteland. Kegs of beer, a giant TV screen with rental fees of twelve hundred dollars a month, some old bicycle painted silver. Hamilton moved in and established a new routine. He would work at Carolina Herrera's on Fifty-seventh Street until five, then go to the apartment.

This was the blue-collar portion of the day. The rubbish was disposed of. The screen was got rid of. As for the kegs, they were five-dollar returnable. "The porters and the doormen were young," Hamilton says. He told them, "I'll give you these beer kegs for free if you get rid of them. You can make two hundred dollars!"

"The bike was there. I was never going to use it. I said to the porter, 'Take it!' "

After he scraped, primed, and painted for a couple of hours, bringing the apartment always closer to a Connecticut standard, he would betake himself to Morgans. This was the domestic part of the evening. He and Steve would have a room service dinner there. A simple, well-cooked dinner. "That way he kept the hotel on its toes," he says. Then the glamor part of the night began. "A driver would pick us up at eight-thirty and take us down to the Canal Bar. That was every night."

The Canal Bar was the hot spot of the time. "But the food you couldn't eat, it was so bad," Hamilton says. "The places we went were the coolest places to be seen. But the food you couldn't take chances on. That was our ritual. That was what we did."

A popular need to punish Studio 54 for the insolence of its celebrity had not been slaked by the jailing of Schrager and Rubell, and opportunities to satisfy that need were arising. One involved Mark Gastineau, a briefly famous New York Jets football player. "What happened was we had a very good-looking bartender who took him down in an arm wrestle," Mark Fleischman says. "Gastineau just couldn't believe it. People started laughing. So he punched this guy in the face.

"I tried to stop it. I flew in the air and ended up on my back."

The punchee sued Studio 54.

Also, a pro basketball player got into an altercation with a Studio busboy over a woman. "It's our fault because our little five-foot-six guy pushed him down the stairs," Fleischman said. "It was a wonderful opportunity for him. He sued us for twenty million dollars."

Frank Cashman, who bought Studio from Fleischman, managed to lose the insurance. Fleischman was quoted a million dollars to renew it when he took back the club. By this time, many of the incidents that had happened in the early eighties began reaching the courts. "It was during the time that insurance went berserk. *Time* and *Newsweek* had covers about the 'Insurance Crisis.' We had claims against us for about twenty million dollars from all these crazy antics. The insurance companies were recognizing that as soon as the jury heard Studio 54, they immediately awarded for the plaintiff.

"They figured Steve Rubell . . . drugs . . . You know what juries must think about Studio 54. They've never been there. But they know it's *bad*. The management must have been doing evil things. They even awarded fifty thousand dollars to a guy who Marc Benecke kept outside. The guy sued for mental anguish because his fiancée broke up with him because he didn't have enough clout to get in."

The club was full as ever, though, when the manager called Gregory Gunsch, who worked the main bar, one March afternoon in 1986. "He said, 'Greg! Don't come in tonight. We're closed for the weekend,'" Gunsch remembers. "I said what do you mean? He says tax problems. We haven't paid our insurance. We'll be open next week . . ."

Actually, insurance woes had closed Fleischman's Studio 54 for good. "I went the Saturday night after it closed. And just stood out in front of the club. For *four hours*. Because it was a very important experience to me," Baird Jones says. "I went with a couple of buddies, and we just sat around, and talked about the old days.

"I really was curious to see how many people showed up. Some cabs pulled up, and people looked, but didn't get out. A bunch of Turks did get out. And a bunch of Israelis got out. There were one or two tourists. And that was it."

Bill Hamilton had been in the apartment about a year and it was beginning to look pretty spiffy. Steve suddenly asked, "By the way. Have you seen a bike over there?"

Hamilton uneasily realized that he meant the silver bicycle—the one he had given to the porter.

"Uhhhh? Why? What bicycle?" he temporized.

"Well, it used to hang in the front as you walked through the doorway. There were hooks on the wall."

Hamilton plumped for the shameless lie.

"No. I don't think I've seen it. Why?"

"Well, it's an Andy Warhol sculpture," Rubell said.

Hamilton laughed uproariously. "It had been signed! It had his signature on the back," he said. "It was a sculpture that was meant for that front hallway. Some porter in New York City is riding around on an Andy Warhol original. I never had the heart to tell him that, oh no! I threw it away . . ."

Baird Jones willingly accepts the responsibility for the destruction of Nightworld. "What I essentially did was completely dilute the prestige of Studio 54," he says with enthusiasm. "I would hand out passes in such numbers that we *constantly* got people who would hand in two hundred at the door. As a joke. It was the clearest sign of contempt.

"They would say, 'Well, Baird, how many invitations did you print for tonight?' I would say four thousand. Actually the number was more like twelve thousand. And I remember Fleischman getting more and more concerned because the crowd were getting younger and younger and younger. He finally came up to me and said we've decided that your parties have gone downhill so much that you can no longer use the Studio 54 logo. You just have to write out Studio Fifty-four."

By this time comps—for complimentary—and drink tickets had become both a sign of nocturnal acceptance and a medium of exchange. They were also the seeds of its ruin. Rudolf says that Steve Rubell originally perfected "the comp thing," but admits, equally cheerfully, that he "massified it" at Danceteria.

Area began with the Mudd Club lists—"They were stolen. I'd assume," Eric Goode cheerfully told writer Michael Gross—and supplemented them with lists from the Eurotrashy boîte Club A. Area sent out two sorts of invitation, comps, and the lesser sort, which required payment at the door. When Limelight opened a few months later, it escalated the stakes, sending out only comps.

Knowing just whom to send them to is as important to nightlife promoters as to any other salesmen. "Promoters come to us with ideas for parties," Paul Garcia of the World told Gross. "Usually we have better ideas, but we want to get a hold of their lists." Private Eyes, a small club where people danced to video, had 30 lists. Limelight had 150, including one of "fashion victims." In Studio days there had been a few dozen people deemed worthy of free drugs and sex and maybe 150 who got free entrance and plentiful drink tickets. By 1986 there was what Jim Mullen, the editor of *New York Talk*, called "the Manhattan 6,000," a mighty battalion of men, women, and near-children who resented having to pay for a single fleeting pleasure.

Milan, a party promoter of orchidaceous exuberance, sounds unnaturally dolorous when he recounts the decline and deeper decline of Nightworld. Milan—he restricts himself to one name, Rudolf fashion, perhaps because his father was a diplomat at the ambassador level—began doing parties for Mark Fleischman in 1980.

"By 1984 the party promoters were making so much money but we were spending so much money," he says. "My houseboy would have to stick me under a freezing cold shower because I was going five nights a week. I was making $5,000 a party and from my private clients I was making $10,000 to $15,000 a party," he says.

It collapsed like a tent with a broken pole. "By 1986 I would be lucky to get $500 for the same party," Milan says.

Whatever happened? Many, many whatevers.

"What killed Studio, besides Steve's bust, and it went on after that, but what really killed Studio was that it was no longer chic to be photographed in a nightclub," he says. Once you would see those klieg-absorbent faces just about every time you opened *People* or wherever. Half a decade on, the faces had fled. "There wasn't that voyeurism and exhibitionism. Everyone was starting to crash," Milan says. "The drugs were starting to catch up with people. They were going into rehab." The days when you popped into a jeweler's and bought a silver straw that you sported around your neck, or an eighteenth-century spoon from the Chelsea Antique Market, were gone, sunk with Lyonesse.

The more dependent club owners became on the legion of promoters, the worse they loathed them. "I remember they didn't want to pay a promoter once," Milan says. "They gave him a thousand dollars' worth of quarters. They gave him all the money from the cigarette machines, because they were so contemptuous of party promoters."

Palladium did well on concerts—Jerry Brandt brought in Kid Creole for New Year's Eve and they did $650,000 in business—but was equally dependent on promoters, and ideas were getting thinner and thinner. It would be tempting to settle on February 1986 as a moment when party promotion went into overload. On Saturday, February 22, Alan Rish, a promoter, gave a bash at Palladium for Glenn Lyons. The point being that Glenn Lyons was a clean-cut but widely unknown twenty-four-year-old carpenter. "It was really cool and it was a joke on cool," Rish explained.

Steve Rubell said that too many celebrities had debased their own currency. "We did this just as a spoof," he told the *News*. "I felt like I didn't merit this," said Glenn Lyons at a lunch with reigning divas Anita Sarko, Priscilla Woolworth, and Janis Savitt.

"Half the people who go out don't merit it," Rish reassured him.

Later in the week Studio 54 gave a party for a red dress. On Thursday February 27 the Saint threw a party for "Nothing." Haoui Montaug, the dry performance artist–cum–doorman said glumly, "It's just the logical progression of what's going on. I don't like it."

There were also problems among the Eurobrats of the Junior International Club. The unstable relationship of Ludovic Autet and Marc Biron had deteriorated beyond repair. At one stage, Biron thought of suing Autet. "But it would have been ridiculous. The newspapers would have laughed," he says. This was actually a bit of a sore point. In 1984 he had given a "New 400 Ball," which was an attempt to retool Mrs. Astor's famous Social Register, and had been asked by Patricia Morrisoe, writing about it for *New York*, why it had not been a benefit. "We could do something like Charity of the Year," he had mused. "But it should be an amusing charity, like for the homeless." The magazine, which called its story "The New Snobbery," had come down heavily on this admittedly clumsy turn of phrase, and the bruise still hadn't faded.

Biron departed the JIC. In January 1986, just a month later, he started a new club. "I tried to find a name but I never found something close to the Junior International Club, which was a great name. So I made it the Club Biron. It was a name that was unusual in a way," Biron says.

Both clubs had supporters—Biron's included Prince Jean de Luxembourg—and a number of competitive parties were given at restaurants and clubs. The to-ing and the fro-ing was polite, more or less. "What his club offers is nothing really new," Autet told *Newsday*'s James Revson. "He's not bright at all. He's very insecure," Biron told the same reporter.

Biron's real feelings can perhaps be glimpsed in a treatment for a screenplay that he tossed off at this period. Variously entitled *Blue Bloods, High Society,* and *East Side Story,* it is "a romantic success story of young Philippe, Lord of Cumberland, who is forced to give up his family's estate and ventures to America. In New York, naïve Philippe, in association with a common manipulator named Dimitri, creates a lucrative party-giving business called the Royal Society of America—RSA. It serves as a social networking system for European and American blue bloods. The film stages an ongoing rivalry between the so-called Eurotrash and unsophisticated Americans . . ." And so forth.

Unfortunately, the timing for this inspired fusion of Henry James and *Hello!* magazine was over. The world's guerrilla gangs had been cracked, aside from a few tough nuts, like Peru's Shining Path. Socialism was less and less a presence, so there was a waning threat of leveling by taxation. Communism itself was on the brink of being disassembled. America was no longer the last safe place, and New York far from being the only possible metropolis. Of course, a sizable wedge of affluent immigrants remained in Manhattan, but the sublime phenomenon of Eurotrash was an iridescent memory. *Quinta Strada* was Fifth Avenue again. Regine's and Club A would have no silken and polyglot successors.

The pressures on Nightworld were the subject of "Nightclubbing," a panel discussion in a midtown hotel, which was part of New York's seventh annual New Music Seminars that August. The NMS always had top-of-the-line panels and the Nightclubbing panel was chaired by Rudolf. Sitting at a long table were the visibly balding Steve Rubell; Steve Gold from the Saint; Dianne Brill, recently separated from Rudolf; Chas Rusinak, the ur-Nightlord, from Brooklyn's 2001 Odyssey; a number of out-of-town club people; Neil Jacobson, who owned a couple of clubs in Boston, one of which had formerly been 15 Landsdowne, briefly Rubell's first club; and Philip Salon, a discontented-looking man, in a floppy sweater and an outsize Dr. Seuss–type hat, who owned the Mudd Club in London, England. Also on the panel was Arthur Weinstein, with Frank Roccio, sitting in a position to offer covering fire in the front row. Other club owners sat throughout the chamber.

The panelists were introduced. They were mostly bland and self-serving. But Weinstein cut in, in darkly raucous good humor, first needling Jerry Brandt in the audience, then turning on a fellow panelist: "Mr. Rubell? You didn't say anything yet!"

"Nobody ever calls me Mr. Rubell," Steve said mildly. His voice was light, scratchy. "All I can say for all of the nightclub owners here is: If you're going to skim your money, don't tell anybody. And count it yourself. And don't trust anybody." There were cheers and clapping as he added, "Because you can't make a dime in this business unless you do."

On the subject of Palladium, Rubell was oddly downbeat. "In trying to top yourself, you build something that's architecturally or technically better than what you did before," he told the crowded room. "But maybe you forget the most important factors in a club are the people who come there. So if I were doing another club—and even though I swear I'll never do it, I know it's in my blood—I think the wave of the future is to build a small club and just have good people there.

"You make a lot more money in a big club. This has become yuppie city. If Jerry Rubin can draw eight thousand people on a Tuesday night, you *know* the city is in trouble. Wherever you go, these big barnlike restaurants. Everything's so *big*." He added that if somebody did go to one of the smaller, livelier—and, naturally, illegal—clubs, there was a fifty-fifty chance of being arrested these days. "I had to run out of the back door of SOBs about three weeks ago because the cops were coming in the front door," he said. "They were really important, the after-hours clubs, and all those things that Arthur provided. They made the city exciting. I love New York, but the edge has to come back. It's losing its cutting edge."

Rudolf began reading out questions: Why had the Saint opened up to a straight audience? "They're making a lot of money," Rubell interjected. "There's one problem with the Saint. It has rules," Rudolf said. "That's why they're still in business. And you're not," Rubell said. Whoops of laughter and applause.

There was another question from the audience, an angrier one, about a club stealing another club's concept. "We all steal from everybody. Are you kidding?" Rubell said hoarsely. "I don't think anybody has an original concept. I mean this. I stole ideas from Jerry Brandt. I can't see a club owner in this room that I didn't steal some ideas from."

Philip Salon spoke up. "It's not true there's no such thing as an original concept," he said, his voice a fierce hiss. "It's bollocks. Just because you haven't got any, it doesn't mean that no one else has. Shit!"

"More! More!" incited Rudolf.

Few in the audience can have been familiar with the London Mudd, which was on the Charing Cross Road. Salon would always be at the door, acting like a bad Rubell, saying stuff like "Okay, you can come in. But you look like shit." At any rate, he now treated the audience rather like his door, saying "What? Pardon? Did you squeak? *Well, don't bother! You can all fuck off! You're shit.* I'm joking.

"But I'm not here to publicize it and say how brilliant it is. It's a club. People basically go to a club to pull each other. That's what it's all about. And it's such a load of hypocrisy. And there's all this snobbishness chucked in like . . . *we don't let in New Jersey people!* . . . What's fucking wrong with living in New Jersey?"

"Have you ever been to New Jersey?" asked Rubell, nettled. "Then you'd know what was wrong with New Jersey."

"I'm not a fucking snob, dear. Like you. I didn't pretend to forget me when I walked in."

"I didn't know you," Rubell said.

"You fucking did!" Salon hissed, paused as applause erupted, and added, "Last time I saw him I was with a pop star named Boy George and he was creeping around him."

"Well, do you blame me for avoiding Boy George now?" Rubell said. "He's an asshole who stuck me with a hotel bill."

"More . . . more . . . more . . ." implored Rudolf.

"You're a fucking snob!" Salon said.

"I am," Steve Rubell agreed. "I am!"

"You're trying to get street credibility again . . . *Oh, I was in prison last year* . . . You know what I mean? Such a cunt!"

"Maybe he's right," Steve Rubell said unexpectedly. "I don't know . . ."

"You're a fucking snob. And you slag off my friend. *Because you're a cunt!*"

"Now this panel is rolling," said Rudolf. "I think it was a good selection of panelists. But I just want to move on a little bit . . ."

"Rudolf is trying to be a diplomat. I don't give a shit," said an unruffled Rubell.

Weinstein had a pointed question. If Salon was so keen on originality, how come he had borrowed the Mudd Club's name?

"In England no one's ever heard of the American Mudd Club," Salon said. The cheers turned to boos.

Rudolf read out a question from the audience: "Since the drinking age went up, you all seem to have forgotten about the eighteen- to twenty-year-olds. You know we dance and socialize too."

"I can solve that problem for you in one second," Rubell said. "On Third Avenue and Eighth Street, just two blocks off the corner, anybody can get to be twenty-one years old."

Rudolf read out another question: "How much money is needed to start up a club? And if you're not fabulously rich, where do you go for backing?"

"To the mob," Weinstein said with massive irony.

"There are people who will always invest in clubs," Rubell said. "The doctors and the dentists and the lawyers, who are looking for a little bit of glamor in their lives. You find those suckers and you get each of them to put up fifty or a hundred thousand dollars. Before you know it, you can raise a lot of money. And all you have to do is give them a drink ticket when they come in."

Rudolf read out another question: "Steve Rubell, some of your Mike Todd private parties are great. But why do you always turn off the air conditioner? Is it to save money?"

"We ran out of money," Rubell said. "Now if you go in there, I think it's pretty cool. We put in a lot of air conditioners."

Philip Salon came back into action. "The reason people turn off the air conditioning is so that you'll buy more drinks. That is a *fact*," he hissed.

"That may be the reason *you* turn 'em off," Rubell said without heat.

"I don't get the drink profit. You do, you little queer! Actually, you haven't patronized anybody for five seconds. What's wrong? I think your club's *so good*. Let's give him a clap. What shit!"

"Take off the hat!" somebody bawled at Salon from the audience. He had lost them. "Take off the hat . . . take off the hat . . . take off the hat . . ."

"Let Steve wear it," Arthur Weinsten suggested. The audience hollered and clapped.

"He needs it," Salon said, nastily.

"I do! I wish I had more hair," Rubell said cheerfully. "Monoxodyl doesn't work. I tried it."

The nighclubbing seminar was, first, a display of grace under pressure on Steve Rubell's part and, second, a display of his intuitive feeling for Nightworld. His "wave of the future in clubland" was just a few weeks short of curling up the shore.

George Pal's movie version of H. G. Wells's *The Time Machine* begins in late Victorian times. Imagine buttoned leather chairs, mahogany, oak, brass, red velvet, dark pictures with gilded frames. The hero fiddles with his contraption and whizzes into a future inhabited by beautiful brain-dead Eloi and dark disgruntled Morlocks. It's like swooshing from a gentleman's club—or perhaps one of the more elegant fin-de-siècle bordellos—into discoworld. In fact, the fair-haired, lissom Eloi and cannibalistic subterranean Morlocks in George Pal's movie version of the fable would hardly draw a glance in uptown and downtown Manhattan respectively. Then Nell's opened on West Fourteenth Street in the fall of 1986, and the time machine whooshed straight back. You could go home again. Nell's was the shock of the old.

The place was financed by Keith McNally and his wife, Lynn Wagenknecht and it was named for Nell Campbell, the third partner and hostess.

Campbell is an Australian, with milk-white skin and red hair in geometrically sheared bangs. She was actually born Laura, but it was as "Little Nell," a name borrowed from the doomed young heroine of Dickens's *Old Curiosity Shop,* that she had arrived in London as a young cabaret performer in the early seventies, and she has been Nell ever since.

When Nell arrived in Manhattan in the early eighties, she was best known for having portrayed a biker babe in *The Rocky Horror Picture Show.* It seemed unimportant that she had had no previous experience in the business end of clubs or restaurants. Keith McNally had started the Odeon, the paradigmatic art restaurant of the eighties, with his brother, Brian. Odeon was still going strong, but the brothers had fallen out, with Brian going on to do Indochine and 150 Wooster, while Keith and Lynn had the Cafe Luxembourg on the Upper West Side near Lincoln Center.

Both brothers have a skillful sense of retro. The Odeon, which had been named not for the Paris monument, but for the chain of old-fashioned British movie houses, looked—and indeed still looks—like a late Depression cafeteria, down to the ghastly cheerfulness of the illuminated clock face. Now they prospected back further. Nell told the *Times* the club would be "the opposite of the sensory-deprivation clubs so popular in New York right now." Meaning the Milkbar. Nell, Keith, and Lynn went antiquing, in Philadelphia and New York State, and assembled nineteenth-century paneling, overstuffed sofas, sturdy old tables, and paintings in gilt frames. Construction began early in 1986, and by the time the club was finished in the former electrical parts store on West Fourteenth Street it looked as if it had been there at least since the time of Stanford White.

Nell's was so small—its capacity, upstairs and down, was 250—that there seemed little reason for the competition to get their knickers in a twist over it, but they did, and they were right. Rudolf told *Vanity Fair*'s Brad Gooch that Nell's was "counterrevolutionary." He said, "It's going backwards in time. It's a place that my grandfather would have felt comfortable in." But the Lords of Nightworld were given scant respect in Nell's. Rudolf didn't get through the velvet cord on opening night. "Rudolf. Rudolf? What kind of a name is that?" an unrepentant Nell Campbell mused to me years later. Gooch also noted that on New Year's Eve Eric Goode had been "involved in a scuffle at the door, knocked over some stanchions, and was pushed off into the night by a guard."

Nell's, consequently, swiftly became a home away from home for that whole Studio 54 generation—from "Suzy" column diehards, like the Herreras and Ahmet Ertegun, to aging Warholites and trust fund brats—whose last serious nightclubbing had been in the Betty Ford cubbyholes in Palladium. There they could sink into languor in the comfy banquettes. Within, the thrum of conversation was as important as the music, and for those with eyes to see, there were such interesting sights as some of the country's most successful bulk drug dealers, Tom Sullivan's former cronies and rivals, hiding in plain sight at the end of the bar.

Howard Stein noted to Brad Gooch that "there's a trend now to smaller, more intimate clubs . . . I'm planning to open such a club." Eric Goode said he was contemplating "a more surreal Nell's. I think I would make it a little kinkier." An impressive ambition, that, because the downstairs bathrooms at Nell's were worthy successors to the temples of plumbing at Studio, Xenon, Area, in every way. One young woman with a crow's nest of blue-black hair returned to the bar one night, and noisily said she was thinking of suing. "I cut my knees on broken glass," she complained. She was dissuaded from taking action.

The Milkbar's success had made Jack Lesco jubilant. One night he told me of ambitious plans to franchise the place. "We're gonna have Milkbars in London . . . Paris . . . Los Angeles," he promised. Actually tensions between Scotty Taylor and him had begun tightening early. Same old same old. "Three months into it, I came in one night and I saw these two tacky women behind the bar," Taylor says. "My two bartenders, funky-looking kids, were sitting on their hands."

He walked up to the women.

"They went, 'Uh, Jack hired us. We met him in Atlantic City,' " Taylor says. "I said, 'Well, I'm firing you. You're outta here!' "

It was always Taylor himself who put together the cash at the end of the night. He had a head for it, as Steve Rubell had accepted when Scotty had worked for him in the Steak Loft. "Steve used to say that at the end of the night, no matter what, I was the one who rang up the registers and made sure everything was in order," he says.

By the end of 1986, Taylor had seen little of his promised money. Tensions between Lesco and him had worsened. "So I was counting the money and I said, 'Hey, Jack! I'm taking two hundred dollars. I got to get some Christmas presents," he says.

"You can't take that!" Lesco said. "I've got bills to pay. I've got people to pay!"

"That's right. And I'm one of them!" Taylor told him.

"At that point he owed me about eighty thousand dollars. For six weeks I didn't even receive my salary," Taylor says. "He told me to forget it! That I wasn't getting the money! And I lost it. I had about two hundred dollars in singles in my hand. And I threw it in his face. I said, 'Jack, I'm not setting foot in this place until you pay me in full.' "

Taylor walked out. It was December 23.

Eric Goode had brought uptowners downtown to Area. Steve Rubell and Ian Schrager had brought them to Palladium. Frank Lynch, who opened 4D, another megaclub on West Fifty-fifth Street, believed he could bring everybody to midtown, much as Studio 54 had done. He hired Cornelius Conboy and Dennis Gattra, who had put on fairly far-out performances at 8BC, a small East Village space with a dirt floor. Lisa E., a much-written-about party girl of the moment, was put on the door. Futura 2000, the Graffiti artist, was commissioned to create a space. Take that, Palladium!

"The Futura Room *is a multicolored, florescent [sic] spray-painted melange of clouds, orbiting planets and rocketships,*" yipped a press release.

Conboy and Gattra left two weeks after the opening. Lisa E. walked shortly after. "I've never been back to that club since I did that," Futura told me. Frank told a reporter that 4D was "more uptown than downtown now." It was soon also more dead than alive.

At the end of December 1986 Rudolf sent out a couple of letters. The one that went out to members of the core began:

NEW YORK CITY, CHRISTMAS 1986.

NIGHTLIFER:

UNTIL YESTERDAY IT WAS ONLY A GIGANTIC ABANDONED RAILROAD TERMINAL. MASSIVE BRICK WALLS AND STEEL BEAMS LAID EMPTY FOR SEVENTY YEARS! SUDDENLY NEW LIFE GER-

MINATES INSIDE THE SOLITUDE OF THIS OLD STONE FORTRESS.

GOLDEN CHAMBERS SPARK AMIDST HEAVY MACHINERY.

A THOUSAND LIGHTS WOUND A REIGN OF DARKNESS . . .

And so on and on the publicity-poetry meanders, until the clincher, which was an invitation to a New Year's Eve celebration, with John Lurie and the Lounge Lizards, for fifty bucks at the door. Or complimentary admission for one the following night. It ends: "In the spirit of the night, Rudolf."

Meantime, though, the inner core had got another letter. This ran:

DEAR TRENDIE:

AN ABANDONED WATERFRONT, DECAYING PIERS. ECHOES OF FORGOTTEN GANG WARS. DARK WAREHOUSES, SPEAKEASIES, AND LADIES OF THE NIGHT . . . THE PERFECT SETTING FOR A NEW CLUB.

AND NOW, THE LAST SEGMENT IS FINALLY COMPLETED:

BASEMENT!

A DUNGEON BELOW IVORY TOWERS . . .

In this case, the recipient was invited to the private opening on December 29. The letter signs off: "All aboard! Choo! Choo! Choo! Rudolf."

The club was the Tunnel. It was on Twenty-seventh Street and the Hudson River, and it had been financed by an Israeli jeans manufacturer, Elli Dayan, who hired Rudolf away from Palladium. The Tunnel actually was an intriguing space, a disused subway tunnel. It was a very long space, with raw brick walls that looked untouched, and were still painted with functional messages, like "Shut Off Valves for Bldg 21." Unpainted pipes ran like ganglia overhead. The Tunnel, in short, had a post-apocalyptic look, like the venue for one of Vito Bruno's Outlaw Parties, but somehow frozen into permanence.

There were some good opening parties. On February 17, Andy Warhol modeled there in a fashion show put together by Benjamin Liu. He confided to Pat Hackett that his dressing room was "absolutely freezing." But, so far as choo-chooing went, the Tunnel was quickly running out of puff.

The Milkbar tottered along a few more months without Scotty Taylor, who took Lesco to court. He got a settlement of $32,000, much of which went to his lawyer. "When all was said and done I got $18,000 and the car. A 1974 Mercedes. At the time, $18,000 was a million," Scotty Taylor says.

So that trip was over. Nightworld.

In January, Area closed. "We were burned out. We just didn't want to do it anymore," Eric Goode says. *New York Talk* folded that same month. Andy Warhol died on February 22.

All these factors were alluded to by Michael Musto in a cover story in the *Village Voice* of April 28, 1987. His subtitle was "Who Took the Life Out of Nightlife?" but his main title was "The Death of Downtown," and it was downtown that he was mourning. "Last September, the phone stopped ringing," Gabriel Rotello, formerly the impressario of "Downtown Dukes and Divas" told him. "It was like a curtain dropped, and nobody wanted shows anymore. I went from being overwhelmed to almost completely unemployed overnight." Musto listed the reasons, from AIDS, through zooming rents, to the neo-conservatism of Nell's. Musto noted gloomily that a trimmed-down Dianne Brill had "showed up at the Tunnel looking like any other tasteful blonde and escorting her good friend Cheryl Tiegs (this was before her birthday luncheon at Le Cirque)." Le Cirque! The agony. Musto's main blame was for Palladium, though. Steve Rubell agreed. "Downtown became completely digested by the rest of the city. It lost its soul," he told Musto, with his usual adroitness. "Palladium probably ruined part of it by exposing the world to it."

Nightworlders are media-steeped creatures, at least as much as any other socialites or performers, and Musto's piece struck a chord. Musto himself says, "Some people were outraged. Those were people who were still clinging to the hope that they could go out every night. It was scary for me. In a way, I felt I was writing my own obituary. Because I was a chronicler of the whole downtown scene. I just had to become more diverse in what I covered."

"That article killed everything," James St. James says. St. James, whose real name is Clarke, had arrived from Florida in 1984 two weeks after his eighteenth birthday and had flung himself into clubland. He adds, "Everybody stopped going out. All the Old School people stopped going out."

Some of the Old School people anyway. Nell's was still prospering, and was soon joined by two other clubs in the same retro vein. Howard Stein started Au Bar in a basement space on East Fifty-eighth Street, importing a young English designer, Emily Todhunter, to make it like a library in an English country house. At the end of the year Eric Goode started M.K., which turned out not to be kinky at all. "I did not want to deal with changing the place," he says. "We wanted to deal with a place that was just going to *be* there. We made a lot more money than we did at Area. But it was more sedate. It had less of that gay energy."

The whole galère of Nightworld, from Rudolf and Dianne Brill to Brett Easton Ellis, was in M.K. for a birthday party for the photographer Patrick McMullan, and it was hectic, with Sylvia Miles, the actress, noisily refusing to have her photograph taken with Robin Byrd, hostess of a porno cable show. The artist Mark Kostabi appeared with Sally Randall and sat at a table directly facing me. This was embarrassing. Kostabi had decided to make a magazine interview with me the conduit for some tasteless remarks about the AIDS epidemic; an attempt at publicity hogging, which had gone badly awry for him. He stared at me, stony-faced.

Then, startlingly, there came one of those flurries in which time is distorted so that things seem to both accelerate and move with creaky slowness. Then Kostabi's face was covered with white gunk, and an aureole of black hair was bouncing toward the door. It was one of those rare moments when a writer can see the physical consequences of something he has written, and it was jolting. Kostabi looked at me, left, cleaned up, and returned. Which was ballsy. The man who had pied him, it turned out, was the gay militant, Michelangelo Signorile.

All of which is not just to bandy about names and allude to odd events, but to say that the times were charged with energies as much as the times of Studio had been, but it was a different sort of energy. Nightworld seemed at once hectic and sullen, Gothic, not rococo, and suffused with a stormlight.

BETWEEN THE ACTS:II
MASQUERADE

ON ST. PATRICKS DAY, 1985, FIVE YOUTHS were hitchhiking through private grounds—technically they were trespassers—in Rockland County, a sedate enclave of upstate New York. They came across a charred door on the ground. Beneath it, they made a chilling discovery: the body of a young man, naked but for a zippered black leather mask. The flesh had been stripped by raccoons but the autopsy showed that he had been brutalized and shot twice through the back of the head. The dead man was speedily identified as a young Norwegian, Eigil Vesti, who had been working in a boutique in Greenwich Village. Some days later two men were arrested. One was Baron Thyssen's art dealer, Andrew Crispo, and the other was Bernard le Geros, who had been working as an assistant in Crispo's gallery in the Fuller Building on Fifty-seventh Street and Madison Avenue. After the arrest, Stephen le Geros, Bernard's younger brother, vehemently defended his brother, not denying that he was a murderer, but saying that he wasn't gay. Peculiar and exotic bloodshed is, of course, a writer's meat and drink, so I was delighted to be assigned to cover the case by New York magazine.

Manhattan was famous for its clubs devoted to gay or specialized sex and a visit had been a favorite way of ending a night for many inquisitive Studio 54 regulars. I had been to the Hellfire Club, which was frequented by men and women, a couple of times. But even though simply strolling around and looking was considered perfectly respectable in the clubs, the certain presence of AIDS was inhibiting and I hadn't been to a sex club for several years. A lawyer, Murray Sprung, told me that Crispo had met up with Vesti in the Hellfire—Crispo told me crossly that ''people like to sensationalize''—so I decided to make the rounds. My guide was an old friend, and an aficionado of the scene, whom I shall call Guy. He warned that I wouldn't be allowed in anywhere inappropriately dressed—a standard club rule, of course—so I put on jeans, battered brown riding boots, and a black T-shirt, which is the *downtown equivalent of a club tie. We set off in a group of four, only one of us being gay. The clubs were on the Lower West Side in the old meat-packing district.*

We began in the Spike, which was a leather bar, meaning that the patrons mostly wore black leather. This was seldom the dourly battered black leather that you might see a biker wearing, but rather the sort of lush and glimmery leather that might be used to upholster a sofa, except it had been made into jackets, and full suits, sometimes worn with black leather caps, complete with visors. The principal nonleather goods worn were glittering chains and handkerchiefs that dangled from hip pockets according to a visual code that indicated the wearer's taste, or tastes. There was a fair amount of pickup action but no actual sex play. We ordered cans of beer, rather than glasses—there was then still much doubt as to just how AIDS was spread—checked out the pool table, and departed. So far, so tranquil.

The Hellfire Club had more juice. At first glance, and this was partly because there were women there, it looked a bit like the club room in a workout center, because there was a bar, a counter to buy sporting goods, and a number of athletic machines. That was at first glance. Then details jumped out. The large mural on the rear wall showed the devil sitting on the lavatory. To our immediate left as we walked in a female rear end was squatting on the floor while its owner busied herself beneath the skirt of another woman who was sitting on a bench and smiling abstractedly.

What the Hellfire Club offered was what Studio 54 had offered, a place to enact fantasies and work out obsessions, but the fantasies and obsessions, unlike those at Studio, seemed sometimes terrifically sad. (A friend told of an elegant couple walking in. The man politely asked who would like to borrow his wife. Several men took him up on the offer. While this was publicly going on, the man was passing around his wedding pictures, and weeping.) That night we walked over to the trinket counter, where a distingué middle-aged man was being fitted with a spiked dog collar, checked out the array of cock rings, tweaks, and thongs, and strolled across to the machines. These included a complicated gizmo constructed from metal and leather, involving hooks and chains; a bulky contraption to which several sets of handcuffs had been attached; and another, which was pink, equipped with several pink leatherette saddles. Reclining there alone in the posture of someone expecting to catch a beating was a pudgy young man wearing only a hopeful grin.

Some specific energy source was sending excitement coursing to our left. A fair number of people—dressed, partly dressed, or naked—had formed a slowly moving line. Guy and I joined the end. The woman on the bench had lost her female admirer but was having a bare foot fondled by a man. She still had that faraway smile. Guy and I were now well advanced in the line which had borne us out of the main room into a space that was poorly lit and subdivided into cubicles. Our line, which was all male, was heading for a cubicle at the back. One by one, the men who had been in the cubicle drifted past us. I looked them over, wondering just what it was they had done there, but found no clue in their closed demeanors. But whatever it was, it was a slow business. A man would pass us, heading back to the main room, and we would shuffle a few paces forward and wait for the next. More than two dozen men had been and gone before Guy and I were close enough to the cubicle to see just what it was we were lining up for.

The head of a kneeling figure was stuck into the groin of the man at the head of the line. All you could see of the kneeler was long shiny dark hair. The male pelvis went shuddery, voided itself, and retracted. By the time the man walked past us, as glazed-looking as his predecessors, the face of the kneeler had taken another penis into its mouth and bobbed back to its task. We had caught a brief glimpse of the face. "I think it's a woman," Guy muttered into my ear.

Another four men were serviced and we were close to the front of the line, looking right into the face of whoever was on his or her knees. It was a handsome enough face, but with a pale, corroded look and it was smeared with what I thought at the time was semen but later decided must have been just sweat. The huge dark eyes looked avid and not completely sane. It was too brief a look to determine his or her sex. Guy and I disengaged ourselves from the line. Our defection didn't even earn us a sidelong glance. Back in the main room the pudgy man on the pink machine was begging a muscular fellow to flog him but the man made a furious gesture and strode off. Disconsolately the pudgy man began pulling on his clothes.

So to the Mine Shaft, which, I had been given to understand, was the most serious of the clubs, hardest of the hard core. A sign inside the entrance warned that patrons would have to get out of "objectionable" clothing and a friend of Guy's was asked to check his sweater, which wasn't a dress-uppy sweater but a keep-warm sweater. As he took it off a man beside him, in his sixties, a banker by his sober suit, was stripping down to his underwear. We ordered beers at the bar, which was on the ground floor. The man next to me at the bar wore a leather jacket, a leather vest, and leather cap, and nothing below the waist. We then headed for the stairs—the Mine Shaft was just that, a shaft—and walked down to the next level.

It was there that I realized that the Mine Shaft was rather a special experience. This was not because of the goings-on. It was more a matter of the staging. First, there was a dead silence, a silence not denied but intensified by the background music—Ravel—and, second, there was the lighting.

This was dim but the dimness was artfully calculated. For instance, a number of the men there—and it was only men—were dressed up in the macho costumes that had once distinguished the Village People, cowboy hats, police uniforms, construction work-

ers' hard hats, and so forth, whereas others were naked, and yet others were at all stages in between, but the lighting, a shadow-less gray penumbra, successfully leached out persnickety details. A way off, the wandering or standing figures seemed insubstantial but as the distance closed you could tell whether they were young, old, fat, thin, bearded, hairless, or whatever, but the quirks and quiddities that make up character were lost in the obscure glim-mer, so the bodies looked at once spectral and solid, like figures carved out of wet chalk.

The men who approached us were polite and if they found no flicker of interest they simply moved on. One offered me his penis as passionlessly as a waiter proffering the check and I hadn't even had to shake my head before he glided away. In one corner we heard loud reports. We went over to have a look—pure voyeurism was clearly okay behavior in the Mine Shaft—and saw that a man chained to the wall was being whipped, then the whipper suddenly dropped his thong and strode petulantly off as though he had bet-ter things to do, leaving the flogged man bereft.

Much, perhaps most of the goings-on around us were run-of-the-mill suckings, fuckings, and masturbations, mutual or solitary—activities of a sort that should not seem too startling to anybody, straight or gay, who has ever leafed through the back pages of a city weekly or logged into the blue channel on hotel TV. But this was fantasyland, so there was some much more inventive stuff. One tableau that hove into sight—literally—was a cluster-fuck on the floor, a quaking mass of buttocks, backs, and waggling mem-bers that looked suddenly like one of those rather too busy chunks of late-nineteenth-century statuary, only with hair.

Beyond was an excellent facsimile of a large jail cell, with real bars, filled with naked "prisoners," standing and staring in the same direction. We watched for a bit. They remained motionlessly in position, a surreal platoon. We moved on to where a nude man was chained to the wall of an alcove, arms slightly raised, in the posture of a crucifixion or the front man of a heavy metal band, except he had his back to us and he was being anally penetrated by another man and a line of about a dozen were waiting their turn.

No, it wasn't safe sex, either.

So we went down more stairs to the lowest level of the Mine Shaft. I couldn't help remembering rumors that cholera bacilli had been detected on the place's walls and I began fancying that I could detect a pale greenish glow. The air was growing smellier as we descended. On the bottom floor three naked bearded men were lying in separate bathtubs. They looked vulnerable as newborn mice, and fixed us with imploring eyes. They were waiting to be pissed or shat upon. It was early in the evening, though, and the action hadn't started, so we left.

We didn't talk for a bit. The gay member of our party, who had lived in domestic fashion with his partner for some years, was the most shaken, feeling that the goings-on in the club would distort straight perceptions of the gay world generally. Wrong, so far as we were concerned. That would be like feeling that Hustler magazine or the more mechanical sort of porno flicks accurately depicted the straight world with all its love aches, humdrum affections, and itches of casual lust. Nor was it news to me that some people have more complicated sex drives than others. What bothered me, simply, was that AIDS was raging through the headlines. "You have to understand," I was told urgently. "The risk is part of the thrill." Truly, the ultimate frisson.

In November 1985, the Mine Shaft was padlocked by the city as part of an anti-AIDS initiative, enforcing new "safe sex" regulations. The Hellfire closed of its own volition at the same time. It was also revealed by the New York Post that both clubs had been evading liquor and tax laws by posing as not-for-profit "social clubs."

In Feburary 1986 several men were indicted as principals, who had operated the clubs "with a complete disregard for the liquor and tax laws.'' They should have learned from Al Capone that crime is crime, but tax evasion is serious. The indictment also charged that they had "conspired to bribe and coerce witnesses in order to frustrate our investigation.'' One of the owners was Richard Bell, a New York city cop for ten years until he had been bounced in 1973, accused of stealing cocaine from some undercover cops. Bell got two to four years.

There was no reason to include any of the above in my reporting on the "Masked Murder." Andrew Crispo was never indicted for the murder of Eigil Vesti. Bernard le Geros, his assistant, was convicted of murder, and is serving fifteen years.

So the hard-core clubs were closed forever?

Well, not exactly. They are now in different venues, but as active as ever.

ACT 3 : NIGHTFALL

KAMIKAZE KIDS

2

JAMES ST. JAMES WAS TALKING INTO MY TAPE RECORDER.
We were in a small room in the Chelsea Hotel on
Twenty-third Street. "This is James St. James. I
moved here when I saw the *Cars* video by Andy Warhol. It was Dianne Brill who inspired me. I wanted
to *be* her," he intoned. St. James has frail, fine features.
A metal crescent several inches long was piercing his
lower lip and chin. Michael Alig, who was alongside
him on the bed, interjected, "With me, it was an Edie
Sedgwick T-shirt. I bought it at a thrift shop in Chicago—"

"Edie!" St. James yelped. "There was a whole
generation of us. When the Edie book came out, we
dropped everything, and moved to New York. I
know *more people* who have said that—"

"The Edie *book*?" Michael Alig said, his voice
moving through several registers. His hair was dyed
various shades of orange and marigold, he threw off
energy like a wet dog shaking off water, and he
seemed genuinely puzzled by the notion that Edie
Sedgwick might have figured in a book. Was he act-

ing? With all of the Club Kids, it could be hard to tell where the acting stops, but especially with Alig, their manic leader.

The Club Kids owed their name to the headline on a cover story by Amy Virshup in *New York* magazine on March 14, 1988, an epithet that quickly became an accepted generic term, dictionary-ready, like "yuppies" or "supermodels." They would be the final working out of some of Studio 54's more exotic energies. Even up until the *New York* cover, though, they were just one nocturnal subculture among a dozen subcultures.

At the end of the bed, another Club Kid was watching *The City of Lost Children* on video. Posters for Alig's infamous Limelight soirees, Disco 2000, were tacked here and there. Gitsie, a slender female Club Kid, her face basted white, like a clown, was preparing herself for a night of dancing topless among foul brokers. Another female Club Kid of heftier build, with hair like a polychrome shag rug and more body rings than James St. James, was getting ready for work too, filling dozens of tiny bottles, made of glass the color of milkless tea. It was getting on for eleven. Party time!

The beginnings of the phenomenon had been innocent enough. James St. James was a trust fund brat. "We were all going to Area and Danceteria. Michael was a busboy and I was . . . fabulous," he says. "We were just *evil* to him. We would throw drinks on the ground and say, 'Busboy! Busboy! Would you come and get that?' We were just awful to him, because he was like this annoying little pest that kept wanting to throw these awful parties." He yelped with mirth again at the memory.

Rudolf, who describes Alig at this time as "a little twinkie," finally let him throw his party at Danceteria. "It was a Filthy Mouth Contest," Alig says. He was the organizer, Anita Sarko was the MC, and the judges included Michael Musto. "People from the audience stood up and tried to outnasty each other," Alig said. He pocketed $500, which was better than the $120 a week he was getting as a busboy. Also, he was launched on his chosen career: Ruler of the Club Kids.

The Club Kids had mostly taken to the nightlife in their mid to late teens, and, as such, they were the heirs of the kids who had overrun Studio and they, too, were mostly white and at least middle-class. But the Studio brats had been straight, for the most part, and their ringleaders had been entrepreneurs, like

Baird Jones and John Flanagan, or social totems, like Cornelia Guest, and they usually dressed as if for a cocktail party or a beach club. Not so, the Club Kids.

Some came from New York but many more from parts of the U.S. where they had grown up feeling freakish and out of place. Most had gotten hard knocks for being girly. In the city, they found safety in numbers. "A lot of us were art students," says Mykul Tronn, one of the more promotionally energetic Club Kids. "People coming into their own." Dressing up was crucial to the phenomenon. At first, it was simply a matter of style. "It was people buying the label clothes, Gaulthier, Mugler, and so forth, and trying to be very fabulous," Tronn says. As any young woman finds when she is pictured naked in a magazine, the evidence gets back to the folks at home in a nanosecond. James St. James was photographed in *Time* and *The New York Times*. "My father saw a picture of me as a mermaid. His friends at the office brought it into him," St. James says affectlessly. "Then there was a picture in *People*. It was at the opening of Nell's. I was wearing a wig. He cut off my trust fund, and I had to get a job."

The job was in a club, of course. Clubs were their laboratories. Mykul Tronn had his bar mitzvah party at Studio in 1983 and he abandoned his "boring" given name of Michael Cooper soon after, borrowing his mother's last name and retooling his first. Warhol superstars, punk anti-stars, even artists like Barbara Ess and Lois Lane, had taken new names, so why shouldn't Andy Warhol's godchildren shed their dull day names by night? Each and every one of them seemed to imagine themselves a pivotal figure in the Factory that had been blown away by Valerie Solanis. Some chose exotic names, as though they were inventing histories for themselves, like Julie Jewels (née Vaynshelbaum), the Pop Tarts, the It Twins, Happy Phace, and Leviathan, but quite often they would simply obliterate their histories, cutting their names into near anonyms—sometimes at their families' request—like Lisa E., Elyn W, and Jonathan Bee.

The male Club Kids were mostly gay or bi, but sex was not what it was about. The phenomenon indeed was partly a reaction to the darkness of sex in a world of AIDS and the Club Kids rationalized it as such themselves. Their attitude was: If you can't get it, flaunt it. The flaunting was their raison d'être. Drugs were packaged energy and instant attitude, and were ubiquitous. Alig and St. James chattered about a particularly sleazy mob-run after-hours joint where Alig had worked for a while with his boyfriend Keoki after Danceteria. "Keoki and I were paid in cocaine. All we did was walk around with a big tray and give it to people," Alig says. "At the end of the night they would give us a rock to play with."

"Do you remember how scary that basement was?" St. James asks.

"There were these big garbage bags full of cocaine down there," Alig says. "Big garbage bags full of money . . . and big garbage bags full of guns . . ."

"Do you remember the time in Milano when the cops came, and everybody flushed their drugs," St. James asked. "And we had to jump from building to building in *platform heels?*"

Another place was run by a wild heiress from the South. "She would walk around naked, and say, 'Feel my pussy.' And people were coming in off the street and fingering her," St. James says. "And I would always see bums jerking off in the pool downstairs. The pool was murky, and black, and vile. There would be goats and chickens running around. She would be having dinner upstairs, and everybody would be naked around the table. *She was marvelous.*"

Another host, Richard Vasquez, would give parties in his East Village house. "They would start on Fridays. He had a five-story loft," Alig says. "You would walk in. He would give you a handful of Ecstasy—"

James: "And that would last you till Monday—"

Michael: "And on Monday, after you had danced for a day, and you had had sex for a day, and you had talked for a day—"

James: "You would leave and come back—"

Michael: "You would leave and come back, and it would still be going on . . . the parties were getting more and more fabulous . . . and the fourth floor fell onto the third floor as everyone was dancing . . . it was hi, girls! And the drag queens fell down in a big pile of rubble . . ."

The Club Kids were perhaps a hundred strong, and Rudolf adopted them en masse when he got to The Tunnel. This was shrewd. Rudolf saw that the Club Kids could be the biggest draw since punk, but there was more to it than this. Rudolf was genuinely amused by the offbeat energy of these elfin brats. The nightlife columnist Michael Musto said, "It may be the one time when Rudolf had an attack of naïveté. I think he really loved them. He thought they were like Alice in Wonderland, except he was too busy seeing how colorful they were to notice the danger."

The Club Kids had the run of the place. Elyn W, a thin girl with an explosion of hair dyed banana-blonde, wasn't allowed to dance until she had done her homework at a desk in Rudolf's office, and her mother telephoned her there to check on its progress. The clubhouse proper was in the basement. "Rudolf invited them free, and they would dress up, and be fabulous," Tronn says. "And everybody would want to go and see them. That's what Rudolf was cultivating in the basement, which was to create very unusual events, which everyone wants to go to, but everyone isn't invited to. It wasn't very sexual and it wasn't very druggy. It certainly wasn't freaky at all."

If sex wasn't the Club Kids' drive—"They dance all night. Then they go home alone," said the Outlaw Party giver, Vito Bruno—this was partly because Tronn's other two categories are more questionable. Cocaine was still all over, as was MDMA. MDMA had formerly been legal—it had been legal in Texas up till the early 1980s—and had been used as an antidepressant. Its early street names had included "Adam," but it was now universally known as "Ecstasy" or "X." Early users remember Ecstasy as inducing a warm glow, and a super-sensitivity of the senses, so that touching human skin was electric and touching velvet, say, was indescribable. Ecstasy was thus too giddily overpowering to be an inducement or accompaniment to sex, unlike such downers as alcohol, or Quaaludes, which had the nickname of "panty removers." It was a drug that gave neural impulses a buzz cut, like LSD, but without the hallucinatory effects.

In the United Kingdom in the late eighties, Ecstasy was the drug of choice of raves. These were huge parties that promoters would throw in unexpected locales, where celebrants would dance to house music and houses successors, sometimes for a couple of days. They didn't eat or drink alcohol, but sustained themselves on an occasional glass of spring water. Deaths through dehydration were not uncommon, though less endemic than readers of the tabloid press might have supposed.

The promoters made money only on the drug itself. Still, a hit of good Ecstasy cost twenty-five dollars and only lasted three or four hours, depending on the quality, so the money to be made was substantial. As always happens with drug scenes, as happened with the hippies, the money created ugliness. UK promotions tended to be policed by Jamaican posses. Stories of rapes and Rottweilers multiplied, and the Ecstasy itself was increasingly cut with speed, low on the fuzzy glow, high on frenzy.

Ecstasy hit New York big time in about 1987. Balloons bearing a hundred hits of Ecstasy used to be launched in the World on Wednesday nights. Nor did you have to be Sherlock to pick up on the drug's presence. I recall being startled when a woman I had seen around but barely knew, came up to me in some club, and was so, so . . . happy to see me. I asked for her number. She scribbled it onto a sheet of paper, adding:

ANGEL OF THE DIAMOND HEART

SEND FORTH YOUR BLESSINGS

OF LOVE & BEAUTY

AND FILL MY BEING WITH

BEAUTIFUL JOY

She had drawn nine stars beneath.

I greeted her warmly when I next saw her. She snarled as she swept by.

A few nights later, she had another lovely smile. I was wise by then. What a fun drug.

A partner had joined the World after the departure of Steve Maas. He was named Peter Frank, and Weinstein had known him since he had installed the video at Hurrah. Frank was a stocky prep, an alumnus of Harvard Law School and the scion of a family that was both wealthy and politically well-connected (His sister had been Mayor Koch's Commissioner of Ports.) He was to be the administrator. Most especially, he was there to get the cabaret license. "We're doing everything in a businesslike way," Frank told me. "I don't see how they can close us. Besides we're upgrading the quality of life in the neighborhood." Frank was also relied on to pump in funds when required, and did so; ultimately to the tune of $1 million.

There were still a few private parties as time trickled by and soon Arthur and Colleen had the look down pat. The World was absolutely the murkiest club I have ever been into with the qualified exception of London's Annabel's, because where the dimness in Annabel's is sleek and refulgent, the World was cavernous, with glimmering lights that were in the sort of colors—prawn, azure, cherry syrup—that were unhelpful in picking up visual information.

Huge rotting rococo sofas were parked here and there and empty gilded frames hung on walls of garishly painted brick.

In the downstairs Crystal Room the walls were marbled like fancy stationery. There were chandeliers and a sharp sound system. The Ballroom, which was up a flight of stairs, looked at once grand and ruinous. In the eccentric lighting—Weinstein's specialty—the dance floor, best seen from the third-floor balcony, leapt like a troubled nighttime ocean. Also up on the third floor a misshapen hole in the wall let the select into the VIP Room, a cubicle of silvery squalor, 1950s furniture, and limitless Stolichnaya, all of which looked absolutely *right*.

The final permits came through in the late summer of 1987. Peter Frank was trying to rein his partners in but they were chafing to go. "We've worked so hard for so many years," Frank Roccio told me. "Arthur Weinstein is like Columbus. Let's get the boat on the ocean. Let's smell the salt air!"

Nightpeople have to have heart. The World opened its doors—legitimately at last—on September 15, 1987. "The night before we opened, I sanded the floor of the Ballroom," Weinstein says. "It's a nice floor. *Needless* to say, I didn't have time to let it dry. I saw something flickering outside. The dumpsters were on fire!

"I was covered with sawdust. I was out of my mind. I knew I was okay. It was going to be . . . The Joint!"

It's hard to say just why one club clicks and another doesn't, but click the World did, and with a striking mixture of revelers. The Crystal Room, for instance, was soon a favorite hangout with the New York chapter of Hell's Angels. The third-floor bar was Bimbo Central several nights a week, except on Tuesdays it became the Rock & Roll Fag Bar beneath the suzerainty of Dean Johnson, a tall, bald man, famous locally for his performances with his band, the Weenies, and for unscheduled improv, like dancing on the bar at the Pyramid. The VIP Room was soon wall to wall with famous faces, not just wrinklies from old Studio nights, but the bands who were gigging there, live performers like The Pogues and Echo & the Bunnymen.

The juves were also wanted, and Alig was an inevitable hire. "Do you know how I first remember Michael Alig?" Peter Frank asks. "I was opening everybody's mail. I *always* opened everybody's mail. There was a letter to Alig with nine dollars and forty-three cents or something in it. There was a letter signed 'Richie,' apologizing it was so little, but he had read Michael's personal ad, and taken the money from his dad's pocket, like Michael said. He said he would see Michael in New York soon.

"I said to Michael, 'Did you put a small ad in the papers telling kids to steal from their parents?' . . . Sure! . . . *He didn't see anything wrong.*

"Then he got a letter from a kid with underwear in it. His father's . . . his mother's . . . his own . . . I don't know. I said, 'Michael, this cannot happen in my club.' He just flicked it off, the way he does . . ."

I wandered around the heaving throng with Paul Garcia one evening. What would it be like if there were only, say, sixty people there, I wondered? "Ominous" he said hollowly. Paul, Arthur, and Frank looked on the disapproval of their neighbors with sangfroid. This was dumb, because that was getting pretty ominous too.

This young black guy, Randall, was a dealer, but clearly an amateur, and likeable. A, who wasn't much of a user, but liked to have some around, for social reasons, had bought small quantities of cocaine from him a few times in the World. Then Randall made a couple of house calls. So when Randall approached A in one of the World's many dark niches holding out what looked like a bottleful of smoke and urged him to inhale, he did so. A balloon suddenly expanded in his head, then was gone just as quickly. No big deal.

Some months later A had started reading scare stories about this stuff called "crack." "What's crack?" *he asked Randall when he next saw him in the World.*

Randall laughed incredulously. "You jiving?" *he asked.* "You and me, we done crack!"

"That was crack?" *A asked. Thinking, well, that wasn't so much.*

Some days later, the bell rang. Randall was at the door with another guy who was older, a soft-spoken fellow in black leather trousers. Randall introduced him as his brother. A let them in, a mite reluctantly. "Have you got a glass of cold water? Mind if we base?" *Randall asked politely.*

A was all attention as the two brought out their product, and a bunch of tackle, including razor blades, glass pipe stems, and cotton swabs, and prepared treats for themselves before setting to work. "Don't start basing," *Randall warned A. Moments later, he was urging* "Want a hit? Want a hit?"

"Hold your breath . . . count to thirty," the brother said. "It's like diving off the high board. Just hold your breath till you hit the bottom."

A took a hit, a small one.

High now, the perhaps brothers started squabbling over a cracked stem. Randall fanned out invitations to scads of clubs and talked with disgruntlement of some long-ago night when he had been tossed out, of all places, the Mudd Club. In due course, the pair had divvied up the crack into small segments and left to distribute their goodies to their uptown clientele.

A, who was $175 poorer, realized he had become a way station on a crack distribution network. He realized the feds might take a dim view of this. They call it conspiracy. He politely made himself unavailable to Randall thenceforward.

Randall had soon disappeared from clubland anyway.

Crack was soon a chill wind howling through Nightworld, and the everyday world too. And the Last Party flamed on.

Tronn appears on *New York*'s cover of March 14, 1988, which was shot in the Tunnel basement, with Alig and another Club Kid, a boy named Magenta. All three have an earnest pale alertness, like extraterrestrials caught in mundane headlights, a look accentuated in Tronn's case by a tuft of bright red hair, like a rhino horn, which rose about ten inches from his forehead and required a can of hair spray a week for maintenance. "It was a total accident actually," Tronn says. "I did it one Halloween. I thought it looked very sharp at night." Virshup described Alig as "a slight young man with a skinny bow tie and blacking under his eyes."

The swelling movement of Club Kids began publishing their own fanzines, with titles like *Incognito, The Ace of Clubs, DV-8*. The leaders of the pack would all be listed on the mastheads, and they would carry gossip columns, illustrated with smudgy photographs of each other, with bitchily inventive text, like this on the opening of one of Suzanne Bartsch's dragfests at the Copacabana:

THE FABULOUS JULIE JEWELS WALKED UP TO THE ROPES . . . AND SAID "I'M JULIE JEWELS AND THESE ARE MY BOSUMS (SIC). SECURITY REPLIED, "WE CAN LET EITHER YOU OR YOUR BOSUMS IN, BUT NOT BOTH OF YOU." SCENE SCRAWLER STEVEN SABAN, 54'S STEVE RUBELL MINUS SANDY GALLIN OR BIANCA, & GADS! RUDOLF &

THE VERY STRAPPED-IN DIANE BRILL ALL WERE HAVING MOLTO PROBLEMES GETTING THROUGH . . . OTHER LUMINARIES, PATRICK MCMULLEN (WHOSE B'DAY PARTY AT MK WAS TO ME DULL DULL DULL B/C I WZN'T INVITED TO THE DINA AND WZN'T EVEN GIVEN A DRNK LAYTAH).

Sic, sic, sic.

Actually, even while the photograph in the Tunnel basement was on the *New York* cover, the club was almost history. Rudolf was looking ahead, cranking up again to create a super club. In 1987, he went to Tokyo. There he was introduced by Yuki Watanabe, heir to a chunk of the Mitsubishi fortune, to Toshiaki Umeda, who had started an after-hours venue in that city some years before. Both men were friendly to the notion of investing. This was, after all, a time when Japanese capital was readying itself to go after Rockefeller Center and Columbia Studios, so taking over Manhattan's Nightworld must have seemed like a stroll in the park.

The World closed for a redo in the summer. On July 29, 1988, there was a preclosing party there hosted by no fewer than fifty Club Kids. Mykul Tronn and Julie Jewels headed a list, which ended with Angel. Angel, whose family was Colombian, and whose complete name was Angel Melendez, was a B List Club Kid. Angel, who planned to be a singer one day, meantime both gained entree and paid his way by dealing drugs. He was not the most inconspicuous of dealers. His working attire was a pair of feathered wings, with something like a six-foot wingspan, red or white according to mood.

Rudolf quickly took advantage of the World's closure. On Friday, July 28, 1988, there was a "Disco Retro Expo '78–'88" at Tunnel. It was an exhibition of over one thousand invitations from STUDIO 54, MUDD CLUB, XENON, AREA, LIMELIGHT, PYRAMID, DANCETERIA, PALLADIUM, TWILIGHT ZONE, (OLD) WORLD, *and dozens more!* FEATURING MEMORABILIA FROM THE PARTIES OF MADONNA, HALSTON, WAY BANDY, BOY GEORGE, DIANNE BRILL, ANTONIO, MALCOLM McLAREN, ANDY WARHOL, GRACE JONES, and so on all the way to LAURIE ANDERSON, DEBBIE HARRY, MICHAEL ALIG, *and hundreds more!*

The free bar at this one ran from ten to eleven P.M. Later that same night

Michael Alig and James St. James hosted a Midnite Swim at the Pitt Street Pool, below Houston. The invitation promised:

MIDNIGHT TILL BUST

FREE DRINKS, TIP THE BARTENDER

BRING YOUR BATHING SUIT (REALLY!)

BATHING BEAUTIES:

JULIE JEWELS, MYKUL TRONN, FASHION PATROL,

OLIVER TWISTED, PROJECT X, CYNTHIA SOCIAL LIES,

KEOKI, MARIA & CHRIS, LARRY TEE, BRENDA A GO-GO,

LAHOMA, OLYMPIA, FLLOYDD, ALLISON WONDERLAND,

GYM, DV-8, LINCOLN, JENNY GO-GETTER, DENISE

ARIEL, BRANDWINE, INTERSTELLA, ARMAN, KAT

SHELTON, ELYN W, KENNY KENNY, STICKY VICKY,

WAYNE FAMOUS, HARLIQUIN ROMANZES, JULIE

FUCHSIA DOLL, CHATHAM & ALEX, DOUG

MICHELLE TANG, ANN CUMMINGS,

ALEXANDER THE GRAPE

ANDY ANDERSON

LIFEGUARDS:

FRANK ROCCIO & RUDOLF

THIS IS OBVIOUSLY A COMP, DUMMY

Michael Alig was the king of the Club Kids, just as he had planned. "They thought he was the candy man. They dropped out of school, and followed him around," Elyn W, now Wollensky, says. "They couldn't go home any more. It isn't like *The Brady Bunch*, where Mom says I forgive you. *Where are they now?*"

REHEARSAL FOR THE END OF THE WORLD

3

STEVE RUBELL HAD BELIEVED THAT PALLADIUM WOULD bring uptown and downtown together. Black Monday, the precipitous stock collapse of October 19, 1987, and the slump that followed, lowered expectations in Nightworld as elsewhere. Uptowners might venture to M.K., Nell's, or—the hard-core—Save the Robots, but that was it, so far as social derring-do was concerned. As for the mood downtown, which had always been a realm of hope rather than hard currency, this was noticeably souring. Emotions had been running high over the gentrification that had followed the Lower East Side art boom. The hardworking local citizenry with their machine shops and bodegas were none too keen on the well-heeled new arrivals, who, for their part, felt poorly disposed to such neighbors as the junkies, winos, and lumpen punks who frequented the parks and burned-out storefronts.

This feeling was returned, with a vengeance. "Death to Yuppie Scum" and similar *pensées* were written on walls and T-shirts. Streets were plastered with posters for the band Missing Foundation, which, according to the scuttlebutt, was part of a Lower East Side cult. This was actually not quite the case, according to Istvan Kantor, a Hungarian artist-activist, who moved to the Lower East Side in 1985, and who would tell people he had come to New York "to start the Revolution." Kantor worked under the name of Monty Cantsin, a shadowy commune, a name usable by anybody. He himself made performances with his blood—"I drank it and splashed it on people"—in such clubs as the Pyramid, ABC No Rio, and his group's own hangout, the No Se No Social club on Rivington Street. "Peter Missing approached me at a party," Kantor says. "I do not know if that was his real name. He was called that because of the band. He's a pretty subversive person. We agreed to work together . . ."

As the decade drew to a close, things became more hectic. There were rumors that occult ceremonies involving animal sacrifices had been held in Save the Robots, for instance. I arrived at one locale where weirdness had been promised but found the windows tin-sheeted, the door multiply-locked. When Daniel Rakowitz, a Lower East Sider hitherto known mainly for carrying a rooster on his shoulder, killed his girlfriend, a Swiss stripper, and boiled her into a soup, which he distributed to the homeless, most thought this wholly appropriate to the locale.

One evening an acquaintance slipped an invitation into my pocket and urged me to visit the Hotel Amazon the following night. It was April 8, 1988. The Hotel Amazon was a club in a deconsecrated church on Suffolk Street between Rivington and Delancey, a neighborhood best known for the ready availability of hard drugs. The occasion, it turned out, was The End of Music (As We Know It) Party, and a DJ was playing noise rockers, like Black Snakes and Prong. The space was big and gloomy. The few people there were wearing mandatory black, and my date, Diana, who was pale, and wearing white, with a bow on the back, was floating around like a silver minnow in a murky puddle.

So far, so ho-hum. But at midnight a line of silent figures began wending their way upstairs. An audience—black leather, shaven pates, pigtails, hair extensions, painful-looking jewelry—was seated in a room on the club's upper floor, facing a makeshift stage hung with Christmas lights. A bearded man came out wearing animal skins, with a toy shop elephant trunk on his penis. A woman followed, howling, her face painted white. Suddenly she was naked, standing on her head, and doing the splits, while he dropped gooey things into her vagina. Diana's notes read: "With full force, he punched her cunt, sending a stream of red running down her buttocks and back. Again and again he punched her, the audience cheering loudly with each blow."

"Wouldn't that hurt?" I asked rather foolishly.

"A lot!" Diana said.

The next performance artist, who was wearing a black turtleneck and jeans and had waist-length brown hair, grabbed the microphone, and began a full-throttled shrieking of fine old Anglo-Saxon words, though, what with the squealing of the amps, few were fully intelligible. He then hurtled around the stage, getting caught up in the Christmas lights as he did so. "Hey! You pulled down the lights!" somebody from the audience complained. "Christmas is over!" the artist screamed, throwing down the mike, and storming offstage.

There was an intermission. We thought of leaving, but some men began swiftly unrolling transparent plastic over the stage and aisles. A promising development. This is an abbreviated version of what took place.

A black-bearded man, apparently misshapen, appeared onstage. The artist was wearing a white jacket, a tie, a shirt, with a pig's snout depending from his neck, a piglet's head covering his privates, and other porker parts dangling here and there. He was misshapen because tubes were strapped to his midriff. He was smoking a cigar, which he nonchalantly stubbed out on his right cheek.

A tall slender woman walked out from the wings. She was costumed to look pregnant. The man spattered her mouth and stomach with a scarlet liquid, pushed her to the ground, and delivered the "child," to wit, a box. He stood up, produced a squirming white lab rat from the box, put its head in his mouth, bit it off, and tossed the body into the aisle. You could see in the audience an extraordinary mix of ecstasy and revulsion, as this performance was repeated with several more white rats. He then produced a lighter and applied it to one of the tubes protruding from his stomach. It went off with a blinding flash. Again. Soon he was almost invisible in the smoke, and firecrackers were blazing down the center aisle sending photographers and black leather toughies scuttling sidewise. There was more. Diana's notes read: "Small headless rat-bodies lay about on the stage and in front of the first row, their necks pinched shut. There were no heads lying about at all . . . What we saw that night was a celebration of destruction, of pain. Does that mean it wasn't art?"

I met the performer later. His name was Joe Coleman and he was also a visual artist, a painter of violently disturbing images. He showed me some admiring letters. One ran: "Joe Coleman has got A MIND PLUS & his art is something else . . . everyone else here likes it." It is signed "Charles Manson."

That summer, the Lower East Side boiled over. Bottles were thrown at the Christadora, a chicly reconditioned high rise where apartments were selling for up to a million. The Christadora overlooks Tompkins Square Park, which housed an encampment of squatters that the city had determined to oust. It happened that Rudolf was on hand on Sunday, August 7, when maddened cops laid into protesters there. Photographs of the clublord, a sort of teutonic male La Passionaria, blood caking his face, were featured both in the *Post* and the *Times*. It suggests his low profile outside Nightworld, compared to that of Steve Rubell, say, or Howard Stein, that in the former he was called only a "bloodied protester" while the *Times* identified him as "Rudolph Pippei, owner of the Tunnel Club."

This suited Rudolf fine. His name does not appear on the invitation to the Outlaw Party to celebrate the riots which he gave that Saturday. "You MUST be at TOMPKINS SQUARE PARK," the revolutionary-red card commanded. A hard core of Club Kids showed up in their finery which looked a bit less fabulous in the light of day and Rudolf dispensed beer alongside a boom box and made political pronunciamentoes. The cops duly showed up. Michael Alig, who was wearing a pigtail wig and a little girl dress over diapers, started screaming, "Arrest me! Arrest me!" but the NYPD looked at his pyrotechnic cavortings, quailed, and refused to oblige.

The last performance of Missing Foundation was at CBGB. "They threw over the speakers," says Hilly Kristal, owner of the boîte, and a veteran of all manner of heavy-duty and hard-core gigs. "They lit a barrel of oil and they threw it into the audience. Not a little barrel but a *barrel*. And I stopped the show. Yeah. I tried to have them arrested. The cops wouldn't do it. They said, 'That's your affair.' That was the end of it."

Peter Missing, in fear of the FBI, justified or not, left for Germany. Word has wafted back that he is doing well in pop music there. "Sometimes Peter Missing likes to be mysterious," Kantor says. Kantor himself has moved to Canada. "That was a very strong group of people, working together in Missing

Foundation," he adds. "And that all completely disappeared. All that lifestyle. Completely."

That particular apocalypse had been, at least, postponed.

When the World reopened after its face-lift in September 1988, innovations included the It Bar, which was in a small slice of the building alongside the front door. It was named for the It Twins, two Club Kids, who were not twins, or even brothers, and it was run for a while by Mykul Tronn, but this was one of the World's less successful ventures. "The Club Kids were about being freaky. The World was about celebrities and sex," a female Club Kid told me sagely.

In April 1990, an edition of Geraldo Rivera's tabloidy talk show, *Geraldo*, was devoted to the Club Kids. It was called "Nightlife: The Agony and the Exxxtasy," so spelled for the dim, and among the guests were Julie Jewels, fake hair piled high medieval fashion, like a double scoop of lemon ice cream; the glossily self-possessed drag performer, RuPaul; Mykul Tronn, slick as a comic strip, with platinum hair and machine-gun emplacement-window glasses; and Michael Alig, who had the eerily desolate look of a Bernard Buffet clown, with bright red nose, thick red lips, and geometrically patterned hair. Rudolf was sitting with them, looking saturnine in a red suit. He told Geraldo how much he loved them all. Ha.

Michael Alig would later claim that it was he who had discovered the five-story building in which Rudolf created Mars. It was on Tenth Avenue and Thirteenth Street, the old meat-packing district, by then best known for its towering transsexual streetwalkers. Rudolf declared that he had been inspired by the movie *Blade Runner,* which effectively meant a noir-cum-pop look, like a giant lipstick on the ground floor, a faux-Oriental opium den, and a conglomeration of lava lamps. Rudolf hired Mykul Tronn, who had moved on from the It Bar and had been doing Tuesday nights at M.K. He was going to hire Alig too. "Michael Alig was going to do the usual debauchery. You know, mayhem and stuff," Tronn says.

He didn't. Tronn apart, Rudolf fired the Club Kids en masse. "They were bugging the shit out of people. I don't care that they didn't have any purpose or goal," Rudolf says. "But they didn't want to change." Stasis is death in

Nightworld. Drugs, and not just coke or Ecstasy, but ketamine, a powerful animal tranquilizer, known as Special K, were destroying the lightness of the Club Kids fantasy just as heroin had sapped the energies of punk.

It was the Last Party, Act III, Scene 3.

According to Mykul Tronn, "What happened is that before the opening Rudolf told Michael that he could no longer be part of it. I'm sure a lot less politely than I just put it. He said the Club Kid thing is *over*."

Rudolf says, with his usual careless effrontery, "I dumped them. You can say that I am the ungrateful father of the Club Kids."

Tronn says of Alig's firing, "That was the only big downer that I can remember in Michael's career. I'm sure that would have an effect. Especially since Rudolf was a father figure to him. As subsequently so was Peter Gatien."

It's true. Rudolf and Michael Alig remained close anyway. "It wasn't his fault. He had no choice," Alig says of his firing. He believes he was dumped on the orders of the seriously freaked-out Japanese.

Regrets over the demise of the Club Kids were expressed even by those who had found them a pain in the neck. They were premature. The Kids were ubiquitous in the Red Zone, a new club opened to compete with Mars by the unsinkable Maurice Brahms. Rudolf, moreover, became a publisher. His magazine, *Project X,* a mixture of fashion and gossip, was edited by Julie Jewels and Michael Alig.

Mars opened on New Year's Eve, 1989. The opening was pandemonium. The sound system on the third floor was such that Mars was quickly noted as the only club in the history of Nightworld where that reliable formula, *if the music is too loud, you're too old,* was not necessarily valid. It was a huge success.

The success of the Tunnel and Mars was almost the death of Limelight, a club that had had its share of celeb shenanigans and wild doings but had never really sparkled with nocturnal pixiedust. The singer Billy Idol actually singled the club out as an example of the malaise that hit after the city had cracked down on the after-hours clubs. "You got corporate clubs, like Limelight," he groused. It takes a Billy Idol to so describe the defrocked house of worship as corporate, but it was true that Limelight—Slimelight as it was inevitably known—had always been a B List sort of club.

Nor had Peter Gatien ever been much more than a B List person himself, which was his choice entirely. It was only Gatien's eye patch that made him recognizable at all, and then only as an occasionally glimpsed figure by the door. Of course not all club owners were as much the lives of their own parties as Steve Rubell, but where John Addison seemed to enjoy the mystique of absence, and Ian Schrager was withdrawn by nature, with Peter Gatien it was all business.

Stella, who had been so close to Steve Rubell, and who has tended bar for Gatien from time to time, found the difference disconcerting. "Steven wanted to get to know each and every person who worked for him, which was a huge, huge staff," she told me. "I work for Peter Gatien now, and do we ever see him? Never."

In business, though, he excelled. Gatien was as ambitious for a club empire as Rubell and Schrager had been in their Studio days, but, unlike them he realized his ambitions, opening further Limelights in 1985, one in London, and one in Chicago. Both were handsome clubs, the Chicago one particularly. "It was a building that once belonged to the Chicago Historical Society," Gatien told me in an interview. "It was one of the first buildings built after the fire. It was a pretty incredible structure." He seemed on the brink of creating a global chain, McClubs, you might say. "I was courted on more than one occasion by people wanting to take us public," he says. But it was not a terrific experience.

"I found when I had clubs in three cities, I was almost like a visitor," he says. "I would come in and it was almost staged for me . . . what I wanted to see . . . but I didn't know how to handle what was going on. I really never had a good gut feeling about was this really the way it should be? Or are we missing a little bit here? You can't just pick up a computer printout the next day, and say, well, we did fourteen hundred people. That looks okay! And put it away. You really have to be there . . . know whether the crowd stayed all night, whether they enjoyed themselves, whether it was really great. Or whether people just went through the motions, and left.

"Different towns have different things that motivate them. You can't just pick it up and move it. Because people in New York think it's cutting edge or whatever. Somebody in Chicago might think this is not for us. In fact, Chicago in the eighties did have a very Second City attitude. When we went and opened up with Andy Warhol, we received a fair amount of criticism. Somebody had done an anti–New York poster campaign. You can't just step in and say I'm a big New York person, I'm going to show you guys what entertainment is about. You can't do that."

Within three years, Gatien had sold both the London and Chicago Lime-lights and focused on New York. In the late eighties, times were tough for Peter Gatien at Limelight. "We struggled financially in I would say 1987, 1988, and 1989," he said. "That was when the Tunnel had opened, the old Tunnel, and Mars opened. I remember picking up these invites and it would say this party on Saturday night . . . open bar till twelve-thirty, comp till one o'clock. And at that point I decided, you know what? We were *not* going to offer four hours of open bar to compete with a three-hour open bar. We were just going to end up going bankrupt.

"So we retrenched. We went more after the tourist industry. And I predicted back then that these establishments would be out of business within two years or a year and a half.

"I had people who worked for me later who had worked at Mars who said the bar downstairs would be packed all night. And it would ring up zero. Like fifty dollars. Exactly zero! It was a total giveaway. I don't know if the owners were partying too much or if they didn't understand they were being railroaded."

The success of Mars added to but did not create the problems of the World. Its causes were more deeply rooted. There were rows between the partners, for one. Paul Garcia had gone to Spain. Peter Frank had recouped most of his investment by keeping a hard eye on the cash register, and was seen there less and less, so it was Arthur Weinstein's and Frank Roccio's club again. "But you have to have a floating fund. To buy the liquor for next week, to pay off the employees for the week before. It adds up. You have to have a floating fund of twenty or thirty thousand dollars a week," Weinstein says. Suddenly this money didn't exist. Another problem was that the East Village art boom was long gone, and the Lower East Side hadn't been that gentrified after all, not the part around the World anyway. An urban folklore sprang up, concerning posses and homeboys roaming the club with Uzis and knives, as though going there were a journey into a combat zone. Perceptions are the stuff of which Nightworld is made, so Eurotrash and uptown attendance at the club slumped, and filmy debutantes were seen among the dark rococo fitments less and less. "Nobody wants to walk the wild side anymore," Arthur Weinstein mourned. "I'm sick of it. But there's nothing I like better. Unfortunately."

A more obdurate problem was the growing enmity of the manifold agencies of the city. If ever there was a club that crossed the line it was the World, and their luck was running out. On the evening of January 31, 1989, Frank Roccio left the club to take his motorbike, a purple Triumph, for a spin. "It was really balmy, sixty-five, seventy-five," he says. "The stick shaft dropped when I was going at thirty miles per hour and I pivoted into the back of a truck. I broke my leg in three places."

The popular wisdom, naturally, was that the purple Triumph had been dropped on Frank Roccio by certain gentry who were upset that he had not gotten them a piece of the club. Roccio was dismissive. "There were all kinds of rumors," he said. "This happened . . . that happened . . . somebody wiped me out with a car or ran me over. All kinds of crazy stuff."

He was still in the hospital on February 3 when the Environmental Protection Agency made an inspection and closed the Crystal Room, citing noise. It was as if the city had decided to close the place down piecemeal, because next the SLA took away the World's liquor license on the grounds that a minor had been served. "Do you want to know what the two saddest things in the world are?" Weinstein demanded, answering himself: "A club without people. And a bar without a liquor license.

"Also the public assembly had been allowed to expire, which meant we had no cabaret license," Weinstein added. "It's only good for a year. It's easy for it to expire, because a year goes by pretty quick in New York. Generally, the Building Department is sort of lax in getting to you." Not in the case of the World.

On April 1 the Buildings Department and the Fire Department both came at 10:30. "A day after that about eighty police came in, harassing guests and opening up their pockets," Weinstein said. "Like I was Carlos Lehder Rivas and the Cali Cartel. I used to think they were persecuting me for my . . . checkered past. But that's not the case. They're *fools*."

A hard core of patrons soldiered on. *Spin* magazine had booked a party and gave it regardless, shipping in beer from a bodega around the corner which had posted a sign OPEN FOR BOOZENESS. But the city had had it with the club, and, as Steve Rubell and Ian Schrager had found out, when the city, or an individual within the city, becomes vengeful, life becomes insupportable in Nightworld.

"It's almost inexplicable what happened to the World," Frank Roccio told me in May, reeling off a list of official strikes against the club. We were in one of the downstairs offices in the World. Roccio was still on crutches, and in black. His hair was long and silver and he had lots of silver earrings in his left ear. Steve Lewis, one of the club managers, slipped in and out, as did Weinstein. Two men came in wearing skirts, one wearing a blue hairpiece; the other, a blond, was thickly lacquered with mascara. "Where the fuck is the staple gun?" the blue-wigged guy asked pleasantly. They were doing the cartoon movies show in the Crystal Room. Just club business as usual.

Roccio was disposed to be philosophical about the nightlife and its often phantasmal benefits. Profits dissolve, what with partners and paybacks. "But you have to understand that what we downtown nightclub owners are able to do is live off the fat of the land," he said. "We live in a microcosmic society where we don't pay for anything. We are virtually required to dress in an outrageous way so very often our clothes range from expensive designer to funky things off the thrift shop rack. And in many clothing stores you get discounts because those people want to come into your club . . . in shoe stores you get discounts . . . many hairdressers would be happy to cut your hair free to be comped and have a couple of drinks.

"So the nightclub business is perhaps the greatest bartering tool in New York. You pay to get in absolutely nowhere. You pay to drink absolutely nowhere. What the hell does it cost? Cab fare? Uptown people go to the ballet or to the theater or to a smart opening. Very rarely do we downtown people go to those affairs. You very rarely see us outside of the nightlife. And perhaps in those trendy restaurants that are part of the nightlife.

"We always look like we have a drink in our hand, which we do . . . we always look like we're having a good time, which hopefully we are . . . we never have a chance to go anyfuckingwhere. We don't go on vacation.

We don't go to . . . *Antigua*. We don't go down to . . . *Mustique*. We don't spend a dime on anything. If you visit most of our homes there's nothing very fancy or elaborate to them because we don't spend very much time in them." He added, "We all have really great Sony televisions."

He said he did not expect to be part of the World's struggle much longer. "I shall slowly, but surely . . . dissociate myself. Dissociate sounds so negative." That's what he meant, though. He, too, it turned out, was planning a superclub. Roccio picked up a plastic beaker, and rapped it. "I've never owned a club which used *glass*," he said. "I've been twelve years in the nightlife. It needs somebody who has come up through the ranks. So that's what the vision is. That's the dream."

When asked to be more specific, Roccio said impatiently, "I don't have a concept. I don't have Rudolf's ego. I don't have to decorate it. I can hire a decorator. Steve Rubell once told me he had never had an original idea in his life. He said, 'I take somebody else's idea and apply it to something I want to do. Every day a thousand people land in New York with plenty of money. Nice people.' "

Roccio paused, and allowed that actually he did have a bit of a concept for his club, aside from real glassware. It was to be a *Playboy* Club for the fin de siècle, a time when, in Roccio's opinion, AIDS fear would be fading. "I've always wanted to do a sex club," Roccio said exultantly. "We're going to get a private membership. We're going legit." Disdain for Rudolf's-style mania or no, he already had worked out a uniform for the female staffers: "Calvin Klein underwear for men. And training bras." He was looking over premises on Leonard Street in TriBeCa. The club was going to be called Lift Up Your Skirt and Fly.

What about Arthur Weinstein? Could he keep the World going? "Sometimes he thinks it's going to close. Sometimes he thinks it's going to . . . change the world," Roccio said, savoring his pun.

Weinstein, who had wandered in, and picked up on the drift of the conversation, said, "Never say die. What they don't realize is this is the time it gets *interesting*."

"Why don't you slow down, Art?" Steve Lewis said despondently.

Frank Roccio, incidentally, had left one item off the list of freebies easily available to the Nightlords: one he started dipping into with abandon.

Heroin.

*   *   *

Vito Bruno's Outlaw operation was still going strong. One day Bruno was outside his office on Lafayette Street. That evening there was to be an Outlaw Party not too far away, on Vandam Street. "I was walking down the street," Bruno says. "All of a sudden, there's somebody on one side of me and somebody on the other and I got . . . trapped. They pulled me over to the side . . .

" 'I'm Detective So-and-so . . . We know exactly who you are and where you are . . . if anybody gets hurt tonight, you're going to jail . . . ' Guess what? That was the last one I ever did."

Nightworld had lost another one.

The last straw for Authur Weinstein was the tree. "Someone came in and cut down a hundred-and-twenty-year-old tree," Colleen Weinstein says.

"It wasn't someone. It was that prick of a next-door neighbor," Arthur says.

"It was Art's favorite tree."

"It was called the Tree of Life. It was a gorgeous tree," Arthur says. "It was in the yard next door. The guy hated our guts. And I don't blame him."

He had resolved to shutter the place when David Bowie wanted to do a concert in the World. "I said you're out of your fucking mind. I'm ready to close the door and walk out of here forever," he told the caller.

Arthur Weinstein went down to State Supreme Court and argued that they should be allowed to reopen if he cleared up the violations. He prevailed. David Bowie gave his Tin Man concert in the club, and it was a smash. But it was the End of the World all the same. Arthur Weinstein still mourns the club. "We did not have our house in order," he says. "If we did, the World could still be open and making plenty of money, believe me."

Rudolf was now Manhattan's Nightlord, but his triumph bore within it the germ of its destruction. "Me and Rudolf, we had this great scam," Michael Alig says blithely. "We would open a club and fill it with comps . . . it would look really good . . . then it would go bankrupt. But by then we'd be on to the next club . . ." This required, of course, that there should be a next club to move on to, and this was not, for the moment, the case. Rudolf resigned from Mars and Quick! in January 1990. Watanabe refused to accept his resignation for several months. Eventually Rudolf just left for Los Angeles anyway. Soon he was running a club there for Mark Fleischman.

I lunched with Rudolf at a babewatch restaurant on Sunset Plaza some months later. He felt he had outstayed his welcome in Manhattan, he said. It wasn't the town he had moved to a dozen years before. "That was something extreme," he told me "It was something that nowhere else could you find. Every night! It never stopped. Every night you could go out and you would find extreme people doing extreme things.

"In these days, New York does not have that. What it has now is okay. Sure. But what is it?" Rudolf said. "Here Melrose Avenue is better. San Francisco. Many cities have it."

Supposing a newly conservative, zero-tolerant America loses it?

"If things become really ridiculous here, we can always go back to Europe," Rudolf said.

Mars did not long survive Rudolf's departure. The Tunnel was soon shuttered too. Peter Gatien had been right. He spoke with Yuki Watanabe later. "He said he had investors who were losing money everywhere," Gatien says. "The money they were losing at Mars was like peanuts compared with the money they were losing on real estate deals. They came and were gone within a period of two and a half to three years. That philosophy of operating a nightclub came and went."

BEYOND THE VELVET CORD

2/4

BILL HAMILTON'S FATHER NEVER MET STEVE RUBELL. "MY mother did. They hated each other," Hamilton says. It cannot have helped that Rubell, presumably nervous, got good and drunk. Nonetheless, in its second year, their relationship was as strong as ever. "He and I never once spoke of the disease," Hamilton says. "I spoke to Ian about this. He said the reason is I brought him the sun—gardening. Not 'Do you feel all right today? Death is coming.' "

In their second year together, Rubell announced that he was going to celebrate with a dinner. "Steve asked me: 'Who do you want to have? Who do you think would be the most glamorous person in the world? And he knew everyone! You name them. Liz Taylor . . . Madonna . . . You name them.

"So it was going to be on Valentine's Day, and it was Carolina, Reinaldo, Ian, Steve, Deb, myself, and the Mystery Date!" Deb was Deborah Hughes. She also worked for Carolina Herrera, and she had been, for a while, engaged to Ian Schrager.

Steve Rubell strung Hamilton along for a month.

They went along at 7:30 to pick up the mystery date, who turned out to be Halston. Hamilton had never met the couturier, who then did little but design costumes for Martha Graham. "Halston, by that time, was totally in. He had not been out in a year. Nobody was seeing him," Hamilton says. "He, of course, was ready when we got there. But he had to make this grand entrance down this staircase that made him glide. He was all decked out in black with his white jacket.

"We went to the Canal Bar. Bianca came too. My head was swirling. It was as if it was ten years earlier at Studio. It was interesting to see Steve's appreciation for him. What glamor meant was Halston." None of that night's conversation remains with Bill Hamilton. "It was his look," he says. "It's all image that your eye sees . . . for look, for color. Halston was fantastic at his gestures."

It was not possible for Rubell or Schrager to forget Studio 54, but they were hoteliers now. "Studio 54 changed our life. And Morgan's changed our life," Ian Schrager told a reporter in the early summer of 1988.

"Jail changed our life," Steve Rubell put in.

Now the Royalton on West Forty-fourth Street was changing their life, then the Century Paramount. As the Rubell and Schrager hotel imperium grew, there were subtle changes in the dual trajectory of their career. Just as it had been Ian who had originally talked Steve into Studio 54, but it had been Steve who had become the public face of the club, so with the hotels, it would still be Steve Rubell who would get the press, whereas Ian Schrager was still the background presence. But he was a sleeker, more formidable presence. It was becoming known that Ian Schrager was more and more both responsible for the look of things, and the motor behind the deals.

In one regard, jail had not changed Steve's life that much at all. His consumption of drugs was as awesome as ever, and this although Bill Hamilton was such an abstainer that he drank beer only to gain weight. "We used to feed it to horses. To gain a stone," he says. "When it came to drugs, he knew it bothered me, because he would get run down, and he would be sick for three days. It was mostly coke.

"There was one night we got back and the TV wasn't working. And he was sitting there in his underwear, *determined* to make it work. I was saying,

'Steve, just give it a rest! The cables are down. It's a brownout, or whatever. You're stoned right now. Go to bed!'

"And he just refused. He sat there for about forty minutes. And wouldn't you know it? He got the fucking thing to work. To show me he was in control. That just because he was stoned, it didn't mean he couldn't think, and see, and hear."

Pertinacious as ever, Rubell went out to dinner with Reinaldo and Carolina Herrera the night before the Royalton opened, and took them for a look at the place before turning in. "It was four in the morning. He moved everything. And that's the way you see them today," Reinaldo Herrera says. The place was an instant success.

He and Bill Hamilton went to St. Bart's in the Caribbean in the winter of 1988. Rubell, the meat eater, who had always noisily said how much he disliked the seaside, took long walks with Hamilton on the beach.

In the spring, Rubell and Schrager plunked down $90 million to begin a condominium project at 105th Street and Central Park West and $50 million for the Barbizon, once a famous residential hotel for women. They also began redoing the Century Paramount. Another $30 million project. It was still an uphill struggle. By May 1989 the unforgiving State Liquor Authority was in its sixth year of routinely refusing liquor licenses to Rubell, Schrager, or anybody it thought too closely associated with the pair. That May, the *New York Post* reported that "the Barbizon restaurant has been shut down, Morgan's Bar is empty, and the Bar-Lounge at the Century Paramount looks derelict." Some of the most successful restaurateurs in New York had tried to get papered up, but to no avail.

But Steve Rubell was as cocksure as ever. Moreover, as he started imagining a way of redoing a once-famous club in the Paramount, the Diamond Horseshoe, his excitement rekindled. Juices started flowing. More so than with Palladium, he could be a Nightlord once again. Characteristically, he discussed it with an eclectic group of hotshots. "He spoke with Hubert, who ran Les Bains Douches in Paris. Hubert did some work on it," says restaurateur Brian McNally. "He spoke with me. I was ready to do it. Steve was one of the few people who could make New York a different place."

★   ★   ★

The ludes and the booze aside, and apart from nursing chronic bronchitis, Steve Rubell seemed fit for anything. In June, he fell sick. He told Jim Fouratt, with whom he was also discussing the conceptual club, that he was taking AZT, but he was still chary of talking about the disease directly. "Because AIDS meant death and Steve was not wanting to die," Fouratt says. Nor, Fouratt adds, was Rubell just blocking it with drink and drugs. It was as if he was using his consuming energy as a force field. "I mean I'm having conversations about opening up a club with a man who has . . . I know what it looks like! I knew what it looked like then! But the mind was still going."

Ian Schrager felt that Rubell somehow managed to ignore morbid presentiments. After all, their property kingdom was erected on loans and guarantees. "We didn't have a partnership agreement—it was a handshake," he later told writer Michael Gross. "Somebody sick doesn't risk what he's spent a lifetime building up. He wouldn't do that to me. It doesn't add up."

Bill Hamilton says, "I think Ian felt very guilty. Why would one of them get sick and not the other? When the two of them were out as much, even though they were in different communities." In the last weeks of his life Steve Rubell's appearance deteriorated with shocking speed. He grew thin and his hair grew thinner, a side effect, he would tell people, of a liver problem. "For the last couple of months I became more or less a nursemaid. Because he didn't want anyone else around him," Hamilton says. He simply wouldn't hear of leaving his room in Morgan's. "He refused to go to the hospital. He did not want any doctors," Hamilton says.

Indeed, according to Bill Hamilton, Nightworld was fading into the background of Steve Rubell's life. He no longer wanted to be out at the current hot club, past midnight every night. "He would show up every once in a while to support a friend. But he was at a different level of his life," Bill Hamilton says. But Rubell was still playing his part on the social stage. The Canal Bar and 150 Wooster were the restaurants of the moment, both being eateries where the haut monde of uptown and fashion people met with the luminaries of the then blazing art world. Steve Rubell would be seen nightly in one or the other, his sad straggle of hair concealed beneath some cocky piece of headgear, with an artificial tan, still with that ingenuous smile on his painfully drawn face.

One night early in the second week of July 1989, Rubell and Hamilton went to 150 Wooster. "Normally we sat at the first table," Bill Hamilton says. That night, though, Rubell asked Brian McNally for a corner table way in the back, an area that was not quite Siberia, but it wasn't the Côte d'Azur either. Steve was as greedy for the whirl of faces and names as ever, but was, for once, content not to be in the middle of it, to be outside the resplendent aquarium, peering in. "He just wanted to observe and not be wrapped up in stuff. He wanted to see what was happening," Hamilton says. "But he wasn't feeling well. At all. And we stopped going out totally from that point on."

That Friday Rubell and Hamilton flew out to Southampton. Steve Rubell's wasted appearance had been exciting increasing attention. If somebody speculates whether so-and-so is "sick," nobody asks which sickness is meant, not in fin-de-siècle Manhattan. As Ian Schrager put it, "In this day and age, when anyone under ninety has a headache, you think it." Now that one of the more visible figures in the city was suddenly offstage, the susurrus of gossip was intensifying. A mini-media frenzy was building up, just the sort of klieg-lit, notebook-waving, pop-and-flash paparazzo tumult that had once been the breath of life to Steve Rubell. It was something he could well do without though, now.

"So there was a lot of press waiting at the helicopters for us. There were cameras there," Hamilton says. "So we would wait and figure out. Because you can either leave from the East Side or the West Side. So we went to the East Side." A woman he knew, a TV gossip was there, flying out. "He was embarrassed to be seen the way he was, by one of his best friends, feeling the way he felt. It was the idea that he was surrendering to his final days. He didn't want to be remembered that way. And he needed help, getting in and out of the helicopter," Hamilton says.

They returned to the city on Monday. It was a progressively more labored week. "He started moving slower . . . vomiting . . . basically, flu symptoms," Bill Hamilton says. On Friday morning, Hamilton was sitting with Carolina Herrera, going over stuff. "And Steve calls. *He didn't know where he was,*" Hamilton says.

He told Carolina Herrera. She said, "That's poisoning of some sort. Go immediately. Leave!"

"Stay where you are," Hamilton told Rubell, "and I'll find you." Hamilton called the driver to find where he was parked. "He was at his doctor's appointment. He just didn't know."

"So we went back to the hotel. We were scheduled to leave for the weekend at one. I called and canceled, because he was vomiting so much," Hamilton says. He rebooked the flight for Saturday morning, on the off chance that Rubell would improve, but he called both Ian Schrager and Don Rubell to tell them that things were worsening.

"He was on just about everything. But the body had gotten to the point where it couldn't function anymore," he says. He told Don Rubell and Ian that he was doing what he could, but it was no longer helping. Both flew in and came by Morgan's. "We decided to wait the night out and see what happened. But it was just getting worse," Hamilton says.

"So on Sunday we went and checked him into Beth Israel. It was ten in the morning but even at that time he didn't want the people at the front desk to know where he was going. He couldn't walk. We physically carried him out in a chair."

The memory remains an intensely painful one for Bill Hamilton. Steve Rubell had been the arbiter of image, the man who had tossed every kind of heavyweight out of Studio 54, simply because he hadn't cared for the cut of the person's jib. Now he was being hoisted past the front desk of his own hotel in a chair as though he were himself being tossed out into the faceless crowd. "He didn't want people to have that last image to remember," Hamilton says dolorously. "That's why he had surrounded himself with just me. 'You can do it!'

"And that's what I had been doing for him. But it got to the point that it was impossible. You know what happens with horses if you cinch them? They get dehydrated. With humans, it's the same thing. He was so dehydrated that he couldn't keep fluids down. We didn't have the ability to feed him IV. He wanted to stay in the hotel. But we just couldn't do it."

They checked Steve Rubell into the hospital under a different name that Sunday. It was July 23, 1989. The nurses were on strike. "We didn't have any help in the hospital," Hamilton says. "So I became the RN. Everybody left. There was a chair, and I was sleeping with him.

"The body was really beginning to give way. On Monday, we got up. The nurse came in. He didn't want her touching him. 'Bill can take care of this!' Then his lungs were filling up. He was uncomfortable breathing. There were difficulties. They had to sedate him and give him oxygen. So the last time that we spoke was that day."

That Monday night, Steve Rubell was out of it. On Tuesday, he was stable, but there was no improvement. "Things were slowly going down," Hamilton says. He had been joined by Ian, Don Rubell, and Deborah Hughes. "We were sleeping in the waiting room and going in to check on him every fifteen minutes. But you're just waiting it out," Hamilton says.

On Tuesday night Reinaldo and Carolina Herrera were on the committee for a gala evening of ballet. The patroness was Britain's Princess Margaret.

"Carolina was chairman of the evening so she had to be there. It was terrible," Reinaldo Herrera says. "We knew he was going from five o'clock in the afternoon, more or less. We kept getting up and calling. Throughout the evening."

Steve Rubell died at ten past seven P.M. This was more or less during the intermission. At the ballet that evening were the Herreras, Claudia Cohen, and Bianca Jagger. "They all just physically felt something was happening at that minute," Hamilton says. He called all four to tell them Steve had died.

Hamilton left the hospital. "I ended up moving in with Ian for a couple of months. We both needed each other," he says.

THE LAST NIGHTLORD

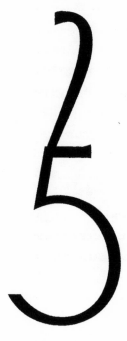

THERE WERE CHANGES IN NIGHTWORLD AS THE NINETIES hove into view. Many were functions of the passing of time, which had conducted its usual strict triage. There was the plague. There had been deaths, for this, and for other reasons, and sicknesses, and the survivors had either mellowed in the normal way, or moved out of town, or were marching sternly through detox, rehab, spiritual regimens, and twelve-step programs. Other formerly numinous Nightworld presences, like Bianca Jagger, would act as though the glorious excess had taken place on a faraway galaxy a long time ago. Others pretended nothing much had happened in the first place. A few, of course, remained incorrigible, reluctant to say goodnight, and they would go to Nell's, Mortimer's, Elaine's. But, so far as the late, late nightlife went, the après-eighties hangover, which had sucked the life from so much elsewhere, seemed to have swallowed that up too.

Those who had been veteran nighthawks since Studio times would complain that things weren't the same, but things are never the same, and a fresh horde of revelers saw no reason to dim the lights. It was pleasantly ironic that Maurice Brahms, the man who had done the longest prison time, was sitting as pretty as anybody in Nightworld. True, because of his conviction, Brahms's name could not be officially an "owner" of boîtes like the Red Zone or the Underground, but there was no attempt to conceal the fact that they were essentially Brahmsian operations. This, though, put him right in the eye of the next storm to break on Nightworld.

There has always been bad blood—often understandably—between clubs and their neighbors. Now, though, partly because of the youthfulness of the new clubgoers, rowdiness and violence were increasing at the same moment that community boards were getting feistier. In the spring of 1989, the City Planning Commission came up with a shockingly timid notion. Closing time until then had been 4:00 A.M. seven nights a week. It was proposed that any new venue that held more than 175 people should close at 12:30 five nights a week and be allowed to stay open until 2:00 in the morning on Fridays and Saturdays.

Nightworld happens to be one of New York's most powerful industries in terms of the money it generates, the jobs it creates, and the visitors it attracts, but club operators had always been too competitive and unruly a bunch to bother with creating any sort of lobby. Now, though, the threat that civic nannies would be imposing nap time accomplished the impossible. Operators of more than thirty of the city's clubs got together and formed the New York Cabaret Association.

"We defeated the early curfew hours," says Robert Bookman, the attorney for the Nightworld lobby. "But they did pass a stricter zoning." This didn't apply to any currently existing clubs, so the cabaret association, satisfied with its curfew victory, swiftly unraveled. The new regulations, though, meant that it would be far harder to open a new club in most desirable locales. The regulations would have made it punitively difficult to start Mars, which had been a meat-packing plant, or Roxy, which had been a factory. The changes had easily foreseeable consequences. "Now it's virtually impossible to open a new club in a lot of Manhattan areas," Bookman says. "So what's happened is that the existing spaces are being recycled time after time. In the old days, people might have to live with a club for two or three years, then it would go out of business, and a restaurant or a clothing store would come in there. Now they've got a club there permanently."

Also, Nightworld *was* getting rougher. A Public Nuisance Task Force created in June 1988 had compiled a list of problem clubs, thirty-five strong, oddly enough, and provided "intensive enforcement," including ticketing and towing of illegally parked cars. At the top of the list had been 1018, a disco on West Eighteenth Street. Captain Daniel Collins, head of the task force, told *The New York Times* that there had been at least twenty shootings and stabbings in or near the club. There had been two killings, and, following one affray, the police had found an armor-plated van loaded with machine guns and thousands of rounds of ammo parked nearby.

That January 1018 went down the tubes. The World, which had also figured high on the list, was also gone. The task force was now hovering around the Underground. "At least one person gets shot there every month," Captain Collins said. Minor rowdyism was endemic. "There was a green market across the street," Maurice Brahms says. "They complained that people leaving the club at four in the morning were taking apples and not paying for them. The general feeling was that they didn't want a club there anymore."

Sporadic muggings in the neighborhood would be blamed on Underground patrons, doubtlessly sometimes correctly. "Palladium had more violence than we did. But Palladium had protection," Brahms says. His reasoning was simple. Alan Cohen, who was one of the owners of Palladium, was also a power on the 14th Street development corporation. "Not that Underground didn't have violence. It did. But not as bad as Palladium's."

Uh-huh. In January 1990 *Newsday* reported that five people had been killed in or near the club the previous year. At any rate, Maurice Brahms realized that the neighbor problem needed to be handled. Accordingly, he hired a publicist, Kelly Cutrone. "Maurice was like the nicest, low-key family man," says Cutrone. "His name couldn't be on anything. There was a guy named Kenny. And another guy who worked there, named Carmen the Ice Pick."

Cutrone is a dark-haired young woman with a heart-shaped face, and her manner can switch from sugar to salt in short order, so I was not too surprised by her approach to the locals picketing the club. "What happened was I got into a fistfight with this guy. He started to bug me so bad that I punched him," she says. "And he started punching me. And it was all over the news. COMING UP AT SIX! NEW YORK NIGHTCRAWLERS GO AT IT! And Maurice got really mad at me, because I had been hired to smooth things down.

"But he said he couldn't really blame me. He said, 'Okay! We'll just close it down and open it up under another name.' We opened it up as the Palace de Beauté."

Cutrone, by this time, was doing promotions, parties, and press for half the clubs in Manhattan. "I did a club called Sweet Dreams," she says. "The Spin Doctors were playing there, and I fired them. I said they were the worst band. And nothing would ever happen to them. Three years later when I was bottoming out on crystal meth in Topanga, the lead singer sent me *Rolling Stone* with them on the cover, and a note, FUCK YOU! I thought that was great."

"Once a month I used to drive around in this car service and spend the night getting paid. I would charge these guys like three thousand dollars a month. Our business would be a cash business. I would have a brown paper bag, and I would walk in. They would say, 'We're really sorry. We don't have any money to pay you tonight.' So I would say, 'Give me fifty drink tickets.' At every club it would be the same story. It was only Maurice Brahms who always paid.

"And right around three in the morning I would go back to each club and say, 'If you don't pay me, this is going to be all over "Page Six" tomorrow.' I would be like a pit bull. One time, they had been keeping money up in the ceiling. It had rained, and there was water damage. They gave me these hundred-dollar bills that were all brown on the edge, and serrated. I was like, 'What am I going to *do* with this?'"

The clubman promised her any bank would change it. She took the spoilage into a bank on Fourteenth Street and Eighth Avenue. "People were coming up to see me. They wanted to know where I got this money from," Cutrone says. "I thought I was going to jail. I told them my grandmother had died and the money had been in her attic."

In about 1990, Kelly was approached by Steve Lewis. After the World closed, Lewis had worked alongside Cutrone at the Underground for a while, but had never got along with Maurice Brahms. He wanted Kelly to come and work with him for his new employer: Peter Gatien.

Michael Alig, who had taken his brood to the Red Zone and the Palace de Beauté after Rudolf had abandoned Manhattan, was at Limelight already. Peter Gatien was ready to make his moves.

Ian Schrager was one of the first to pick up that something new was in the air. "I noticed something at restaurants in the late eighties," he told a *Times* reporter. "At eleven P.M. the lights would dim, the music would turn up, and the people would start to table-hop." He felt, he said, the same energy that had eventually culminated in Studio 54. He added, "The idea of the huge nightclub has to be reinvented." Whether this was a real need or the phantom ache from a missing limb that can never be regrown was as yet unproven, but Schrager, of course, had no intention of being the re-inventor. Others felt the same, though, Peter Gatien among them.

Gatien had been the stealth fighter of the Nightlords. He was simply *there*. Kelly Cutrone's first meeting with him was in Limelight. "They were redoing all the furniture in his office. It was very, very high end," she says. " 'I'm going to be a major force in the business here.' That's what he said to me," Cutrone says. "He said he had these big, big plans. He wanted to be relevant. He wanted to start getting press beyond clubs."

Gatien was becoming a producer. Gatien gave a busboy in the club, Chazz Palmenteri, $25,000 to stage Palmenteri's play, *A Bronx Tale,* in Los Angeles, and was listed as a producer when it was made into a movie. He was preparing to back a second movie. He had taken over as publisher of *Project X,* the Club Kid faux glossy, from the departed Rudolf. He started a record label, Vortex. Simply put, Gatien was preparing himself to make the sort of transition to a wider world of media that Steve Rubell and Ian Schrager would have made if they hadn't been giddy with narcotics and acclaim.

He was not losing touch with his core business, though. "He said he was going to redo Limelight and make it cool again," Cutrone says. Some of the Club Kids had been appalled when Michael Alig started doing his nights there in 1989. "At that point, you couldn't get any more unhip. I mean, like, *Limelight?*" says James St. James. "You would no more think of going to Limelight than to . . . the Yonker Bonker Ballroom in Jersey. It was considered so tragically uncool.

"But Michael wanted more control over what he was doing. The money was there, and the offer was for Michael to have complete creative control. Peter gave him carte blanche. The place was a sanctuary for his growing little movement."

Alig called his night Disco 2000. It was actually a pumped-up version of something he had already done at the Tunnel called Celebrity Club. "Celebrity Club was a mix of everybody . . . a little gay . . . a little straight . . . a little black . . . a little white . . . a little poor . . . a little rich," Alig says. "And we had a Celebrity of the Week. A Michael Musto, a Dianne Brill, a Billy Beyond." Disco 2000 was bigger. "There were probably about fifty people involved in the Tunnel Kid scene in 1987, 1988," James St. James says. After the *New York* magazine cover, the number swelled to several hundred. Trash TV swooped. The Club Kids would appear on *Geraldo*, for instance, no fewer than four times, and each appearance would create more Club Kids from attention-hungry waifs in the hinterland.

Some have studied the parallels between rise and fall of hemlines and the Dow Jones. Here, too, an iron skeleton can be discerned beneath the froufrou. It happened that Black Monday. The market collapse of October 19, 1987, was followed by a recovery, but then lean times began in earnest, and it was just when the mood seemed glummest that surfaces began to glitter. The supermodels were conjured up, for one. "The supermodel thing happened immediately after the market crash," says Michael Gross, who has written extensively about the business. "That phemonenon began when Elite Paris began to market Christie (Turlington), Linda (Evangelista) and Naomi (Campbell) together in 1990, 1991. The bottom fell out of the fashion business so the models became the magnetic core of attention."

The cult of the drag queen flowered in orchidaceous mimicry of the cult of the supermodel. "There's always been drag. Divine was just beginning to make breakthroughs when she died. And that was already well after the Warhol superstar period," says Michael Musto. "So there were all these sputterings. But America was ready for it. The gay culture had come to the forefront, directly as a result of AIDS. It came to fruition in about 1990. RuPaul, singing 'Supermodel.' And then Madonna, with the voguing. Then there was *Paris Is Burning*."

"Voguings," of course, were the burlesqued catwalk routines that had first begun in the drag queen section of jail on Riker's Island. *Paris* was the drag documentary. "Everything happened at once," Musto says. The Club Kid cult included.

Another way of reading it is this. "Real" celebrities were now increasingly wary of the appetites they were feeding, and the relentless machinery of surveillance that had grown up, and they were increasingly remaining in their private reservations. But the hunger for visible celebrities in clubland was as demanding as ever, Hence, the Club Kids.

The Club Kids also made a strategic alliance with another subculture, drag queens. Drag icons, like Divine and Joey Arias, had always featured in nightlife, but somewhat on the fringe. The Club Kids made them central. Their costumery began moving toward shock, the taboo.

The Club Kids weren't all kids. Disco 2000 party hosts would include not just such temporary Alig favorites as Clara the Carefree Chicken (who wore a chicken costume), Lizzerd Souffle, and Kenny Kenny, but such relative oldsters as the demi-star Susan Anton, Sylvia Miles, and the Baroness Sherry. The parties were inventive in their themes, throbbing with music and light, powered by ingestion of drugs. Manuel Toledano, a young Spaniard, a film student at NYU, says, "Michael hired twenty, twenty-five people, and everybody had a personality well defined.

"Michael was aware it was important. He put out Disco 2000 trading cards, and each one was a character. James St. James is the Man with a Thousand Faces. Keoki was the Superstar DJ, who goes to the club in a limo, but can't afford to pay his phone bill. Michael himself was the Egomaniac. It was a complete orgy, where everything was allowed." Toledano began writing the script for a movie. He called it *Shampoo Horns*, for the games infants play with their hair in a bathtub. Quickly, and with Peter Gatien watching from the shadows, everybody, including kids from the boroughs, and from out of state, were falling all over themselves to shell out $30 to be part of the action. Limelight was, for the first time, white-hot.

In May 1992 Gatien acquired the shuttered Tunnel. The artist Kenny Scharf put together a VIP room, the Cosmic Cavern. It had lurid fake fur on the walls, amoeboid metal and vinyl seats, transparent columns with luminous bubbles rising through liquid walls of lava lamps like reptile brains in motion, and pumpkin-sized light bulbs that spat interior forked lightning. It was not, of course, wildly different from what Scharf had done at Palladium—"Peter has never had an original idea in his life," an associate says acerbically—but it looked pretty good anyway.

Work on the club was still under way when Ian Schrager called Arthur Weinstein to tell him about a promising site, the former Minsky's burlesque theater on Forty-seventh Street just off Times Square. Weinstein, who was then working for Gatien at Limelight, took him there. Gatien took that over, too, and hired Serge Becker and Eric Goode, who were already working on the Tunnel, to design the new place. The Tunnel had opened early in 1993. The new place, Club USA, cost $8 million and opened in December 1992, with decor that included a giant slide, a Thierry Mugler Room, and mannequins decked out in S&M apparel in glass vitrines.

In 1992, Gatien also bought Palladium, which had been in a long-drawn-out decline. "It had turned into a Spanish dance club. Do you remember the lambada?" Kelly Cutrone says. "The reopening was my birthday party. Debbie Harry sang." The landlord's bankruptcy had closed Club USA, but Gatien simply focused on finding other spaces to develop. He was in a remarkable situation. The plans for a superclub in the Paramount had died with Steve Rubell. Ian Schrager was in the hotel business. Au Bar was a money spinner for Howard Stein, but it never came within a whisker of being The Joint. Mark Fleischman owned Tatou, a cabaret-cum–supper club on East Fiftieth Street, and a club in Los Angeles. Eric Goode was in the restaurant business. Arthur Weinstein was doing the lights at Limelight. Frank Roccio was deep into smack. Nell's was Nell's, and Maurice Brahms was beavering away in the shadows, but Peter Gatien was what Jerry Brandt had called the "Grand Man." The least considered of the Nightlords had become the biggest. Ever.

Gatien's private life had been transformed, too. Until the end of the eighties he had lived on Central Park West with his second wife, with whom he had a young son, and usually with his two daughters from his first marriage, Jennifer and Amanda. His relationship with Claire O'Connor had also been exceptionally close, though sexless. Indeed, in 1987 he gave her away in marriage to the singer Adam Bomb. With a touch of the insouciance that sometimes lightened his ungiving demeanor he wore a rhinestone-studded eye patch for the affair.

In 1990, though, Gatien had met a woman, Alessandra Kobayashi. She was twenty. Until recently she had lived on the demesne of Rocky Aoki, owner of the Benihana chain, in Tenafly, New Jersey. One of her jobs there was managing Aoki's team of hot-air balloonists. Peter Gatien told Frank Owen, a reporter for the *Voice*, that he and Alessandra had met when her brother applied for a bartending job, but Aoki himself said to another female friend that it was Alessandra herself who wanted to work at the club. "She was spending more and more time in the city," the restaurant magnate sighed.

Ambiguity has always hovered around Kobayashi. For a while, she claimed that the wealthy Aoki was her father. Indeed, the "brother" she had spoken of to Owen actually was Aoki's son. Aoki ultimately had his publicist send out a release denying a blood relationship, but Kobayashi had been part of his broader family, and Aoki hasn't wholly forgotten her. A friend who visited Aoki's mansion in mid-1996 saw that there were still photographs of her there, and a bathrobe with ALESSANDRA lettered on the back.

Claire O'Connor duly left Limelight. So too did Fred Rothbell-Mista. "My marriage to Peter ended well. Fred's ended badly," she says dryly. Gatien's real marriage also splintered. In 1993, he and Alessandra had a son, Xander, and he made her president of Palladium. She put what had been mostly a cash business onto paper, put Gatien on a stringent budget, and made Palladium the most profitable of all the Gatien clubs. This, although she was a remote presence in the nightclub business that she had entered with enthusiasm, and distrustful of the nocturnal denizens whose company Gatien so enjoyed, and most particularly of Michael Alig. She made herself thoroughly unpopular, but put the business onto a sound footing. Now every smidgen of work was papered over. Or so it seemed. The empire was not just the biggest ever, but the most professional.

In December 1993, Scott Covert, an artist, ran across Victor Hugo. Hugo, Halston's former paramour, the notorious livewire of Nightworld, had AIDS, and was sleeping in the park at Twenty-second Street. He had been staying in the Chelsea Hotel, but had left to live on the street after running out of money. "You know those box seats they have in the lobby? He had his things in there. Different changes of clothing and stuff," Covert says.

Halston had treated Hugo well, Covert says, leaving him several million dollars, and the Halston estate had been fairly openhanded too. "They gave him more money. They gave him money not to write a book. He went nuts. He went through it all," Covert says. "None of his old friends from Studio were talking to him. So I asked him to come and stay with me. Then he got sick. Then he started dying. He stayed three months . . . four months . . . we were together for Christmas."

Covert was living in the Chelsea, too, and he and another hotel resident, Colleen Weinstein, settled down to do their best for Hugo, who had cancer. Covert took him to Mother Cabrini Hospital when it got too bad for him to handle. "When he died, we didn't have the money to bury him. It took us two weeks to raise the money. We buried him in the cemetery out in East Hampton. We buried him on Halston's birthday," Scott Covert says.

Scott Covert has himself left Manhattan for the Midwest, where he has inherited some land beside a lake. "I might do a pet cemetery. That might be sort of fun," he says.

Few Nightworlders, of course, would do anything as banal as draw lessons from such dismal endings. That same year, for instance, a shady Indian-born entrepreneur, who was using the title "Prince," was bloodily murdered in an apartment on New York's Park Avenue. "Prince" Teddy had been a lover of Screamin' Rachel, and the media descended. "I was in the *Post*, the *National Enquirer*, the *Globe*," she says. "My friends within the club scene all thought it was really fabulous.

"And you're thinking hmmm! This was my friend, he was murdered. But everybody is like, *oh, wow! Fantastic!* . . . *I read about you here, there. Could you say I knew the prince?* . . . Everybody wanted to be involved. We were doing parties about it. We had a great memorial service in the chapel at Limelight." Screamin' Rachel went into therapy, and wrote a pop song with a "house" beat about her tragedy, but failed to crack the top forty.

Drugs were increasingly rife. Ecstasy was being cut with anything from cocaine to heroin—cute code name: "H-Bombs"—and heroin itself was making its umpteenth comeback. Cocaine had never gone away, and there was a new killer thrill, ketamine, a colorless liquid used by veterinarians for such chores as tranquilizing racehorses. Baked to a powder, it could be inhaled, and had the entertaining effect of metamorphosing users to zombies. It had the street name Special K, but it was not as yet illegal.

The drugs played into a new mood. "When Disco 2000 opened, the Club Kids were really cartoony, really playful," says the photographer Tina Paul. "There were stuffed animals and clowns. Then it went into a dark period."

"It's like the beauty in horror," the Club Kid Kenny Kenny told a reporter.

"We were all trying to outshock one another," James St. James says. "I would paint my face white, and splash blood all over me, and glue bugs over my face, and carry a butcher knife around, and the next week there would be thirty little kids from New Jersey doing the same thing. And then we would all laugh. And we would have to come up with something that would top *that*."

Sources of inspiration included the British performance artist Leigh Bowery. "The bruises came from Leigh Bowery," James St. James says. "We all started having oozing sores on our faces. Leigh was the Club Kid god. He was the one who outdid everybody. He grossed out all of us. He used to do his enema act. The next day, everybody would send their dry-cleaning bills to the club. We all loved Leigh. Michael would fly Leigh over at the drop of a hat. And pay him an exorbitant amount of money, just to show up, and be fabulous. And show the kids how to do it. He was just the sickest puppy of all time."

Well, Michael Alig was coming up on the inside track there. "Leigh was like Quentin Crisp," St. James says. "If you're going to be shocking, you had better make everybody feel comfortable. You have to make sure nobody is scared of you and everybody loves you. That's where Michael and I differ. I used to get very upset with his obnoxious antics. Giving people glasses of vomit. How many nights have I turned around and Michael has been peeing on my leg? Or I'll say, Michael, I need a drink, and he'll hand me a glass of urine, or something. It's not very much fun. It's more fun to read about in a column the next week."

Peter Gatien's role was a curious one. He was the watcher from the sidelines or the wallflower at the orgy, to use Nora Ephron's phrase, and he seemed to inhale energy off the giddy antics. "Peter has always been a very hard guy to put a finger on emotionally," Kelly Cutrone says. "He reminded me of Andy. He seemed like somebody who was really together. But he had a lot of really sick people around him.

"He was very, very controlling. He was like the king on the throne, and you were the jester. And then he would decide if he was going to pay you or not. He would sit there. Right? And there would be that eye thing going on. Right? And there would be every freak and their brother there. Even then, when I was a little out of my mind, I would think: How can this guy have this going on around him all day? I didn't understand control and power in the sense of what it means to be a voyeur.

"Michael Alig and Fred Rothbell-Mista and Steven Lewis and the others would sit there and fight. And Peter would just sit there. And at a certain point, he would just go . . . like this"—she flapped a hand—"and that meant it was time for you to go . . ."

The space that had housed Studio 54 had gone through various permutations since the retreat of Mark Fleischman. It had been run by Hasidic Jews. It had been this, it had been that, but in Nightworld terms it had been strictly nowhere. That it became a contender again was largely because Peter Stringfellow, a London club owner with a hectic explosion of yellow hair, had fallen on his face while trying to run a fancy club in New York.

"I closed Stringfellow's during the recession. It went into Chapter Eleven," Peter Stringfellow says. "Then I brought back into New York the all-girl cabaret club. I turned it into a topless club. That was a phenomenal success. But I sold it. I was under pressure from the IRS."

The new owner was Lebanese. He was named Salah Izzedin. He was not a stranger to Manhattan—he had been a partner in Uva Hardin's model agency, Ten—and he was far from a stranger to topless clubs. According to his business card, at least, he was an executive with a public company called Casino Royale, and he would claim to be involved with successful strip clubs in Texas and Mexico City. Now Manhattan.

"Salah did a deal with a guy called Brian Travis," Stringfellow says. They took on the old Studio 54 club. They renamed the place Studio 54. They relaunched it as a nightclub-cum–strip club, but their plans were much more ambitious. "The whole idea was to put 54 and Stringfellow's on the stock market. As a combination," Stringfellow says. "The beginning of a Girl Empire." Peter Stringfellow remained aboard as a consultant, Rubell-Schrager style.

It was visionary, in its way. New York was going to be like Paris. It was going to be the Naughty nineties, part 2, with the gloriously reborn Studio 54 functioning as a Toulouse-Lautrec-ready Crazy Horse Saloon. What Izzedin had not allowed for was this: Dallas and Mexico City were fresh markets, but Manhattan was already up to its neck, so to speak, in toplessness, and there was barely a flicker of interest in their plan. Travis and Izzedin fell out, the deal fell apart, and the Lebanese entrepreneur was left holding the husk that had been Studio 54. Just what to do with it—that was something else.

Peter Gatien was approached. Naturally.

"Everything evolves," Gatien told me at the time. "Music has splintered so much. The day of the large club with one large room ended a lot of years ago." No deal. Mark Fleischman also met with Izzedin. "He was very sleazy, and dead broke. He wanted to sell me Studio. Again," Fleischman says. No deal there either.

One day Colleen Weinstein got a call from Maurice Brahms. "He had a deal, and he really wanted me involved," Colleen says. "Couldn't tell me the location until the day of the meeting. Okay? He said, 'Top secret! Right? I'll call you on that day and I'll let you know where.' "

Brahms telephoned again. "So he told me. It was in the old Studio 54. Top secret. 'You can't tell Arthur!'

"I can't even tell Art?"

"That's who you *really* can't tell."

"I went up there. Maurice was there with Errol Wetson," Colleen says, one of the self-styled progenitors of Studio 54. "Errol wanted to take over the place. He was working out a deal with Salah Izzedin. He wanted to bring it back. He wanted to do this, he wanted to do that . . . in the meantime, there was Errol . . . Maurice . . . me . . . a bartender . . . a girl answering the phones . . . and a girl gyrating and stripping away onstage . . ."

She laughed convulsively. "It was in the afternoon. And I think there was one guy, literally one guy in a chair, in the audience. There was no one there, right? But it was all hush-hush. We had to talk backstage. Backstage was three wooden steps up to the main stage. And there were the girl's props. Like some kind of old wooden bathtub, and a shower stall. One of those metal shower stalls. It was kind of a little decrepit. And some of those fluffy drag queen feather boas. That was where we had to talk.

"Errol said, 'Colleen, what do you want to do?' I said, 'What do you mean, what do I want to do? What do *you* want to do?'

"Maurice had told me he was going to get everybody there and Errol was going to bring in the money. Then Errol was going, *'Maurice, Maurice! We don't need any money. We don't need to do much!'* Errol literally took me through every inch of the space, and told me how he was going to move the two couches that were upstairs in the bar to where the rest rooms were. He was going to move them to these two points downstairs. Because they were just in the wrong place. The furniture was just . . . in the wrong place. If we rearranged it, it would make a tremendous difference. This girl was still stripping onstage. I thought I was in the Twilight Zone. And then Errol missed the step and tumbled down the three stairs, and fell on his head, and continued the meeting. I said, 'Errol, you can't just move furniture around. What's going on here?' Even Maurice is quiet. What can I say? I don't think I've ever seen Maurice really quiet. Except then. At a certain point, at that meeting."

The Maurice Brahms deal was a no-go.

Izzedin, his money hemorrhaging, his entire girl empire foundering, decided extreme measures were necessary if Studio 54 was to be what it had been: a cover-up. In the fall of 1994, he approached a duo of party promoters, Michael Ault and David Sarner.

Michael Ault is from a blue book background and grew up in New York and Palm Beach. He gave his first parties in Europe, at clubs in Ibiza and St. Tropez. In 1986, when he was in his early twenties, he threw himself a birthday dinner for a hundred at Annabel's in London. "It wasn't business. It was for my friends," he says. Upon returning to New York, it speedily became business. He worked with Marc Biron, and in 1987 he began throwing parties at Tunnel.

Ault had a job at the Bank of New York but found the people stuffy concerning his other life, particularly if he had been out sick, and a party he had thrown at the time was duly bannered across *Women's Wear Daily*. Things got to the point where a junior partner took him aside and said fretfully, "Your phone volume is twice what mine is. And you're a *trainee*." By then, he had formed a partnership with David Sarner, another New Yorker. "We were hired to produce Comic Relief for HBO," Ault says. "And that was the end of my banking." By the early nineties, Ault and Sarner were heavyweight party promoters among the preps.

"Salah asked us to do something there in addition to the strip operation. So the stripping would run some nights and the club would run others," Ault says. But Ault and Sarner didn't like the piecemeal approach. They thought the time was ripe for a big club again. "The fashion was back, the bell-bottoms and everything," Ault says. "Everyone was wanting Gloria Gaynor. So we convinced them that we would be able to pull off this Studio 54 rebirth. With the music, with the fashion, with some of the old personalities as well. He only gave us two and a half weeks to do it."

The promotional opening party was planned for October 1994. "How many invitations did we send out?" Ault asked.

"Thirty thousand," said Sarner.

"Thirty thousand . . . several colors . . . folded, stuffed, sealed . . ."

"Stuffed with *confetti*," Sarner reminded.

"Confetti," Ault agreed. "For days and days, we had a staff of twenty people, stuffing and sealing. All at $10 an hour. And we had a lot of promoters on board . . . and the ads . . . and the DJ . . . the lighting man . . . security . . . twelve, fourteen security men at $125 each . . ."

The opening was a success. "Six thousand people showed up," Ault says. "There was a Sandra Bernhard show. We had the naked girl on a horse. She was gay. We reconstructed the confetti cannons and the Man in the Moon and the spoon from the old blueprints. We had Gloria Gaynor . . . Vicki Sue Robinson . . ."

"Sister Sledge," Sarner says.

Ault and Sarner next began a face-lift. The basement was a changing room for the strippers. They were going to turn it back into a VIP room. "We were going to call it 'Jerry Hall,'" Sarner says. It seemed like happy nights were there again. Indeed, Ault and Sarner began negotiating for Donna Summer to sing at Studio on Halloween.

I paid Studio an occasional visit for old times' sake and found the silver ball twirling. There was a chorus line of beefy transvestites, blips of crimson and yellow light chased themselves across the rear wall, and semi-dressed urban nymphs would play suggestively with the stripper's poles, but the night I realized that the place was running out of steam was when Michael Ault was reduced to doling out drink tickets one by one.

I handed my own Ault-authenticated drink ticket to a blond woman who looked as though she had done time in Vegas, not on the Strip, but in Glitter Gulch. She eyed it somberly. "I don't think it's any good," she said, but handed it on to a long-haired man, who looked as if he'd just come off a twenty-year road tour with a metal band, who okayed it. I was handed a Heineken, went up to the balconies, and looked down. What had been a shimmering dance floor was sullen and turgid, a Sargasso sea. That was my last time in Studio as a live club.

The Stringfellow deal had left Izzedin with a hefty debt. He was to pay the landlord $150,000 at the beginning of 1995 or forfeit the space. The New Year's Eve party went off well.

By morning, Salah Izzedin was gone. "He grabbed the money, and ran," Michael Ault says. "*They literally ran out of the back door!* The next day, a truck came along and took out all the lighting and the sound system, and put it in a warehouse in New Jersey. Within a couple of days, papers were filed for bankruptcy."

"It has been very . . . meaty," Sarner says.

Neither Ault, Sarner, D'Alessio, nor any of the promoters were paid.

There was a gloomy justice to this, and Michael Ault will cheerfully rail away about the rapacity of promoters, which is as if a Salah Izzedin were to lament the lusts of the flesh. Ault points out that in other cities with a famous nightlife, London, say, or Paris, promoters are insignificant. "People have a couple of clubs that they have had for years, sometimes for decades. And those are the places they go," Ault says. Not so, the novelty-crazed citizens of Manhattan, where the clubs are now at the promoters' mercy. "The problem in New York is that promoters pirate away profits from the door. And we're as much to blame as any of them," Ault says. "So nightclubs have only one source of profit and that's the bar. And clubs can't operate on just the bar. But promoters take your door. They take everything. *They take your firstborn!*"

Ault zeroed in on another, more specific foe: Peter Gatien. "He's the last of the old evil emperors," he says. "The warlords! He runs a classical, feudal operation over there. He knows everything that's going on. Not just in his own clubs, but in everyone else's clubs.

"There were so many dirty tricks. He would call in bomb threats. He would send in fire trucks. In Studio we literally had to hire a security guard to stand all night in front of each fire alarm. Because what he would do is he would send these Club Kids in, they'd pull the fire alarm, and they would clear out the club."

Peter Gatien not only denies such mischief making, but says that he has often himself been the target of such stunts. Still there is no doubt that at the political level he could be the wiliest of strategists. Susan Wagner, formerly an influential pol in the Koch administration, was hired in 1992 to represent him with community boards. He handed over checks to several political campaigns in the city, including that of Rudy Giuliani. In this, he had moved on beyond Schrager and Rubell. "The feeling on the street is that if you open an establishment that affects any of his businesses, he'll see that you are closed," Michael Fesco told me in 1995. "He can call up various cops and cause you problems. And if he can't do that, he'll buy you out."

At the beginning of 1995, Peter Gatien was riding high. The Olympic Committee, aware of his previous record in Atlanta, had asked him to build the official nightclub for the athlete's village. He had put in bids for properties in SoHo and on Forty-second Street. The Forty-second Street club would make him a part of the transformation of one of the most famous city landscapes in the world.

Times Square had long been best known for sleaze, and, like Hollywood and Vine in Los Angeles or London's Piccadilly Circus, it had become a checkpoint for out of towners rather than natives. So squalid and dangerous had the area become that in the early 1980s the city developed an urban renewal plan, designed by Philip Johnson and John Burgee, that would condemn the old theaters and replace them with towers faced with reflective glass. The development was greeted with widespread dismay, and the slump of the real estate market at the end of the decade meant the towers were not going up any time soon, but many of the theaters had been boarded up, and would come down anyway.

The president of the 42nd Street Development Project, Rebecca Robertson, described what she called a "pivotal moment" to Paul Goldberger, cultural editor of *The New York Times*. It was the opening in the spring of 1992 of an outlet of The Gap on the corner of Forty-second Street and Seventh Avenue. "Our retail guys said their numbers were incredible, and suddenly we realized what was possible here," she said. In March 1993, Robert A. M. Stern, the architect, and a board member of the Walt Disney Company, was asked by Michael Eisner, Disney's chairman, to look into the possibility of Disney acquiring a theater on Forty-second Street. Stern showed him around a 1903 Beaux Arts theater, the New Amsterdam, the following morning. Eisner said go.

It took two years, and there was heated criticism at the time, because Disney was given a $26 million low-interest loan and had put only $8 million into the project, but where Disney trod, others poured in, and the result would shortly be a $1.8 billion make-over of Manhattan's leprous and risky "crossroads of America." Paul Goldberger would write, "Disney came to 42nd Street not so much because Disney was ready to become like New York as because New York was ready to become like Disney." That is to say that Rudy Giuliani, who promised "zero tolerance" of lifestyle crimes, planned a Manhattan as family-oriented and spic-and-span as, say, the new Las Vegas.

It was going to be Manhattan as Toon Town, and Peter Gatien planned to run the ultrabrite clubs.

DARK SIDE OF THE MIRROR

26

EARLY IN THE MORNING ON SATURDAY, SEPTEMBER 30, 1995, Limelight was raided by fifty cops. This was the fruit of a two-month investigation by the New York Police Department and the Office of Special Narcotics and it had been hoped that at least thirty dealers would be roped in. As it happened, just three people were busted, one being a Limelight busboy, for the unspectacular crime of selling pot. This simply made the lawmen mad as hell. *New York* magazine later disclosed that a promoter had been circulating a paper with forty names around the crowd in Limelight some hours before the bust. The paper had been headed: IF YOUR NAME IS ON THIS LIST, YOU DON'T WANT TO BE HERE TONIGHT. Limelight was closed. It reopened a week later after Gatien agreed to pay a $35,000 fine, post a bond of $160,000, which would be forfeited if the problem recurred, and hire Kroll Associates, a straight-arrow company, to beef up the security.

The bust certainly made a nonsense of Peter Gatien's fabled clout with the city and the cops, though.

Just what had set the city in motion against his empire? There were many working theories. There had been a newspaper report of a kid being bundled into a taxi after being clubbed into a coma at Palladium. Another youth, from Hanover, New Jersey, had died after a night in Limelight. Supposedly his family had been politically connected, and Governor Kean had personally called Mayor Giuliani. Drugs had been ruled out as a cause of death, though. Probably there had been no single cause, just too many reports of unbridled drug use, and growing violence. What was certain was that Giuliani and the city agencies had again decided to make war on Nightworld, and upon Peter Gatien in particular. That October, the D.A.'s office began an investigation of his cash flow.

Peter Gatien reacted to the increasing heat in his usual way, with a sort of stubborn nonchalance, as though he were a voyeur of his own travails, wallpaper on a particularly unyielding wall. He was always woodenly professional around his clubs. He was never to be seen, rubber-legged on ludes, like Steve Rubell, or dreamily escorting his seventh Stoly, like Arthur Weinstein. "I've never even seen the guy do the occasional line of coke," another Nightworlder says.

Gatien apparently had one fling with a young woman, whose *nom de Club Kid* was Jennytalia. With Alessandra extending her power over Gatien, this ended. Mostly he was aloof. He told the *Voice*'s Frank Owen in October 1995 that he was "the most responsible nightclub operator in town." He said, "I've worked very hard to dispel the stereotypical image of the New York club owner as someone who's a big womanizer, drug taker, and drinker who stiffs everybody and then goes into Chapter Eleven after eighteen months."

This baffled other Nightworlders. "I don't know what he *wants* from the business," Michael Fesco told me, a bit fretfully. Claire O'Connor, who worked for Limelight, says when she first met Gatien he was withdrawn but pleasant. "He was a Canadian in a down jacket. He didn't know anything," she says. Fred Rothbell-Mista, who worked for Limelight in New York from the opening night, believes that Gatien was naïve in his first dealings with other Nightworlders, and that he has resented the way he was taken advantage of ever since. "Steve Rubell enjoyed the party. The money overwhelmed him, but his motivation was the party, I think.

"Peter always wanted to be Steve Rubell. But he hated him, because he could never be him. Because he did not get . . . the party! *He didn't get it!*

Someone like Peter Gatien is a miserable person. Never enjoyed his clubs. He didn't care about meeting celebrities. All he cared about was charging people and making money. He sits in his office the whole time. And he used to say that Rubell ruined the nightlife by giving it away. But I felt that he ruined nightlife. Because money is his god. That's all he cares about. It changed the way things are done."

What Peter Gatien made possible, Rothbell-Mista thinks, was a new de-personalized Nightworld. "In the nineties they opened up all these theme things. Like Planet Hollyood," he says despondently. Celebrities had taken the logical step. They stopped coining money for the Nightlords. They wanted it themselves. Big clubs had simply become money machines. "Money is Peter's god," Rothbell-Mista repeats. "He used to say to me, 'I have no friends. *If anyone mentions my name at the door, I have no friends!'* He has no joy. It's a loveless life."

An austere assessment, and by no means shared by all.

Peter Gatien, whom I found oddly pleasant under intense stress, once said to me, almost jauntily "It's like the old proverb says. 'Beware what you wish for. You may get it.' "

Eva—this is not her name—is blond, with a pale baby face. She works for a Catholic charity and has written social chitchat for magazines that cater to provincial smart sets. She and I have been close, but until she chose to tell me, over several bottles of hot sakè, I was wholly unaware that she had also an interesting other life. She had been, by fits and starts, what some nowadays prissily call a Sex Worker.

In about 1991 a female buddy in another city had called Eva to say she had a friend who was "lonely" and wanted company on his birthday. Eva, who had worked on Seventh Avenue, knew a bunch of available babes, mostly un-super models. She and one of them duly made their way over to the "friend's" apartment. It was on the West Side. A doorman building.

Eva recognized the Nightlord from the door of his club. She had always seen him as a controlled presence, and she was startled to see that he was wearing a sort of rock star toupee and that his nostrils were encrusted with cocaine. They all got undressed, as pro forma, and Eva was concerned to find herself tripping over rubber duckies in the bathroom, and children's toys. "This is someone's home," she said to herself. "Suppose they come back?"

They watched porno movies, but no sex occurred. The Nightlord didn't even seem to have that in mind. She and her friend were paid $200 an hour. To her irritation, he insisted that she take a check. "He said he didn't have any money," she says. The check bounced. She went around and collected on the debt, successfully. But the vibe was bad. "It was like he resented paying," she says. "I always had problems with him. He wasn't a good client. I think he has all this heavy guilt."

The next party Eva catered for the Nightlord was in the Parker Meridien. This time she took six women. He was the only male. Again they all got naked and there were quantities of coke and room service champagne, but again there was no sex, or none involving the Nightlord anyway. "He just wanted his harem around him," Eva says. It went on for two days plus. The women got $2,000 apiece.

The third party was, she thinks, in the Mark on Madison Avenue, and this was the one where he started freebasing. "That made me really uncomfortable," Eva says primly. It went on for three days. At one stage the coke ran out and he went out to get more. He returned with the dealer, a black woman. "I assumed it was a referral. She was lighting his pipe," Eva says. She was startled to find he had found the dealer on the street, and she insisted on cash payments from then on. The woman in charge of disbursements at his club would have to messenger the cash to that night's hotel of choice.

The sporadic blowouts continued. The Nightlord freebased more and more. "He would stay up for three days and he began getting paranoid. It was not a pretty picture," Eva says. "He was hearing things . . . seeing things . . . looking through the curtains . . ." The mood worsened. "It changed when he started bringing the Club Kids," Eva says. "It wasn't a party after that. It was more like a show." More and more also it became a display of raw power. The Nightlord would insist that all the naked and semi-naked people play Scrabble or charades. The Club Kids despised this. They could seldom remember any Scrabble-worthy words and why play charades when your whole life is a sort of charade? There was almost never any sex involving the Nightlord himself. "Somebody who lost at Scrabble might have to give him a blowjob," another orgiast says indifferently.

The Nightlord's wife, who had caught wind of the goings on, started telephoning, and trying to get him to come home. Finally, she arrived, began hammering on the door, and threatened to call security. Eva invited her in. An odd friendship sprang up between

the two. "I love him," the Nightlord's wife said despondently. "He's killing himself."
She made Eva promise to warn her when another party impended.

The next party was in the Presidential Suite of the Four Seasons. Eva called the
Nightlord's wife. "You've betrayed me," the Nightlord told her morosely. He and a
bunch of Club Kids were cutting up pills, popping them, and watching porno, and soon
he was freebasing. Eva remembers that he, she, and the leading Club Kids were soon
lost in an interminable discussion about Catholicism, about their guilt, about their appetite
for decadence. "Meanwhile, these carts were coming in," Eva says. "With bottles of
champagne, four or five at a time, and vodka . . . mixers . . . caviar, and shrimp cock-
tails."

The Nightlord's wife arrived and holed up by herself in a small room. "She was
making sure he wasn't going to jump out of the window," Eva says. "He would walk
out onto the balcony. He was getting very paranoid . . . thinking that things were moving
in the room or that people were spying on him . . . he would go up to the front door
and watch for shadows underneath it." Eva, who likes an occasional line of cocaine, was
induced to try Special K. She quickly felt as bad as she had ever felt in her whole life.

That was the end of it. For Eva, anyway.

It was March 1996. Arthur Weinstein was ruminating about Nightworld
in his room at the Chelsea Hotel, when his tone changed, his voice dropped.
"Something really weird happened in the club," he began, then hesitated, and
became reticent. "I can't talk about it," he decided. Some time later, though,
he said that he supposed it was okay to tell the story so long as he didn't tell
me the names. His manner was so uncharacteristically hesitant that I was all
attention.

A man had come into the downstairs bar at Limelight about a week before,
Weinstein said. Weinstein said the man looked "weird." Looking weird
enough to be noticed in the Limelight bar is *special*, so much so that Weinstein
had asked if the guy were okay. He volunteered that he had a "problem." The
problem was that he had got into a fight with a drug dealer. His roommate/
lover had arrived in the middle and had hit the dealer on the head with a
hammer. They had then finished the job by shooting him up with Drano.
"Drano!" Weinstein repeated, marveling.

The corpse had been in a bath for four days. *That* was the problem.

Weinstein heard him out. After he had left Weinstein told the doormen never to let the guy back in again.

He was back in the bar four days later, though, and aggrieved at the attempt to exclude him. "How did you solve your, uh, problem," Weinstein asked.

"We cut him up and dropped the body into the East River," the guy said.

Could this be true? Weinstein, a man cynical even about cynicism, was clearly a believer. I took to reading the metro items in the *News* and the *Post* with great attention. Nothing. Then gossip began surfacing. Astonishingly, it suggested that Michael Alig, supremo of the Club Kids, had been involved with a killing and dismembering, and that the victim had been Angel, the Club Kid and drug dealer. The rumor first saw print as a blind item in Michael Musto's column in the *Voice*. Then an item headlined PETER GATIEN'S LOST ANGEL? appeared in *New York* magazine's "Intelligencer" column. The reporter, John Connolly, wrote that Alig had been questioned by the police. The item quoted Alig saying he had "heard that his hand is in a freezer somewhere in Staten Island. I don't really know, but I'm going to Europe this weekend. There's nothing left for me here.'"

Alig was nowhere to be found. The mention of Europe was intriguing. Another of the swarm of rumors had Alig saying he was going to see Rudolf in Germany, that the Mephistophelian clubman was going to "save" him. I had spoken with Rudolf just a couple of months before in Los Angeles, where he was managing the Century Club for Mark Fleischman. I called his home number there. His recorded message ran: "Well, the rats are still jumping off the ship and sharks want to eat them. But the truth is that both are very sick and tired of this game and they are looking for better things to do." Rudolf has always had rather a German sense of humor. I left a message and rang off.

Peter Gatien's only public comment about the affair was that he had nothing but "compassion" for his former aide. I called Gatien. Are things getting tougher in the club business? I asked. Yes. Back in the days of Studio 54, club operators "were really pushing the envelope," Gatien said. They got away with it. He added "There's definitely a lot more pressure today from community boards and from police. There's been a number of task forces set up that incorporate everything from Consumer Affairs to the Buildings Department to the Fire Department to Narcotics. To regulate underage drinking, whatever, you name it.

"It's a cover-all task force whose job is to go after . . . well, I don't know 'go after,' but to monitor clubs. Whereas in the earlier part of the eighties, the police attitude was basically that if you didn't have violence, if they weren't called three or four times a week, there was not a whole lot of pressure on the operator." Gatien, who was presumably under considerable pressure, sounded emotionless. It was like listening to an auditor reading a company report. We agreed to meet at the Tunnel at two in the afternoon on May 16.

Before dawn in the morning on May 15, Gatien was rousted out of bed by four DEA agents. Other squads of agents made citywide arrests of more than twenty other characters on an array of drug charges, including Steve Lewis, the former manager of the World, and a bunch of others identified both by birth names and street names, like "Baby Joe," "Flip," and "Victor Extraordinaire."

Arthur Weinstein, who was not among them, called that evening from the Chelsea. He was filled with a dark and glittering hilarity. "Did you get to-morrow's *Times?*" he demanded. "What are you waiting for? It's one of those classics. And they've got a *picture*. The pictures were taken when they were doing some stories about Peter, when he was a good boy. You know, his best angle is from the left. This is when you know you're in the soup. When you pick up the Metro section and you're the headline . . . U.S. CLAIMS TWO NIGHTCLUBS ARE DRUG BAZAARS . . ."

He read passages of the piece. Gatien was being accused of participating in a ring—"a multimillion-dollar ring," inevitably—that was smuggling Ecstasy in from Holland. "It's a feeding frenzy," Weinstein said. "Steve Lewis called twenty minutes ago, and he didn't realize that he actually made *The New York Times*. I was able to tell him that." The *New York Post* had weighed in with a quote from U.S. Attorney Zachary Carter to the effect that "the drugs were the honey trap that attracted young people to the clubs in the first place."

I asked Weinstein if I should phone him back. "No. I won't be here. I'll be at the Limelight. I do have a job to go to, you know. Meanwhile we have got every TV station in front of the club. I tell you it's one way to get the club going again . . ."

It so happened that Rudolf called me minutes later. He was in Hamburg. "So what's happening, man?" he asked in warily hipsterish fashion.

He had not known about the misadventures of Michael Alig, or about Peter Gatien, and reacted with perfectly mundane shock for a moment or so but quickly recovered. "Heh-heh-heh!" he chortled. "Now I feel like coming back to New York. Now you've got some action. For the last few years it has been asleep. Well, it sounds excellent to me, all this!"

Peter Gatien's bail was set at $1 million, and he was put in a jail in Brooklyn. He spent several days there while the bail was being raised. "I was offered cocaine my first evening there," he told me with his usual sardonic impassivity after his release.

The genesis of the Gatien bust proved to have been convoluted. In October 1995 a couple of undercover DEA agents, Bob Gagne and Matt Germanowski, bought drugs from two Israelis. In conversation, the Israelis identified the Gatien clubs as major distribution outlets for their wares. In November 1995 a nineteen-year-old was arrested for passing counterfeit money in a New Jersey mall. Rather than finger the supplier, he promised to get DEA agents an entree into the drug underground of the clubs. He was handed over to Gagne and Germanowski, who enthusiastically got themselves up in drag and set to infiltrating Gatien's sector of clubland.

The affidavit they submitted to support their arrest warrants records their adventures. There is some surreal comedy about this document, as when the agents were in the Tunnel and "entered a room denoted as the 'Police Room,' which is decorated with 'police' wallpaper, signs on the walls indicating that drug use is illegal and police barricades, which . . . were used at the time of the September 30, 1995, NYPD efforts to close the Limelight nightclub. The undercover agents were granted access to the room by a male transvestite known as 'Gravity.' " And so on.

Peter Gatien was mostly remarkable by his absence from the report, with this singular exception. "Your deponent and other D.E.A. agents conducted periodic surveillance of the third floor office of the Tunnel nightclub . . . from the third floor of the building across the street." They claim to have seen Gatien "sniffing an object in his hand. Your deponent believes that Gatien was sniffing cocaine throught a device known as a 'one-hitter.' " I have checked out this office. Gatien's desk is in an alcove, utterly invisible from the other side of the street. I suppose he could have been swanning around his office, doing drugs in full view of the windows. But, at work anyway, Gatien has always had the reputation of being drug-free.

That December, the two Israelis were busted. That December also the city of New York began investigating the Palladium's finances. In February, DEA agents arrested four people for selling cocaine in Limelight, and fifteen IRS agents raided Palladium and carted off documents. The untouchable Peter Gatien was now a target of both the feds and the NYPD, and the subject of a tax probe, which is doubtless where his greater vunerability lies.

Michael Alig checked out of a rehab in Colorado and returned to Manhattan in September 1996. I went around to see him in the Chelsea Hotel. Jaunty was not the word. He was talking about rehab and methadone while writing out entrance passes and drink tickets for a party he was throwing that night. It was to be at an instant club, which he was thinking of calling, rather pointedly, ILL EAGLE. Suddenly, he made a fist and began snuffling up Special K. "Give me a bump," another Club Kid pleaded. Alig obliged, then inhaled another hillock of the drug.

"Michael, I thought you weren't using," I said.

"Heroin. I'm not using heroin," he said patiently, as though I were extremely dense.

He, James St. James, and I went to grab something to eat on Eighth Avenue before party time. They were both full of both the Angel killing and of Peter Gatien's troubles, but spoke of them as if they were quasi-fictional, scenes from some movie that had not yet been fully edited, and in which Michael Alig and Peter Gatien were both playing important parts.

"They're going to get Peter," Alig said.

Rumor had Alig cooperating with the feds. Was this the case?

"What? Turn on Peter Gatien? Michael Alig!" James St. James said.

"Michael Alig?" Michael Alig said. "How can he stand to look at himself in the morning? How can he stand to see his face in the mirror?"

But Gatien, they said, had condoned the drug traffic in his clubs rather than controlling it. "He wants full, happening clubs," St. James said. "Bring in the drug dealers!"

As for Ecstasy, though, Alig spoke of it with disdain. "Ecstasy was for the eighties. The line was always that Ecstasy was a reality drug. But Ecstasy was a fake reality," Alig said. "You thought you were happy but it was just a cover-up, you understand? You felt happy while you were on it, but in reality it wasn't happiness at all.

"K is nineties. K is reality. When you're down the K-Hole that is reality. Do you understand what I'm saying? All the stuff you don't want to face? It forces you to face whatever has happened to you."

"Who wants that?" James St. James shrieked.

"K is reality," Alig repeated doggedly. "That's very nineties, I think."

Out in the street, insanity returned. Alig passed a restaurant he identified as one of the haunts of the departed Angel, and peered anxiously through the window.

"Look! They're looking at me!" he said.

"Of course they're going to look," St. James said. "If they see you jumping up and down, pointing, and making faces like a monkey."

"I did it!" Michael Alig screamed, full throttle. "I did it! I couldn't stand him anymore. HE BORED ME! I KILLED HIM!"

They scampered gleefully back to the Chelsea. Why did you say all that, I asked. Was it a joke?

"I don't think it's a joke," Alig said, suddenly sobered.

I asked what happened to Angel Melendez.

"He was a drug dealer," Alig said, his voice gone faraway. "Drug dealers disappear . . ."

Angel disappeared from the conversation. In inconvenient actuality, he turned up, though. His body, which had been in the morgue for several months, mislabeled as Asian, was ID'd on a slab in Staten Island. The City Medical Examiner's Office made an announcement on November 2, 1996. Angel's legs had been cut off and he had been throttled. Also, though the announcement did not specify this, his hands had been cut off, and he had been injected with "a toxic substance." So the killing had been very much in the manner Alig had described to several people.

In the weeks that followed, though, there were no arrests.

Michael Rodriquez, an investigator with the Manhattan D.A.'s office, who, according to the *Voice,* was working from a secret location above an art gallery in SoHo, did call Screamin' Rachel, and asked to interview her. She told Michael Alig about the call. "He had the federal DEA people call me," she told me. "They said pay no attention to the New York D.A. Because we have taken over this case.

"The next time the D.A. calls, just say he is harassing you, and you are talking to us. We are Michael's friends. We seek to protect Michael."

So Alig's latest straight middle-aged mentors, heirs to Rudolf, Maurice Brahms, and Peter Gatien, were none other than the DEA. Screamin' Rachel was told the DEA were building a big case. "They said they followed the case from here to Amsterdam," she says. They speculated also that perhaps it was Peter Gatien or even Alessandra who had had Angel done in. "They are thinking maybe he would want to discredit Michael. Michael is their strongest link," she says. "They are saying they believe Michael. They are trying to help Michael." They also told her not to worry overmuch if Michael Alig were arrested. "Don't be upset," she quoted them. "I should just realize that they've been doing their best . . ." It all seemed rather simple. Why should the DEA let a small-time dismemberment stand between them and nabbing the Last Nightlord?

Soon Michael Alig was blithely giving a party every Friday in the Mirage, a club on West Fifty-sixth and the river. This was at the suggestion of another of his straight middle-aged supporters, Maurice Brahms. "Michael couldn't commit murder. No way," Brahms said. Brahms, like Anita Sarko, like many nightpeople, simply couldn't imagine that the mercurial Club Kid could have committed such a brutal act. It must be a stunt, a gothic joke, like the times that he would show up at parties wearing a neckbrace, or the time he had showed up on a Geraldo Rivera show, "Klub Kidz '94," made up with purplish-green bruises on his forehead and on both sides on his neck.

Geraldo defined the look on camera as "accident-victim drug-addict" and asked Alig what the look was about.

"I guess I'm bored. I don't know," Alig said, and shrugged.

Geraldo said, "I love the bruises. The bruises have a nice—"

"Do they look real?" Alig shot in, with hyper-real sprightliness, arching his throat around for the audience's benefit.

At this moment, the camera cut to an audience member, Angel, who was wearing a red vinyl cap, blood-red wings, and a gleaming grin. No wonder many thought the "disappearance" was a stunt, perhaps a promotion for a new club, and that Angel would feature at the opening.

Nonetheless, doubts were settling in as the weeks passed, partly because Alig was forever making tauntingly provocative comments, like "Do you know the difference between me and a murderer? I haven't been caught," but not least because Johnny Melendez, Angel's brother, had arrived in New York and was forlornly looking for information. But Michael Alig, apparently convinced that his cooperation against Peter Gatien was buying him immunity, was braving it out. With brilliant effrontery, he called his club-within-the-club at Mirage the Honey Trap, profiting from the phrase used to attack Gatien's clubland by U.S. Attorney Zachary Carter.

The parties had an odd feel to them all the same. The scandal guaranteed plenty of press, and a lot of unbridled gossip, and there would be a slew of Club Kids there in all their finery, but the parties were pervaded by the drear feeling that they were just reruns, and that a whole culture had been brought back from the dead by a death. Peter Frank, who had come to one of them with Arthur Weinstein, was half enraged and half amused. "He's an accused murderer. He did it! Look! Nobody cares!" Frank said as "We Can Dance! We Can Dance!" came over the sound system.

"And the DEA are supporting this little freak with his Lewis Carroll stories because they think he can give them Peter Gatien. Steve and Ian broke the law. They stole. But Peter Gatien is a businessman. They're prosecuting him for lifestyle crimes. It's disgusting. Do you know what I think happened here? I think it's because Limelight was a church. I think he should have given up the church a long time ago . . . "

The final Honey Trap was peculiarly drear. Its bizarre high point was the arrival of Screamin' Rachel to promote her new single, "Give Me Freedom/Murder in Clubland." It was, at least, newsy. Sample lines run:

THE D.A.'S ON MY PHONE, GOT TAPS ON MY PHONE.
THE ONE-EYED DON'S IN JAIL, AND HOPES TO MAKE BAIL . . .

Michael Alig was delighted.

The party shambled on, with a whirring and stuttering of cameras, and interviewers scribbling. The shamelessness of Studio 54 had been, I think, a excellent thing, in many respects. There had been an opening up, and some hitherto dark places had been flooded with light. Everything evolves, though, and this was where that fine freedom had ended.

But the Honey Trap was closed down that week. It was over a dispute about money. Of course.

Alig telephoned me in late November. His manic recent plans had included starting a glossy magazine of his own or, maybe, moving to California. Now he was full of his Next Parties. Indeed, he proposed giving a party for "my generation and your generation." I told him that many of my generation were dead. "Mine too," Alig said brightly. It sounded as though the party was already blazing away in his head.

Early on Thursday, December 5, Alig was arrested in a motel in Toms River, New Jersey, where he had taken shelter with his twenty-two-year-old lover, and hauled back to Manhattan. His roommate Robert Riggs, whose club name was "Freeze," was picked up later that morning and invited to "answer a few questions." Freeze, a twenty-eight-year-old milliner, whose hats had been displayed in Barney's and shown in *Vogue*, could have refused. Instead, he accompanied the D.A.'s investigators, including Michael Rodriguez, to the Wooster Street office of the D.A.'s anticorruption unit. There, without asking for a lawyer, he made a full confession, both in writing and on video, to the motive for Angel's murder, a tawdry argument about money, and the way that he and Michael Alig had chopped up the body.

Finally it became clear how Alig had solved the "problem" he had complained to Arthur Weinstein about. They had packaged the body well in duct tape—if there's one thing a Club Kid can do, it's dress up a body—and put it in a crate. They had then hailed a cab, driven to the Hudson River, and chucked it in.

Alig and Riggs were both put into the gay block of Riker's Island. Alig was soon savagely beaten up there by four inmates, who took away his one link to the clubland he had ruled, his phone card. Most believe his attackers were Hispanics, avenging Angel, but one fierce clubland joker said, "Perhaps they were guys he wouldn't let into Disco 2000." In the wake of his arrest, he was said to be going cold turkey there. One last go at rehab.

Peter Gatien and Peter Gatien's clubs, and the waning force of Club Kids who had frequented them, were, of course, not the whole of New York's Nightworld. A slew of "lounges" sprang up in the mid-nineties, places like Spy, Wax, and Chaos, places that were for walking around and talking, or just sitting, not dancing and drugging; places, in short, for grown-ups. Jackie 60, which became Mother, remained a fine haunt for freakishness. In mid-December, Steve Lewis showed his face again. "It's a whole sick sandwich and everybody wants a bite," he had told me, dolorously, after being indicted in the Gatien bust. Now he popped up fronting at Life, a small dance palace in a former jazz club, the Village Gate, on Bleecker Street.

It would be easy, but wrong, to put too much symbolic weight on one horrid crime. Not everybody who has become reality-impaired through multiple drug combinations has done a murder. But some connection can be made. "Michael was trying to achieve a Sodom and Gomorrah, but it became too decadent, and there was no glamor to it anymore," Lincoln Palsgrove III, one of the doorpeople at the hot club Twilo, told Michael Musto in the immediate wake of Alig's arrest. "There was no sense of responsibility like Studio 54." An amazing remark; partly true.

"I had a great reputation, both as a club owner and a serious business person," Peter Gatien told me in his office at the Tunnel. "Dealing with the Forty-second Street area is a concerted effort of the state, the city and whatever. They would never entertain me as a tenant anymore. Not a chance. Even if . . . even *when* I'm vindicated. My life has been turned upside down and sideways."

This was true, but spoken flatly, without any (fairly justifiable) whining. One November night I had accompanied him on his club tour. He moved lithely and with speed, the unnecessarily long cord that secured his eyepatch snaking out behind him like the tail of a black kite. In August, cocaine charges had been added to Gatien's indictment. If he felt pressure from what he is facing—an (improbable) jail sentence of twenty years, an (unlikely) million-dollar fine, and (very possible) ruin—he showed no sign of it. Indeed, he was as impassive as when his empire was at its peak. As Claire O'Connor put it, "Peter loves trouble. He loves problems. They make him come alive. He's never been happier."

Suddenly, Gatien mumbled a few pro forma words, vamoosed off to one side, and disappeared. He had retreated back to his office. "Who was that?" a young woman asked me, curiously. "Doesn't he have something to do with this place?" She seemed to be the only one who had even noticed him: doubtless just what he wanted.

FINALE

ALL TOMORROW'S PARTIES

*IAN SCHRAGER HAS BEEN THE SURVIVOR. HOTELS, he once said, are in
certain important ways nightclubs for grown-ups. "When you're in
the nightclub business, you have no product. You just have
magic," he told a reporter. "That production you create . . . that
cachet. So when Steve and I went into the hotel business, where
we had a real commodity that people wanted, we didn't rely on
that. Our approach wasn't, well, we have a bed. Our approach was
we want to make it something magical."*

*Never wholly at ease in Nightworld, Ian Schrager has left
it with relief, if some ambivalence. "If they had a dance floor
in this hotel, it could be a nightclub," he said to a reporter
of the Mondrian Hotel in Los Angeles. "It's getting closer and
closer and closer." Steve Rubell would, of course, be in Nightworld, were he still around. "Steve's story wasn't a sad story,"
says Don Rubell. "Like Halston's wasn't a sad story. None of these
stories were sad. These people didn't end up living happily ever after. But I think none of them would have traded. That's the essence of it.*

*"Ian and Steve's comeback was a grown-up comeback. Studio
54 was the moment of youth. That was their magic moment. What
Steve wanted out of life, he achieved. He didn't achieve the lon-
gevity of his desire, but he achieved his desire. They all lived in a
dreadful fear of growing back into their roots, and they didn't.
They wanted this energy, and this fame, and this freedom. And
they got it. For a time."*

*The human lights that burned so bright in clubland have
mostly, as is the way of things, gone out or dimmed. Certain Studio 54 veterans in particular seem to look back on their heyday
with alarm. The people who made the wheels of clubland turn are
of tougher stuff. "I sort of want to be in Europe for a while," Rudolf said after moving back to Germany. "Hamburg is practical.
Also, it has the greatest red-light district in the world. So it keeps
me busy. But I'm going to Paris for a while. Then to Lisbon. I think*

it can be the new Spain. It may offer interesting opportunities to people who are on the ball.''

Actually, he got no farther than Paris, where he began preparing to open up a new boîte, possibly near Les Halles.

''The club scene keeps going in phases . . . cycles . . . there's an upside and a downside,'' Michael Alig had told me in a rare moment of temperate lucidity. ''The upside may be a great party . . . the opening of a club. Everybody says, 'Oh, it's never going to get better than this! We should enjoy it while we can. This is it!'

''Then you have a club closing . . . the closing of Danceteria . . . the closing of the World. The closing of these clubs had such a dramatic effect on us. You remember all the good times you had. This is the worst!'' He added, ''It's like a person dying . . .'' Death was much on Michael Alig's mind.

There is an ominous atmosphere around New York's big clubs these days. ''Now there is a real fear in my heart. Each time I go out to a club I wonder who's looking at me. And I don't think I'm being paranoid. I think I'm being realistic,'' one nighthawk told me. ''There's a backlash. It's horrible. Everyone is watching their backs,'' the doorman Kenny Kenny says dismally. ''There's no color anymore. No eccentricity.''

Perhaps it's a matter of the mood of the times. Steve Rubell once said of Studio 54's success, ''I think if you had opened it two years earlier or later, it wouldn't have worked. Because while Watergate and Vietnam were going on, there was a bigger cause than yourself.'' At the time of this writing, certainly, Manhattan's nocturnal energies are focused in the so-called lounges, which tend to resemble the bars of peculiarly funky hotels. Perhaps Manhattan is getting too bland, too homogenized. The lead story in the November 1978 issue of Life *was ''Disco! Hottest Trend in Entertainment'' but the cover story was about Disney, predictably. It can easily seem that New York is the scene of an unequal battle between squeaky-clean Disneyworld and Nightworld, which, despite*

its ferocious vitality, its allure, its enticing risks, will be leveled,
like some picturesque Dickensian slum.

It won't die easily, though. Nightworld has deep psychic roots
and Nightworlders have sweet, devouring dreams. These, for in-
stance, are Arthur Weinstein's plans. "In the year 2000, you've got
to open the greatest club in the world," he says. "You've got to
build it from the ground up. It has got to be symmetrical. The most
beautiful shape is the sun." He gave remarkably detailed plans and
ended, "Instead of a play dome, I want a real dome. It's only going
to take about forty million.

"Here's what the guy who puts up the money gets. Nothing!
But he gets to be a big shot. And all the drink tickets he
wants . . ." he laughed savagely, but wasn't wholly joking. He and
Scotty Taylor, last I heard, were looking at a space.

CAST LIST

John Addison: Model, club owner, RIP

Barbara Allen Kwiatowski: Party girl; society woman

Michael Alig: Club Kid, murder suspect

Princess Dialta Alliata di Montereale: actress, director, Euro-diva; mother & hostess

Diana Anderson: Actress

Patti Astor: Gallerist, star of *Assault of the Killer Bimbos*

Ken Auletta: Writer

Michael Ault: Party promoter; publicist

Ludovic Autet: Impressario, actor, diamond publicist

Bill Avery: Publicist

Baccio: DJ at Studio 54, Plato's Retreat

Karin Bacon: Maker of events

Brad Balfour: Pop music journalist & archivist

Jean-Michel Basquiat: Artist, RIP

Peter Beard: Photographer, adventurer

Angus Beavers: Club owner

Claude Beer: Rackets and backgammon player

Sidney Beer: Entrepreneur

Marc Benecke: Doorman; Los Angeles restaurateur

John "Jellybean" Benitez: DJ; music producer

Glenn Bernbaum: Restaurateur

Richard Bernstein: Artist/designer

Christine Biddle: Publicist

Marc de Gontaut Biron: Eurotrash party promoter

Christopher Blackwell: Music & movie producer

Susan Blond: Music publicist

Ruza Blue: Impressario

Joyce Bogart: Producer, widow of below

Neil Bogart: Head of Casablanca Records, RIP

Robert Bookman: Attorney

Fran Boyer: Model, Studio 54 party person

Maurice Brahms: Club owner, ex-convict; businessman

Jerry Brandt: Club owner, producer; Sweden-based promoter

Bea Breuer: Pseudonym; former ingenue

Scott Bromley: Architect of Studio 54; architect

Peter Brown: Manager of the Beatles; Manhattan publicist

Vito Bruno: Party promoter, talent manager

Ben Buchanan: Punk band manager; photographer

Gail Lumet Buckley: Writer; mother

Guy Burgos: New York socialite, Miami socialite

Count Roger de Cabrol: Interior designer

"Screamin' Rachel" Cain: Queen of House Music, Club Kid

John Cale: Musician

Nell Campbell: Actress, diva, hostess

Paul Caranicas: Artist/designer

Robert Caravaggi: Maître d'

John Carmen: Publicist

Barbara Carrera: Model; actress; Beverly Hills socialite

Nicholas Cerman: London restaurateur

Ricky Clifton: Picture framer

Kip Cohen: Herb Alpert manager; director of the Herb Alpert Foundation

Nik Cohn: Writer & journalist

Richard Corkery: Photographer

Scott Covert: Artist; would-be proprietor of pet cemetery

Joanne Creveling: Fashion publicist

Frankie Crocker: DJ

Kelly Cutrone: Addicted party promoter; sober chanteuse; survivor

Carmen D'Alessio: Party promoter, globaltrash queen

August Darnell: Musician

Rick Dees: DJ, creator of "Disco Duck" & "Discorilla"; radio show host

Nigel Dempster: Gossip columnist for London's *Daily Mail*

Dan Dorfman: Financial reporter

Richard Dupont: One of the "Fake Dupont Twins"

Robert Dupont: See above

Jack Dushey: Partner in Studio 54; businessman

"The Elf Queen": Supplier of controlled substances to the gentry

Ahmet Ertegun: Founder of Atlantic Records, socialite

Joe Eula: Fashion artist

Jonathan Farkas: Businessman, socialite

Ron Ferri: Artist

Michael Fesco: Actor, club owner, promoter

Annie Flanders: Publisher of *Details*; Puerto Rico resident

Mark Fleischman: Club owner in Manhattan; club owner in Manhattan & Los
   Angeles

Jim Fouratt: Club owner, gay activist; music publicist

Diane von Furstenberg: Designer

Prince Egon von Furstenberg: Eurotrash star; designer

Futura 2000 aka Lenny McGurr: Graffiti artist

Steven Gaines: Writer

Larry Gang: Partner in Xenon; attorney

Chuck Garelick: Security chief of Studio 54; security company head

Peter Gatien: Club owner; federal target

Gloria Gaynor: Disco diva; disco comeback diva

Fred Gershon: Music lawyer & executive

Vitas Gerulaitis: Tennis player, nightperson, RIP

Ed Gifford: Studio 54 publicist; retired Southampton resident

Gitsie: Club Kid

Al Goldstein: Pornographer; retired-to-Florida pornographer

Eric Goode: Club owner, artist; owner of Bowery Bar, New York

David Granoff: Publicist

Steven A. Greenberg: Club owner, entrepreneur

Bob Greene: Chicago-based syndicated columnist

Michael Gross: Reporter, writer

Gregory Gunsch: Model, Studio barman; Mortimer's barman

Maaret Halinen: Model; Sotheby's client services

Halston: Couturier, RIP

Bill Hamilton: Steve Rubell's amour; Carolina Herrera designer

Keith Haring: Mudd Club doorman, busboy, artist; RIP

Nikki Haskell: Promoter, TV interviewer; health food entrepreneur

R. Couri Hay: *National Enquirer* columnist; nightclub entrepreneur

Carolina Herrera: Couturiere

Reinaldo Herrera: Socialite; *Vanity Fair* editor

Jeffrey Hogrefe: Writer

Geoffrey Holder: Designer

Michael Holman: Musician, writer

Joanne Horowitz: Party planner; actors' manager

Fred Hughes: Warhol intimate; chairman emeritus, Warhol Foundation

Victor Hugo: Halston's lover, window dresser, night person, RIP

Celine Hurley: Comedian

Bohdan Huzar: IRS agent, raider of Studio 54; accountant

Billy Idol: Singer

Mark Jacobson: Journalist, novelist

Bianca Jagger: Studio icon

Baird Jones: Preppy, party promoter; *Daily News* gossip writer

Grace Jones: Diva

Istvan Kantor aka "Monty Cantsin": Drinker of blood, industrial musician

Ulla-Maia Kirimaki: Model; designer

David Knapp: Rubell chauffeur, Palladium manager; playwright

Bitten Knudsen: Model

Jesse Kornbluth: Writer; on-line entrepreneur

Lech Kowalski: Moviemaker

Eleanor Lambert: Fashion publicist

Joe la Placa: Studio 54 jack-of-all-trades; Paris-based music producer

Robin Leach: TV reporter

Victoria Leacock: Studio 54 secretary; moviemaker

Dr. Timothy Leary: Behavioral pied piper; RIP

Stuart Lee: Writer

Francine Lefrak: Moviemaker

Nina Lerner: Sixth wife of Alan Jay Lerner

Larry Levenson: Proprietor of Plato's Retreat, convict; recluse

Perri Lister: Dancer; singer

Gail Lumet: Writer

John Lyons: Nightclubman; Boston nightclub king

Kevin McCormick: Producer of *Saturday Night Fever;* Fox producer

Earle Mack: Balletomane, horse breeder; New York cultural commissioner

Malcolm McLaren: London-based punk promoter, Paris-based musician

Mahim de Maleret: Designer, socialite; Paris resident

David Mancuso: Organizer of pioneer disco, the Loft; private party host

Richard Manning: Paparazzo

Jack Martin: *New York Post* columnist; Los Angeles–based columnist

Richard Meinards: TV gossip; British royalty watcher

Alex Melamid: Artist

Milan: New York party promoter; Los Angeles resident

Sylvia Miles: Actress

Liza Minnelli: Singer, Studio icon

Haoui Montaug: RIP

"Dr. Moon": Narcotics retailer

Giorgio Moroder: Composer, Eurodisco prince; Los Angeles–based movie composer

Gordon Munro: Photographer

Michael Musto: Tyro; columnist

Philip Nobile: Writer

Bill Oakes: Music producer

Glenn O'Brien: Writer; copywriter for, among others, Barney's

Roger Parenti: Doorman; time-shares entrepreneur in Boca Raton

Stephanie Parker: Art dealer

Lester Persky: Movie producer

Rudolf Pieper: Club owner; departed for Paris

Robin Platzer: Paparazzo

George Plimpton: Editor, writer

Amos Poe: Filmmaker

Yoram Polany: Entrepreneur

Countess Antonia de Portago: Punk singer; animal rights activist

Pierre Prudhomme: Pseudonym

Dotson Rader: Writer

Sally Randall: Doorwoman, musician, artist

Marcia Resnick: Photographer

Renny Reynolds: Florist & designer

Elisabeth Rieger: Kid; agent & editor

Gwynne Rivers: Ingenue; slightly older ingenue

Frank Roccio: Impressario

Nile Rodgers: Musician

Peter Rogers: Adman, creator of the Blackglama campaign; society portraitist

Michael Roth: State Liquor Authority chairman, lawyer

Howard Rower: Dealer in macrobiotics food, Australian aboriginal art & TriBeCa real estate

Don Rubell: Gynecologist, art collector, Steve's brother

Steve Rubell: Nightlord; RIP

Mimi Rubin: Entrepreneur; married to Mark Fleischman & Los Angeles resident

Hollywood de Russo: Party girl, makeup artist

D. D. Ryan: Halston's muse, socialite; Manhattan resident

James St. James: Club Kid, doorman, promoter

Anita Sarko: DJ

David Sarner: Party promoter, publicist

Francesco Scavullo: Photographer

Kenny Scharf: Artist

Myra Scheer: Publicist

Neil Schlesinger: Restaurateur, partner & friend of Steve Rubell

Ian Schrager: Nightlord, hotelier

John Scribner: Party guy; artist

Mary Seymour: Chanteuse, IBM employee

Brooke Shields: Jeans model; actress

Ira Silverberg: Kid; publisher

Nicolas Simunek: Entrepreneur

Liz Smith: Gossip columnist

Trey Speegle: Entrepreneur

Howard Stein: Rock concert producer, club owner

Stella: Dancer; bartender

Cyndi Stivers: Reporter; editor *Time Out*

Richard Stolley: Editor *People*, Time Inc. executive

Michael Stone: Socialite; writer

Peter Stringfellow: Club owner

Peter Sudler: Federal prosecutor; real estate developer in New Jersey

Chris Sullivan: Studio 54 doorman; video producer

Tom Sullivan: Narcotics smuggler, Warhol crony, RIP

Donna Summer: Singer

Scotty Taylor: Club owner; Peter Gatien's chauffeur

Thierry: Pseudonym

Jane Thorvaldsen: Model

Manuel Toledano: Filmmaker

Neil Travis: Columnist

Tolly Travis: Married to above

Mykul Tronn (Michael Cooper): Club Kid, job seeker

Richard Turley: Publicist

Craig Unger: Editor *New York*; editor *Boston*

Peppo Vanini: Clubman

Andy Warhol: Andy Warhol, RIP

Don Was: Musician

Arthur Weinstein: Club owner; lighting director in Limelight

Colleen Weinstein: Designer, troubleshooter

Max Westerhart: Bond girl in *For Your Eyes Only*; New Age zealot

Chris Williamson: Night manager of Studio 54; concert promoter

Anna Wintour: Editor of American *Vogue*

Elyn Wollensky: Club Kid; writer and editor

Holly Woodlawn: Warhol superstar; Los Angeles resident

Randy Wren: Publicist; New Orleans resident

Cristina Zilkha: Diva, writer

Michael Zilkha: Founder Ze Records; Texas oil executive

INDEX

74532378R00267

Made in the USA
Middletown, DE
26 May 2018